AND LIFE IS CHANGED FOREVER

AND LIFE
IS CHANGED FOREVER

Holocaust Childhoods Remembered

Edited by Martin Ira Glassner and Robert Krell
Sponsored by the Holocaust Child Survivors of Connecticut

WAYNE STATE UNIVERSITY PRESS   DETROIT

10 09 08 07 06   5 4 3 2

Library of Congress Cataloging-in-Publication Data

And life is changed forever : Holocaust childhoods remembered / edited by Martin Ira Glassner and Robert Krell ; sponsored by the Holocaust Child Survivors of Connecticut.
p. cm. — (Landscapes of childhood)
Includes bibliographical references.
ISBN 0-8143-3173-4 (pbk. : alk. paper)
1. Jewish children in the Holocaust—Biography. 2. Holocaust, Jewish (1939–1945)—Personal narratives. 3. Holocaust survivors—Connecticut—Biography. 4. Holocaust, Jewish (1939–1945)—Influence. 5. Holocaust, Jewish (1939–1945)—Personal narratives—History and criticism. I. Glassner, Martin Ira, 1932– II. Krell, Robert. III. Holocaust Child Survivors of Connecticut. IV. Series.
D804.48.A53 2006
940.53'18'0922—dc22

2005024382

Designed and typeset by Maya Rhodes
Composed in Adobe Garamond Pro and Bernhard Modern Std

*Dedicated to the memory of **Hilde Scheraga,***
late president of the Holocaust Child Survivors of Connecticut,
who conceived the theme of this collection of stories

CONTENTS

CONTENTS

CONTENTS

PREFACE

The Holocaust Child Survivors of Connecticut (HCSC) was created only months after the first international conference of child survivors was held in New York in 1991. Our members came together, little by little, cautiously at first, still not entirely sure that they were ready to speak about their painful past. Since that initial meeting the group has cemented together, closer than friends, feeling that all are accepted like family, like siblings. The members spent years talking about their painful past, the effect of their broken young lives on their families, on their children and grandchildren. The experience has been and continues to be one of healing and slowly coming to terms with their past, although the wounds will never be closed.

In addition to acting as a support group for its members, the HCSC has been developing a number of outreach activities. In 1998 it published *Childhood Memories: Jewish Children Who Survived the Nazi Peril Speak,* designed for and widely used in secondary schools; it is still available from the organization. In 1998 HCSC also produced an award-winning video documentary, *One out of Ten,* now also in DVD format. The organization continues to maintain an active speakers' bureau, providing speakers for schools, churches, civic groups, synagogues, community commemorations, and the like. Its latest project is an annual essay contest on the Holocaust for high school students, with cash prizes awarded in a special ceremony. In January 2000 Hilde Scheraga, then president of the HCSC, asked me to help the group develop its most ambitious project to date: a full-scale, booklength collection of child survivor stories with some uncommon features.

From January to May 2000 Hilde and I and the board of directors of the HCSC discussed the proposed book and agreed on its basic objectives and a plan of action. We sent a letter to each of the approximately one hundred members of the organization, informing them of the project and soliciting written contributions that would follow our guidelines (see the appendix). We also placed articles and requests for stories in the *Connecticut Jewish Ledger* and the newsletter of a national child survivors group. In addition, word spread rapidly through the proverbial grapevine. Eventually, we received forty-seven submissions from as far away as Ukraine and Australia. We rejected eleven as unsuitable for a variety of reasons, leaving thirty-six under active consideration, including several that I constructed from raw materials—newspaper and magazine clippings, audio and video tapes of interviews, outlines, sketches of narratives, and so forth—sent to me by child survivors. I also interviewed several contributors and used the tapes of the interviews to supplement or substitute for documentary material.

In September 2002 Hilde and I went to Detroit for two days of consultations with Jane Hoehner and Annie Martin of Wayne State University Press. The four of us sat around a conference table with stacks of manuscripts and selected twenty-seven for inclusion in the book. We were looking for interesting, insightful, and reasonably well-written narratives that represented a variety of countries and experiences. Early in 2004, for lack of sufficient space, we had to delete seven more, an agonizing experience for Hilde and me, because even these seven were very good.

The editing process stretched out over more than two years, during which I also designed and supervised creation of the maps, solicited and organized contributors' photographs, worked with Robert Krell on his contributions, and created the front matter and back matter. I edited all the manuscripts, and the authors approved the editing of their contributions, even those that had to be drastically reduced in length.

The result is a book that is unique in that it incorporates several features not found together in any of the multitude of Holocaust books extant:

1. It includes only survivors who were children during the Holocaust.
2. It consists mainly of twenty first-person narratives.
3. The stories represent a great variety of countries and experiences.
4. Most writers emphasize their postliberation experiences and the effects of the Shoah on their lives.
5. It includes an analytical introduction and three psychosocial commentaries on the narratives by Robert Krell.
6. The unifying principle is date of birth because, as Krell points out, people's memories and reactions to trauma tend to differ by age. We considered and rejected classification by country of birth and by method of survival as less appropriate for this particular project.
7. The book includes twenty-four specially commissioned maps and many photographs submitted by the contributors.

I wish to express my gratitude to the Holocaust Child Survivors of Connecticut for the opportunity to participate in this demanding but most gratifying project; to the late Hilde Scheraga for her close cooperation throughout; and to the group's board for its continuing support and willingness to deplete its treasury to finance this enterprise. I should note here that *all* the participants contributed our services pro bono; no one is receiving a penny for it. Finally, I wish to thank again Jessie Jones of Southern Connecticut State University in New Haven, who has been typing my manuscripts for more than twenty years, always with great skill, patience, and good humor.

Martin Ira Glassner
Hamden, Connecticut
October 15, 2004

PROLOGUE:
Where Did They Go?

Where did they go, my little sisters and my brothers,
Murdered in cattle-car masses long before their prime,
Crying to the very last to join their mothers?
World, tell me what was the nature of their crime?

Was it perhaps the God they worshipped strangely
Or the synagogues where their fathers prayed,
Their books, their garb, their foods or how their names sounded,
Or the religious objects they displayed?

World, you were so cruel and thunderingly silent
When the jack-booted sadists crushed their dream.
Why were you paralyzed by gross indifference,
Blinded to their tears and deafened to their scream?

More than a million of these babies, boys and girls
Went to their untimely deaths and no one cared.
Murderers did whatever they wanted,
Gassing and burning decency beyond repair.

Why did you die, my little brothers and my sisters?
Why did I live to see my life fulfilled
While you were cast into the nightmare's chasm,
Brutally tortured and wantonly killed?

Where are you now, my little sisters and my brothers?
I'm in a safe land, far, far across the seas
While you are but splintered bone and ashes
Carried in the air upon the breeze.

I lived to tell my story of survival
While you knew pain and died a martyr's death.
If God now wills it, I'll give voice to your existence
While I have life and strength and draw my breath.

Stephen Adler
Seattle, Washington
December 2000

Child Survivors of the Holocaust: The Elderly Children and Their Adult Lives

AN INTRODUCTION BY ROBERT KRELL

How did the Holocaust affect Jewish children who survived it? We know that some cannot or will not speak of it to this day. And those who now are able to relate their stories often required a distance of forty to fifty years in order to do so, for what happened to Jewish children during the Nazi reign of terror surpassed the imagination and exceeded the limits of human suffering known to that time, particularly in supposedly civilized, modern, and modernizing societies.

That the world of a child Holocaust survivor is exceedingly complicated, perhaps uniquely so, is not surprising. The Holocaust was a unique event in human history, a massive genocidal assault on a people whose birth status determined that they must die. It mattered not whether they were citizens of France or Holland, Poland or Czechoslovakia. It was enough to be a Jew. Jewish children, many so young that they were entirely unaware of being Jewish, were condemned to death. Those few who eluded the murderers remain afflicted with the effects of the existential threat of outright annihilation.

The murder of Jewish children in Europe was nearly total. Deborah Dwork estimates that only 11 percent of Jewish children who were alive in 1939 survived the war.[1] That estimate includes children who escaped in the Kindertransport (the program to move children out of Austria, Czechoslovakia, Germany, and Poland for passage to Belgium and England) or through the efforts of the Palestinian Jewish organization Youth Aliyah. In Nazi-occupied territory after September 1, 1939, only 6 to 7 percent of Jewish children survived. Dwork's study is an important account of the suffering of these children, as well as of the adaptation and resilience of children who managed to survive.

Roughly 1.5 million children and adolescents were murdered. At liberation there were perhaps five thousand young camp survivors, about one thousand of whom were found at Buchenwald. Each major camp still in existence yielded but a few hundred living children. In a little-known 1949 booklength report, the Irish historian Dorothy Macardle described the plight of refugee children, primarily those who were Jewish.[2] She estimated even then that two million Jewish children had been slain. According to Macardle, the two largest groups to escape were "about 30,000 children under age 16 in 1939 from Austria and Germany" (thanks to the Kindertransport) and about 12,000 rescued throughout Europe by the Youth Aliyah. She wrote that about 500 children were found at Theresienstadt (Terezin), 500 at Bergen-Belsen, and 800 at Buchenwald. Two hundred twins survived Josef Mengele's gruesome experiments at Auschwitz. In Poland 5,000 Jewish children were registered as surviving; in Holland, 15,000 (20,000 others were deported and killed); and in Belgium, 3,000. But of the 4,363 Belgian Jewish children who were deported to the camps, only 39 returned.

Thus the accounts of child survivors represent the experiences of a comparative handful when measured against the hundreds of thousands who were slaughtered. This alone should make us mindful of the inherent good fortune of those who survived, for they were no more clever or resourceful than countless other children who tried so hard to live but were killed, sometimes because of a single misstep.

Virtually no child had a chance to survive without the assistance of adults. Fate, luck, and the help of strangers all played a role, but the children who lived took actions that contributed to their survival, and they displayed remarkable resilience in constructing their postwar lives. Sarah Moskovitz traced the lives of twenty-four war orphans brought to England from Prague shortly after liberation; twelve had been at Theresienstadt (Terezin).[3] The author, a developmental psychologist, found all the survivors nearly forty years later and described their reentry into life in their adopted countries. Martin Gilbert, the British historian, documented the stories of 732 young concentration camp survivors, including about eighty girls, although generally this group refers to itself as "The Boys."[4] And Judith Hemmendinger and I described the efforts to rehabilitate the 426 youngsters found at Buchenwald and brought to France.[5] Mental health professionals told members of this group that they would never recover, but they have mostly succeeded in raising families, finding success in work, and contributing to their communities. A few achieved fame, such as the writer and Nobel Prize–winner Elie Wiesel and Israel Meier Lau, who served as an Ashkenazi chief rabbi of Israel.

One thing is clear. These are children who were deprived of childhood and who were forced to grow up, literally overnight. One day they were at play. The next, they were foraging for food for their entire families or were responsible for the welfare of their younger brothers and sisters in horrendous circumstances. One day a child was a member of a large family; the next day found this same child abandoned and hiding in caves, forests, and convents, usually with strangers. They were indeed children grown old before their time, elderly children. Irene Frisch writes here of herself at twelve: "I was afraid, I missed my family, and I worried about them. Even so, it never occurred to me to complain. I was a child, but children matured quickly at that time."

The effects of traumas sustained in early life are apparent in most infants and children who suffer malnourishment, abandonment, and separation. In the Shoah, Jewish children suffered these and more in rapid succession without pause for recovery. Research conducted into child development confirms that the first three years of life are crucial to successful development. Important factors include the health and circumstances of the mother during her pregnancy; the temperament of the child, which is both genetically determined and influenced by parental expectations; the mother-child attachment; and the need for a child to be in the care of at least one loving person. Consider this requirement of constancy with what happened to children at Theresienstadt.

The garrison town of Theresienstadt in Czechoslovakia was emptied of its 3,000 inhabitants and transformed into a Nazi concentration camp that held 74,000 Jews. In all, 150,000 people passed through Theresienstadt on the way to death camps, including 15,000 children. The adults tried to care for the children in the ward for "motherless children," but eventually each loving caretaker was taken from them, a never-ending series of psychological blows that Sarah Moskovitz summarizes in her 1983 book, *Love Despite Hate*.

A proper childhood is an important time of discovery, curiosity, exuberance, playfulness, and joy. However, as André Stein once noted, "Playfulness and joy for hidden children changed from 'hide and seek' to 'hide or die.'" Stein chronicled ten stories of child survivors—including his own and that of his sister—in his book *Hidden Children: Forgotten Survivors of the Holocaust*.[6] Following the first International Gathering of Children Hidden During World War II, held in New York in 1991, Jane Marks and Paul Valent each wrote books describing the entire gamut of child Holocaust experiences.[7]

A commonly accepted guideline for determining who is a *child* survivor suggests that any person who was sixteen or younger in 1945 may be considered a child survivor, whereas those who were seventeen or older may be categorized as adult survivors. The reason for this differentiation has much to do with the course of their postwar lives and the decisions made by those who were temporarily responsible for the care and rehabilitation of these youngsters.[8]

Generally speaking, children who were younger than seventeen when the war ended were placed under some kind of guardianship that led to their placement in homes or orphanages and their resumption of schooling. They had relatively little say about their destiny. Those who were seventeen and older were more likely to seek independence, search for their missing family, arrange for their early emigration, and/or seek work and vocational training. Many were married in the displaced persons camps and started families. Their caretakers sent the younger orphans to Palestine; to countries such as Britain and the United States, where their relatives had settled before the war; and to Canada, where the Canadian Jewish Congress had persuaded the government to accept 1,116 children, who arrived in Canada between September 18, 1947, and March 10, 1952.[9]

But such definitions are problematic. For example, a Polish youngster who was 13 when Germany invaded Poland in 1939 endured six years of extreme danger before being liberated at 19, whereas a Hungarian youth who was 13 when Germany invaded her country in 1944 was actively endangered for one year and liberated at 14. The war consumed the adolescence of some Jewish youngsters who found themselves to be young adults at war's end. Kuba and Helen Beck, for example, were 17 and 14, respectively, when they were caught up in war, but they were 24 and 21 when they married in December 1946.

Although the Kindertransport children did not suffer the deprivation and torment of Jewish children on the continent, they were nevertheless torn from their families, and most never saw their parents again. Their sense of loss and grief cannot be denied. In order to include all children who suffered such losses in childhood and adolescence, some experts have proposed defining as a child survivor any survivor who was nineteen or younger in 1945.

Because Jewish children were subjected to severe trauma, it is pointless to attempt to determine who suffered more, the hidden children or the concentration camp children. People often think that those in the camps suffered more than those in hiding and that younger children suffered less because they were assumed to have no memories. Similarly, a common assumption is that Kindertransport children led normal lives because they were sheltered and fed. But all these experiences were off the scale of what could be considered a secure and normal childhood. The suffering was so enormous, no matter the individual's precise experience, that the majority of children who survived bear emotional scars from the experience.

Another widespread assumption is that children in hiding with Christians were treated kindly. In the life-and-death context of the Holocaust, rescuers deserve extraordinary credit for saving lives, but the day-to-day existence of a Jewish child in hiding was not a secure one. Renée Glassner describes overhearing her hiders planning what they would do with her if they moved to another city. She recalls thinking: "What should they do with me?" She heard them agree that there was only one solution: "Jurek [her hider] would soon take me out to the cemetery and shoot me. As the days passed we talked very little. . . . I never revealed what I knew of their secret plan."

Sarah Moskovitz sent a questionnaire to child survivors inquiring about their treatment while in hiding; she received twenty-seven responses.[10] All were from people who had been younger than fourteen at liberation; seventeen came from survivors who had been younger than eleven. Fourteen people knew that their hiders had been paid. Children hiding in thirteen places felt that they had been treated warmly. The remainder felt they had been treated with "cool indifference."

Gentile children living in convents received packages from home and were allowed to go home for Christmas and other holidays. Imagine a Jewish child who watched them open their packages. And discipline of Jewish children was frequently enforced with threats to turn them over to the Nazis. Such threats were common in hiding families as well. Moreover, six people told Moskovitz that they had been sexually abused, including a male respondent who reported that a priest had molested him. Moskovitz points out that some children were moved as many as nine times and that these moves were not necessarily to homes or convents but included attics, cellars, pigsties, garbage dumps, fields, and ditches. In Paul Valent's book Bernadette describes staying with a Polish Catholic peasant whose alcoholic husband regularly beat Bernadette and her sister.

In the concentration camps younger children were expendable because they could not perform useful work. Of the approximately one thousand children found in Buchenwald at liberation, very few were younger than thirteen. The majority were older adolescents and youths. The French child rescue society Oeuvre de Secours aux Enfants, which arranged to receive 426 child survivors for rehabilitation, had prepared hundreds of little beds, unaware that small children had not survived.

A study carried out in Israel in the early 1960s by Leo Eitinger, the Norwegian psychiatrist who had himself survived Auschwitz, found that the very youngest survivors were the most likely to require permanent institutionalization.[11] Their experiences during the most sensitive time of their development had rendered them psychotic. Instead of offering them protection, their youth had left them most vulnerable to the loss of parenting, multiple separations from caregivers, and exposure to cold and malnutrition. Only in hiding were younger children able to receive sufficient care to avoid the most extreme outcomes of massive, unrelenting trauma.

Interestingly, although older children suffered enormously because of their more mature conceptual abilities and hence greater awareness of their hostile surroundings, they nevertheless benefited from having had a secure and normal upbringing during the crucial developmental years of infancy and early childhood. In childhood a few years make an enormous difference to a child's later well-being. Again, a Jewish child born in Poland in 1933 had only six years of comparative safety and nurturing, whereas a Jewish child in Hungary born in the same year would have been eleven before the full force of the Nazi terror enveloped him.

Such facts are crucial to an examination of the postwar adaptation and coping of child survivors of the Shoah because the developmental stages are the primary determinants of the child's ability to remember, and memories are, in turn, a major determinant in the shaping of identity. "Looking back at my life, I realize that the most precious possessions I have are my memories," says Dori Laub, whose memories begin at age two. However, a child born during the war might have little or no conscious memory of wartime events yet can be profoundly and permanently affected by them. If the child's earliest years were marked by deprivation, loss, and separations, all in a climate of oppressive danger, she may have experienced the consequences of the trauma without an awareness of the causes.

The scraps of memory of child survivors may make little sense and in any case are a double-edged sword. For example, the meaningful recollection of a mother's face may also be the memory of seeing her for the last time. The effort to remember that loving, perhaps tearful, countenance comes with the emotional price of reminding the child of his greatest loss. In light of such a complex memory, one can begin to understand the child survivor's struggle to recapture memories on the one hand and, on the other, to suppress them. On balance, those with the ability to remember achieve greater peace than others. Child survivors have fought valiantly but not always successfully to remember. Hilde Scheraga describes how, between the ages of eight and eleven, "my memories faded with the passing years, as I struggled to remember what my parents looked like (I had no photographs) or the sounds of their voices."

Younger children, usually those in hiding, were often unaware that they were Jews, and those who were aware were forced to relinquish their religious identity. Retaining a Jewish identity was intimately connected with death, whereas being a devout Christian promised life. Children who were indoctrinated in Christianity found it difficult to give it up after they were liberated and learned that they were Jews. Many children whose parents died remained with their rescuers and were lost to Judaism, while others were swept up into Jewish orphanages, taken to Palestine/Israel, or fostered by Jewish families around the world. Even in Israel, not all children were able to construct a Jewish identity free from the traumatic past. Older children, with prewar memories, were better equipped for the resumption of Jewish life, for they could rely on their recall of Jewish family traditions, attending Jewish schools, and participating in various meaningful rituals.

Parents who survived and found their children often experienced a painful process of convincing them to adopt a Jewish identity and abandon the Christian one. Some children in hiding with decent Christian families grew so attached that they resented the return of their parents. Often they no longer remembered their parents, and if they did, the bond had been disrupted. Hilde Scheraga was reunited with her mother: "I recognized her immediately, yet she looked so different to me. . . . I was now fifteen. I no longer spoke German. . . . I was a little child when I left home. I was now, or so I thought, an adult who still looked like a child."

Nor were the parents in any sense the same people of a few years earlier. Those who returned were weakened and tormented, not the emotionally and physically strong parents that the children needed. Eva Metzger Brown was only eight when her mother was plunged into depression after escaping from Germany and trying to adjust to life in the United States. As Brown recalls, "I spent all my free time at home, often sitting at the end of my mother's bed, telling her about my day, and thereby filling up hers." The child survivor in a survivor family frequently ended up with responsibilities far beyond her years. A surviving parent sometimes returned with a new spouse or partner. A young child might not be told that the partner was not his natural parent, only to discover years later that his natural parent had been murdered.

The children who somehow survived ghettos or concentration camps were reminded daily that they were Jews, but those in hiding were reminded daily to hide any evidence of their identity. The majority proved to be quick studies, for their lives depended on mastering catechism and liturgy in order to pass for Christians. But doing so often caused postwar complications. As Renée Fritz relates, "I became an ardent Catholic convert." It makes sense that in later years, while attending Hebrew classes to prepare for her bat mitzvah ceremony, she reports: "I attended the classes, and right after each class I went to church to confess. I did become a bat mitzvah—and went to confession right after!"

Memory remains a contentious topic. Many experts agree that traumatic conditions can sear some dramatic events into a child's memory as early as ages two to three. Felicia Graber had images and fragments of her life from when she was younger than five. Upon returning fifty years later to a Polish farm where she had been hidden with her parents until liberation, she was able to confirm her recollections: "The cow . . . the planes . . . I am starting to tie things together."

But not all accounts of childhood during the Shoah, or descriptions of such childhood memories, are true. Some writers have distorted their personal histories and portrayed themselves as survivors when they were not. Others have written credible accounts as fiction, thereby blurring the lines between fact and fantasy. Fortunately, following a few pioneering works,[12] a vast literature of child survivor memoirs has emerged since 1990,[13] revealing the powerful hold of memory on those who endured the Shoah.

For therapists who work with child survivors and for those who document their stories, it is evident that recapturing memory and making sense of it is a healing enterprise. When placed in a sensible chronological frame, the memory fragments help the child survivor to achieve a better sense of what happened and thereby reconstruct an identity, even one permeated with recollections of trauma. The offering of sequential testimony has proved to be a powerful tool in creating a narrative that allows child survivors to regain some control of their life story.[14]

A topic not sufficiently considered is the anger or, rather, the rage so intimately connected with living in constant fear of death. Even a very young child in hiding, protected by adults who themselves live in fear, absorbs their anxieties and develops an awareness of imminent danger. In addition, persecuted and hunted children may know or sense that they are the focus of the danger and may feel responsible for the predicament. It is not a major leap for persecuted Jewish children to think that they must indeed be bad people or that they did something awful to be the object of such hatred. Self-blame quickly turns to shame, and the child feels powerless to deal with that emotion and becomes angry. Attempts by child survivors to control the shame, curb any expression of anger, and absorb a continuing series of traumatic psychological assaults, all with life-or-death consequences, led to their building up a reservoir of rage.

In other cases helpless victims witnessed atrocities inflicted upon family and friends and could not act on their anger. In fact, survival required them to force retaliation out of their mind. Nearly all who physically resisted were murdered on the spot. And in most instances it was bare hands against guns. What is surprising is that in the postwar period so few adult survivors allowed their rage to dominate their lives.

Child survivors were more likely to vent their anger initially—as did the children who came to France from Buchenwald, trashed the furniture, and set fire to their dormitories. Their initial outburst was followed by a period of adjustment and settling. To my knowledge, none of the 426 youngsters turned to crime in their adult lives.

Rage was not visible in the younger children, but it may account for their development of various problems. Not only were children pursued relentlessly by the enemy, they were also forbidden to cry or protest. Silence thus became an integral component of the child's being. Could the rage at being persecuted and driven into silence at such a tender age disappear with time? It is not likely. The combination of a fragmented memory, an ambivalent identity, and the likely presence of unfathomable rage usually makes for a pessimistic prognosis. And herein lies an enduring mystery. Developmental psychologists know that a single significant trauma in early childhood will often have permanent negative consequences. Holocaust children suffered the chronic, unrelenting blows of the most massive psychological traumas. How were they able to study and work again, raise families, and contribute to community life wherever they lived?

Those who were able to acknowledge rage also developed an awareness that a successful life requires its control. Many developed constructive responses, including recording audiovisual testimony, teaching children about the Holocaust as a means of countering prejudice and racism, and writing books for children, as well as creating art and music. Another important factor was their memories of family and tradition, real or imagined, which helped them to rebuild their lives in familiar ways.

Undoubtedly, an important factor in the surviving children was their temperament, which may have helped them to adapt to a variety of situations. Being smart enough to make rapid decisions and learn quickly during the war also helped these people after the war. Several recent books on child survivors shed light on the adaptive strategies used by some to reconstruct their severely disrupted lives. Mary Gallant, a sociologist, scrutinized and described the accounts of eighteen survivors, eleven of whom were children and adolescents, for the strategies that they used to stay healthy during crises.[15] A recent book by Kerry Bluglass, a psychiatrist, provides an intimate look at the lives of fifteen child survivors and examines the effects of the Holocaust and what ingredients were required for "surviving well."[16] And Peter Suedfeld, a psychologist, provides a telling commentary on the influence of the Holocaust on the ultimate career choices of other social scientists, some of whom were child survivors.[17]

Surviving after surviving the war required a return to functioning in a long-forgotten world, one where food was available and danger had receded. Once children became aware of the possibility of becoming "normal," their determination to achieve normality was unrelenting. They set aside their experiences as if there were a compartment reserved for grief and bad memories and went about the business of learning at a ferocious pace. Most had lost many years of schooling and caught up or surpassed their grade level within only a few years, often in a brand-new language.

The traumas were not erased; they were kept under wraps, indeed, psychologically compartmentalized. During the Holocaust children had learned not to complain or cry, even when they were terrified. Nor did they complain or cry after liberation. It served no purpose. Those who could cry shed their tears—torrents of tears—privately or with other survivors but not in front of family and certainly not in the presence of strangers.

In my work as a psychiatrist or as a colleague in Holocaust education, all survivors whom I have encountered allude to carrying two selves within them. Over the years they have come to view that child of the ghetto, or of the camps, or in hiding as an important part of their being but not necessarily important in their day-to-day interactions and definitely not relevant to their loving relationships in the present. The only problem with this remarkable adaptation is its considerable success, which has resulted in child survivors' revealing so little of their past that many of their children know little or nothing of their parents' history.

Professional observations of the successful adaptation and coping of child survivors of the Holocaust are divided. Some studies reflect a degree of pessimism, others of optimism. A study of 664 questionnaires (of the 5,200 mailed out) of child survivor respondents around the world suggested that even though these particular respondents had done fairly well, more than half reported severe and permanent physical damage as a result of their experiences, and three-quarters reported lifelong emotional suffering because of loss of family.[18] Although it is now commonly accepted that all trauma survivors will have some symptoms of posttraumatic stress disorder, Suedfeld's studies of videotaped interviews of survivors revealed that 40 percent reported no symptoms and 30 percent reported only one symptom.[19] Perhaps such findings reinforce those of the surveys discussed earlier, in which self-reporting child survivors claim physical and emotional damage. However, the perceived damage has not kept the vast majority of survivors from becoming successful by any measure.

It makes sense that child survivors struggle with certain fears and preoccupations. They *are* more cautious with strangers. Work success *is* exceedingly important. The self-recognition that they have suffered profound psychological damage does not necessarily mean that they function as if they are psychologically damaged. Far from it. But difficulties arise when the past self intrudes upon the present self. This commonly occurs when the child survivor retires from work, the children are gone, and the cat dies. The danger lies in this period of nostalgia, when the survivor reflects on life, just as other retirees do. The person fortunate to have lived a life of relative comfort is able to recapture joyous moments. When a child survivor reflects nostalgically, memory propels her directly into the abyss of terror and hunger.

Thus this latter stage of life presents a new danger to the child survivor's well-being and makes it important for the aging "children" to gather in groups and at conferences in order to confront the past in the presence of people who have had similar experiences. They alone understand each other. They alone are able to encourage each other to relate their stories and to share them with family. The unburdening of the child survivor's traumatized self has resulted in a recent outpouring of published memoirs. I expect there will be many more.

In reviewing the precious accounts in this collection, I noted that the writers have identified themselves as the parents of 48 children. Of the 42 offspring identified by gender, 29 were female and 13 were male, a 2:1 ratio. Given that Jewish lineage is determined by the mother, according to Halacha (Jewish law), is it possible that survivors of genocide produce more female offspring? Whatever the reason for this particular statistic, the pride inherent in forming families and having children is evident in almost every story. After all, there could be no more effective method of thwarting the enemy's intentions of total annihilation than having children and grandchildren.

Notes

1. Deborah Dwork, *Children with a Star: Jewish Youth in Nazi Europe* (New Haven, CT: Yale University Press, 1991).
2. Dorothy Macardle, *Children of Europe: A Study of the Children of Liberated Countries—Their Wartime Experiences, Their Reactions, and Their Needs* (London: Gollancz, 1949).
3. Sarah Moskovitz, *Love Despite Hate: Child Survivors of the Holocaust and Their Postwar Lives* (New York: Schocken, 1983).
4. Martin Gilbert, *The Boys: Triumph over Adversity* (Toronto: Douglas and McIntyre, 1996).
5. Judith Hemmendinger and Robert Krell, *The Children of Buchenwald: Child Survivors of the Holocaust and Their Adult Lives* (Jerusalem: Gefen, 2000).
6. André Stein, *Hidden Children: Forgotten Survivors of the Holocaust* (New York: Penguin, 1993).
7. Jane Marks, *The Hidden Children: The Secret Survivors of the Holocaust* (New York: Fawcett Columbine, 1993); Paul Valent, *Child Survivors: Adults Living with Childhood Trauma* (Port Melbourne, Vic.: William Heinemann Australia,1994).
8. Robert Krell, ed., "Child Survivors of the Holocaust: 40 Years Later," *Journal of the American Academy of Child Psychiatry* 24, no. 4 (1985): 378–412.
9. Fraidie Martz, *Open Your Hearts: The Story of the Jewish War Orphans in Canada* (Montreal: Véhicule Press, 1996).
10. Sarah Moskovitz, "Barriers to Gratitude," in Yehuda Bauer et al., *Remembering for the Future: Working Papers and Addenda,* papers and addresses delivered at the International Conference—Remembering for the Future, Oxford, July 10–13, 1988, and at a public meeting in London, July 15, 1988 (New York: Pergamon, 1989), 2:494–503.
11. Leo Eitinger, *Concentration Camp Survivors in Norway and Israel* (The Hague: Martinus Nijhoff, 1972).
12. Jack Kuper, *Child of the Holocaust* (London: Routledge and Kegan Paul, 1967); Jona Oberski, *Childhood,* trans. Ralph Manheim (New York: Doubleday, 1983); Saul Friedlander, *When Memory Comes* (New York: Farrar, Strauss and Giroux, 1979).
13. Nechama Tec, *Dry Tears: The Story of a Lost Childhood* (New York: Oxford University Press, 1984); André Stein, *Broken Silence: Dialogues from the Edge* (Toronto: Lester

and Orpen Dennys, 1984); Frida Sheps-Weinstein, *A Hidden Childhood: A Jewish Girl's Sanctuary in a French Convent, 1942–1945* (Toronto: Collins, 1985); Yehuda Nir, *The Lost Childhood* (San Diego: Harcourt Brace, 1989); Renée Roth-Hanno, *Touch Wood* (New York: Puffin, 1989); Walter Buchignani, *Tell No One Who You Are: The Hidden Childhood of Regine Miller* (Montreal: Tundra, 1994); R. Gabriele S. Silten, *Between Two Worlds: Autobiography of a Child Survivor of the Holocaust* (Santa Barbara: Fithian, 1995); Magda Denes, *Castles Burning: A Child's Life in War* (New York: Touchstone, 1998); Robert Melson, *False Papers: Deception and Survival in the Holocaust* (Urbana: University of Illinois Press, 2000); Roman Frister, *The Cap: The Price of a Life* (New York: Grove, 2000).

14. Robert Krell, "Therapeutic Value of Documenting Child Survivors," *Journal of the American Academy of Child Psychiatry* 24, no. 4 (1985): 397–400.

15. Mary J. Gallant, *Coming of Age in the Holocaust: The Last Survivors Remember* (New York: University Press of America, 2002).

16. Kerry Bluglass, *Recovered Voices: Reflections of Resilient Hidden Children of the Holocaust* (London: Greenwood, 2003).

17. Peter Suedfeld, *Light from the Ashes: Social Science Careers of Young Holocaust Refugees and Survivors* (Ann Arbor: University of Michigan Press, 2001).

18. Sarah Moskovitz and Robert Krell, with Itzik Moskovitz and Ariella Askren, "The Struggle for Justice: A Survey of Child Holocaust Survivors' Experiences with Restitution," in John K. Roth and Elizabeth Maxwell, eds., *Remembering for the Future: The Holocaust in an Age of Genocides,* vol. 3 (New York: Palgrave, 2001), 923–37.

19. Peter Suedfeld, "Life after the Ashes: The Postwar Pain and Resilience of Young Holocaust Survivors," Monna and Otto Weinmann Annual Lecture, May 15, 2002, United States Holocaust Memorial Museum Center for Advanced Holocaust Studies, Washington, D.C.

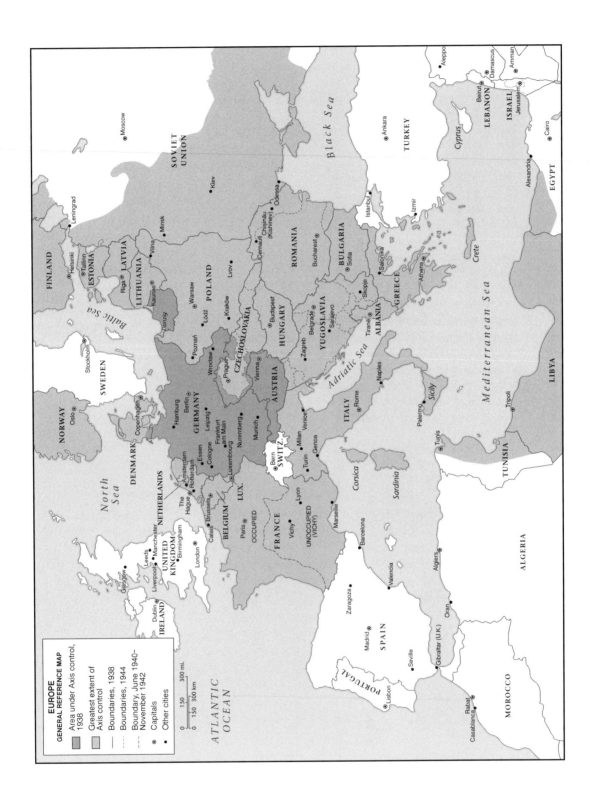

EUROPE
GENERAL REFERENCE MAP

Area under Axis control, 1938

Greatest extent of Axis control

Boundaries, 1938

Boundaries, 1944

Boundary, June 1940–November 1942

⊕ Capitals

• Other cities

0   150   300 mi.
0   150 300 km

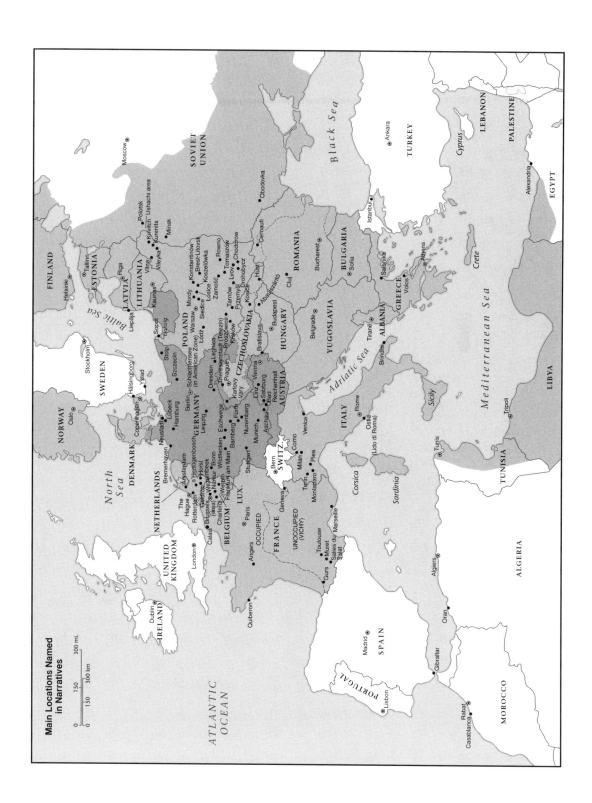

Main Locations Named
in Narratives

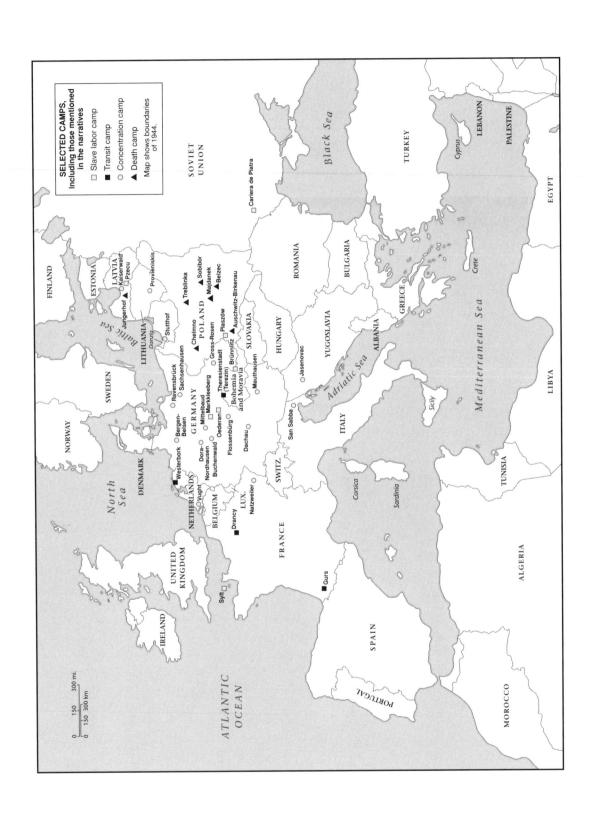

SELECTED CAMPS,
including those mentioned
in the narratives
☐ Slave labor camp
■ Transit camp
○ Concentration camp
▲ Death camp
Map shows boundaries
of 1944.

GROUP 1: SURVIVORS BORN AFTER 1935

Irka Beyond Irkutsk:
Vignettes of Escape from Poland and the Soviet Union

JUDITH TRAUB
(b. 1936, Poland)

Judith, or Judy, was not always my name. In reverse chronological order I have been called Irene, Irina, Irena, Ida, and Irka. When I arrived in the United States in 1951 at fifteen, I abandoned "Irene" and chose "Judith"—the equivalent of my Hebrew name, "Yehudit" (Jewess).

My birth certificate is dated April 26, 1936, although, according to my parents, I was born April 20 in Zamość, an architecturally distinguished city in southeastern Poland, founded around 1600. It now consists of the old town, considered the prestigious area, and the new town. Before World War II it had a population of thirty-four thousand, half of which was Jewish. It was home to the well-known socialist leader Rosa Luxemburg and the famous Yiddish author I. L. Peretz.

Zamość was also home to both my parents. They were born in the early 1900s and met in the mid-1920s. My father, Uszer Hechthopf, was then a handsome young man, sensitive, intelligent, and well educated in Talmudic studies. By profession he was a bookkeeper employed by a wealthy Polish flour mill owner named Badzian. My father was also a volunteer bookkeeper for a charitable Jewish organization chaired by my maternal grandfather, Eli Zwilich, who recognized my father's merits and arranged a match between the charming bookkeeper and his own daughter, Rywka, my mother. She was twenty years old, strong willed and stubborn, beautiful and sophisticated, educated at a secular gymnasium (European high school).

My father arrived at the prearranged rendezvous in the park wearing peasant boots and an outlandish hat. Mother was appalled. If it had not been for her parents' perseverance, she would not have pursued this relationship with my father. He, on the other hand, intentionally wore this costume to test my mother's character. Were appearances more important to her than character?

They were married on a Friday in February 1927. Many Jewish weddings took place on that day of the week and ended before the onset of the Sabbath, thus shortening the celebration and lessening the expense.

My parents had a good marriage. They lived in a comfortable apartment in the old section of Zamość, near their families. My sister, Tosia, was born in 1928, and I followed eight years later. We were surrounded by loving relatives and close friends. I was cared for by a Polish nanny, Marianna Szczuz, who accompanied us each summer to Zakopane, a fashionable resort in the Carpathian Mountains.

In 1937, after managing one of Badzian's flour mills on consignment, my father built his own mill in Tomaszów Lubelski. We moved into a large house in Tomaszów, only twelve miles from Zamość. For the next two years life was normal and uncomplicated.

The events of September 1, 1939, changed everything. At lunchtime that day my mother tried to bribe my sister with two zlotys to eat a *kotlet,* a hamburger. The negotiations were interrupted by a loud explosion. We ran into the garden; fiery colors illuminated the skies, and sulphurlike fumes filled the air. The first German bombs had fallen on Poland and World War II had begun.

Panic set in. Everyone scrambled toward the ditches in the yard, which had been dug during the previous few weeks in anticipation of war. In the evening, when the all-clear sirens blared, we returned to our homes, where the windows were covered with lightproof window shades. During the next few days we attempted to make contact with our extended families to consult, discuss, make plans. But confusion reigned and rumors, rather than facts, prevailed.

The Nonaggression Pact between German Foreign Minister Joachim von Ribbentrop and Soviet Foreign Minister Vyacheslav Molotov, signed on August 23, 1939, provided for the division of Poland between Germany and the Soviet Union. Zamość came under German rule and Tomaszów under Russian authority. Thus our families were separated and unable to reunite.

My parents joined a multitude of other refugees on a trek east. They stopped in Chodorow (or Khodoriv), in Ukraine, a place known for its wooden synagogues. My father's two younger sisters and their families lived there. They provided temporary accommodations during this time of chaos and havoc.

Although I could not know it then, my short childhood of three and a half

Left to right: Tosia; nanny Marianna Szczuz; Irka (now Judith) in Marianna's lap; and Rywka Hechthopf, Tosia and Irka's mother, in Tomaszów Lubelski, Poland, 1937.

years had come to an abrupt end. My family became homeless and helpless, persecuted and hounded. My normal life did not resume until 1962, when I settled on Long Island as a married woman of twenty-six.

The ground was damp and cold. I could barely breathe as I lay facedown in the narrow ditch by the side of a rural road. My sister's knees pushed against me, and my mother's trembling body pressed down upon us. She was shielding her children from the bombers flying overhead. We were fleeing from the Germans and traveling by horse-drawn wagon along a crowded, refugee-filled road when the bombing attack began. By the time it was over, the whole area looked like a battleground, but instead of soldiers in uniform, we could see only dead civilians in ordinary clothing.

We reached Chodorow in the autumn of 1939. One night, June 29, 1940, we heard a knock on our door, and three Russian soldiers entered the simple wooden house. They instructed my parents to pack within the next half hour and take only as much baggage as they could carry. We were going to a distant, unidentified place.

After many weeks of travel by wagon, boat, and train, we were placed in communal barracks in Bodaybo, Siberia, on September 5 to await transportation for the next stretch of our odyssey. By now my father was very ill with bleeding ulcers. The hospital was overcrowded and admission to it impossible. Frequently, my mother would disappear for hours, while my father lay listless on a cot, and my twelve-year-old sister took charge of me.

One day my mother returned from a secretive expedition in a jubilant mood. She had approached a high-ranking official's wife and had given her a priceless, cherished dress. This was how my mother gained access to the woman's important husband. The official was impressed by my mother's argument. His sense of empathy emerged and with it an admission slip to the hospital.

Does a three-and-a-half-year-old have memory? Perhaps not continuous memory but memories of isolated events that engrave themselves upon her subconscious mind. My first remembrance of Uncle Kisil is when he came to visit my parents, Tosia, and little me in Chodorow. He was one of my mother's six siblings, sent as an emissary by my grandparents to convince us to return to Zamość.

He arrived unannounced. He was young, tall, slender, and handsome. He brought me a present. It was a two-piece, pale blue, woolen knit outfit, most appropriate for the late fall weather. As everyone admired me in it, I admired myself in front of the mirror of the armoire.

Two days later, after persuading my parents to come back to Zamość, Kisil left. Shortly thereafter we left too but not for German-occupied Poland, as planned. When my father applied for a travel pass from the Soviet authorities in Chodorow, they labeled him disloyal to Russia. We were exiled and sent as political prisoners to an outpost in a most remote region of Siberia, where we remained for two years. Eventually, we were relocated to Samarkand in the Uzbek Republic in Central Asia.

It was here in Samarkand that I began an infrequent and one-sided correspondence with Uncle Kisil. Although my parents tried to discourage me from engaging in such a hopeless endeavor, I continued to write postcards with short childish messages. One day, three years later and shortly after the war, while we were living in Stuttgart, my uncle Kisil appeared at the door of our apartment. He was barely recognizable after seven years. He no longer looked like a young man. His posture was stooped and bent; his sparse hair was mostly gray; his once-smiling blue eyes were vacant and full of sadness.

On Kisil's right forearm was tattooed a ten-digit number preceded by the letter A. The tattoo revealed that he had been an inmate at Auschwitz. The thumb of that hand was missing, and its absence was self-inflicted so that he would be exempted from fearful work assignments. While he was confined to the infirmary, one of the last Nazi death selections took place. Almost all the inmates of Kisil's regular barrack were sent to the gas chambers, while he escaped their fate.

After liberation at Auschwitz, Kisil returned to Zamość to search for his immediate family. He found that all had perished in the Holocaust. His prewar home was in shambles—the walls had crumbled, the rafters were hanging, and all fur-

Ikutiel Zwilich (Uncle
Kisil) and Judith's sister,
Tosia, in Zamość, Poland,
1936.

nishings were gone. But under the rubble Kisil spotted a piece of white paper. It
was one of my postcards from Samarkand. That's how he learned that his sister and
her family had escaped Nazi annihilation and were probably still alive.

After months of extensive personal inquiries and information from acquaintances and strangers, my uncle located us in Stuttgart. Our reunion was joyous yet
sad, uplifting yet desperate. Kisil set out for Palestine. Despite the British blockade
and his imprisonment at a detention camp on Cyprus, he reached his destination
in time to participate in Israel's war for independence.

At the end of 1951 my family emigrated to the United States. During the
ensuing years I visited Uncle Kisil in Israel several times. Each time he lavished on
me gifts that he could barely afford. (He was offered monetary reparations from the
West German government but refused to accept them.)

Many years later my children still read from the now-stained Passover Hag-
gadah, my husband wraps himself in the frayed tallith (prayer shawl), I wear a frag-

ile silver bracelet, all gifts from Uncle Kisil. And each day as I look at Kisil's photograph on the piano, my heart fills with emotion and my eyes with tears. I loved Kisil for his devotion and dedication to me, and for being the only surviving composite of all the dead relatives.

Uncle Kisil died at fifty-five of a broken heart and the lack of will to live. At his death his wallet contained a folded, time-worn, and badly torn piece of whitish paper. The writing on it was illegible, but the faded stamp was recognizable and the postal cancellation decipherable. It read "Samarkand."

Late August of a Siberian summer (1940). The rocky and mossy embankments were identical on both sides of the wide river. They rose steeply toward the evergreen forests of spruce and pine trees, interrupted here and there by flat and flowering plains. The river served as the primary highway for the infrequent boats, barges, and rafts that provided access to the scattered settlements along its banks.

In two months, by mid-October, the waters will begin to freeze and navigation will cease. Once solid, the river will continue to provide passage, for horse-drawn sleds and wagons. The plains will be transformed into white wasteland, and endless snow-covered taiga (subarctic forest) will dominate the forbidding landscape. By early April the thick ice covering the river will begin to crack and break. Transportation will come to a standstill, until the ice melts completely and the river again becomes a flowing waterway.

A lone raft rode rapidly downstream on the raging waters. The raft was primitive, consisting of about a dozen logs tied together by thick interwoven ropes. A local Russian peasant was guiding it. I was four and squatted in the center of the wet raft, wedged between my mother and my sister. An overwhelming fear of both the hostile surroundings and the freezing spray of the river water sent shivers through my body.

An object in the middle of the river just ahead of us attracted my attention. It grew progressively larger as we sped toward it. I recognized it as a motorboat with a single passenger standing by the rail, staring at us in disbelief. As I studied the expression on his face, I was suddenly jolted into reality. The man was my father! We had been separated for three weeks, while he remained in the hospital with his bleeding ulcer. We were exiles en route to the hinterland of Siberia.

When we passed each other, the boat from the netherworld and the raft to nowhere, we were too stunned to utter a sound. Mental paralysis let the rare moment of contact evade us. Will I behold my beloved father again? Will he disappear forever?

Thankfully, we reunited two days later, on October 5, 1940, in Syniuga, our final destination. It was a small settlement, 930 miles east of Irkutsk. This desolate, God-forsaken place became our open jail for the next year. There were no barbed-wire fences or armed guards. It was a natural prison where the rugged terrain and the harsh climate prevented escape.

Winter. The log barracks in which we lived were subdivided into small cubicles, each housing three or four people. Adults were allotted a cot, and children shared one, sleeping head to foot. The narrow cots were placed away from the permanently frost-covered walls lest the warm human body adhere to the cold ice on contact. A black metal coal stove sat in the communal hallway. Its long pipe exited through the roof, and its cooking surface held a greasy skillet. It heated oil in which we dipped black bread, our staple food. We obtained water by lowering buckets into deep holes in the ice of the river. The filled pails were suspended from the two ends of a pole placed across the shoulders and carried home.

Adult exiles were assigned to fell trees in the taiga, in subzero temperatures. Most suffered from frostbite, and many died from the shortage of food and medication. My father, however, was assigned (through back-door connections) to work as a bookkeeper in the heated office of the lumber production control center. He became a Stakhanovite, a top-producing worker whose name was posted on the weekly honor roll bulletin.

As a result, he was dispatched monthly to other lumber camps to inspect their production records. He traveled by horse and sled, the horse leading the way through the almost continuous darkness of the winter days and nights. Upon his return he would tell us in detail about his encounters with wolves, reindeer, and foxes. During my father's prolonged absences I lived in a state of constant panic, envisioning his being attacked by wild animals. His safe return was a miracle that repeated itself over and over.

The endless frozen steppe stretched beyond the horizon. The only reminders of civilization were a solitary hut, a horse and sleigh next to it, and a group of three adults with two children. The adults were my parents and a hired sleigh driver. The children were my sister, Tosia, and me.

We all wore multiple layers of clothing and fleece-lined boots. The men wore hats with flaps covering their ears, my mother and sister had babushkas (scarves) wrapped around their heads, and I wore my Polish winter outfit, skimpy and outgrown. The air was about zero degrees Fahrenheit on this spring morning (April 15, 1942) in Siberia. Dead silence dominated the solemn landscape. As we stood there, tapping our feet and clapping our hands to keep from freezing, faint sounds from a distant, invisible source interrupted the quiet. As the sounds grew louder, I could see an airplane approaching, growing larger and larger in the sky. It landed a few feet away from us, slipping and sliding on the icy surface of the "landing strip." The plane was very small and dilapidated, used for transporting freight and unimportant passengers such as my family.

My father had finally been granted a transfer to a regional office in Bodaybo, a major town in central Siberia where we had stopped briefly in September 1940. His objective was to relocate closer to Western Europe and the Iranian border so that we might some day escape from the Soviet Union.

We had reached the "airport" via a frozen river, but since the waterways had begun to thaw, we could travel to Bodaybo only by air. Such luxury was a rare privilege. We were lucky, or so I thought, as I ascended the wooden ladder that was leaning against the plane's open door. Once inside, I changed my mind. The pilot's stern face, the two metal benches, and the ripped rubber mats on the floor presented a grim scene aboard this barely heated monster. Immediately upon takeoff, I was motion sick and began retching violently. The vomit froze as soon as it made contact with the cold air.

When we arrived in Bodaybo, we were housed in a two-room log cabin. One room was occupied by a Russian peasant woman and her teenage son, the other by the four of us. We all shared a hearth with a stove for heat and cooking, tin pitchers for water, a wooden tub for washing, a couple of kerosene lamps for lighting, and a barrel of pickled cabbage (sauerkraut).

Food was scarce that summer of 1942, and by autumn there was a famine in Bodaybo and the surrounding areas. Each evening during the harvest my mother, sister, and I went to the potato fields to scavenge for leftover or discarded spuds. From these my mother prepared delicacies. She wasted nothing. She transformed the peels, considered food suitable only for animals, into delicious pancakes. My mother discovered an edible variety of poison ivy that she picked with rag-wrapped hands. She boiled it and served it (with blistered fingers) as soup. We shared these foods with our roommates, while they shared their barrel of sauerkraut with us.

I was sickly and skinny at six and looked younger. My parents registered me in the children's communal kitchen as an eligible five-year-old, entitled to receive free cooked meals.

I was present when my mother bartered a fashionable black woolen coat that she had purchased in prewar Warsaw. It was a Parisian model, with weights sewn into the hem to give it shape and a permanently pressed look. She traded this valuable coat for counterfeit transit papers. My parents were determined to escape a winter of starvation in Bodaybo, and the negotiator was eager to complete the transaction quickly. I was amazed at how fast the man departed, hugging the coat to his chest. Later my parents explained that the coat buyer probably thought that he had found an overlooked treasure, mistaking the weights in the hem for hidden gold coins. We left Bodaybo in a hurry. Weeks after, in the fall of 1942, we arrived in Samarkand, after a sojourn of several weeks in Tashkent. Perhaps survival was possible after all.

A pair of silver candlesticks were miraculous objects to me at the age of six, at sixteen, and still at sixty-six. These family heirlooms were given to my mother by her grandmother on her wedding day. During normal times in Poland my mother, like her female ancestors before her, lit the candles in the candlesticks each Friday night to usher in the Sabbath. In Bodaybo, Siberia, they were my security blanket. Whenever I was alone, I would surreptitiously crawl beneath the bed where they were hidden, unwrapping and rubbing them like Aladdin's lamp, hoping for a magic genie to appear and grant me my wishes.

I repeatedly recited the same supplications: "Please don't let my father have another ulcer attack . . . and stop those nasty boys from beating and tormenting my sister on her way from school . . . and Mother, poor Mother, don't let her be burned again by the steam in the bath house . . . and if I have any wishes left, please take away my cough from tuberculosis. I want to go to school."

Many years later I began to wonder about my origins. In 1983 I traveled to Poland to examine my roots and to ground myself. Armed with a list of places that my parents provided, I retraced my steps and visited sites of the annihilation of my people. Upon my arrival in Zamość I inquired at the city hall about an attorney to discuss my family's properties, a still-existing house and a working flour mill. I was directed to a Mr. Richter.

Richter, in his late fifties, was a *Volksdeutsche,* one of many Germans settled by the Nazis in the early 1940s in Poland to balance the Polish population with German nationals. He invited me to his home and was charming and hospitable. As he conducted a tour of his comfortable apartment, he pointed out his valuable acquisitions: a statue of General Josef Pilsudski, a Polish national hero; a wall-hanging depicting a scene from local history; and a pair of silver candlesticks, almost identical to Mother's.

Mother's candlesticks are now mine. I light the candles in them each Friday night to usher in the Sabbath. In their flames, I see my mother's face and hear her voice whispering: "Good Sabbath, my child."

The courtyard was surrounded by a crumbling stone wall. Three mud huts and an outhouse stood in the corners of the yard, and a well was in the middle. One hut housed an Uzbek couple, another a Polish Jewish expatriate, and the last was occupied by my family.

It was hot. My parents and our expatriate neighbor sat on a makeshift wooden bench in front of his hut. They were engaged in a serious, hushed conversation. It was interrupted by the chanting call from the minaret of a nearby mosque that was summoning Muslims to evening prayers. When their chat resumed, puzzling words reached my ears: "Roosevelt . . . president . . . peace."

It was mid-April 1945, a week before my ninth birthday. In Samarkand in the Uzbek Republic a time of celebratory anticipation became a time of deep mourning. Our "savior," Franklin Delano Roosevelt, president of the United States of America, halfway across the world, had died and with him our hope for peace.

On the morning of my birthday, April 20 (in common with Hitler), I was awakened by my sister's scream. A deadly scorpion was crawling across our shared pillow. While our father disposed of the venomous creature, and our mother sprinkled water and swept the dusty earthen floor of our one-room hut, I rehearsed a many-versed poem that my sister had written at Mother's request for me to recite on my birthday. I was nervous, dreading the task that lay ahead. I don't recall the birthday celebration, but I vividly recall my father's taking me at its conclusion to the local photographer. There he presented me with a typical Arab head covering worn by males, and I wore it proudly as I posed for photographs. I looked emaciated, however, because I had had a serious bout with jaundice. I missed second grade and was tutored by my mother in school subjects and instructed by my father in Hebrew.

In the spring of 1945, shortly after the war in Europe had ended, we were traveling again. It was Passover. The train was heading toward Szczecin, a Polish town on the escape route from Eastern to Western Europe. All along the rail tracks were German prisoners of war engaged in forced labor. As the train moved slowly past the staring Germans, my mother kept throwing pieces of homemade matzoh at them. I could not understand why she would waste our limited food on these much-despised people. When I questioned her, she firmly replied: "To let the Germans know that the Jews are still alive!"

My mother did not receive rewards or medals. But to her family she was a hero through whose efforts and resourcefulness we survived the war. Whenever I think of the many acts of courage that she performed, a smile spreads across my face and a warm sensation surges through my body.

I am proud of you, Mother.

It was early spring in 1946 in Szczecin, Poland, and the mood among the fifty people sitting on the floor of the cold, barren room was somber. As a ten-year-old I could sense the tension among the adults and the restlessness among the children. There were only a few boys present. The occupants of the room, all strangers, had gathered early that afternoon in a small abandoned house on the outskirts of the city. My family had arrived last. A middle-aged Polish man added our names to a list. He seemed to be in charge of the group and was assisted by a younger Russian.

This would be a crucial night for all of us. After months of arduous search, negotiations, and preparations, we surviving remnants of World War II were about to be smuggled out of Russian-occupied Poland. We would be crossing illegally through East Germany, and we hoped to enter West Berlin, the gateway to Western Europe.

The afternoon dragged on forever, but night finally arrived and with it a small army truck. Everyone was excited, rushing to put on their outer garments, gather the children, pick up their meager bundles, and head for the door. But the Pole and the Russian stopped us, and the Pole began to read the names in the order in which they appeared on the list. But when our names were read, instead of being led outside, we were informed that there was no space left for us on the truck. Despite much arguing, begging, and cajoling, the situation remained unchanged. We heard the engine start and the lorry depart. That night we slept fully dressed, anxious and miserable, on the floor.

The next day we were joined by new arrivals. Close to midnight, we were loaded into the truck. Freezing and hungry, we sat on wooden benches underneath a tarpaulin cover. A while later, after a bumpy drive, the truck stopped. I heard a conversation, mostly in Russian, between the driver and male strangers. And then the truck started up again, carrying us through the quiet night. At daybreak we reached Berlin. After a stopover in the French sector to wash, eat, and sleep, we were delivered at Schlachtensee, the DP (displaced persons) camp in the American sector, also known as Düppel Center.

Only a few years ago I learned the logistics of this operation from Rabbi Herbert Friedman. He had been a chaplain in the U.S. Army in 1946, stationed in Berlin. He was assigned to care for the needs of the two thousand Jewish soldiers in the four Allied armies, but at the same time he was a secret member of the Bricha.

This organization was composed of current and former members of the Jewish Brigade of the British army and financed by the American Jewish Joint Distribution Committee (known as the JDC or simply as "the Joint") and the Jewish Agency for Palestine. The Bricha was responsible for bringing Jewish survivors out of Eastern Europe to Berlin's American sector and thence to Mediterranean ports. The chaplain and others secretly commandeered U.S. Army trucks, which held fifty people each. The drivers, gunners, and mechanics were all Palestinian Jewish soldiers. They would set out from Berlin at dusk and arrive in Szczecin (formerly Stetin) by midnight. They had arranged to pay the bribes.

The guards on our side of the crossing point were Polish, and on the German side they were Russian, because this was the Soviet zone of occupation. The bribes, divided between the two sets of guards, amounted to one carton of American cigarettes or US$150 for each Jew on the truck. The money and cigarettes were contributed by Jewish soldiers or sent by donors in the United States and funneled to the Bricha by the Joint.

For the Holocaust survivors liberation was the end of a nightmare and the beginning of a painful process of readjustment. They came to West Berlin from the corners of Eastern Europe and from various Soviet republics. They came from concentration camps and hiding places. They had a look of both despair and hope on their gaunt faces and sadness in their eyes. They were dressed in worn clothing, crudely mended and patched, and carried meager belongings in bundles or frayed suitcases. My parents, sister, and I were among them. It was May 28, 1946.

We were assigned a room, to be shared with four other people, in a barrack of block number 46, at Camp Schlachtensee. This camp was sponsored by the United Nations Relief and Rehabilitation Administration (UNRRA) and operated by the

U.S. Army. It was located on a recently vacated Nazi military base on the outskirts of the bombed-out city.

Schlachtensee was administered by Harold Fishbein, a UN official and a former American army officer. He was compassionate and sensitive to the Jewish internees' recent painful past and current needs. The camp became an autonomous, all-encompassing community where we felt safe. It had a school, library, synagogue, medical clinic, and sports center. A weekly newspaper was published in Yiddish, the common language; political parties were represented at meetings; and attempts were made to resume a semblance of normal life that fulfilled the emotional and social needs of the residents. Official weddings, brises (circumcision ceremonies), holiday celebrations, burials, and other rituals were observed for the first time in many years. But there were hardly any bar mitzvah ceremonies.

Accommodations at Schlachtensee were Spartan. We slept on army cots, ate food supplied by the army, and dressed in either surplus military garb or second-hand clothing donated by Americans. I recall a pair of laced brown shoes that I wore even though they were much too narrow for my growing feet. I still blame those shoes for my painful bunions, which have plagued me ever since. Aside from daily tasks, we spent most of our time in conversation and exchanging information about the fate of relatives, friends, and acquaintances. In the beginning the stories of concentration camp horror seemed fabricated to me, but each narrative confirmed the content and veracity of the preceding one.

In the early days of postwar freedom someone wrote a song that expressed the common sentiments of the refugees. It became the hymn of the homeless everywhere. The lyrics were in Yiddish: *"Wuahin sol ich gayn, az dos ghetto iz farmacht?"* (Where shall I go now that the ghetto is closed?)

Schlachtensee closed in 1948 because of the Russian blockade of Berlin. We were flown out by American airplanes that brought in supplies. We were landed arbitrarily in Stuttgart.

"Herzl School, Schlachtensee Reunion 1991" read the banner outside a motel in Lancaster, Pennsylvania. The lobby was filled with well-dressed, middle-aged guests, the men clean-shaven and groomed, the women bejeweled and coiffured. They had come from the corners of the world. The participants were engaged in animated, overlapping conversations punctuated by exclamations of laughter and weeping, surprise and recognition.

In the center of the group sat an elderly gentleman. When I approached and identified myself, he did the same. He was Harold Fishbein, now ninety-three, the former director of Camp Schlachtensee. We reminisced, reviving long-dormant memories of remote places and forgotten events, identifying faces in the almost fifty-year-old photographs that accompanied each of us.

One of my pictures was inscribed on the back in childish handwriting in pencil. It read in Polish: "To my friend Irka, forever. Masza, Berlin, 1946." The photo showed two young girls, me and Masza. "But where is she presently?" I asked a woman standing next to me as she examined my album. She pointed at a woman nearby. Masza materialized out of the past. She is now a prominent businesswoman in New York City.

I was lonely in Munich during the summer of 1951. We had moved there from Stuttgart in 1949, and I attended a school sponsored by the Sochnut (the Jewish Agency for Israel) on Mehlstrasse. All my classmates and teachers were DPs and survivors. Although the teachers were not accredited professionals, they were educated, knowledgeable, and motivated. They taught every subject in Hebrew, the required common language used by the multilingual student body. The Jewish Agency supplied the textbooks.

After-school activities included ORT (Organization for Rehabilitation through Training), where I learned how to sew and embroider. I also visited the ice-skating rink in cold weather. But mostly, my friends and I were involved in common teen pursuits: socializing, boy-girl romancing, gossiping, playing, and dreaming. None of us discussed our wartime experiences; they lay dormant in the back of our minds. Subconsciously, we tried to recapture our lost childhoods and pretend that we too were normal youths.

One of my closest friends was Rut. She was Lithuanian and among the few whose two parents had survived the war. In school she stood out in science, and at play she distinguished herself as a tomboy and mischief planner. My bosom buddy was Yadzia. She was Polish like me. She and her widowed mother lived near me, and we spent most days and many nights together, sharing secrets and intimacies. She was feminine and sensitive. Yadzia excelled in the arts: she drew beautifully and played the violin. And I, Irka, stood out in the liberal arts, especially languages and literature.

The Jewish community in Munich at that time was transient. By 1951 most of the DPs had emigrated to the new State of Israel, the United States, Canada, Australia, South America, and South Africa. Rut left for Canada, and Yadzia moved to Berlin after her mother remarried. I felt isolated and abandoned. My parents applied for emigration to the United States and awaited sponsorship papers from my mother's uncle, who was a prewar resident of New York.

Our school did not reopen in September because there were so few students. A former classmate, Shoshana, and I reluctantly enrolled in a German public school. Our proficiency in German was limited and our cultural differences obvious. We were either ostracized or ridiculed, at best ignored by the German students and faculty. Shoshana and I clung to each other like drifters in the sea, as if we were drowning in the ocean of hostility. After five weeks of misery among the enemy, we quit this school with relief. We stayed at home, awaiting emigration.

When we finally sailed from Bremerhaven in mid-November, I was excited and impatient to reach Milwaukee, the destination assigned to us. Our ship was the USNS *General A. W. Greely.* It transported army troops from the States who had been assigned to Europe and on the return journey brought refugees emigrating to the United States. My sister, who had married two months before we left, remained with her husband in Munich; both would graduate from medical school at the end of the semester, then would join us in America.

Aboard ship, men and women had separate accommodations. My mother and I were directed to bunk beds in the hold, with about one hundred other women. My father's situation was the same among the men. For privacy we had crude curtains between rows of double-decked sleeping platforms, which were reminiscent of wartime labor camps and postwar DP barracks. At mealtimes we stood in line with metal dishes and canteens in the malodorous mess hall to receive our ration of food.

The thirteen-day ocean passage was difficult for me. The waters of the Atlantic were turbulent and the weather stormy. I was seasick most of the time, lying on a cot in the infirmary.

At last, on December 4, 1951, we reached New York harbor. It was dusk. I was elated by the breathtaking view of the illuminated Statue of Liberty, the tall skyscrapers in the background, and the light-studded bridges in the foreground. It looked like a fantasy world created from sparkling jewels. I stood on the deck mesmerized, glad we had to remain on the ship overnight.

The following morning I eagerly ran back to the deck. I was shocked. To my great dismay the scene of the previous evening seemed like a mirage. Gray bleakness enveloped dilapidated buildings facing the pier; cloudy skies hung heavily over garbage and debris-strewn paths, and a damp and misty blanket covered everything.

My eyes filled with tears as I followed my parents down the gangway. After extended immigration processing, we were met by a representative of the Joint, who informed us that our destination had been changed from idyllic Milwaukee to earthy Chicago. Opportunities for physicians were better in large cities, and the Joint did not want to separate families, in our case, my sister and brother-in-law.

December is not my favorite month, and that was especially true for December of 1951. My parents and I arrived in Chicago at the beginning of the month, on a cold and rainy day. We were met at the railroad station by a female representative of the Joint and taken by bus to an apartment in a Jewish neighborhood on the South Side. The apartment was occupied by an elderly woman who made two rooms available to us, "the green immigrants," in order to supplement her income. The Joint paid three months' rent for us. The premises were dark and musty, poorly furnished, and very depressing. The whole scene was a sad introduction to life in the U.S.

The next day my father took me to the Ida Crown Hebrew Academy. It was an Orthodox parochial school that offered secular studies in English, and Jewish studies in Hebrew. I was enrolled in tenth grade and began attending this school in midsemester. Once again I was a stranger in a strange land, an outsider in an established student society, a nonobservant pretender in a religious educational institution.

As a fifteen-year-old I wanted to acclimate and be part of the group. But I was different: my speech, my dress, my lack of makeup, my non-English-speaking parents, and mostly my self-image. I was conditioned during the war and afterward in Europe to be ashamed of being Jewish. I knew the Christians only as enemies and persecutors. It took me many years from that December of 1951 to gain self-confidence as a person and pride as a Jew.

My passage led through undergraduate college in Chicago and Brooklyn from 1953 to 1956 and a semester of study in Israel in 1956. While I was there, the Suez Crisis broke out. Both my parents and I panicked. This war came only ten years after World War II, which was too fresh in our memories. Although I could have remained in "dangerous" Israel, I returned to "safe" America. Because of that decision I have felt guilt and regrets for years. In Israel I felt a sense of belonging, identity, and self-confidence. There I was at home. In the United States I was still in exile.

When I returned to the States, I boarded with my mother's widowed aunt in Brooklyn and supported myself through teaching at Hebrew schools. In addition, I studied at the Jewish Theological Seminary and earned a master of Hebrew letters degree. I was now a practicing Orthodox Jew. Initial pretense had led to genuine conviction.

I was of marriageable age. Whom did I date? Definitely not survivors! After all, I considered myself unaffected by the Holocaust. I reasoned that I was too young at the time to be influenced by wartime events. I wanted a normal life with a mate who was American-born, representing stability; a professional, representing security; an observant Orthodox Jew, providing commonality. The man I married in 1959 met all my requirements.

My husband, Gerald, is a dentist who volunteered for the U.S. Army and was stationed as an officer in Pirmasens, Germany. After he finished his military service, we settled on Long Island in a predominantly non-Jewish community. My husband opened a dental practice. I resumed graduate studies, this time at C. W. Post College, and earned a master's in library science. We raised two children, Shari and Jeffrey.

I searched for religious liberation yet kept traditions and rituals. Our daughter and son attended a Hebrew day school outside our residential area. I began to feel like a fish out of water as a traditional Jew in an assimilated community and a primarily Gentile world. Even at fifty I had still not found a comfortable niche for myself and my family.

To separate truth from fantasy, to ground the facts of my origin, I made that trip to Poland in 1983. This odyssey became a milestone in my life. It made me

Judith Traub, Long Island,
New York, 1995

aware that the years of war had left an undeniable imprint on my psyche. After the pilgrimage to the land of my birth, I accepted the reality of the effects of the Holocaust upon me, and my need and right to identify myself as a survivor. Ever since, I have immersed myself in issues relating to the Shoah and exposed myself to the subject through books, lectures, films, docudramas, conferences, and symposia.

In 1995 I retired after twenty-five years as a teacher-librarian. It was then that I participated in the videotaping project sponsored by Steven Spielberg. I am a donor of war-related materials to museums and institutions and an organizer of functions. But, most important, I am finally at peace with myself. Since 1986 I have lived in Great Neck, a predominantly Jewish community on Long Island. My friends are a mix of survivors, American-born Jews, foreign-born Jews, and observant and secular Jews.

My children are successful professionals, dedicated to Judaism and their Jewish heritage. My three grandchildren are named after my parents and Uncle Kisil.

In 1959, eight years after I arrived in the United States and three years after becoming a naturalized American citizen, I returned to Germany. This voyage across the Atlantic Ocean, heading eastward, was much different from my westbound trip in 1951. This time I sailed aboard the luxury liner SS *Bremen* on its return maiden voyage. My private cabin had a porthole, the new linens were made of damask, the towels of plush terry cloth. The dishes in the elegant dining room were fine china, and champagne filled the crystal glasses.

I came to Germany as a newlywed, wife of an officer in the U.S. Army Dental Corps, and as a teacher at the American Dependents School. For two years we lived among Germans in the town of Pirmasens near the River Saar and worked among Americans on the army base. My relationship with the local population was limited by choice and based on past experience. Although the tables had turned—I belonged with the victorious, they with the vanquished—I was not jubilant, just suspicious and mistrusting. I mentally questioned every German over a certain age: "Where were you during the war? How many Jews did you murder?"

The highlight of this sojourn was my reunion with Yadzia. We spent time together before she emigrated to Israel, where she met and wed an Israeli book publisher. Our relationship had not changed; the years of separation only reinforced our mutual affection. The one thing that had changed was her name: Yadzia had dropped her Polish name and assumed the Hebrew name of Tova.

We have maintained contact ever since, through personal visits, correspondence, and long-distance telephone calls. Tova is an established artist whose paintings are exhibited in galleries and museums in Israel, the United States, and Europe. She is also known in Israel as a stage and costume designer for major theaters. That is her public image. In private she remains a warm and caring person, but, like other survivors, permanently affected by her wartime memories. She has yet to speak of them.

Rut, now Ruth, on the other hand, shares the memories of her wartime experiences by writing and lecturing about them. When she was seven and an inmate in a Lithuanian ghetto, Ruth was responsible for her four-year-old sister while her parents worked at a labor camp. In their absence a *Kinderaktion* (children's death selection) took place in the ghetto. An SS officer decided that Ruth should live, but her sister, Tamara, was torn from her grip and placed on a deathbound truck, never to be seen again. Ruth survived the rest of the war as a Christian child in hiding with an Aryan Catholic peasant family.

Although I was not a hidden child, I was drawn to the first International Gathering of Children Hidden During World War II, held in Manhattan in 1991. Twelve hundred people participated in numerous workshops, lectures, and events. While observing a psychodrama workshop, I was stunned. A familiar female figure approached the microphone. As she spoke, her voice awakened a long-dormant memory. After forty years I still recognized my childhood friend Rut from Munich. I called out her name from across the room. She responded with "Irka?" We hugged and kissed and gave vent to our emotions, while the audience shared our momentous reunion.

In June of 2001 we organized a fiftieth reunion of students who attended the school on Mehlstrasse. Tova, Ruth, and I participated in this milestone event in Munich. Many others joined us from around the world. Few reside in Germany, and some refused to set foot on German soil. We, the child survivors of the Holocaust, mature adults today, have developed different attitudes as a result of our experiences. We act and react according to the dictates of our psyches and interpretations of our minds. Yet we were all branded by the catastrophes of our childhood.

I Was Only Three Years Old

RENÉE FRITZ
(b. 1937, Austria)

During 1939–45 thousands of Jewish children across Europe escaped Adolf Hitler's systematic genocide. They hid in basements and sewers, joined Christian families, and took refuge in convents, monasteries, and orphanages, where they concealed their identities from all but a few.

The children were witnesses to one of the darkest periods in history. They felt guilty for being alive when a staggering six million Jews perished around them, including more than 1.5 million children. Psychologists agree that hiding was often quite traumatic, leaving their lives blemished, scarred, tormented, anguished, and mystifying—and robbing a generation of its childhood. Instead of playing with dolls as a young Jewish girl, I was learning to recite the rosary. Instead of singing, I was learning prayers. Instead of going to school, I was hiding. Instead of being with friends and family, our families plotted ways to evade the Gestapo's spontaneous searches in a never-ending series of raids.

I was born in April 1937 in Vienna, the only child of Nicholas and Sabina

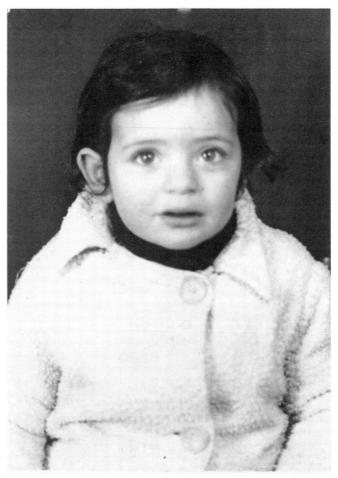

Renée Schwalb,
Vienna, 1939.

Schwalb, a middle-class family whose comfortable existence ended when my father was abruptly arrested a year later. His crime? He was a Jew.

Hitler's troops entered Austria in March 1938, announcing the Anschluss (the annexation of that country) two days later in Vienna. Jews soon learned that they were targets. My father, who was a retailer, was immediately arrested. My mother learned that he had been taken to the concentration camp at Dachau. She also found out that she might be able to obtain his release if she could prove that he would leave Austria immediately upon his release. Obtaining the visas and other necessary papers was not easy, but she was able to purchase them on the black market. In 1939 my father was released from Dachau and left Austria; we did not know where he went.

Life for us was so dangerous in Vienna that I was placed on a Kindertransport in 1939 and sent to Belgium. I was two years old and had never been separated from my mother. Fortunately, my grandmother lived in Brussels, and I stayed with her until my mother joined us later that year.

After a few months my mother and I left for Calais, France, hoping to catch a ship to the United States. The French authorities arrested us because we spoke German. They thought we might be German collaborators. I wonder how a child of two could be considered a collaborator. After spending weeks in jail, trying to convince the French that we were not German sympathizers, we were finally released and returned to Brussels.

The Germans invaded Belgium in May 1940. I had just reached my third birthday. Rumors were that Jewish people caught with their children would automatically perish. Through a connection my mother made arrangements for us to be hidden in the confined quarters of a Mme Degelas. But my mother soon realized that our being hidden together was too dangerous. Our chances of survival were greater if we were separated and hidden in different places.

So, with the assistance of Mme Degelas, I entered a Catholic convent in 1940. I was three. My name was changed to Suzanne Ledent—the name I would keep throughout the war—and I was to answer only to my new name, the Mother Superior told me. She told me that she was going to go to church and showed me all the nice medals that I would get if I knew the right prayers and the right things to say. She also told me that, from now on, I would celebrate my birthday on Saint Suzanne Day. I didn't even know what a birthday was. Then the Mother Superior gave me a huge safety pin and told me that every time I learned another prayer, I would get another medal that I could slip onto the safety pin.

I quickly assimilated into my new church life. I became an ardent Catholic convert. My Yiddish and German gradually gave way to French and Flemish. Existence within the convent was strict, lonely, and intimidating. I was assigned to a nun and told never to go anywhere without her. She and I shared a space in a dormitory and went to church together. I spoke to no one else and saw no other children, except those who came to day school from the town. But I wasn't allowed to mingle with them or even speak to them. The motivating factors of survival were the daily prayers and religious experiences. My religious medals and rosary beads slowly increased my sense of belonging. They became my security blanket. They made me feel safe. I became a very reclusive child. I never left the confines of the convent, never interacted with anyone except the formidable nun to whom I had been assigned.

I was put to bed right after evening mass, and I was frightened of being alone in the dormitory. The metal partitions between the cubicles created strange vibrations that terrified me. The space I shared with the nun had a bed, a sink, and a bench on which to kneel. A huge cross and a picture of the Virgin Mary hung on the wall. I had no toys, no books except religious ones. I did what I was told and tried to be a very good child. While my "Christian soul" was well nourished and cared for, my emotional and physical needs were being starved. No one bothered to bathe or wash me. I never changed my clothes, which became infested with lice. Food was very scarce and I was always hungry. In the winter we had no heat and I was always very cold. I remember freezing each time I had to attend church services on the grounds of the convent. We had to step outside to reach the chapel. I never complained, I never cried. I had been told that I must not be noticed and that I must be good. To me that meant that I had to remain invisible and not make any noises that could attract attention. I really tried to be good and not let anyone see that I lived in constant terror. I thought that my life was not unusual in any way. I believed that all children lived that way.

In spite of my difficult life in the convent, I was getting used to it. In fact, I have one good memory of this institution, one little incident that left a deep impression on me. While I was there, the observance of Saint Suzanne Day was significant to me because the saint and I had the same name. On that day when I exclaimed, "It's my birthday," I was rewarded with a box of biscuits. To most of us a box of biscuits would not be very exciting. If you were starving, you too would celebrate any holiday where food would be offered as a gift.

Then in 1943 I was abruptly uprooted once again and taken to a farm to live with a family in the Belgian countryside. I later learned that the Nazis suspected that the nuns were hiding Jews in the convent. It was too dangerous for me to stay there. A strange man picked me up in the middle of the night, and I was ordered to follow him. This was another new environment for me. I had never met the family I was going to live with. Yet I was, at the age of six, expected to immediately adjust to my new situation. Fortunately, this family was very good to me and I learned to love them very much. They took care of my lice, supplied me with clean clothes, and gave me real food. Jeanine, the daughter who was two years older than I, became my friend. But the neighbors became suspicious and once again I had to leave. This time Mme Degelas picked me up from the farm where for a few months I had been so happy. I also recall seeing my mother at that time. She spent a few hours with me and then disappeared again.

Today I know that hiding Jews was very dangerous. During those unsettled times all Europeans were in constant fear for their own lives and the lives of their kin. No one was to be spared, regardless of their religious commitment, if they were guilty of concealing Jews.

Mme Degelas now brought me to a Protestant orphanage in Namur, Belgium. I was confused and bewildered. With Nazi headquarters across the street from the orphanage, every day I felt like a criminal in hiding, and I was terribly hungry and cold. This orphanage was a terrible place. No one looked after us. At seven years of age, I was supposed to take care of myself. I became so infested with lice that I got sick. Later on, after we were liberated in 1945, my head had to be shaved in order to get rid of the lice and allow my scalp to heal.

In this awful place starvation, fear, and loneliness were my sole companions. I had learned in the convent not to speak or interact with people I did not know. I remembered the admonitions of the nuns. My lonely and sad existence continued. Was I being punished because I was Jewish? Actually, I did not know what being Jewish meant. I thought that it must mean being bad. After all, I kept on being moved from one place to another. I could only assume that I was being punished for something.

At the end of the war in 1945 the Americans took over many Nazi headquarters, including the one that was near the orphanage where I was living. One day an American soldier came to the orphanage to look for a child to adopt. He chose me because I was the smallest child there and because I looked so sad. He brought me food, which was the greatest gift he could have given me. He took me out for rides around the town. We became good friends, and I was really looking forward to being adopted by him. I was now eight years old. Until he showed an interest in me, I could not recall being cared for so lovingly. Then I was reunited with my mother, who had survived Auschwitz.

Her survival was truly a miracle. When she arrived in Auschwitz, she was immediately selected to stand in one of the two lines that were being formed. She had no idea what the lines signified. At that point a Nazi officer appeared, pulled her out of the line, and ordered her to go to the other line. He recognized her from his school days in Vienna. He saved her life that day. Those who stood in the first line she had stood in were immediately sent to the gas chamber. She was then given a job in a munitions factory, where she labored long hours with very little food.

When my mother appeared, I cannot honestly say that I was happy to see her. I remembered her, yet our reunion was very difficult. We were not then, or later, able to resume normal relations. I truly wanted the American soldier to adopt me. My mother and I had been separated for five years. Our bonds had been broken.

My mother was very sick with typhus when she found me in Namur, and she had to be hospitalized. I remained in the orphanage for some time until she was well enough to remove me from that dreadful place. We returned to Brussels to a tiny apartment provided by the refugee relief agencies. With minimal rations and a coal stove for heat, we recovered from starvation and disease. The apartment in Brussels was also home to my maternal grandmother, who had survived the war in a Christian nursing home. She had been placed there by Mme Degelas, who felt that the Nazis would not find her there.

Sometimes we had no coal and no heat in the winter. I recall that my mother washed the floor every Friday night and lit Shabbat candles. One very cold Friday night she boiled a floor rag. After it dried, she unraveled it and with the wool she knitted a sweater for me with cap sleeves.

We were so poor that when my grandmother died, my mother could not afford to have her buried. It was several days before my grandmother was picked up by a Jewish agency and given a proper burial in a Jewish cemetery in Dilbeek, Belgium. My maternal grandfather did not survive the Holocaust. I have one last memory of him. While my mother and I were hiding in Mme Degelas's home, my grandfather came to see me. I was very proud that he invited me to go to the Orthodox synagogue with him that day. It was the last time I saw him.

I never attended school. In the convent I had taught myself to read French so I could learn my prayers. Now my mother ordered me to go to school. I had no intention of going to school and so wandered around Brussels, making her believe that I was in school. She never found out. My lonely existence continued. I spent my days on my own.

After my father was released from Dachau, he had embarked on a journey to a new country where he hoped to build a new life. He initially found a home in Montreal. His next stop was the United States, the home of distant cousins in Manchester, Connecticut. With the help of the International Red Cross, my mother and I were eventually reunited with him. Unbelievable as it may sound, after losing total communication for eleven years, we were reunited in the United States in 1950, when I was thirteen. For a teenager it was simply another move, another country, another way of life. The endless cycle had begun again.

When I arrived in the United States, I had to go to school, but I had never attended any school. I was taken to a public school and registered there. Because I was thirteen, I was placed in the eighth grade. Needless to say, I was in no position to learn English and make up eight years of schooling in that one year in the eighth grade. My teachers decided that the best strategy for getting me caught up to my contemporaries was for me to spend a few hours every day in the different grades leading up to the eighth grade. At the same time my father insisted that I attend Hebrew school in preparation for my bat mitzvah ceremony. I resisted but was given no choice. I attended the classes, and right after each class I went to church to confess. I did become a bat mitzvah—and went to confession right after!

The following year, after only one year of schooling, I was enrolled in the local high school. School was a nightmare for me. Loneliness and isolation continued to haunt me. I did not know how to make friends. I was miserable at home. My parents did not know how to nurture their only child. Their predominant interest was my grades.

I tried to learn. I took a college course because I wanted to be with the smart kids. I felt I could learn from them. In order to learn English faster, I bought sheet music and stood before a mirror speaking the words of the songs and making sure that I enunciated them as clearly as possible. Little by little some of the other kids took notice of me. Yet my sense of loneliness and isolation remained.

A funny incident remains in my mind from those days. I had been taught in the convent that I must always obey my superiors. In hygiene class we were taught to go to the dentist twice a year. When I noticed a dentist's sign in the neighborhood, I went to see him. My parents were very upset when they saw the bill.

My high school grades were not good enough to get me into college. Yet I desperately wanted to go to college—I saw college as the only way to escape from life with my mother and father. Since I could not get into a university on the basis of my SAT scores, I pleaded with the principal to arrange a personal meeting for me with an admissions official from Boston University, where I wanted to go. The principal picked up the phone and made the call. At that point I had only five years of schooling, and I did not know what my chances of being admitted were. Yet I had to try. I was admitted conditionally to Boston University. I was thrilled.

I left home, determined never to return. Fortunately, my roommate was very smart and very nice. She agreed to tutor me and help me with all my assignments. All my professors agreed to allow me to take my exams orally rather than in writing, for I felt very insecure when I had to write exams. I graduated with honors with a major in education. I was so determined to create a life for myself that I sent applications to all the airlines to become a flight attendant. I did not want to return to my parents' house. I felt that I had to make it on my own.

As it turned out, I did not need the airlines. I was married to Jesse a few weeks after graduating. My father had wanted me to be active in Jewish organizations, and Jesse and I met in the United Synagogue Youth, the youth group of the Conservative movement. Since our marriage I have become a practicing Jew, as have our two children, who both married Jews.

My parents were and remained very unimportant in my life. While I was living with them, they did supply me with the basic necessities—and I know that they did their best to be good parents. But they did not know how to raise a child. We were unable to bond with each other—to show warmth, love, and affection. Yet my mother adored my children—her grandchildren—and developed a wonderful, close relationship with them. She was also very close to one of her sisters. I was very jealous of her warm and close ties with my aunt. As I reflect on my relationship with my parents, I can only surmise that their experiences during the war severely and irrevocably damaged our family life. My mother's incarceration in Auschwitz, the separation from her young child and her husband, the loss of her father and her brother in the concentration camps surely had a very damaging effect on her life with us.

My father's long separation from his family, the loss of his four siblings in the camps, the guilt he must have felt because he escaped to this country while his wife and child were left behind most likely created obstacles that the three of us could not surmount. Perhaps my father felt that he had abandoned us. An invisible wall made of cement separated us permanently. We lived in our own worlds, incapable of surmounting the terrible past that had been thrust upon us.

My husband was born in the United States. He had lots of friends and enjoyed socializing with them. I began to suffer from terrible headaches whenever I was to meet his friends. I seemed to be unable to deal with crowded rooms. Getting together with friends seemed to be a very American thing to do. I remained mired in my lonely existence. Whenever we joined a group of people, I felt that I had nothing to say, but they always seemed to have something to discuss. I really wanted to blend in, to be part of the crowd, but all I could do was retreat to a corner or leave early.

I did not, at that time, realize that my experiences as a hidden child affected my life. I never thought about my past. I washed it out of my mind. When we traveled to Belgium in 1971 to retrace my life there, the war years came flooding back into my consciousness, and I had to get away from that. My husband and I visited Mme Degelas and then quickly left Belgium after spending only twenty-four hours there.

When my children were born, I again experienced great anxiety. How does one raise a child? Why is discipline necessary? I recall an experience I had shortly after I graduated from Boston University. I got a job teaching in an elementary school. I could not understand why children who had everything—the opportunity to go to school, food, a home, parents, friends—would be unruly and need discipline. It was a mystery to me. After all, I had never needed discipline. I knew when to speak and when to keep silent. I knew how to obey orders. Why did these students not know the same thing?

With my own children I was able to reinvent my own childhood. My girls had music, singing, and dancing lessons. I had dreamed of becoming a ballet dancer. I recall that after the war, when I lived with my mother in Brussels, I escaped into a life of fantasy by running to the theater, sneaking in, and staying there for hours. I would do that day after day—or as often as I possibly could. I would also run to see an open market near one of the larger railway stations in Brussels—the Gare du Nord—where there was a beautiful flower display. I loved the breathtaking beauty of flowers and still do. These experiences provided me with a sense of serenity and peace that I could find nowhere else. My mother thought that I was in school. I know now that I was escaping the reality of my existence.

The reality of my past returned to me in 1988 when the United States Holocaust Memorial Museum in Washington invited me to go there and be interviewed on tape about my Holocaust experiences. I felt that because I was not a camp survivor, I would have nothing to contribute. After all, I was only a hidden child. My life had been very normal and my childhood would not be of any particular interest to anybody. Or so I thought. At first I refused to go, but Jesse prompted me to accept this invitation. When a second call came from the museum, I agreed to go, but I warned the caller that I would not have anything to say. The interview lasted four hours. It opened up a can of worms for me. I cried a lot.

I had met Anne Shore, the president of the New York–based Hidden Child Foundation of the Anti-Defamation League. She invited me to attend the support group meetings that were being held in New York. These meetings were very helpful to me, but the defining moment that brought my childhood into sharp focus occurred during the Memorial Day weekend of 1991, when an extraordinary gathering of hidden children was held in New York. Until that time, hidden children had not been considered to be Holocaust survivors. More than sixteen hundred people from all over the world attended this gathering. It is not easy to describe the feelings that I experienced during those few days. For the very first time in my life, I realized that my childhood had been difficult and traumatic. Until then I had no way of comparing my life to other children's lives. I used to think that I was quite normal, and that if anyone was abnormal, it was the Americans. Only when I at-

Renée Schwalb Fritz,
Bloomfield, Connecticut, 1989.

tended the conference did I begin to understand how much my wartime experiences as a hidden child had influenced my life.

Today I feel quite comfortable dealing with and thinking about my past. But although I have experienced some healing and gained a deeper appreciation of the effects of the Holocaust on those of us who were children at that time, the wounds have never completely gone away. Yet I can talk about it today. I no longer feel stressed or get headaches when I mingle with a crowd. I have gone back to Europe several times, and I have retraced the route of my childhood path to survival.

I was lucky to have survived. Although the loss of childhood creates unique memories of this long, dark period in history, many of our stories are too valuable to be forgotten. We need to clarify why we see the outside world the way we do, and we need to tell our children and their children about our well-kept and long-hidden secrets. We bear witness to the Holocaust and remember the voices that were silenced.

Sparkling Jewels in a Sea of Terror

DORI LAUB
(b. 1937, Romania)

Looking back at my life, I realize that the most precious possessions I have are my memories. They do not constitute a continuous, even flow over the years. They don't even feel to me as if they possess a temporal sequence. Rather, they are discrete experiences that stand out, powerfully etching their contours against a background that can feel rather amorphous. They are like islands that possess both clarity and force and create a field, a ripple effect, around them, with wider waves of imagery and associations. I know I can rely on them for the lessons that I learn in and through them. The confluence of these various strands seems to have formed the very Gestalt of my life. What existed between these islands seems to matter little. Yet each island in itself contains very special realizations, cornerstones of my

45

Dori in his pram with
his mother, Clara Laub,
ca. 1937.

own identity mosaic. I often marvel at what enabled me to experience such clear
and precise knowledge of detail and of the general overview, followed by reflection
and self-reflection, that is behind the richness, the power, and the radiance that
these memories exert.

As I try to understand this, I have to think of my mother. To the last days of
her life, she represented the same kind of clarity of vision, of absolute lack of com-
promise regarding what is true, as well as the total embrace of living that I find in
this testimonial dimension of my own life. She never changed in this respect, despite a life fraught with a reality full of insurmountable dangers, massive losses, and
courageous and difficult split-second decisions that she had to make. When in her
eighties she had lapses into regression, I felt afraid and deserted. I did not want to
believe that she was aging. My reactions most probably kept her both alive and
younger for many, many years. I think I owe the brilliance of my memories to the
uncompromising trust she provided for me.

Dori with his parents, Moshe and Clara Laub, on Dori's first birthday, June 8, 1938.

My earliest memory is of awakening in a pram in Cernauti, Romania, where I was born on June 8, 1937. The pram was covered by a blanket, so it was dark and cool inside. I could sense the rhythm of the pram as it was being pushed. I even knew what street it was. There was something very calm and very safe in that moment. I have no idea why I remember it or why I feel so sure about the whole situation. The experience of that moment was not of a little child but of someone who knew what was happening around him.

My next memory comes from when I was three. The occasion was my governess's departure. She had brought me up since I was a few months old and now had to go back to her homeland, Germany. She was an ethnic German, and after the Molotov-Ribbentrop Pact (also known as the Nazi-Soviet Nonaggression Pact) between Germany and the Soviet Union, she was part of an exchange of ethnic populations that the two countries had agreed on. Her name was Berta Stark, and she had become a member of the family and a very close friend of my mother's. There are many photographs of her with me. She is heavyset, wearing a white bonnet, and appears to be self-possessed, usually smiling.

I have no memory of any direct contact or exchange with her, except that on that fateful day, she walked arm in arm with my mother to the train station, and I followed them at a little distance. I was pretending that I was driving a car and running after them in circles. I was dimly aware that she was going to be gone, but I apparently had no feelings about that. I was just accompanying her to the train station, following the two women while driving my fantasy car.

The next memory dates to age five. I was wearing a newly tailored suit, and a studio photographer took my picture. I have that photograph. In it I am standing in front of a screen, facing the camera and smiling, my right hand in my pocket. I

Dori on his tricycle at
age three, 1940.

had a sense of the gravity of the moment, that this was going to be the last photo taken of an era, that somehow my childhood was at an end. I remember no particular sadness, only a certain determination and even excitement about what was coming, together with a sense of fear.

Other memories are more like glimpses, without that sense of being present, almost as if they occurred to another child. I remember the granddaughter of the horse and wagon driver from across the street. She had been baptized and was returning on Sunday from church, with an elaborate braided hairdo and flowers in her hair. She seemed to me fascinating and beautiful. I think she liked to play with me, perhaps even put me to bed for my afternoon nap and tuck me into my little brass bed.

Another such glimpse is of sewing the Jewish star on clothing after the edict to wear it came out. Children were exempt, yet as a proud Jew I insisted on wearing it. On another occasion I apparently overheard my parents talking about conversion to Christianity in order to escape persecution and deportation. I vehemently objected, insisting that I wanted to remain a Jew. A somewhat nightmarish, though completely unreal, memory is of a knight on a horse that reared almost upright with its legs on my bedroom window, as though threatening to break into it.

I have no other memories before the big divide in my life, the deportation to the camp.

It was a sunny early summer afternoon. I think that the date was June 22, 1942. I was roaming around the veranda on my tricycle. Men in uniform came in and spoke to my parents. The next thing I knew, we were packing to go to the train station. It felt almost transitory, as if we were going to come back. We probably said good-bye to my grandparents on my mother's side, with whom we lived, with the same expectation. My father, after all, had a permit issued by the mayor saying that he was a much-needed municipal employee. But the permit was red, and that was the wrong color.

I remember the train station vaguely. I think we were searched, perhaps given a loaf of bread by representatives of the Jewish community, and ordered to the trains. I remember the journey into the night. People were standing; it was quite crowded. Some were sitting on their luggage. People started crying. I did not know why, but I started crying too. My mother asked me why I cried, and I answered that I missed my little brass bed. She said she would sell one of her two coats and buy me another brass bed. I remember that promise very clearly. The journey continued. At some point, probably after one or two days, it was hot and we were thirsty. The train stopped and the doors opened. My father got off the train to look for water. I remember the panic I experienced for the first time, fearing that he would not return in time and that the train would depart without him. He made it, and we continued our journey to the River Dniester, the border between Old Romania and the now Romanian-occupied part of the Ukraine, where the camps for Jewish deportees were set up. The name of the area was to be "Beyond the Dniester," Transnistria.

I do remember the river crossing. We were in a wooden boat built of quite narrow wooden slats, like those of park benches. My gaze remained focused on the floor of the boat, until we reached the other side. There was an adventure in this journey, and my love for boats has continued since. On the other side was an embankment near a railway track. We must have spent a couple of days there, cooking, building a fireplace from stones that we gathered, and using splinters for firewood. Trains were passing us with troops, artillery pieces, and armor moving toward the front, but none of them stopped. These were not "our" trains.

Eventually, we must have been picked up by a train and our journey continued to an abandoned stone quarry that the Soviets supposedly used as a penal colony. In Romanian the name of the place was indeed the "stone quarry," Cariera de Piatra. Barracks surrounded a square in which the *Appells* (roll calls) took place. It was three or four hundred feet from the River Bug, which was the demarcation line between the Romanian- and German-occupied territory in Ukraine. We had free access to the river, and I spent hours sitting on its bank with a little girl whose family befriended mine. On that other side of the river something mysterious was going on.

When I think of the "stone quarry" camp, I have both distinct memories and something like fantasies of memories, which are either reconstructions from what I was told or come from events that I do not quite remember. Basically, our stay there lasted one summer. The winter belonged to another experience. During that summer I didn't want to eat. My mother wanted me to accumulate a reservoir of fat from which I could draw in future times of need. I vaguely recall being fed and keeping the food in my mouth, whereupon one of my parents would say, in German, "Chew, swallow, chew, swallow," to set my eating back in motion. How they were able to get the food is still a riddle.

Our camp was surrounded by a barbed-wire fence, and soldiers guarded the gate. Once a week peasants were allowed in with their food products, and people would barter in the makeshift marketplace—a piece of clothing—a shirt, trousers—for food. I have images of such market days, except that they don't feel like real memories.

I also remember a totally different side to eating. Among the inmates were patients from a psychiatric hospital who had been brought to fill up the train. They were distraught, dirty, crazed figures that roamed around and particularly rummaged in the garbage. Potato peels were a delicacy. I have images of emaciated, worn-out bodies with haunted faces. How in the midst of all this I still refused to eat and had to be force-fed, I don't quite understand.

I think I was quite aware of what was going on but later on refused to know and remember it. Years later, when I was two weeks into psychoanalysis with a Swedish analyst while I was serving on the staff of a small psychiatric hospital in the Berkshires, in Massachusetts, I recounted a memory from my time in the camp. I was sitting with a little girl on the west bank of the Bug. It was summertime, we had a lovely view of a winding clear blue river and lush green meadows, and we were having a lively debate about whether one could be harmed by eating grass.

My analyst interrupted me at this point with an anecdote of his own. "It was," he said, "a Swedish Red Cross unit that was the first to enter Theresienstadt (Terezin) after its liberation. Depositions under oath were taken from many of the inmates. Several women declared that conditions had been so good that they received daily breakfast in bed, served by SS officers." My analyst said nothing more, but his remark was the most powerful commentary on my denial of what I had experienced in that camp. It was his having been a historical witness to the Nazi deception of Theresienstadt that enabled him to see through my defensive position. His perceptiveness in turn helped to open the door that I had closed on my own story, which is part of a larger historical experience.

I stopped talking about casual chats with little girls on days of beautiful weather and started my own journey of recovering the gruesome events that I had lived through and witnessed. I really did continually feel a prevailing sense of dread and an urge to flee. I often argued with my parents to let me go. They had lived, I said—they had visited spas and vacation places. I had seen so little, lived so little in my life, and wanted to experience that too. My mother argued with me, and I think that they literally had to watch me and prevent me from running away. According to my mother, I did escape once, and they were able to locate me at night, freezing, under a bridge.

I distinctly remember several scenes from the "stone quarry" camp. One is of the whipping of an inmate over his naked upper back, with the other inmates forced to watch it as they stood in a circle. He was getting twenty-five lashes for some misdemeanor. Afterward the onlookers were allowed to disperse, but I was fascinated by what this man had gone through and wanted to find out what he thought and what he felt. I approached him and watched him in silence. I could see the bloody streaks that the whip had left on his back. He was crouched over and smoking a cigarette, saying nothing. How could he smoke a cigarette, I thought, but I did not dare to ask. I do not remember how this ended. I regard this moment as quite decisive in my life, because the urge to know and to bear witness to the experience of others who suffered pain was very evident to me. It might have had something to do with my becoming a psychiatrist and psychoanalyst and also with the witnessing project that I carry out in my professional life. I really, for the first time, felt the inner compulsion to know, to imagine what was going on in another person's mind. I have an inner certainty that I must have watched other things, other scenes with much more brutality. While I can retrieve no clear memory of them, in some way I am certain that I watched a public hanging, and this occasionally occurs in my dreams. Only after my mother's death did it occur to me that I could have asked her whether such public executions indeed took place. I never raised that question, although I always wanted to know.

I have another distinct memory from this time. Rumors spread about the liquidation of this camp, and money was gathered for a group of people who would be evacuated before that. My parents were able to gather the proper amount, and on a sunny day we were taken in a convoy bound for a nearby town, Ladizin. The only thing I remember is walking behind a cart that was carrying our luggage, accompanied by Romanian guards. All of a sudden, the Romanian officer in charge had a change of mind and ordered us to return. Tumult ensued, with people trying to grab their luggage from the cart. The Romanian officer took out his pistol and started shooting. Apparently, he was aiming at my father, and my mother threw herself in front of him, to prevent the killing. I think I see her image behind the cart and a soldier's rifle butt descending on her head and shoulders. I imagine her to have been bloodied, but I have no clear memory of that or of our journey back to the camp. But I do remember having a sinking feeling that something that we tried had failed and that the danger that we had tried to escape was still with us.

My most outstanding memory of the time we spent in the camp is of the day of its final liquidation. My memories are of both knowing and experiencing the events, far more than a five-and-a-half-year-old could have been expected to understand. I might have overheard people talking and gathered my information that way, but many memories are of actual moments that I lived through and visual experiences that I had. They are in front of my mind's eye.

A rumor was spreading that something was going to happen and that whatever it was related to total evacuation. That evacuation had an ominous quality to it, and an inmate, a lawyer named Stoller, was making a list of people who could pay a certain amount of money and would be considered "experts," or specialists, that the camp commandant had to retain in order to be able to manage the camp. Of course, the money was going to be a bribe for him to do so. My parents did not have the amount required to become members of that exclusive list. I remember the gathering of all the inmates, numbering in the thousands, early the next morning in the *Appell* place. Lots of soldiers were milling around, mostly Romanians but some Germans. There was a certain disorganization everywhere. The inmates were in groups of thirty, with a group leader who kept them under control. My father had that role with one group.

Attorney Stoller, the maker of the list, was in the group adjacent to ours. I distinctly recall that suddenly Stoller and his family picked up their luggage and started moving out of the group. My mother turned to him and asked loudly where he was going. His answer was, "Where I go, you do not have a place, it is not for you." She promptly grabbed our luggage, took me by the hand, and summoned my father to join us. He was hesitant, claiming that he had a responsibility to the group he was leading. She replied, "If you do not come, the child and I will go alone." He joined us somewhat reluctantly, following at some distance. We followed Stoller and his family, and after maybe six or seven hundred yards we arrived at a house that was set somewhat apart from the barracks. All the doors were closed and the windows were boarded. My mother knocked but did not gain admission. She pounded on the door forcefully, yelling, "If you do not open, I'll turn you over to the Germans." Finally, we were allowed inside. It was completely full, with perhaps two to three hundred people. We squeezed in too, and everyone remained completely silent.

As hours passed, we heard the sounds of trucks arriving. The inmates were loaded into the trucks, their transportation across the River Bug to the German side of the occupied Ukrainian territories. We heard screaming and crying. I also think that we heard shots. The atmosphere was one of dread and suspense. We all knew what was going on and tried to maintain our complete silence. I had pertussis but contained it and did not cough.

Sometime in the early afternoon, all of a sudden we heard steps outside the house. A German patrol had discovered us and started shouting, "Jews out" in German: "Juden herraus." We were expecting the worst. I remember that my father said good-bye to my mother, knowing that one of the first things that would happen was that men and women would be separated from each other. He gave her his watch in case she could sell it for food. In the commotion someone had the idea of calling the Romanian commandant, and a messenger slipped through. Luckily, the commandant arrived and made his claim that the Jews in the house were indeed the specialists that he needed to keep the camp running after everyone was evacuated.

As the afternoon wore on, things began to quiet down. I think I remember the fading sound of roaring motors, but that could be a fantasy. Then it was completely quiet. I remember our return to the empty barracks. This, I think, was early October of 1942 and a cloudless night, bright with stars. I looked up into the infinity and asked my father how deep the sky was. He understood the real nature of my question and told me, "Churchill and Roosevelt will not allow this to happen." This was my last memory from the stone quarry camp. I know that we were advised to avoid being seen from across the Bug, because the Germans might come again to fetch us. After some time we were also told that from then on, we did not exist on any books. The camp population was no more.

It was a cold November day when we left the camp in a small convoy guarded by Romanian soldiers. I remember stopping at night and staying in a barn to sleep. My mother was trying to get a soldier to buy some milk for me in the village and succeeded. We continued the next morning. My next memory is of being sick and wrapped up in many blankets and that the snow on the ground was almost knee deep. My father was carrying me on his right shoulder, while my mother carried the remaining luggage. I was thinking what a burden I must be and that he might want to find relief by dropping me to the ground somewhere.

The next thing I remember is our arrival in Obodovka. At this point we had a cart and a horse, which the luggage was on, and so was I, a feverish child bundled up like a piece of luggage. The Jews from the town started grabbing the luggage and one of them took me. The next thing I knew I was in a room, and people were unpacking the bundle and surprised to find a little boy in it.

Somehow we found a distant cousin of my father's in the town, and she took me in for those first few days. Later on all of us found a place to live with a farmer family in the woods because we were still illegal. Some partisans had their base in that house, and I know that they tried to get my father to join them. He refused because he felt that, both as a partisan and a Jew, his fate, if he were caught, would be immediately sealed. Eventually, we became more connected with the ghetto in the town and with the Jewish community there, particularly a man named Yanko Vindish, who later became our protector.

I remember one night when my father was taken away on some sort of transport. Another couple lived with us, and the husband was also taken away. The wives spent all night awake, waiting and hoping. My father eventually did come back. I also remember from around that time that my parents were fighting with each other, my mother urging my father to hide out and try to avoid being caught. He was afraid that if he were found, he would be shot on the spot, and he preferred to present himself when asked to. In one of her angry outbursts I remember her throwing a boot at him. It was a startling awakening for me.

Two more incidents stand out in my mind from the time we spent in Obodovka. At some point, I assume in the winter of 1943, a plan was devised to send the children away, ostensibly to Switzerland. I prevailed on my parents to let me join the transport. My father took me to a group of horse-drawn sleds. He accompanied me on the trip because he wanted to make sure that it worked out. Sometime in the afternoon an accident occurred. Two sleds collided and children were injured. My father promptly decided that this was not going to work, and we left the transport and spent that night in a little village. I remember sleeping with him in the same bed and having mixed feelings. On the one hand, my hope of escaping had been thwarted. On the other hand, I was grateful for his presence and his protective judgment. For once he put his foot down and acted decisively in a moment of crisis.

Late in our stay in Obodovka we lived in a room with a window that faced the main road. I spent endless hours watching this road. It was the route that the Romanian and German troops took to go to the front line. Infantry, tanks, artillery, armored cars, motorcycles, and ambulances kept moving nonstop, day and night. Once two German soldiers in gray-blue uniforms came into our house. I was paralyzed with fear, but all they were looking for was a piece of rope. I remember seeing two youngish men, perhaps even boys, who were confused by our response. They definitely had no intent to harm.

One day in 1944 I noticed something strange. The movement on the road was now in the opposite direction. Infantry, tanks, artillery pieces, armored vehicles, motorcycles, and, most of all, ambulances, in an endless stream all day and night. I did not understand the reversal of direction. It lasted for about seven days or longer. Then the road was quiet for hours. In the distance we could hear the rumbling sounds of artillery. All of a sudden a group of motorcycles appeared. The soldiers wore different uniforms. Something was totally changed. These were the first Soviet scouts to enter our town. We were liberated.

We joined the Soviet troops and began our journey back home. We hitch-hiked on trucks, buses, trains. Jews came out from everywhere: ghettos, hiding places, forests. No one knew who was still alive. My mother and I accidentally encountered my father's sisters and their five children in a little donkey-drawn cart. That's how my two aunts found out that their husbands were dead.

I remember sitting on a cart with our luggage and entering the street where my grandparents lived. From a distance I could see my grandmother cross the street. My mother ran to embrace her, but my grandmother didn't recognize her at first. Both grandparents had considered us all dead for about two years.

The first thing I did on entering the house in which I was born was to run to my toy cupboard. I opened it with excitement and hope. What I saw was pitiful. It was mostly empty; only a few broken toys were left on one shelf. Forty years later, when my mother gave testimony to the Fortunoff Video Archive, she described with pride my joy as I ran to the toy cupboard and found it full of toys, exactly the way I had left it. I was sitting next to her as she said that and I had to correct her. My memory was totally different. She was crestfallen and said that perhaps I was right. She had so much wanted to bring me back home to the childhood that had been interrupted and now could resume. Perhaps her memory was what she wanted to find and not what it really was.

Indeed, I had not returned to my interrupted childhood. Had I continued with the children's transport, I do not know if I would have returned either. I had no childhood to resume, nor did I have a father of whom I could ask questions. I developed a fantasy world and found other children my age with whom I played it out. We were going to build a huge army and invent new weapons with which we were going to be victorious against Hitler. I realize now that I never resumed a normal childhood or a normal life upon my return from the camp. Perhaps the rest of my childhood, and indeed of my life, was driven by the need to deal with what I had lived through in those early years.

When I review the pages that I have just written, what stands out glaringly to me is what I've left out, the reflections that come with the memories that I have omitted. I mentioned the fights between my parents. On thinking about them, it strikes me that they were much more profound than what I have described and in a way continued in me throughout my life. My mother had an eagle's vision for recognizing danger and finding impromptu solutions. She had almost an uncanny ability to find herself and her bearings in dangerous situations. She felt frantic and quite threatened when she found herself to be the only person who perceived the danger at hand.

My father took a quite different position. He was not echoing her sense of danger or even the urgency and the resoluteness with which she found and followed through with solutions. He probably was too scared to know what was going on when he said that he preferred to volunteer for the transports rather than risk the dangers of hiding out, being discovered, and being executed on the spot. His way of dealing with the situation was to not recognize, or at least not acknowledge, the deadliness that permeated our lives. This is a conflict that raged in every single Jew in one way or another, from the partisans who fought back to the *Kapos* who bought their lives through collaboration and the masses who indeed believed that "work makes you free."

This conflict also continues in me and has for all my life. On the one hand, I'm quite astute in picking up dangers and seizing on solutions, sometimes unconventional ones. On the other hand, I also take unnecessary risks, like leaving at the very last minute for a place I need to be at on time. I do not do enough to avoid dangers yet continually live in their shadow. More threatening to me is a situation in which I alone recognize the danger, and no one heeds it despite my warnings. Most hurtful and threatening of all is when I find myself alone and deserted as I try to marshal the resources to face the danger.

I find little solace in knowing that, time and again, I come up with solutions to the impossible situations I have gotten myself into. A bitter lesson for me is that no one else had learned a lesson from it, and I must prepare myself for yet another situation that I need to solve alone. On the one hand, I feel frantic and desperate that no one seems to have learned a lesson or even to have paid attention to what has happened. On the other hand, after a moment of pause and reflection, I wonder what lesson, if any, there is to be learned. Wasn't I the one who allowed the situation to become dangerous and stayed in it for far too long? And is that not the single most important lesson that I need to learn from this?

Another pervasive experience that I left out of my first draft of this paper was the almost continuous sense of dread. Throughout my days in camp I experienced sheer terror. I knew quite accurately what was happening. My so-called composure was really both detachment and a facade, a thin exterior veil with an inner sense of being flooded by dread. There were moments when it was obvious that something was imminent, that something new was going to happen. I could envision the gray-uniformed soldiers. I saw mostly their legs, raised high with their knees unbent, marching. This was probably what I saw as a child; my gaze was focused on their shiny boots. When I looked up, I saw baby faces topped by steel helmets. I can remember their heavy belts, the shiny helmets tightly fitted on their heads, and rifles hanging loosely on their shoulders. I was sure that these soldiers were going to come and do something to us with the bayonets stuck on top of their rifles.

I did not allow myself to feel any further. The terror bored through my body, almost paralyzing me. I can almost feel it now when I merely think about it. It travels to my fingertips, accompanied by a weird sense of numbness. I can hardly move. Some sounds are droning in my ears. I am almost outside myself. I am nauseated and start to retch. I may have screamed while retching. I was terrified that the soldiers were coming.

My mother used to spank me on my behind. When I felt the pain, I started crying and stopped retching, and the terror would begin to subside. A paralyzing terror that slowly spreads and flows through my body is very familiar to me, now, to this very day. It is an almost regular occurrence at night when I sleep, accompanying every dream, every nightmare. No other impression, no other feeling, can reach me at such moments, nor can I tear myself out of this state. Even remembering the origins of this terror does little to make it subside. Everything around me and in me feels different when I experience it, or when I am in the midst of such a state. There is no texture, no color, no timbre, no pleasure, no vitality. Essentially, there is no future to experience or look forward to. It's something very, very frozen and barren that allows for no other feelings to exist. It is also impoverished and closed, and fantasy does not have free rein. My memory is limited, and no creative solutions are available to me at such moments.

It is obvious to me that my leaving out these observations was an attempt to keep my childhood memories separate from my present life, as though belonging to a world of their own. It is a version of my father's refusal to recognize the deadliness that permeated every corner of our lives. It's similar to his attempt to believe that by following orders, he could keep the disasters at arm's length. The oversights

I mentioned put in question the integrity and the completeness of my testimony, the very testimony and reflection that are included in each one of the memories themselves. Like any other survivor, I therefore personify the conflict I mentioned before.

After taking this detour to describe my terror and before I return to my memories, I have to ask myself this: How does testimony hold up when the reign of terror is complete? The answer to this question is unwelcome. It does not. When terror prevails, it eclipses everything else, including memory. It is like a hurricane that leaves only destruction in its path. But like a hurricane, it passes and the sky clears up, and then a clearer vision, a more accurate memory, is back, and the hurricane that has just gone by seems quite unreal, incomprehensible. Were it not for the destruction it left in its trail, one could almost deny its occurrence.

Editor's Note: Dori and his mother remained in Romania until 1950, when they emigrated to Israel. He studied at the Hebrew University–Hadassah Medical School in Jerusalem from 1955 to 1961, when he obtained his medical degree. After additional study and internship, he served in the Israeli army from 1963 to 1965. He earned a master's degree in clinical psychology at Bar-Ilan University in Ramat Gan, Israel, in 1966 and emigrated to the United States later that year. He held positions in Massachusetts before coming to Yale University as an instructor in psychiatry in 1969.

Through the Concrete Wall

EVA METZGER BROWN
(b. 1938, Germany)

I remember being in summer camp and watching children run one to another, holding a stick and passing it on to the next person, who would then run with it and pass it on to still the next person, who would run farther with it and then pass it on to yet another teammate. I did not know what the children were doing. I did not know the name of the game. I could not ask because I did not speak English. Instead, I watched.

I was an outsider and a bystander with all those feelings connected with being left out and ignored. But the game looked like fun. One day I was going to learn how to play it and join in with the others—I was going to love it, and I was going to be good at it. The game was called "relay races." I had been sent away to sleep-away camp one year after I arrived in America. I was four years old.

I wrote those words in 1995, after I met with Elie Wiesel, who said, "Write down your story and send it to me." I was already fifty-eight years old, but I had never organized the story of my life during and after the Holocaust.

Mine was not a talking family on matters of the Holocaust. My father spoke not at all of the murder of his mother in Theresienstadt (Terezin), and my mother, whose leg was blown off in the bombing of Angers, made me feel that the topic of her amputation was off limits. After our arrival in America, the focus in our family was not on looking back at the major catastrophes that the war had inflicted on our lives or on examining the difficulties that my parents and I faced thereafter. Rather, the focus was on recovery and looking ahead. My father directed all his energies toward re-creating a life that felt financially secure. My mother focused on regaining her strength and her spirit.

I think I took my parents' example to heart and got busy also with learning how to become American and how to deny and minimize the impact of the traumas in Europe and the difficulties that I faced here. So going to camp so young just did not feel like a big deal to me then or to anyone else either. I must have figured that no one would have the time, interest, or energy to deal with what had happened to me, and I certainly did not want to cause my parents more difficulties by bringing it up; they had had enough difficulties already. Yet I know now that I was affected, deeply affected, by their silent sufferings and by my own.

After some years I got used to camp. Eventually, I found it to be a really fun place, where I could meet lots of children, see the different ways that people behaved, learn new things, and leave the sadnesses of my home behind for the summer. I was naturally athletic, I loved nature, and I began to look forward to the camaraderie of other children. Still, I think now, being sent to camp so young, so soon after I had come to the States, was too soon. I can say this now, after decades of silence, recognizing that it is okay to feel bad about bad things and say these things out loud to others, without feeling guilty. After all, one should feel only grateful for surviving at all and surviving with parents who did the best they could, given the circumstances. But let me tell my story from the beginning.

I was born in Nuremberg, Germany, on July 13, 1938. The family history, as recorded by my grandmother and her two brothers in a red leather-bound book, told of generations of our family in Germany. No doubt, these deep roots contributed to the family's disbelief that Hitler could or would be allowed to carry out his threats. Even so, with Hitler's rise to power in 1933, the first family members began to lose their jobs, and our emigration began. By the time of Kristallnacht, on November 9, 1938, the night when German thugs entered the apartments of Jewish families, my own included, and with clubs broke everything in sight—including furniture, dishes, and crystal—few remained blinded to the true threat. German Jews everywhere began trying desperately to leave.

The day after Kristallnacht my father, who had a passport because of his international business connections and had tried to get a passport for my mother for more than a year, went to the passport office once more. This time he threatened the local official with the crime of murdering my mother if a passport was not issued to her immediately. The next day a passport was waiting. Two days later we left for Paris. I was four months old and by this time had already lived in an atmosphere of great panic and with a succession of caregivers, each of whom had left Germany—and me—as soon as she could emigrate.

Our decision to go to France turned out to be a poor one. A year after we arrived, the French rounded up all aliens, including my father, and sent them to detention camps. The decision was made that my mother and I should move to Angers, a smaller, safer town southwest of Paris. Unfortunately, Angers proved not to be a safe haven for us. On June 17, 1940, the Germans bombed Angers while my mother and I were walking on our street, Rue Fulton. An explosion pitched us into a doorway. I was wounded in the head and on the left side of my body; my mother's left leg was shattered.

We were taken to the local hospital, where I was stitched up. Upon my release I was hidden in a Catholic orphanage, and shrapnel in my brain remained undetected for decades. My mother remained in the hospital for four months. The doctor thought that she would die, but, determined to recover from her wounds and the amputation of her left leg, she survived.

I have little memory of this period, though I do remember two things. I remember the sensation of warm blood running down my face right after the bombing, and I remember the nuns' hats, the big white hats that they wore in the orphanage. For the longest time I thought that these images were insignificant, as they had no words attached to them and fit into no story that I knew. I would learn, decades later, that this is how very young children remember things, not with words (explicit memory) but through snippets of imagery and sensations (implicit memory).

In October 1940, as northern France began to fall into the hands of the Nazis, the expanding web of detention camps collapsed. Freed, my father began to look for my mother and me. He was unable to enter occupied France and therefore Angers, so he contacted the International Red Cross, in the hope that it could find us. In time the Red Cross did, and the family was reunited in Toulouse. Without delay, my parents and I headed west, toward the Pyrenees and the ports of Spain, only to learn that ships there were no longer accepting refugees.

Retracing our steps, we headed for the port of Marseille and found that visas for America were waiting for us. We had made the American quota! Immediately, my father called people he knew in the business world and asked if they could help us secure passage on a boat out of Marseille. They did, and two and a half years after we had emigrated from Germany, we were able to leave the chaos in Europe for good. We sailed aboard one of the last boats out of France. Luck was with us.

However, our passage across the Atlantic was not without further ordeals. The British stopped our French-owned ship, which now was under Germany's control, at the Straits of Gibraltar, refused it clearance, and directed the passengers to Casablanca. After some time my father's business connections gained us passage on a

The Metzger family reunited in Toulouse, France, in October 1940: Ernest from an internment camp, Doris from a hospital, and Eva from an orphanage.

Portuguese ship, the *Guinea,* a barge outfitted for refugees. I remember nothing of our stay in Africa and little of the trip to America. I am told that my mother stayed in quarters on the upper deck, unable to maneuver the stairs to where my father lay ill below with the malaria he had contracted in Casablanca. I stayed with him, perhaps because it was safer for a three-year-old not to be running on the deck with a handicapped mother.

My only memory of this time is the sensation of being rocked back and forth. Was it by my father? Or was it the boat's movement? I do not know, but I used to wonder whether my love of the cadence of raindrops on rooftops is related to this memory of movement and sound, as the boat rocked back and forth and the waves lapped rhythmically against its sides.

Before we arrived on the shores of America, we would be forced to make one more stop: Martinique. This presented a new set of problems. Martinique functioned as a gateway to the United States, and we had to pass inspection there. I think my parents feared that after their long and arduous escape from the horrors of Europe, they might be denied entrance now, because of my father's illness. In addition, my parents were informed that they would need transit visas, papers that they did not have, in order to leave Martinique.

Unexpected complications seemed to arise at each turn, yet fortunate rescues would appear as well. We were among the lucky ones. Through the efforts of our family and Rabbi Steven Wise in America, we received an exit visa. And after my mother courageously complained to the authorities that "too much was being asked of us refugees after our ordeals," they waved our family through the inspection line. Finally, it was time to take our last boat.

We arrived in the United States on August 6, 1941. I was three years old. I once asked my mother what it felt like to see the Statue of Liberty come into view. She said solemnly, "We stood on the deck in silence. No one said a word. We did not know if America would take the boat." Two years earlier the *St. Louis* had been returned to Germany.

A gripping story in itself, our flight from Europe is only part of any survivor's story. Coming to a safe country after such an ordeal as the Holocaust does not ensure that a person will feel safe and protected in the New World. For me, coming to America would close one chapter of my story of disruption and instability, only to open the next one, with its own accounts of continued separations and uncertainties.

Upon our arrival in the States, my parents again left me in a strange place and with people I did not know, no doubt to ensure that my mother could get some rest, but I did not understand that then. The strangers were my paternal grandmother's brother and his wife and their four teenage children. They had come to America some years earlier and were "settled." I met with one of these "teenagers" recently and asked him how long I had stayed with his family. John, now eighty, told me that I had stayed for several months. I wondered why and why I was there for so long. He did not know, but he told me that he had seen me in Paris twice before our emigration, and then he told me about myself back then—a rare gift for a person who has no stories of herself from this time. He smiled when he told me these stories, and I smiled with the warmth of his memories.

He was my mother's first cousin, and I was the first baby to be born to that generation. John led me to believe that this made me special. As the only baby of that generation to be born in Europe, I was the only child survivor in a family of survivors, which left me, an only child, with no one to talk to—if, indeed, I would have talked to anyone at all about the war. After my parents retrieved me from John's family, we moved to a small apartment. I recall having fun playing with another child there, on an enclosed fire escape that we used as our playground. After a few more moves we settled in Kew Gardens, in New York City's borough of Queens, for some years.

In Queens I was enrolled in a French-speaking nursery school "to meet other children." Years later my mother told me that I then stopped speaking. Concerned, my parents called the doctor. He felt that the people around me were speaking too many languages: French at school, German at home, and English in the streets. He advised my parents to choose one language, preferably English, and suggested that they take me out of my nursery school, which they did. I do not remember nursery school, and I do not remember going from French to English, but I know these things leave their mark on very young children.

My new school was a long walk from my home, and I remember that my father brought me to PS 99 that first day. I think I was a little afraid, and my father, who loved to tease me, was not very helpful. Even so, I was always happy to be with him and entered the school, as I did most new things, with a curiosity and a desire to do the right thing and fit in. I remember that kindergarten started out as a scary place. I had no idea what to expect, and my parents did not or could not help me with this.

I found my class picture once. I am the only child sitting very, very straight, with my hands clasped on the little desk in front of me. I think I look as if I am trying very hard to do what I think the teacher wants, without knowing exactly what that is. Yet even though I was very shy in school, and stayed very much in the background, I think my desire to learn and my ability to do so helped me to adjust in school and not stand out as too different from the American children.

I remember Mrs. Fuller, my fourth grade teacher. She would tell stories about herself, personal stories about her family and especially about her children. I had never heard a person talk about her children in this way, so personally, and happy and carefree. We were not carefree at home, in the beginning. One Easter Mrs. Fuller brought in little yellow, sugar-covered marshmallow duckies that she put by the side of her desk. We could buy them for a few cents each. This seemed like a marvel to me. Perhaps every teacher had a box like this by her desk, but I did not ask. I asked as few questions in school as I did at home. It was as if I were afraid to make waves and chose instead to learn things on my own, through my readings and my observations.

Two years before, when I was eight, the family suffered a major catastrophe, at least that is how it felt to me. My mother collapsed; perhaps one would call it depression now. I remember feeling that something was terribly wrong when my father talked to the doctor on the telephone, in a tone that was very serious and that frightened me. I asked him if my mother was dying. She was lying on her bed a lot or, rather, upon the pull-out couch where she and my father slept in the living room, having generously given the one bedroom to me. My father reassured me that my mother was not dying, and I think he reassured himself that this was not so serious, for he left on a business trip shortly thereafter. However, in so doing, he left me alone with my ill mother. I have a sense that this scared me dreadfully. I am sure that I did not understand what was going on or how to deal with my mother's unhappiness and frustrations. My mother needed me, now more than ever.

I spent all my free time at home, often sitting at the end of my mother's bed, telling her about my day, and thereby filling up hers. I did this for many years, even after my mother got better, and only later would I realize that this habit contributed to my limiting the exploration of my own life and the number of friendships that I could make with children my own age.

I do remember that my mother made a concerted effort to help lead my Brownie troop, and once or twice she even took me sledding. But I felt an increasing sense of responsibility for her well-being over my own and maybe for my father's too. It was not that I was heroic, though I think, looking back, that I was a courageous child. I did what I understand that many young children do when they feel that family security is shaky: I helped, in whatever way I could, to maintain the delicate balance, as I perceived it.

Somewhat later that year my maternal grandmother emigrated to America from Israel, the country to which she had emigrated after Kristallnacht. I was told that she came here to take care of my two cousins, but I secretly believed she came to America to help my mother and me. With her arrival, I began a new chapter in my life.

I remember the first time that I opened the door to Granny. She was not as old as I expected, and she was smaller than I thought she would be. She looked tired too, very, very tired. Yet upon seeing me she smiled and reached into her purse to pull out a candy for me, a Swedish fish. It tasted as if it had been there a long, long time, waiting for me, just as I had been waiting for a grandmother to give it to me. Then she said hello to me in English. No one had told me that my grandmother would speak English.

Granny moved into our apartment house, an arc of three floors of apartments surrounding an inner courtyard containing the largest hydrangea bushes I have ever seen. I was allowed to go from my home to hers, on my own, once a week. Her apartment was small, and her front door opened into a narrow hallway with even narrower bookcases on either side. Each was lined with a variety of jars, filled with different things that Granny collected: buttons, yarns, string . . . things with which her grandchildren were allowed to play. There was a large multipurpose room with a railroad kitchen on one side, the kind where the refrigerator, sink, and stove are lined up against the wall. At the far end was a window from which Granny taught me to feed squirrels from a pie tin. Her other window held rows of tiny shelves, upon which were plants that we watered together.

A dining room table filled half the room, and once a week Granny taught me German grammar and German writing there. She would say, "Unless you can read and write in a language, you will forget it." Every so often I would watch her make *Schnecken* there, rolling the dough out flat and spreading it with a mixture of raisins, cinnamon, and nuts. Then she would roll it up again, cutting it into seven or eight chunks before baking it. The other half of the room contained a sofa in front of which were two chairs separated by a table on which she taught me to play bridge. No grandchild was allowed to enter her bedroom. Granny was a very pri-

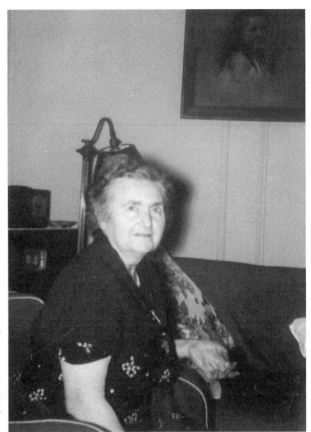

Betty Bamberger Bancroft, grandmother of Eva Metzger Brown, in her apartment in Kew Gardens, Queens, ca. 1968. On the wall is the portrait of herself as a child that she brought from Germany via Israel in 1948.

vate person, but from the doorway I could see piles of the mystery stories that she loved to read, and I could see the eiderdown comforter that she had miraculously brought from Europe.

Later on, Granny took me to the Metropolitan Museum of Art and introduced me to Rembrandt. And she would take me with her to visit Aunt Lina, a dear elderly relative of hers who had survived Theresienstadt, and to Kennedy Airport when it was still called Idlewild. Wherever Granny took me and whatever we did together, she taught me something. I loved Granny and I admired her, and while she was somewhat stern in manner and not overly affectionate, she was the first person in my life who had time to pay attention to me—and did. Yet she, like my parents, did not talk about what had happened to her in the war—her losses, her regrets, and her grief—or how she had lived before the war. I learned much later that she had lost her mother in Theresienstadt and that she left behind, in Germany, wealth, social position, and a household full of help. Still, I never heard her complain about her small one-bedroom apartment in Queens or about the jobs she had taking care of other people's children.

Occasionally, my mother and her sister and brother and their families would gather at my grandmother's apartment for high tea, a simple spread crowned with Granny's *Schnecken* or her "bittersweet" *Pflaummenkuchen*. Outside of this, I do not remember that she cooked very much, or perhaps it was that she just cooked simply and lived simply.

My mother cooked simply too. Perhaps it was because my father was away for weeks at a time or perhaps it was because standing and cooking were too much of a strain for her. In any case, I remember feeding myself, often by eating things that were left in the icebox. I do remember that my mother sometimes prepared cocoa and cookies for me after school. This was a real treat. So were the visits of two peddlers, Mrs. Wertheimer, who arrived to great excitement and sold an array of the most delicious European chocolates and candy, and a gentleman whose name I do not recall, who sold linens and underwear. Both were survivors who made their living by selling their wares door to door. Back then it seemed that the only people my parents had to the house were survivors.

My mother's sister and her family lived up the street, and her brother and his family lived a few towns over. And a stream of relatives visited from different countries: Israel, Germany, England—all places where different branches of our family had settled after the war. One of my father's sisters passed through from Sweden, where she had fled during the war. However, I never saw her after that one visit. I never met my father's other sister or her family.

There was a rift between my father and his sisters. It had started before the war and was exacerbated by misunderstandings about who-did-not-help-who-enough during the war and who was responsible for their mother's death in Theresienstadt. I think my father suffered greatly from this, though he never spoke of sad things with me, and my mother told me not to ask him about such matters. Yet I knew something was missing, for him, for me.

After a few years we began to celebrate Hanukkah. Back then it was the only mark of our being Jewish. We never celebrated other Jewish holidays or lit Sabbath lights, and I did not go to Sunday school. It was not that my parents had turned their backs on their Jewish identity; I think they just did not have the energy for things like this until much later. But with Hanukkah, somehow it was different. I realize now that a part of my father was truly a child at heart; when he allowed that child to escape, I had a sense of having a playmate. At these times he would tease me, and my mother would reprimand him, saying, "Ernstle bitte hörauf" (Ernest, please stop), but I did not mind.

The Hanukkah gift that stands out most in my mind, after all these years, was one that I received when I was about twelve. It was from one of my parents' friends from Europe—a box filled with books of literature and poetry, all for me. I own some of these books still; others eventually fell apart from my reading and re-

reading them. Those were the first books I ever owned. Maybe all parents refrained from buying books for their children back then, but I think my parents did not buy things like this for two reasons. First, they were always trying to save money, and, second, the Holocaust had taught them that everything could vanish overnight.

Between Hanukkah celebrations it seemed like my father was away on business for most of the year. When he came home, he would go to sleep for what seemed like days on end, to wash away the tiredness from the intense daily efforts he was making in his toy business. He sold toy cars, tops, dolls, doll houses . . . and entertained buyers at night in Canada, South America, and Japan. From England he brought the Matchbox cars to the United States. He became a great success here, but it came at a cost to me—his presence in my life. After he retired and his grandchildren arrived, I could see what I had missed because of his absences. At home he liked to listen to classical music on the radio and kept up with the newspapers, but he never talked about these things with me, except for occasionally reciting poetry by Goethe—*auf Deutsch*. I loved poetry and music too, but I do not remember sharing these interests with him.

By the time I entered high school, my father was a financial success, and we moved to Forest Hills, a Queens neighborhood with a better high school, which my parents wanted for me. Even though I do not remember my parents ever reviewing my homework or asking me if I had done it, I did get the message that they supported my education, and I knew by their behavior that they believed that great effort and perseverance would provide their own satisfaction.

My education began with the English lessons that they gave me to rid me of my guttural German "rrr," and then I had many years of violin lessons. They supported me financially at college and graduate school, at a time in the sixties when marriage and childbearing were the only options for most women my age.

I was not immune to society's message. I married a nonsurvivor, Norman Brown, a gastroenterologist, and had three wonderfully healthy children: David Frank, named after my husband's paternal grandfather; Carolyn Metzger, named after my maternal grandmother; and Michael Harold, named after my husband's maternal grandfather. For me, having children, especially children who remained Jewish and raised all seven of their children as Jews, was like a miracle, and I know my father felt that way too. By 1967, when I was twenty-nine, I had received my PhD in clinical psychology and had a family of my own. As I look back now, my studies started me on a journey of research and practice geared to learning about trauma and what it does to human souls. I did not realize at the time that I was seeking to learn what had happened to my soul too, given the many traumas that I had undergone.

In 1979 Granny died after a long debilitating illness, and I was asked to give the eulogy. It was the first time I spoke publicly to the family at large. The Holocaust was not in the forefront of my awareness at this time, and so I did not speak about it. No one in the family was speaking about the Holocaust then. No one in the world was yet paying much attention to it either. Instead, I spoke about my memories of a woman whom I loved deeply and who had made an enormous difference in my life. When my grandmother's household was dispersed, I asked my mother for one thing of my grandmother's—an oil painting, a portrait of her as a child. I always wondered how she had decided to bring it, instead of some of her other possessions, from Europe. And I wondered how it had survived the journey.

My mother gave me some other things too, including some children's books in German and my grandmother's eiderdown comforter. To these were added one tablecloth with the letters *BB,* for Betty Bamberger, her name then, and her cookbook. I was very happy to have these mementos, reminders of the life she had left behind in Europe.

My parents had left Europe almost two years after she did and came with far fewer things. However, among these possessions was a photo album of my mother's family and me as a baby. This is one of my most treasured possessions. I know that many child survivors have no pictures of the past, and I had no picture of my father's family. I did not know what my paternal grandfather looked like until I was in my sixties, but I did have the pictures in my mother's album, and I looked at them often, sometimes wondering what life would have been like if the Holocaust had not taken place and I had grown up among all these people.

In the early 1980s my father asked me to help him for the last time. He said, "Eva, help me . . . I am losing my mind." He had dementia. I was heartbroken. However, this time I knew I could not help him in the way that he meant. Oh, I did want to, but I could not, no matter how hard I tried. Also, my mother quite abruptly decided to move with my dad to Florida, far away from the family. Some might think that this made it easier for me, but I did not think so. All I was aware of was that I felt bad, very bad. That was when I decided to meet with a psychiatrist to try to deal with the effects of my father's impending death on me, its impact on the family unit, and my profound sense of loss.

For a long time I did not speak to my doctor about the Holocaust; instead, I focused on the present and made little of the past. It was easier that way, though it was not easy. I think I needed time, a lot of time, to see whether I could trust another person to understand what had happened to me, when I did not understand it all myself. I knew that I would need a doctor who could care enough and be empathetic enough, even though he did not—could not—know the extent of my Holocaust wounds because he had not been there. I think too that my fears kept me silent. I was afraid of what might emerge: feelings that I had not allowed myself to feel, that come from being abandoned, losing my way, and being overwhelmed by the unfamiliar.

My history was one of broken and rebroken connections, with no control over how I was left or when I would be picked up—in the hospital in Angers, the orphanage, my great-aunt and uncle's apartment when we came to New York, camp, kindergarten, the time when my mother took ill, the many times when my father disappeared with no advance notice and no idea when he would return. So many people had said to me growing up, "You were so young, you could not have been affected." Even professionals I had met, before *trauma* became the buzzword in psychology and psychiatry, made incorrect assumptions. All these experiences inhibited me from opening up. Instead, my feelings went underground, into hiding, as I see it now—into a deep freeze behind a concrete wall. I would not be able to break through the wall easily, yet I think there remained a lingering hope to reconnect—both with what I truly felt inside and with others.

How I began to open up is complex, but it did require two things. One was a growing awareness that, for me, keeping my pain closed in my heart, silently, like a secret, created more pain, not less; and that it was not enough to have a doctor who would reach out to me. What was essential was that I open up the wall surrounding the core of my inner self and let him in. When I began to trust him, truly trust him, and trust myself too, the concrete wall surrounding my inner self began to crack. It is still hard for me to explain in words how this happened, because it was not words I found . . . but tears.

I thought I would never stop crying. My doctor reassured me that I did not have to. He understood something that I had not allowed myself to feel. He let me know that Holocaust losses are worth remembering, worth grieving, and worth working through, even decades later. He let me know that the oversights of the past were important and that he had the time and patience to listen to them. I asked him once if it had been hard for him to hear my story. He said, "No, it was a pleasure." He said what was difficult for him was listening to me all those years before, when I did not remember and did not allow myself to feel the feelings that must have been connected to those enormously difficult times.

As I began to talk with my doctor about the war and the years after the war, the walls of silence began to crumble. Feelings that I had blocked began to flow in a continuous stream. That was when I allowed myself to realize how much I had lost, how much I had denied, how much I had avoided dealing with my sadness, loneliness, and grief. Perhaps it would have been too much to deal with when I was small; perhaps it was too much to deal with when I had no one to tell it to.

Slowly, I began to put things together, unconnected bits and pieces of my memory and my feelings that I had minimized before: the sensation of warm blood running down my face, a glimpse of the nurses in what to me were their strange and unfamiliar hats, the rocking of the boat as it crossed the Atlantic, going to camp when I was so young, entering kindergarten alone, eating meals from the icebox by myself, watching my father as he slept off his exhaustion after a business trip, feeling the pain of sitting by my mother with her missing leg, befriending the new and lonely children who appeared and disappeared at school. I had kept so many feelings to myself, buried, hidden, and beyond my awareness.

I had been taught that these feelings were connected to my past and the past was over: deal with today's challenges, submerge the past horrors, and face the future with courage and determination. Maybe this approach was helpful in 1941, but it was not helpful to me now, because what was submerged was still there in the different levels of my consciousness, and in my heart and in my soul.

The Metzger family, 2003. *Standing:* Eva Metzger Brown. *Seated, left to right:* Eva's cousin, Ursula; Eva's mother, Doris Metzger; and Eva's daughter, Carolyn.

As I faced letting go of the pain surrounding the loss of my father, I let go of my silence, and with it all the unwept tears of my childhood flowed up into my eyelids and flooded over. It seemed to me that the streams of tears would never end, but every so often they did, and then I would begin talking with my doctor. And slowly, I began talking with others too.

In 1988 I was asked to speak to my congregation on the occasion of Rosh Hashanah. I retold the story of the Akeda, the Torah text read on the second day, in terms of the meaning of the survival of Isaac. Then I talked publicly, for the first time, about my own Holocaust survival. The response to my talk was overwhelming. Friends, acquaintances, people I did not even know came into the aisle as I returned to my seat, to press my hand or give me a hug. I felt overwhelmed. I could have cried, but I did not. However, the experience changed something for me. I saw, I learned, I felt that some people out there were not as afraid of my past as I was and had the kindness to show me. I had taken the critical step of "coming out" as a survivor; it was now in the open.

In 1990 I began to study to become a bat mitzvah, motivated in part to fill a gap in my life, that of a Jewish education. Although I had helped my children prepare for their bar and bat mitzvah ceremonies, now I wished to learn Hebrew and study the sages for myself. Another reason was that I had just become a grandmother, and I wanted to know enough so that I could answer my grandchildren's questions or at least know where to direct them to find answers. In the end I created a bat mitzvah service that celebrated my "coming of age" and commemorated my Holocaust beginnings.

In 1992 I left the confines and safety of my Jewish community and accepted an invitation to speak at my first survivor reunion, the Nuremberg-Fürth reunion, called "The Golden Reunion Plus," at Kutsher's in the Catskills. After I finished speaking, a member of the audience came up to me and said, "You are a child survivor. You should call Doctor Judith Kestenberg in New York." Her words struck me like a thunderbolt. I had never heard the term *child survivor* before, but I knew it was mine. (I would learn later that it was coined in 1980.)

I had always felt that the impact of the Holocaust on me was different from how it had affected my parents, but I did not know that there was a name for who I was or what it implied. I would learn that for a very, very young child to survive the Holocaust, during her developmental years, was different—very different—from surviving as a teenager or as an adult. It seemed that with each step I took on this path of going public, I discovered something important about myself.

Now I started to travel. I went from my home in Massachusetts to New York to meet with the inspiring Dr. Kestenberg, the founder of Child Development Research, which is conducting the International Study of Organized Persecution of Children, and I went there again to meet with Dr. Helene Bass-Wichelhaus, who interviewed me. It was she who validated for me that blood running down my face was a childhood memory and not an incidental thought with no meaning. I traveled to Israel to meet with Dr. Yolanda Gampel, a psychoanalyst who worked with Dr. Kestenberg and her project. After meeting her, I wrote my first poem, about tears. I went to Boston, not to give a talk but to participate in the Boston Child Survivor Group founded by Freida Grayzel, where I was welcomed with open arms as the "sixth Eva" in the group. Growing up, I had known no other child with the name of Eva. In this group I realized that not only had we child survivors been raised in silence but that in turn many of us had raised our children, the second generation, in silence too. This led me to create the project called Intergenerational Healing in Holocaust Families at the University of Massachusetts, a project that has attempted to bring together members of the second and third generations.

And I traveled back to Europe to find the graves of my paternal grandparents. One was buried in the old cemetery of Nuremberg, where headstones still lay smashed and overturned from the war, and the other was buried in a mass grave in Theresienstadt. My maternal grandfather was buried on the Mount of Olives in Israel, and my Granny was buried in New York.

Everywhere I went, I laid stones for me and for each of my children and grandchildren, to let the dead "know" that they had a family, a growing family. It was as if in visiting the cemeteries of all my grandparents, dispersed as they were in different lands, I was looking for one place for all of them to be. I found that that place was within me, within my heart and within the memories that I was creating by visiting them in their last resting places. My travels proved to be a way not only to mourn my losses but to connect with that part of my Holocaust family tree that had been lost to me.

In 1995 I returned to Angers, I think to capture something that I could not quite identify. Angers was a place I could not remember, but I had arranged to meet there with Mme Hélène Vernhes, who had befriended my mother and me during the war. At our first meeting she embraced me, saying over and over again, "Ma petite bébé." I cried as I hugged a woman I could not remember but whose open arms made me feel accepted. She cried too. Hélène had hired an interpreter for our meeting, a second-generation German who was fluent in French, German, and English. He was warm and friendly and, in his own way, wounded too. He would tell me his story later, but first he told me that he had been hired to give me a choice of the language in which to communicate. I used English and a broken French, and he interpreted it all. We talked for a full day in the lobby of our hotel and I taped our conversations. The next day we walked around Angers.

Hélène brought me to where I had lived on Rue Fulton and where I had been bombed. She brought me to where the hospital and orphanage had stood all those years ago. I remembered nothing of the place, but something miraculous did happen. On Rue Fulton and in front of the church, which had stood near the orphanage and which was still there, I began to feel an overwhelming feeling of sadness, and I began to feel a new compassion toward myself. Many feelings were surfacing, and as they did, I began to write them down. When I left Angers, I started writing "Through the Concrete Wall," a poem in which I begin to talk not about what had happened to me in Europe or in America but about my inner experience of "breaking through the wall," of truly shedding my silence and coming out of hiding.

I had been wanting to meet Elie Wiesel for a very long time but had not had the courage to ask. In 1996 I sent him a piece of my writing and asked if we could meet. To my great joy an appointment was arranged. He asked me, "What can I do for you?" and I asked him the question that was the main reason that I had come. I asked him how he had broken his silence "so soon." He smiled and sighed and told me, "It took me ten years." I thought, "For me, for whom it took five decades, that would have been a very short time." But then I understood what he was trying to tell me. For the silent a decade, a year, a month, a week of silence is too long a time. And then he smiled at me again and asked if I would write my story for him and send it to him when it was done. He said it was the most important thing a survivor could do. I think he thought that I needed a push to do it, and he was right. He gave me that push and helped me start to collect the smashed glass and shrapnel of my life in Europe and in the United States.

For me, writing is like having a conversation with myself. It is how I find the words for the inner story that was kept so long in hiding. Every writing and retelling, every response and every new scrap of memory that emerges, every visit "back" shifts the picture in some important way. Every step in the process of breaking my silence can create a broader and more balanced perspective for me.

Today I try to live my life in the present, without denying the details of my past. One and a half million children died in the war. They never got the chance, as I have had, to find their voice, to find a loved one, and to have loving children who begin new generations. For them I will never stop grieving, but I feel that I am now free to move on to the next chapters of my life, less burdened by the things that were once kept so hidden, so immobilized, and so fearfully inside.

Editor's Note: This essay is adapted from an unpublished memoir on healing, Through the Concrete Wall: A Child Survivor Comes Out of Hiding.

Child of Four Families

MARIAN NACHMAN
(b. 1938, Holland)

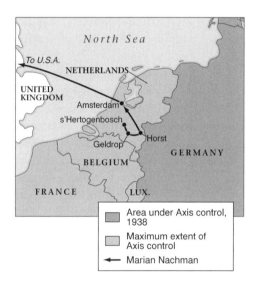

I was born on May 8, 1938, in Holland, in s'Hertogenbosch in the province of Braaband. My parents, Martha Davids and Arthur Neuhaus, had emigrated independently to Holland from Germany and had met and married there in 1936. My mother came from a small town called Darfeld, where she had grown up as the oldest in a large family. She had gone to Amsterdam to become a saleswoman and governess for wealthy relatives who owned (and still own) the Bonneterie, a famous and fashionable department store. My father came from Herleshausen, an equally small, if not smaller, town where he was one of four sons of Joseph and Minna Neuhaus.

Why Arthur and Martha emigrated to Holland is not exactly clear. It was too early for them to have been escaping Nazi persecution, so in all likelihood my mother wanted to experience the glamorous life of a big city, and perhaps my father was looking for better business opportunities. From what I have pieced together from various sources, he went into the women's sportswear clothing business with a Dutch partner, Erich Voss.

What I know about my parents and my early years I learned much later in my life. Since I was just three years old when I was sent into hiding, I have no recollection of my mother or father. My grandfather apparently also lived with us. Though I don't remember him either, I have a large photograph of him that was dedicated to me on my third birthday. I gathered much of this information on a trip that I made to Holland in April 1996. I went to Horst, in Limburg, a very small town near Venlo, not far from the German border, where I spent the war years. I had returned to visit the Martenses, the family that had hidden me. The occasion was the ninetieth birthday of Christine, my *onderdaag,* or rescuing mother. Albert, her husband, had died several years before. Now, after thirty-six years, I was again to see Ton, one of my two "brothers" from the war years who is just about my age, and to meet his wife, Mariet, and their son and daughter, Bart and Doreen, who are almost exactly the same ages as my son and daughter, Alex and Juliet.

We had been in contact through the years, with occasional letters and photographs, but I had not been back to Holland since 1958–59, when I made a trip during Christmas vacation of my junior year in college, which I spent in France. The following summer my aunt and uncle were traveling in Europe, and they met the Martenses and Marianneke, the Martenses' niece who is now their adopted daughter. In 1972 Christine and Albert made their first and only visit to the United States, and while they stayed with us, we talked about the war years. Despite the many problems and hardships then—there was no school for a while, and twenty-seven people were living in their house at one point—we always had enough food and no one was ever in a bad mood. The children slept in the basement for months and railroad ties were fixed to the windows.

My parents had gone into hiding in 1941, in a place that was too dangerous to take me along. I went first to live with the Bruning family in the nearby town of Geldrop. Mr. Bruning was a business associate of my father's who had twelve children and felt that one more child in the family wouldn't be noticed. I was there only a few months, because one of the children mentioned in her kindergarten class that a Jewish girl had come to live at her house. Her father thought it too dangerous for me to remain with them and sent me to live in Horst with his sister-in-law and her family—Christine and Albert Martens, and their two sons, Ton and Jan, who were five and three years old at the time. I was able to live in the open; the only people who knew that I was Jewish were the town priest and the Martenses.

Neighbors believed that I was a sickly cousin from the city, where people were starving. I had been brought to the countryside to benefit from the more plentiful food and the fresh air. I vividly remember that the Martenses told me again and again that my real name was Marianne Martens, not Marianne Neuhaus. (In the United States, about 1950, I changed the spelling of my name to Marian.) I really became a member of the family and called the Martenses Papa and Moeder. I was brought up as a Catholic child and so went to the local convent school, where I was a top student and knew my prayers. (I also learned to knit and crochet.) I studied for my first Communion and was devastated to learn that the church would not

Marian and her "brothers," Ton and Jan Martens, ca. 1942 (*above*) and ca. 1946 (*below*).

Marian and her father, Arthur
Neuhaus, in s'Hertogenbosch,
Holland, ca. 1941

permit me to go through with it. The priest could not allow my Communion, because he was aware that I was a Jewish child.

It was a low point of my life. I had studied long and hard and knew everything inside out. I was six years old and really looking forward to the whole festive occasion—an important milestone in a Catholic's life. I was allowed to wear the white dress and carry the flowers, but I learned at that moment that I was an outsider. I had come to believe that I was a real member of the family and did not understand why I could not participate fully in this ceremony.

Not too long after the Communion, some time after May 9, 1945 (VE Day), my uncle Kurt (my father's brother) appeared at the house, very impressive in his American army uniform. Although I didn't know him, I was immediately drawn to him and went to sit on his lap, perhaps because, as I was to learn later on, he bore a strong resemblance to my real father. I must have had his picture somewhere in my memory. Then the Martenses started talking to me about going to America to

Marian, dressed for her first communion, with Jan Martens, in Horst, Holland, 1945.

live with an aunt and uncle. I absolutely did not understand. I could not figure out why I had to leave. Of course, I did not want to leave what I considered to be my only family, and I had almost no memories of any life before the Martenses. I had been there from about the ages of four to eight.

I clearly remember that when the Nazis invaded and occupied our town, they came to live in our house and turned part of the house into their headquarters. The *Hauptman,* who was a major and their commanding officer, was a fairly decent fellow. Christine's brother was allowed to stay in the house and did not have to go into forced labor like all the other townsmen, because he was needed, supposedly, to cook for the Nazi officers.

We children were told not to speak to the Germans. We pretended that we did not understand them, yet we really did understand, because the local dialect was very similar to German. I knew that the Nazis were bad and were to be feared and avoided. At school we used to have regular bomb drills—we would have to get

under our desks and face away from the windows. A bomb actually did fall not far from the school building, leaving a huge crater that filled with water. The town's imposing church was bombed to the ground.

It used to be my job to ride my scooter into town very early in the morning to pick up bread at the family bakery. One morning a military truck slowed down and stopped next to where I was stopped on the sidewalk. The soldiers in the back were pointing at me, and I was sure they would pick me up and take me away. I tried to hide behind a lamppost. But then they decided to move on. I was really relieved and remember it as the most terrifying moment of my life.

The major also warned us about impending bombings and suggested that everyone seek shelter in the cellar for several nights. Relatives joined us there for safety, and we slept there for several nights of bomb attacks. I felt very safe there, tightly surrounded by so many people.

After the war our *Hauptman* was sent to a "reeducation camp," but his wife stayed in touch with the Martenses. After he got out of the reeducation camp, he came to visit the Martenses and learned then that I, the child he had playfully bounced on his knee in the mid-1940s, was Jewish. The officer was particularly concerned about the hatred that Ricki, an older girl whom the Martenses were also hiding, might feel for him.

In July 1946, shortly after I turned eight, Papa and Moeder brought me to Amsterdam—my first view of a big city and the beginning of many firsts, including staying in a hotel, smelling perfume, and going to a movie. We went to a newsreel, and I saw an airplane taking off and coming right toward me. I actually ducked! I was scared and didn't understand. I was, for the very first time, experiencing many new and exciting adventures. Until then I had lived in a small quiet village with familiar routines and people.

The plane trip from Amsterdam to America was long and lonely, but I had my stuffed doll, which had been sent to me from America to keep me company. I also remember that the stewardess was very kind to me. My aunt Ellen and uncle Fritz, another brother of my father's, were at New York's La Guardia Airport to meet me. They were total strangers to me and they did not speak Dutch. They spoke both English and German, but I spoke only Dutch. I cried for several days and would not and could not speak to anyone, because no one spoke Dutch and I was so very homesick. Ellen called an elderly cousin who spoke Dutch, Annie Cohen, for whom my mother had worked in Holland before the war. Annie could get me to talk. I don't remember that it helped me; I felt so very lost and abandoned.

Bob, the son of Ellen and Fritz, was sixteen years old, a senior at the High School of Music and Art in New York who was spending the summer away from home. I remember meeting him later that summer at some relatives' chicken farm near Camden, New Jersey. I adored him. He was like an older brother for me. He must have had very mixed feelings about me, because he had been an only child for so long. My isolation was relieved somewhat by the appearance of my uncle Kurt, who had found me in Horst and had made the arrangements with the Martenses

for my transfer to America. I liked him and was comfortable with him. I did not want to let him go and clung to him. In those days, however, bachelors were not permitted to adopt children, so his brother Fritz was the next best choice.

We lived in Washington Heights, a big center then for German Jewish refugees in New York. At that time I was still not aware that my real parents were not the Martenses and that the Germans had killed my biological parents in a concentration camp. As a teenager, I learned from Red Cross records that they were killed in Sobibór, in Poland, in 1943 after being arrested and taken first to Westerbork, a holding camp in Holland. But I did not learn the details of what had happened to them until 1996.

In September 1946 I started third grade at PS 173. I had already finished third grade in Holland but had to learn English and cursive writing to catch up. There were no English-as-a-Second-Language courses in those days, yet I don't recall being uncomfortable in school. In fact, I liked school very much. I was a very good and very conscientious student and learned English rapidly. At the same time, at home I was learning German, which was the language of the household. Meanwhile, Aunt Ellen and Uncle Fritz formally adopted me.

My adjustment to life with the Neuhauses—my uncle and aunt—was problematic. The relationship was difficult. They were well-meaning people, but my uncle was distant and my aunt was a critical and dissatisfied individual whom I viewed during my youth as having deprived me of the warm relationship that I had had in Holland with the Martenses. In Holland I was a lighthearted, happy, and outgoing child. I had become a sad, well-behaved, lonely, and timid girl. I was still a young child and feared that even mild misbehavior of any sort might lead to my being taken away again.

Ellen and Fritz had had their own adjustments to make when they came to America, just under the wire, but they remained very German and lived almost entirely in the German Jewish community of Washington Heights. Fritz was a doctor and had to learn English and take his medical board exams before he could make any money. Ellen came from a wealthy Berlin family. Although the first years were very hard, eventually Fritz established a successful practice and their fortunes improved considerably. Yet I continued to feel alienated, even as I desperately wanted to fit in. Fortunately, I met a girl in that third grade class who became a lifelong friend. Her mother took me under her wing and became the adult with whom I could feel comfortable and whom I could trust completely, something that I was never able to feel toward Ellen.

I always stayed in touch with the Martenses—during the first years reluctantly because I was so angry that they had sent me away. As an eight-year-old I could not understand why unknown relatives had the right to demand that I move in with them in an alien land. It would be many years before I could come to terms again with the family I had loved and who had cared for me.

Christine would write to me, signing her letters *Moeder*. I, on the other hand, no longer addressed her as Moeder. I now knew in the back of my mind that neither she nor her husband was my real parent. Also, my anger at having been sent away caused me to be ambivalent toward them. Christine was ninety-three when she died in October 1999, and I went to Horst for the funeral. I had seen her that summer when I stopped in Holland on my way to Israel. It wasn't until almost at the end of Christine's life that I called her Moeder again. My adoptive mother (from whom I had been estranged for several years) died in 1998, also at the age of ninety-three.

I remained conflicted for most of my life about the complex relationships and loyalties with the Martens and the Neuhaus families. Ellen was a very controlling individual who gave me little freedom to make my own decisions and to choose my own friends—especially boyfriends. I wasn't allowed to attend Wellesley College near Boston because my current boyfriend would have been able to visit me there too easily. I was a pliant and dutiful daughter but seethed inwardly.

Much later on—in 1996, when I went back to Holland for the very first time since 1958–59—a woman who had known my real parents related an anecdote about my mother and me when I was a willful and stubborn little girl of about three. I had been offered some candies by a neighbor and I took them. Despite my mother's request, I refused to say thank you. My mother told me that I would have to give the candies back—and without hesitation, that is exactly what I did.

During that same 1996 trip I met a former playmate, Corey van Gelen, who had been trying to trace me through the Red Cross. Her mother and mine had been friends and neighbors before the war. While Corey was going through her mother's things after she died, about a year before my trip, she found some memorabilia belonging to my mother, including some photographs, which are incredibly precious to me. One shows the silhouette of my grandfather and me when I was three, together with Corey and her twin sister, in my family's living room.

Although Corey and I are the same age, she has some memories of our time as playmates and remembers how my mother cried when she knew that she had to give up her little girl, her only child. When Corey told me that, I finally understood how my mother must have felt when she had to give me away, and how Christine, whose only "daughter" I was, felt when she also had little choice about giving me up. As a mother myself, I could imagine what it must have been like.

Most important was that meeting these two people finally gave me some real connection, beyond photographs, to the first three years of my life. I went to visit the house where my parents lived when I was born, the house that my parents bought—which is lovely—and the house in which they lived after they were forced by the Dutch Nazis to give up their own house, and from which my parents disappeared forever. I also learned from Corey that it was her father who had arranged for my parents to go into hiding. This trip gave me back a vital part of my life and with it a stronger sense of my identity.

In 1998 my son, Alex, went to Holland and visited the Martenses: Christine, Ton and Mariet (her son and daughter-in-law), and Bart and Doreen, her grand-

Marian at the wedding of her
daughter, Juliet, in Spokane,
Washington, 2001.

children. He saw the house where I lived during the war. He saw the cellar where
we had spent many nights during the bombings, and he saw corners in the attic
that had been set up as hiding places for people who needed temporary shelter. In
telling me about his visit, he seemed especially moved by how Christine had expressed her strong feelings of love for me. Interestingly enough, it was not until my
last visit, in 1999, that Christine told me that just before Uncle Kurt had come to
claim me, she and Albert had begun adoption proceedings. After so many years I
finally learned that the Martenses really had loved me and had wanted to keep me
with them always. I learned that they hadn't wanted to interfere when members of
my real family appeared. Yet the hurt I felt when I was sent away so many years ago
still surfaces to this day.

The trauma of the numerous sets of families and parents that I had during my
childhood obviously affected my adult life and still does. The broken bonds were
never completely healed. I did go to Smith College, where I majored in French and
made the dean's list. I worked for a while at the United Nations as a guide and as a

photo researcher at the *New York Times*. I worked for an architect, art galleries, and a museum. I gained a lot of satisfaction from school and work, and from my children. My marriage ended in divorce in 1976.

And my story does not and will not end—nor can or should it. The latest chapter occurred at Christine's funeral, attended by many Brunings, the first family that hid me. At the reception after the service, a woman somewhat younger than I extended her hand to me and blurted out, "I was the one who betrayed you." I was stunned and couldn't say a word. Later I thought of how relieved she must have felt after being burdened for so long by this childhood guilt.

The oldest Bruning sister (who had physically brought me to the Martenses for safekeeping) had told me some years earlier in a letter that I had arrived at their house wearing a fur coat and with a toy sewing machine, among other fancy— for their large family—toys. I, an only child from a wealthy family with her fancy clothes and toys, must have created some envy when I arrived on the scene. I will go to Holland again, and maybe I'll learn some more about my past. Those visits and the support of the Holocaust Child Survivors of Connecticut have helped me reconnect to my past and present.

And She Lived Happily Ever After

FELICIA GRABER
(b. 1940, Poland)

I have always said that, unlike many of my peers, I was and still am a very lucky woman. Even my name, Felicia, comes from the Latin word for luck, happiness. In fact, for me the war years were a breeze compared to what other Jewish children experienced. But still there remain residues, as well as some glimpses, of early childhood that are burned into me as if with a branding iron:

Mobs . . . noise . . . shouts . . . screams . . . dusk . . . train fumes . . . a locomotive whistling . . . a steam engine hissing . . . people pushing, trying to get on the train . . . a woman standing on the tracks, halfway under the train, only her upper body showing—arms raised: "Please take my child, what about my child?" "Give me the child." "No, I'll not let go of her!" Where am I going? Where am I? A garden . . . trees . . . a white rabbit in a cage . . . yelling up to Mother from the garden.

Bullets flying through the window . . . crouching down on the floor . . . running to the basement . . . bombs exploding. . . . A soldier in knee-high black riding boots standing outside the open door of our house, a rifle in his hand. A potato field, a cow moving steadily into the field. I am four years old, the cow is so big, and I feel so helpless and small as I keep hitting her and she keeps moving farther into the field. Muddy streets, a few scattered farmhouses . . . thatched roofs . . . Russian planes . . . people shouting . . . running . . . happy . . . a group of men coming down the street yelling, drunk, happy: "We are free!"

I am in horrible pain. All night I am being held and walked. All I feel is my ear—will it never stop hurting? Someone (the doctor?) is putting an instrument into my ear, my mother (or is it my "uncle"?) is holding me. (Recently, I had an ear infection and went to a doctor, who told me that I had had my eardrum pierced many years ago. So I am not imagining things.)

My mother and I arrived at a house where my "uncle" had found a place for us to live. There was a big bed; on the bed sat the most gorgeous doll anybody has ever seen. My doll, my first doll. I do not remember ever playing with her, but I will never forget seeing her on that bed. The year must have been 1945 and I was five years old. The war was over.

Sometime later, I'm told, my mother married my uncle, although—as I keep telling anyone who wants to listen—I never saw a wedding. My brother was born. But he was born ill, with a hernia and rickets. He was not allowed to cry, lest he strain himself. My mother was very ill and was taken to Kraków for a major operation. When she returned, her recuperation period was lengthy. I was left in the care of a nurse who was hired to care for my brother. I didn't like her; she was tall, wrinkled, old, and mean. The feeling was mutual. She disliked the little "Miss Bigmouth" who faithfully reported all her comings and goings to her employer. Finally, a young woman came to take care of me. I got to go to church with her. One day she pointed out some dark-looking men on the street and declared: "Those must be Jews." I looked around, following them with my eyes. Already the word *Jew* had a vague but distinctly negative connotation—of somebody sinister, mysterious, someone to be afraid of. Where did I get this negative notion of a Jew? I do not know.

But I loved going to church. I remember pushing my way through the crowd to be in the first row. Being there gave me a warm feeling. For Christmas my young caretaker made me an angel costume. It was beautiful: I had wings, a white robe, and a halo. I was supposed to recite and sing for my parents. But something went wrong. In the middle of my performance I broke into tears and ran to my mother, unable to finish. I remember her saying to my father: "You would think the child knows." I did not understand what she meant, but I do remember what she said. Why do I remember these little tidbits from my early years, while other things are totally gone?

We were sitting in a large kitchen in our small apartment. We had left Poland. No more nurses, maids, mother's helpers. We had come to Brussels, where my father had a distant cousin. The next day I was to start in my new school, in second grade, learning to speak French. My mother was holding my year-old brother on her lap. This scene is engraved in my mind. I had been listening as my mother again

Felicia Graber with her parents, Shlomo Lederberger-Bialecki and Tosia Fallman-Leder-berger-Bialecki, in Sopot, Poland, late 1945 or early 1946.

told my father: "You must tell her—I do not want her to go to school before she knows." Was I curious about or interested in what I was supposed to know? I don't remember. But I clearly remember the scene in the kitchen. My father told me that I am a Jew and that he is one too, as are my mother and my brother. He told me that his parents were Jews and so were my mother's parents. He also told me that he is my real father, not an uncle who married my mother—that I never had a father who was a Polish soldier and who was killed in the war as I had been told. I do not remember how I felt; in fact, feelings seem to have played a very small part in my life.

Sometimes I think that I was, and still am, incapable of feelings. Yet I still burst out crying for the slightest reason and often flare up in anger. But what I do remember from that night is that I went to my room, as if in a trance, took out the beautiful white and gold Catholic prayer book that my young caretaker had given me as a present, and tore it to pieces. Why did I do that? To this day I have no explanation. I don't even remember feeling guilty, but now I wish I still had it as a memento. I still do have a little gold pendant depicting Mary with her infant that I wore later in Sopot, and I have resisted many attempts to make me give it up. For reasons that I do not understand, I find it very precious.

These are some fragments of memories that I have from my earliest childhood. I am extraordinarily lucky that I had my parents, who filled in some of the blanks of what really happened in those first seven years of my life. Throughout my life people have often told me how lucky I am to have been such a young child during those war years—because I could not possibly remember the terrible things that happened. Yes, I am truly lucky because both my parents survived, I was never separated from my mother, and I do not remember hunger or any feelings of fear.

Sometimes, though, I wish that I could remember. When talking to older child survivors who remember their grandparents or happy scenes from their early childhood, I wish I could be hypnotized. I wish I could go back to the first months of my life to see my father's father, who, I am told, adored me and came to see me daily as long as he could. I wish I could remember some scenes of the "life before," see my mother as a young mother and wife, my hometown of Tarnów as it was then, a small town whose Jewish life was strong and vibrant. I wish I could remember my father as a young man whose only worries concerned running his father's prosperous jewelry business.

But the only memories I have of those early years of my life are the fragments that I have described here. Yet those memories have haunted me throughout my life. I have had frequent dreams about a little girl riding in a train. It took me years to understand why I experienced panic attacks whenever I was in a big crowd or why I have uneasy feelings whenever I am on a train or in a subway station. These fragments are not my memories but those of my parents, especially of my father, who had an unbelievable memory and who was almost obsessed with talking about the war years.

I was born in March of 1940, a few months after Hitler invaded Poland. I was told that my mother, like many of her contemporaries, had planned to have an abortion. Who wanted to bring a Jewish child into such uncertain times? A child is a burden when you want to flee to Russia, as many young people did. But my mother did not go through with the abortion partly because my grandfather, a very religious man, begged her not to. Then, because my mother was five months pregnant with me, my parents could not run to Russia. The first time I heard that story I broke out sobbing with immense feelings of guilt that I had prevented my parents from running to relative safety from the Germans.

When I was two, we had to move into the Tarnów ghetto, and there my father managed to get a forged ID for my mother and a Catholic baptismal certificate for me. This happened after we were miraculously taken out of a transport that was awaiting the train to the Belzec death camp.

I never fully appreciated the task that my mother undertook at the time. She was raised in an Orthodox family, had led a pretty sheltered life, and was an ardent Zionist who had gone to Palestine, only to come back when her mother was dying. Now she was thrown into a Catholic world that she knew nothing about. Except for a few rare meetings with a Jewish man who was helping his coreligionists in hiding, she was left to her own devices. My father had not been able to procure papers for himself; besides, he would have been a liability. Young Poles had been conscripted into the army; how would he explain his presence? His "Jewish" appearance did not help either, nor did his poor command of Polish. (He had been raised in a totally Yiddish environment.) He remained in the Tarnów ghetto.

So my mother had to fend for herself. She had to learn how to behave, what to say to whom. She had to invent a past that was foolproof, explain why she was alone with a young child. She had to watch her every word, every gesture, lest an eager Pole become suspicious and run to the Gestapo. And she had to brainwash a little girl. She had to change homes, move to another town a couple of times, until she finally trained the little one about what she could or could not say to strangers, and until she had turned her daughter into a pious little Catholic girl whose highlight of the week was going to church.

Later, when my father managed to escape from the ghetto himself and join us in Warsaw, my mother faced the double task of hiding him in her one-room apartment and redoubling her brainwashing that nobody lived with me but my mother. As I was often told in later years, I was literally "pulled out of Hitler's clutches" and then had my parents' life in my hands . . . all at the ripe age of four as I was playing downstairs with other children. (The white rabbit . . . the garden . . . calling up to my mother.) There really *was* and still is a garden; I saw it in 1994 when I went to Poland and found the house.

After the Warsaw uprising, which started on August 1, 1944, was crushed, the three of us were driven out of our home, along with thousands of other Poles (those riding boots), forced westward toward Germany. Only luck and quick thinking helped us escape being shipped to Germany as forced laborers. We managed to find shelter with a farmer, who lived in one large room with his wife and two daughters. They never knew we were Jews, and his daughters, whom I traced on that trip to Poland, still don't know. Sitting in the farmhouse fifty years later, I was afraid to tell them that we were Jews after I heard an angry outburst by the husband of one sister: "Lech Walensa is a traitor; he is selling Poland to the Jews." My parents and I had stayed on that farm until liberation. (The cow . . . the planes . . . I am starting to tie things together.)

In the spring of 1945 my father left to look for a place to restart our life. He did not go back to Tarnów. He knew there would be nothing there. He had seen the liquidation of the ghetto; he had been made to sort clothes to be shipped to Germany. He had no illusions. He found a room in a big city for us. (Was it Łódź or Lvov?) I became very ill there, first with typhus and then with the ear infections that resulted in my eardrum's being punctured. I don't remember the typhus or that my mother quarantined herself in the room for weeks because she would not allow me to be taken to a hospital, but I do remember the pain.

Finally, my father was able to literally dig up tools from the ruins of a watchmaker's store in Sopot, near Gdańsk (formerly the Free City of Danzig) in northern Poland. How did he get there? By hitchhiking on Russian army jeeps and trucks. Why there? I do not know. He also found a place for us to live and sent for us (the mobs . . . screaming . . . whistling . . . shoving). It must have been dusk because I am still uncomfortable in a crowd after dark.

Was it also dusk when the Germans put me on that truck, to be taken away, back in '42? I never talk about that. At the last moment my parents had a change of heart and voluntarily joined me on that truck, an act that saved me from being sent to Belzec. Here is all I know about what happened: in 1942 my father had a hiding place in our room in the Tarnów ghetto, and members of the Jewish Council convinced the Gestapo chief that they needed him to run things smoothly. So the three of us were taken out of the transport. Is this why I have those horrible feelings of being abandoned and become panicky when I think that I have displeased someone I love or someone in authority? I don't think I'll ever know.

Anyway, it was in Sopot in 1945 that I found my doll. Sopot also was where my brother was born in 1946 and where my mother got sick.

In 1947 the Communist regime was targeting all "capitalists." Life was getting too dangerous so my father bribed a Belgian consul to issue us a visa to Belgium. Again we started a new life. My parents had lost everything for the second time in their lives. My father had to start from scratch to build up a business. And I discovered a new identity.

I was asked recently whether I ever discussed my feelings with my mother and whether I missed going to church or even sneaked into a church. I don't remember discussing any feelings with my mother or ever going into a church to pray. When I do go into a church now, it is as a tourist, sightseeing. But I do have to admit that I have a funny feeling when I do enter one, a feeling that I cannot describe in words but one that stirs some deep-seated emotions in me.

One time, shortly after my father's death in 1991, as I was sitting in the synagogue on a Saturday morning, I suddenly smelled a whiff of incense that was inexplicably very real. For a very, very brief moment I was transported back into my childhood and had the feeling of being in church. This feeling was so strong that I almost panicked. What was I to do? Why did I feel that way? Was the past catching up with me? The feeling and the smell never came back, but they scared me because they put my whole current life into question.

But in 1947 my parents had other worries than the feelings of a seven-year-old. They had to rebuild their lives for the second time in two years. My mother was still recuperating from her surgery, she had a sick baby on her hands, and she was thrown into a new world again, one whose language she did not speak or understand. Belgian authorities were quick to give asylum to refugees from the Communist world but would not allow them to earn a living. Belgium was rebuilding after the war and was not about to allow foreigners to take jobs away from Belgian nationals. So my father ended up "commuting" to Germany. He spent weeks there, building a business, pulling himself up, making life financially more comfortable for us.

I have mostly fond and happy memories from those years in Belgium. I remember moving several times, each time to a better and bigger apartment. I remember going to school, being happy, being put in charge of my brother, and taking him to the park after school. Even though I did not always enjoy being his "nanny," to my recollection I never rebelled, never complained. My mother later often told me that I never gave her any trouble. I was a "good little girl," doing what I was supposed to. If I was terrified at being left alone at night in charge of my brother, I never let my mother know. If I resented having to walk my brother to sleep for hours, I did not complain. I was well trained to do what I was supposed to.

I do not remember having many friends during those years. Only two come to mind, sons of friends of my parents, also survivors, who were in transit to other destinations—Argentina and Brazil—and who soon left. I do remember being an avid movie fan, of American movies especially. I can still recall being allowed to go to the movies alone every Sunday. It was the highlight of my life. I still recall some of my heroes: Burt Lancaster, Errol Flynn, Maureen O'Hara, and Yvonne De Carlo. And I will never forget Lana Turner in *The Three Musketeers.*

In 1951 my mother finally capitulated. She had resisted moving to Germany and raising her children there, but my father's commuting became too much for all of us, and we moved to Frankfurt am Main. At first I was put in a boarding school for children of French occupation troops because my mother resisted putting me in a German school. At the French school I boarded with two other Jewish refugee girls, and the three of us became inseparable. Both girls were child survivors, but we never broached the subject of our war years. Today they too live in the United States, but it was only a few years ago that we finally discussed our past and were amazed that we had never done so as teenagers.

After two years of indecision and being shuttled between the French boarding school (in which I was very unhappy) and a German private school (which was even worse), I was finally but reluctantly enrolled in a public German girls' school from which all former Nazis had been purged. Ever since we'd moved to Germany, I had been engaged in a constant mental tug of war. I was living in enemy territory. I kept thinking, "What did my classmates' fathers do during the war?" I felt isolated and had no friends, and at home the situation was becoming unbearable.

My parents, who had never really had a chance to build a foundation in the early years of their marriage, were not able to do so now, either. I became my mother's counselor, friend, and confidant. She instilled in me that I was to get an education and be able to stand on my own two feet, and that she would do anything, make any sacrifice, for my benefit.

Those years in Germany stand out in my mind as bittersweet (more bitter than sweet). As I said, I had no friends. I remember spending my weekends with my American movie magazines, cutting out pictures, writing to Hollywood, and hoping I would not be forced to take a Sunday ride with my parents and their friends. Being alone was preferable to that.

But I did have a bright star in my life. Israel had sent an envoy, a *shaliach,* to help the Jewish community and its children and to instill a sense of identity with

Israel. He and his wife became my heroes. He introduced me to Israeli culture, its songs, dances, and language. We had a weekly youth group, and although I was the oldest of its five members, it was my lifeline. I could not get enough. He also introduced me to Freud and psychology (his hobby). I started to study psychology and almost became a psychologist because of his influence. And his wife showed me that marriage could be a wonderful experience.

In 1956 I was sixteen. My mother decided that I could not live in Germany any longer, so she settled me in a boarding school in England, a small international girls' school not far from London. It was not Jewish—but not German. My year at Pax Hill, as it was called, was great. I loved it. It was liberation all over again. For the first time in a long time I did not feel different. All the girls were different. They were daughters of ambassadors, diplomats, and high-ranking officials from all over the world. They had been sent to England either to finish their education or get a Western education in order to be more attractive as a prospective wife or just to get out from under their parents' feet.

I worked very hard, determined to pass the required five exams to get my General Certificate of Education, the equivalent of a high school diploma. Contrary to the predictions of the headmistress, who claimed I could not possibly pass them in just one year with my poor knowledge of English, I passed all my exams. Now I could go to a university; my door to the United States had opened.

In the spring of '57 my parents' visas for the United States came through. We all went to New York during my spring break, immigrated officially, and went right back to Europe. My parents intended to liquidate my father's business and move permanently to the United States. That fall I was told to enroll at the University of Frankfurt while awaiting our move. Well, the move did not happen. For reasons that I was either not told or that I do not remember, my parents let their visas lapse, and I was once again stuck in Germany.

I was determined, however, to bide my time and to work toward admission to an American college. That first academic year as a student at Johann Wolfgang University in Frankfurt was not much different from my previous experience in a German school. The only difference was that I was now able to mingle with foreign students, join the foreign student organization, and have more of a social life, or so I thought. Dating a German was unthinkable—it was treachery. I did date a couple of foreign students, but I never really felt comfortable among them either.

I still had my youth group, which had gained more members because many German Jews were returning to their *heimat* (homeland), lured by the financial incentives of the German government. A Jewish summer camp was started in the summer of '57 for children born after the war, many in displaced persons (DP) camps. A Jewish rebirth was underway in Germany. I was one of the first counselors who volunteered to work at the camp. The following year a few Israeli students appeared at the university. They were sons of expatriate Germans who had returned to their parents' homeland to get a free education. In the fall of 1958 I got together with a couple of them, and we formed the first Jewish Student Club in postwar Frankfurt, the Israela.

At home things were not getting any better, however. My father and I never had gotten along. I could never get close to him. Was it because I always had doubted that he was my real dad, even though I looked so much like him? Was it because he never attempted to establish any kind of relationship with me? Whatever the reason, only after he died did I begin to look back and try to understand him. Too late I realized that, in his own way, he did love me, even though he never told me so or even showed me any affection. Mostly, he was dictatorial and did not believe in discussion. His way of showing love was to shower me with jewelry whenever he could. He loved jewelry. It was not only a business but also a hobby for him, and he drew pleasure out of seeing me wear some of the beautiful things that he gave me. But I can remember only one time that I had a real heart-to-heart conversation with him—and it was not a pleasant experience.

One scene, however, stands out in my mind. He was in a nursing home, here in the States. I went to see him and he seemed to be sleeping, so I sat down on his bed with my back to him. Suddenly, I felt his hand gently on my head. I will never forget that feeling. No word was spoken, none needed to be. In that one small gesture he had said it all.

A few months after his death, I was sitting in the synagogue one Shabbat morning when I physically felt my father looking at me from behind. I do not know how I knew it was him, but I could swear I saw his face hovering above and behind me, and a strange feeling came over me: he did love me!

Finally, in the fall of 1958 I prepared to go to the States. I had made arrangements to stay, at least temporarily, with a cousin of my father's, a survivor of the camps who had emigrated to New York. Although all my attempts at getting into Barnard College were unsuccessful, I was sure that I would work something out. My parents, especially my mother, were worried about sending an eighteen-year-old alone to the New World. So they made me an offer that they knew I could not and would not refuse: a chance to travel—to Paris, Rome, Greece, and Israel—if I would postpone my plans for a year. It did not take any effort to convince me. I would have been willing to do anything for such an opportunity.

Again, someone was watching over me, for the day after I returned from the first installment of my "bribe"—an unforgettable trip to Paris—I was called by a friend who was working in the office of the Jewish Community. She had a dilemma. A young American Jewish GI had come to see her with an unusual request. He was homesick, wanted to meet a Jewish girl, and was very persistent. Since I was the only person my friend knew who spoke English, she had thought of me. With my mother's permission, I invited him for dinner to check him out. During dinner he informed me that he had arranged for a double date with the new American Jewish chaplain, who was also a bachelor and who had just assumed his position in Frankfurt. So I agreed to go out, and the moment I saw Howard Graber, it was love at first sight. But I had been brought up with stories of European rabbis: they were to be honored, revered, followed but not dated. So when Howard called me for a date a few days later, I was in shock. That was April of 1959. We were married in December, and a new life started for me in more ways than I can count.

In December 1963 Howard was reassigned to the advanced chaplain school at Fort Hamilton, New York, and we (the children and I) of course went with him. Then we were transferred to Fort Bragg, North Carolina. In 1965 he was sent to the Dominican Republic with our army field hospital. We left the army later in 1965, and he took a position as rabbi in Ellwood City, Pennsylvania. In 1968 we moved to Pittsburgh, where he became principal of the College of Jewish Studies. In 1972 we moved to St. Louis, where he became vice president of the Central Agency for Jewish Education. He retired in 1997.

I had been brought up with a very strong feeling for Judaism and had never given a thought to my Catholic past. I had heard stories about the Orthodox ways of my grandparents and their religious life in prewar Poland, but we were not observant at home. My mother always lit candles on Friday night, fulfilling a promise she had made to her mother. Friday dinners and Shabbat lunches were always a family affair, with the traditional chicken soup, chicken, and *cholent* (a Sabbath stew). The Passover seder was always a big event, but we went to the synagogue only three times a year. My mother had converted her kitchen to observe the dietary laws when my brother had a brief encounter with religion, but we did not observe any of the restrictions of the Sabbath or High Holidays. But I had absolutely no problems slipping into the Orthodox lifestyle of my husband. He never once asked me to do or not to do anything in Orthodox practice. I just naturally adopted all those practices, way before talk of marriage even came up.

Friends have often asked me whether I found it difficult to change my lifestyle so drastically, but I found this so natural that I never gave it a thought. They have also asked whether I may have married an Orthodox man to prove to my parents that I was a "good girl." I really don't think so. In fact, my mother was very worried that I would not be able to maintain this commitment in the long run. Both my parents were afraid that I was too young, too inexperienced, to know what I was getting into, that my emotions were overshadowing everything else. They were right: my emotions were pushing all rational thinking away, but I never swerved from my commitment in the now forty-three years of my marriage.

Looking back, I realize how young and inexperienced I really was at that time, how much growing up I would do over the years, how many obstacles, problems, insecurities I would have to overcome. How much of a makeover I would have to do to turn an introverted, shy, very reserved girl into a chaplain's wife, a mother, a *rebbetzen* (rabbi's wife) in a small Pennsylvania town, and finally the wife of a prominent community leader. I not only changed my lifestyle but came into a new culture, adopted new customs and a new language, and finally a new personality. I also had to overcome the antagonism of my husband's family. Except for my sister-in-law and a cousin, his relatives felt that he had been trapped into marrying a foreigner who did not measure up to their standard. He was, and still is, the darling of his very large family, and I was this stranger with no college degree who spoke with an accent and had all kinds of foreign ideas and ways.

Over the years I overcame many of my insecurities, went back to school, and got my bachelor's and master's degrees and a teaching certificate. I raised two children and worked, and my early childhood years seemed to have disappeared into oblivion. If somebody had suggested to me that the Holocaust years would come back to haunt me, I would have called that person crazy.

Looking back now on the years from 1959 to the mid-1980s, I see a woman who struggled with many issues without realizing that most had their roots in those early years. My feelings of insecurity, of being inadequate, of not being good enough for my bright, handsome, successful husband— my inability to understand and express my constant need for approval, acceptance, and reassurance—led to many heartaches but also propelled me to achieve more than I would have otherwise.

I still struggled with my parents' problems, was constantly feeling guilty for not doing enough to make my mother happy, still trying to be the "good girl" who was indebted to her mother for all the travails and sacrifices she had endured. It was not until my daughter was an adult that I was made to realize how much she had resented my total dedication and attention to my mother whenever she came to visit or whenever we went to Belgium, where my parents had moved again after my marriage. I was torn between the need to please and my own needs and desires. My mode of operation, though subconscious until recently, was to go along with my husband's, parents', and colleagues' wishes until the situation became unbearable. Only then did I react, sometimes too strongly, changing course to do what I wanted.

This need to make sure everybody was happy must have influenced my raising of my two children, especially my daughter. I remember her telling me, "This is America, Mom; we are not in Europe any more." Recently, while going through some old papers, I found a letter that she wrote me while she was working in Israel. In it she chides me for "stifling" her as an adult. She reminds me that "we are, thank G-d, no longer living in the era of the Holocaust and there is no need to be so overprotective. I'm just asking that you be less overbearing in your demonstration of that caring." She is now a speech pathologist in Cleveland and has two girls and a boy. Our son is a certified public accountant in Baltimore and has three boys and two girls.

In 1987 I brought my parents to the States. My father was not well, and my parents could no longer live without support and help. My mother was terribly unhappy here. She missed her friends and her old lifestyle and could not adjust to life here. Her English was poor, and she could no longer adapt to another new culture and way of life. She became terribly angry with me and resentful because I had been instrumental in moving her. When my father had to go into a nursing home, she became an extremely devoted wife, spending every day of the week with him. I often felt—rightly or wrongly—that she somehow blamed me for his fate. I never remember her hugging or holding me. After my father's death in 1991, my mother went into a deep depression, refused to take her medication, and kept talking about how she wanted to die. She had a heart attack in my house one Friday night during dinner and died a few hours later, leaving me with the impression that she had never forgiven me, that she died angry at me, even though I do not know what I could have done to make her life happier.

To this day, in my senior years, I still struggle to uphold my identity as an individual. It took professional help to understand that I do not need permission or approval from my family if I want to do something, that I am not responsible for my children's or grandchildren's happiness. I am entitled to have my own wishes and needs fulfilled before I am pushed to the edge and react. Will I ever "grow up"? Is there such a thing as an adult? It would seem that I should have the answers to these questions at my age, but I don't. I struggle to understand how much the Holocaust years have shaped my personality. Would my parents have been able to be more parental, functional, had they not been traumatized during those years when they had to fear for their lives, struggle to survive, and later rebuild their lives twice? I do not think that there are answers to these questions.

There have been so many fateful events and ironic twists in my life that I have a hard time believing them myself as I write them down. How many times have I been saved from death, separation, and harm? How many people appeared to help as if sent by some invisible hand? How did my husband show up in Germany, of all places, to literally carry me off into forty-three years of happy life? And how did it happen that my two children, both healthy and successful, married well and have given us eight beautiful grandchildren, all but the youngest of whom attend Orthodox Jewish schools?

The ironies? I, the fervent, pious Catholic, married an Orthodox rabbi and raised two Orthodox children who married Orthodox spouses and whose lives have become much more traditional than mine. I, who used to run away from any uniform, who had nightmares about marching soldiers, married a soldier who wore his army blues at our wedding. I was a good army wife, living on an army base for the first five years of married life. I had the horrendous experience of seeing my husband called off to an unknown destination in the middle of the night during the Dominican crisis in 1965, leaving me alone and helpless with a toddler and a four-year-old. I, who had hated Germans and Germany, found that teaching their language as well as French—which I do love—gave me marketable skills in later years.

Through it all I survived. I became stronger even though I am still striving to connect the missing pieces that formed me, and I am still trying to find myself. However, looking back, I feel that someone is watching out for me and gently directing my life. I am truly a very lucky woman.

The Caveman Triumphs

ASHER J. MATATHIAS
(b. 1943, Greece)

I was born in Volos, Greece, on December 3, 1943. The actual place of my birth was several miles away, in Ayos Lavrentios, a village of several hundred people on Mount Pelion. I was born in a small cave embedded in rugged mountains while my parents were hiding from the Germans. But the story really begins a few years earlier when my father, a young Jewish businessman and itinerant peddler living in Volos, fell in love with a young woman from Salonika.

Although Athens is the best-known Greek city, Salonika, a city that Jews set-tled more than two thousand years ago, has played a more important part in the country's Jewish history. Of the eighty thousand Jews in Greece before World War II, sixty thousand lived in Salonika. In this drama the protagonists were related, and the two families had occasion to come together during the Jewish holidays. By and by, my parents fell in love and corresponded. Even as he traveled, the lad risked capture for violating military regulations to visit his maiden in Salonika. During the German occupation, however, they faced certain choices. Should they marry and risk living together? Should they separate, with the understanding that they

97

would meet again, to resume their lives after the war? Or should they separate and say that this is fate, their marriage was not meant to be, with each returning home and forgetting this romance?

They chose the first alternative, to speed up their plans, and on September 6, 1942, Jacob and Nina were married in Volos. It was an omen of good fortune because the Nazis had occupied Salonika first, in April 1941. Many of the city's Jews did not realize or accept the extent of Hitler's plans. Consequently, they were hesitant, and they rebelled at the thought of leaving the main city to seek refuge elsewhere. Therefore, the Germans often sent entire families to concentration camps, never to be heard of again. One such family was my mother's parents and brothers. My maternal grandparents had a business in Salonika. My grandfather, Daniel Atoun, was a restaurant owner who kept it open to the very end. That might have prevented him from taking the decisive step of leaving. One of my mother's younger sisters, Mendi, chose to go with my mother and her new husband in their new life in Volos.

Life continued for a while under normal conditions, even though it was an occupation period. When Hitler's soldiers and decrees reached Volos, my parents had no time to agonize about having a family. My mother was already pregnant.

My father's business associates came to him with news of the imminent roundup of the Jewish population. Members of a family named Stamos took it upon themselves to impress on my father the utter seriousness of the Nazis' plans for the Jewish population of Volos and to induce him to leave his business and follow a friend of his to the mountains.

A pivotal factor in our—and other Jews'—eventual survival was fluency in Greek. Salonika's importance had grown after many Jews settled there following their expulsion from Spain in 1492. Others had arrived from Italy and eastern Europe. They were gladly and grandly received by the Ottoman Empire, which controlled the city until it was given to Greece in 1912. This large and thriving colony of Jews never developed a facility for the Greek language, preferring to use Ladino in secular as well as sacred matters.

In the Holocaust period Salonika's Jews were easy to identify because they were homogeneous and insulated from native Greek cultural currents and influences. The Nazis destroyed 87 percent of the country's Jewish population. Today only two synagogues remain. The Jewish population now numbers fewer than fifteen hundred people. Because my father's family had a Romaniote (Greek-speaking) background, they were better able to adapt to prevailing conditions, which required the appearance of assimilation. Using Christian-sounding names was a common subterfuge, for example.

In the midst of a fierce winter and Hanukkah my mother gave birth to me. No hospital or any other medical attention was available. A midwife living in the same village took three days to reach the cave because of a severe snowstorm. Fortunately, the delivery was without complications. We lived in that cave for two more years, until liberation in 1945.

I have been told that we came close to being captured by the Nazis several times. Upon their arrival in Volos, the Germans had lists containing the names of resident Jews. The Nazis were to round up the Jews systematically and ship them to concentration camps and subsequent annihilation, the final solution. Since the population of Volos had early warning, based on the unfortunate experience of Salonikan Jews, many fled to wherever they could, to hide and save themselves. When the Nazi dragnets failed to yield all the people on their lists, they figured out that Jews would be found on the outskirts of Volos. On a bright spring morning in 1944, the Nazis began to comb the Volos suburbs, villages, and countryside and were successful in augmenting their catch. My parents tell of close calls that they had and of the heroism of Gentile families, who faced summary execution for harboring Jews if they were discovered.

My father supported the work of the underground, so he would not be found at home during the day. However, he would return in the evening. Families with babies ran the grave risk of being discovered if the babes cried as the frequent patrols passed by. Several infants died when anxious parents covered their faces with pillows, out of anxiety or accidentally. It is sobering to think that this could have happened to me.

Deprivation was commonplace. My mother could not nurse me properly and I was fed goat's milk. To overcome my aversion to its taste, my parents added coffee to the milk. Our diet included cheese, olives, olive oil, and bread—plentiful and brought daily, very often hot, by the family that was protecting us. Food was prepared in clay ovens, outside, under coals. People brought their stuffed leaves and peppers and tomatoes to cook their meals in the community oven. It appears that we were not deprived of food, but it was not the diet we were used to in the city. I do not recall how many families were hiding in our place. Others were hiding in nearby villages. Many Jews who lived in Volos managed to survive, absorbed in the fraternal bosom of their Christian compatriots.

Alas, one Nazi patrol was able to locate our hideaway in the mountain, where we spent daylight hours. With guns poised they knocked the door down and came upon a nativity scene, a mother and a child only. Of course, instant death could have followed. Instead, the German soldier smiled broadly. A man in his twenties, he said that he had someone just like that baby in Hamburg. The image of the family was enough to overcome the seriousness of the situation that he discovered. He left us in G-d's hands.

Years later, having thus been spared from harm, I have no animus toward Germans, do not avoid visiting Germany, and discourage any boycotts of German goods. Although Hitler had many willing executioners, there were also Germans who protected Jews.

With V-E Day people returned to their homes in cities, ready to resume their lives. But many Greeks returned to several years of fierce civil war between government forces loyal to the king and leftists who wished to usher in a workers' socialist republic. The timely American intervention, through the Truman Doctrine, infused prostrate Greece with needed economic resources and the military materiel to stave off the Communist challenge. The crisis forced an extension of my father's military tour until September 9, 1948. Meanwhile, my sister Miriam was added to the family in 1945.

The cataclysmic events during the 1930s and 1940s culminated partly in the establishment of the modern State of Israel on May 14, 1948. My father's younger, unattached brother, Moshe, had braved the British blockade of further Jewish immigration into Palestine to become a pioneering settler. He and my father arranged that Moshe would contact us. In time, he was to signal to my father the propitious time for us to move to the Promised Land. But it was not to be.

Instead, we composed our lives in Volos—father in business, mother a busy housewife, a third child, Rachel, who arrived on January 11, 1952. This was a calm period, but as the early 1950s progressed, Greece suffered a series of devastating earthquakes that brought terrified residents to seek shelter in tents courtesy of America's Marshall Plan. Also making a debut into our lives was an organization that specialized in disaster relief, the American Jewish Joint Distribution Committee, or, as we called it simply, the Joint.

It was at this juncture that we got a tantalizing offer. The quota system for American immigration, based on the National Origins Act of 1924, allowed only a tiny number of people to immigrate from Greece each year. However, because of the extraordinary conditions of suffering, and on an emergency basis, the quota was waived. My parents, then in their thirties, decided to rebuild in America. An exciting period ensued: trips to Athens for emigration papers, passports, medical examinations, and a round of visits to friends and relatives. We also had to decide whether to travel by air (thirty-two hours) or by sea. My father instantly concluded that an ocean voyage would afford us the opportunity to digest the latter-day wonders unfolding in our lives, as well as take in some sightseeing.

On January 18, 1956, we set sail from Piraeus, Greece, on a local steamer, *The Aegean,* for Brindisi, on the east coast of Italy, after stops in the Ionian Sea isles, including Corfu. We boarded a passenger train for Naples. It was at this teeming port that we first cast our gaze at the flagship of the American Export Lines, the ocean liner SS *Constitution,* which would transport us to the New World.

Most people on the ship's passenger list came from Italian locales, including Sicily and Genoa, the first legs of our journey. While aboard ship we made use of my parents' linguistic facilities: Italian, which they had learned during the relatively benevolent occupation by Italian Fascists prior to the Nazis' arrival; Spanish, from Ladino, which we used as we befriended our waiter, Pedro, a Puerto Rican living in New York; and French, in which my mother had been educated in Salonika, at a school sponsored by the Alliance Israélite Universelle.

The second and third days of our voyage were also spent in the Mediterranean Sea, calling at Algiers and fathoming the wonder of the Rock of Gibraltar—where the continents of Europe and Africa almost touch each other. The massive Atlantic Ocean lay ahead. For six days the thirty-five-thousand-ton ship was the ocean's plaything, mounting winter waves easily and emptying the dining rooms of their patrons. Finally, on January 30, 1956, a rainy, cold day (but one to celebrate each year) the Matathias family made a triumphant sail past the Statue of Liberty and into New York harbor. Awaiting us, after we cleared customs, were our sponsoring relative, the noted philanthropist Jesse Colchamiro, and representatives of the Hebrew Immigrant Aid Society (HIAS). Jesse escorted us to a Greek restaurant, the Pantheon on Eighth Avenue, for lunch, while the HIAS officials arranged for us to stay in their building on Lafayette Street, Manhattan, while they found work for my father and permanent lodgings for the family.

Brooklyn then held a gravitational pull for many Jews, including the Sephardim, as parts of it still do. We were introduced to the United Sephardim of Brooklyn, and to a young rabbi, Arnold B. Marans, who is now the distinguished spiritual leader of the Sephardic Temple of Cedarhurst, New York. Our lives have been linked ever since.

Now, years later, Rachel is a happily married teacher who lives with her husband and four children on the West Coast. My brother, Daniel (my only sibling to be born in America, after my sister Miriam's untimely death of leukemia in 1956), is a pediatrician, a graduate of the Columbia University College of Physicians and Surgeons. He is married to Amy Shedroff and they have two children.

As for the first-born, the erstwhile caveman, I am the president of Long Island Lodge #1353 of B'nai B'rith, serving in the tradition of the original tribe of twelve German immigrants who founded the world's largest and oldest Jewish service organization. My cup runneth over, in the words of the psalmist, for in every important respect I am the ever-evolving, ever-growing, ever-aspiring product of this blessed land. My formal education included the completion of coursework for a doctoral degree in political science, and I have taught at both secular and religious schools. I have run for political offices and am actively involved in communal affairs. I am married to Anna, my helpmate, and we have three daughters, Miriam, Joy-Simha, and Sara. We have no grandchildren yet, but we have an Ashkenazi son-in-law whom we love dearly. This is an auspicious point at which to return to an incomplete account of my life in America.

In 1970, as a twenty-six-year-old bachelor, I had my first opportunity to return to my roots in Greece. I reflect upon the fateful moment when my heart and eyes met those of Anna on August 16. She had decided to make aliyah to Israel and was in Volos to visit her parents for the summer. Life has since taught us that love does not consist of gazing at each other—though we do that often—but of looking outward together in the same direction. We had a whirlwind romance—thirteen days from introduction to proposal and nuptials.

I had gone to Volos to meet the family that had helped us and to see whether I could bridge the gap and learn more about what had transpired during those critical years. The Stamos family had now also acquired a place in the suburbs of Volos, just beyond Agria. As I entered the courtyard, an old man, who must have been several hundred yards away, yelled at me and said: "Asher, you are Asher!" He had recognized me instantly, even though he had not seen me since 1945. Of course, we embraced and we kissed. He immediately went to call his grandchildren from the fields and the neighborhood, and when they had gathered, we sat and he retold the story of our survival. It was a wonderful experience for me, for his narrative confirmed many of the details of my early life. It was the last time I would see him alive.

Whenever I travel to Greece, I visit the Stamos family, although now I am seeing his grandchildren and other relatives. They, of course, always receive me with open arms. I have strong emotional ties to this family. Their heroism might have been prompted by a need to demonstrate patriotism at a time when they were suspected of being leftists. To the extent that the Greek cause was associated with saving other Greeks who happened to be Jewish, the Stamoses went out of their way to save us. They were also personal friends. There was never a monetary payment to these people. Years later I learned from a reluctant source that my parents had arranged that were they not to survive the war, the Stamoses—who were then childless—would adopt me, have me baptized with the name Apostolos, and would never reveal my true origin. Thus they would be "saving a life for Jesus."

Some Jewish survivors in Greece picked up where they left off before the war, with businesses inherited from their families, and they in turn pass them to their descendants. Many other Greek Jews have emigrated to Israel, others to the United States. And the younger generation of Jews continues to forsake Greece, leaving behind the legacy of anti-Semitism and whatever else existed for the Jews in Greece. The older generation, those who are very well-off financially, find themselves less willing to forsake old and comfortable ways. My in-laws are a case in point, refusing to emigrate, settling for periodic visits to and from their children and grandchildren. Life is very pleasant in Greece, with the siestas and a tempo appropriate to successful middle age and even for elderly couples.

As for me, my personal saga began with my birth in a remote spot and was nurtured by faith, hope, and love—always love—rising from the ashes of the Shoah. Despite the trauma of starting over, my parents embraced an uncertain future in the New World as immigrants who spoke no English. I praise G-d, inspired and humbled by the generosity of a land and its people worthy of the phrase "God Bless America."

Commentary on Group 1

ROBERT KRELL

One question posed to very young child survivors of the Holocaust is compelling, namely, "Do you have any memories?" A fair question and far better than the oft-repeated statement, "You must have been too young to remember anything."

Young Holocaust survivors, particularly those who offer memories from ages two or three, are suspect. After all, memory is a complex phenomenon, and child-hood recollections are often disguised or embellished with stories and information provided later by adults. Although most people fortunate enough to have lived a "normal" early life later can remember, at most, a memorable birthday party or picnic at age five or six, their normality in fact is defined by the absence of early trauma. In other words, if all goes reasonably well, there may be little sufficiently dramatic to remember.

Not so in the early lives of child survivors. Dangerous incidents, frightening events, the presence of anxiety-ridden adults were features of their earliest life experiences. Their memories were formed in periods of extreme crisis and retained in fragments lacking the coherence of conscious understanding but nevertheless are eventful and powerful. The postwar attempts by children to relate their experiences were discouraged by adults, including mental health professionals. Few children were afforded an outlet to describe their fears and grief, mainly because adults assumed that the children had no memory and therefore did not suffer like the older survivors, particularly those from the concentration camps.

This was a total inversion of the premise that psychological health requires at minimum a first two years of safe and secure nurturing. Preferably, this period should last at least five years, to provide the child with a solid emotional foundation. One may assume that any child whose earliest developmental years were filled with dread and anxiety will in fact struggle throughout life with traumatic memories, nightmares, and unexpected depressions. It is the normal consequence of an abnormal experience.

The accounts of this age group were written more than fifty years after the events that they describe. Although their experiences were vastly different, all suffered the consequences of massive early life trauma, irreparable losses, pervasive grief, and unresolved mourning. Yet most somehow achieved a life that includes successes in work, family life, and community.

If there is any discernible mechanism that allowed these youngsters to function, it was the ability to compartmentalize their war experiences and separate that part of themselves from the trials and tribulations of living ordinary lives after extraordinary experiences.

Judith Traub asks, "Does a three-and-a-half-year-old have memory?" She answers, "Perhaps not continuous memory but memories of isolated events that engrave themselves upon her subconscious mind." Her memory of Uncle Kisil is one of those sustaining memories, for he reappears from Auschwitz as the lone survivor of his entire family. Another is the silver Sabbath candlesticks she uses in her home, the same ones lit by her mother throughout their long exile. As a teenager she made friends who have found each other again recently. Their reunions reinforce their memory and provide continuity to their postwar lives.

Memory links these children, for they suffer either from hypermnesia (unusually vivid or complete memory) or from a variant of amnesia (far too little memory). I discussed the complexity of memory in the introduction as the struggle of child survivors to recapture memories in order to make sense of what happened or to suppress them in order to reduce the pain of what they do or might remember.

Renée Fritz was three when, after the German invasion of Belgium, she was placed in a Catholic convent, where she became an ardent Catholic. She recalls being frightened, cold, hungry, and alone. And she states clearly what so many hidden children report: "I never complained, I never cried. I had been told that I must not be noticed and that I must be good." Felicia Graber and Eva Brown reacted similarly during and after hiding. This attempt to cooperate in their survival by maintaining their silence also explains in part why silence, which once was a survival strategy for them, remains a theme in their later lives. The comfort with and need for silence was an important factor in the hesitance of child survivors to share their experiences.

The identity of Jewish children hidden and saved as Christians was fragile at best, as we observe in the stories of Renée Fritz, Judy Traub, and Felicia Graber. Fritz was so conflicted that even in the United States, as she prepared for her bat mitzvah ceremony, "right after each class I went to church to confess. I did become a bat mitzvah—and went to confession right after!" Graber observes, "I, the fervent, pious Catholic, married an Orthodox rabbi and raised two Orthodox children who married Orthodox spouses and whose lives have become much more traditional than mine."

Few surviving children shared their earliest memories even with each other. It took more than forty years for that to happen. As children, they lived in the present and focused on the future. In addition to being discouraged to speak of the past by well-meaning adults, few wanted to reveal themselves for fear of being perceived as not normal. Child survivors strived to fit in and not be noticed, except perhaps for scholastic and/or athletic prowess.

Dori Laub's capacity to remember and the eloquence with which he describes these memories are astonishing. Memory may precede by years the ability to describe that memory with words. His memory becomes more distinct during his family's deportation to a labor camp in Transnistria, although he wonders whether some memories are a reconstruction of what he was told. He also unlocks the key to a commonplace feature of childhood traumatic memory, that of denial, when he states matter-of-factly, "I think I was quite aware of what was going on but later on refused to know and remember it." Laub's memories from the age of six are so vivid that his understanding reflects the awareness of constant danger. Real memories have replaced uncertain memories. But some things he still simply cannot talk about. Laub's father disappears halfway through his narrative. Apparently, he died. Every survivor's story has secrets that cannot be told, not necessarily because of an absence of memory but as a result of unbearable pain. Some things must remain unspoken.

Eva Metzger Brown's family managed to escape to America, but the unsettling experience of separations, uncertainty, and different countries and languages seems to have been etched in her unconscious memory, for she stopped speaking altogether when she was enrolled in a French school in the United States. Her speech returned in an English-language kindergarten. When she sought therapy in the 1980s, she was at last able to connect her feelings to her childhood memories, with the inevitable sequence of grief, tears, and mourning.

"Second separation" is a constant theme in the lives of children who became attached to their hiding families. Some hiders gave up "their" children to allow them a chance to reconnect with their Jewish roots. Others refused and often lost them to surviving family members in prolonged court battles. The tensions between competing adults added to the child survivor's trauma, particularly if the young child could not yet appreciate the complexity of the situation. Marian Nachman, for example, was three years old when she went into hiding and has no recollection of her parents. She was in "open" hiding, a member of a Christian family, as opposed to "closed" hiding like Anne Frank's. After the war Nachman was sent to the United States, desperately upset to have to leave the Martenses.

Because an understanding of being a Jew was beyond the comprehension of most of the youngest child survivors, their postwar lives were marked by a conflict in personal identity and, for many, a confusion of belief in G-d. After all, most were saved by the "Christian" G-d and were left unprotected and vulnerable by the "Jewish" one. Some abandoned all belief. Whether they re-embraced Judaism depended on who raised them and where. Some stayed with their Christian foster parents, others ended up in Jewish orphanages and displaced persons camps.

The particular group of children whose essays appear here became Jewish and raised Jewish children. However, they may not be representative, for while some child Holocaust survivors have come forward and broken their silence, others remain in hiding to this day and may never reveal themselves.

In reading these accounts we encounter the memories of young children as filtered through the eyes of the adults they have become. Some memories are offered in thoughtful, coherent language with words that were not yet available to the children as they were engulfed in the madness. Some experiences were preverbal or lost in the original language of these children, whether Polish, Dutch, or French. But the memories are not necessarily gone, only the ability to find the words to describe them. Is it any wonder that children of this age have remained silent for so many years? Is it any wonder that to speak at all is an act of personal courage?

From understanding the power of memory in these children, so often thought not to have memories, we can begin to understand the impact of the Holocaust on children who were slightly older, the preadolescent group, whose stories follow.

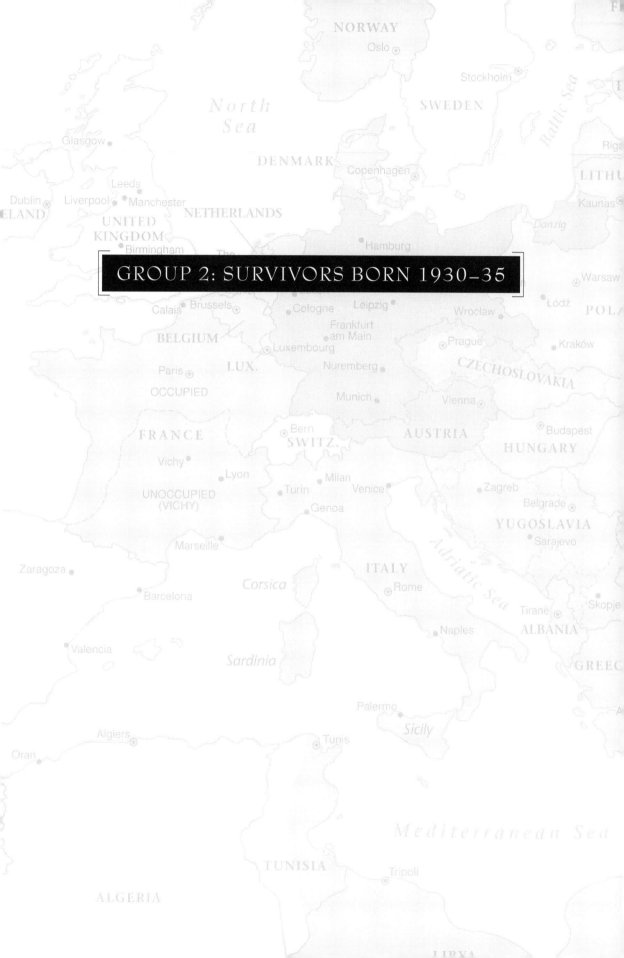

GROUP 2: SURVIVORS BORN 1930–35

And Somehow We Survive

RUDY ROSENBERG
(b. 1930, Belgium)

In 1902, in what is now Poland and was then part of Russia, my father, Hillel Rosenberg, was born in a very small village called Łopuszno, west of Kielce. His parents were well-to-do farmers. Through all the tribulations of his life, my father always carried pictures of his mother and older brothers that were taken in the late thirties and sent to me by his sister just before their mother died in 2000. Unfortunately, no pictures of my grandfather survive. All of my father's twelve or thirteen brothers and sisters died during the Holocaust.

In 1917, when the Russian Revolution started, my father was fifteen years old. He was a very resourceful young fellow. He worked for a while at a variety of jobs, including ferrying horses to the Austrian/Prussian army that was besieged by the Russians in Przemyśl. Then he realized that it was much safer to take the horses and harnesses, sell them to somebody, and stay away from the war as much as possible. You could say he started his career as a horse thief.

He was very capable. He went from job to job, working on leather, doing carriage work. In 1919 or 1920 he worked in Germany as a mason's apprentice and learned German. One of his important jobs was taking down a huge industrial smokestack. Inflation was rampant in Germany at the time, so he asked the fellow who hired him to pay him with a railroad ticket to Paris instead of cash. My father demolished that smokestack stone by stone, and he got his train ticket.

He met two Polish fellows who were also looking for work, and they told him they were going to Charleroi. He asked, "Where is Charleroi?" They said, "It's in France. We understand there is work there." They took a train to Charleroi, but it was in Belgium, not France. Of course, they spoke no French. My father spoke Yiddish; the Polish fellows did not. The only work that was available was in the coal mine, but nobody wanted to work below. The coal mines of Charleroi were about the most dangerous, filthiest, hardest work, but my father began to work in a coal mine and was almost killed in a mining accident. To the end of his life he retained a piece of coal in his wrist of which he was very proud. This was his badge of honor for having worked in the coal mine.

One day he was walking near a furniture store, and he asked a friend of his to introduce him to the store owner, Mme Cousin. He explained, by gesture, that whatever they were doing, fixing sofas and the like, he could do. To the end of his life his trade was interior decoration. He was a master at it. He even worked on furniture restoration for the queen of Belgium in later years.

From Charleroi he went to visit a friend in Altena, Germany, not far from Cologne. When he left, someone said, "Do me a favor. I know some people in Cologne named Friedemann, and I would like you to take this can of coffee to them as a gift." He went there, and that's how he met my mother, Frieda. She was born in Cologne, where her father, Phillip Friedemann, had a wholesale kosher poultry business. Her mother was Emma Wolfe. My mother had one older brother, Richard, and a younger brother, Paul. A while later, after a dispute with her family, Frieda came to live briefly with my father in Charleroi, although she always maintained that she was a virgin until her marriage. In July 1927 my parents were married in a civil ceremony in Charleroi and in a religious ceremony in the Cologne synagogue. That's why I was born in Belgium several years later to a Polish father and a German mother who were both Jewish.

My sister, Ruth, was born in Cologne on July 31, 1928, because my grandmother thought that there was better obstetrical care in Cologne than in Charleroi. So my mother went there to give birth, then came back to Charleroi. Cologne was a beautiful city and my mother loved it dearly. Charleroi was a coal-mining town with clouds of smoke and pollution all over, always black soot over everything, miners sitting on their doorsteps coughing blood. But I loved it. For years after we moved away, I was homesick for Charleroi.

Belgium had been destroyed, decimated, and raped by imperial Germany in World War I. My father's name was Rosenberg, which is a very German-sounding name, and when he opened a furniture store, it could not have survived with the name of Rosenberg. His first name, Hillel, did not exist on the saints' calendar, so he used the French name Hilaire, which is Hilary in English. From then on he was known as Monsieur Hilaire. The furniture store was Maison Hilaire, my mother was Mme Hilaire, I was *le petit* Hilaire, and my sister was *la petite* Hilaire.

I was born on February 26, 1930. I was named Rodolphe because Belgium is a Catholic country, and at the time the only names that could be used were those on the saints' calendar. I always knew I was supposed to be aborted because my mother never made any secret about it, especially when I was hiding with her during the war, but she told me about it with affection. My mother was very unhappy in Charleroi. She had fits of depression. I have a mental picture of my sister and me when I was about two. Alida, my nursemaid, is holding us as we are perched on a window ledge to get some fresh air, because my mother had turned the gas stove on and had tried not only to commit suicide but also to take us with her.

My first remembrance of Jewishness is, I believe, from 1935. I was five years old, and it was the High Holidays. Once a year a Jewish man who was a part owner of a string of movie theaters would convert one theater, the Cinéma Eden, into a temple for the High Holidays (Rosh Hashanah and Yom Kippur). I vividly remember sitting in the balcony with my mother, looking down and seeing some Jews rocking back and forth, praying. But by and large I was not aware that I was Jewish. My family wasn't observant at all. My father came from a religious family and was even sent to become a cantor. He had some ideas about kashrut (the dietary laws), but that was about all. My mother's family was not religious at all, as far as I know, but they did go to the High Holiday services. The Jewish community that I was exposed to was so small that, to my knowledge, there was not even a synagogue in Charleroi. I went to the regular public school.

In the summer of 1938 my parents put us in a day camp run by the Catholic school. We went there every day by streetcar, and twice a day we would recite Catholic prayers with everybody else. It never came to our minds to question it. That's really the first religious instruction that I ever had. We were so immersed in the Belgian lifestyle that Christmas was an important day.

About 1934 or 1935 my parents discovered gambling, and it became a sickness with them. This was the middle of the Depression. Things were very bad, and the gambling didn't help at all. My parents were gone all the time, mostly to Namur, where the biggest casino was. My father's business went bad because of the gambling and the Depression. We began to move, from one house to a smaller house to an apartment to smaller apartments. By the time I was eighteen, we had moved eighteen times and usually without furniture or anything. Everything was just left behind. By then my parents didn't get along any more. They stayed together after a fashion, but they argued a lot, mostly in German. For some reason it's easier to argue violently in German than it is in French. Ruth and I learned German pretty well, and it became our second language.

My parents commuted almost every day to Namur's big gambling casino, but in 1938 my father disappeared. He left us. He was broke. My mother decided to move to Namur so she wouldn't have to commute, and she could go to the casino every night. Things were very bad there. My mother left every day to gamble, or

The Rosenberg family on Boulevard Anspach in Brussels, September 1939. *Left to right:* Rudy, 9; Frieda, 37; Ruth, 11; and Hilaire (Hillel), 37.

whatever, and she won every day. She always came home with enough money to feed Ruth and me. Later on we realized that maybe our mother didn't go to the casino after all. But whatever she did, she did it for us to survive, and we did survive.

In 1939 we left Namur for Brussels, where we were reunited with my father. This in the long run saved our lives, because Charleroi and Namur were small towns where it was very difficult to hide during the German occupation. For a while we all lived together in a suburb called Jette, which was Flemish speaking, and I felt extremely out of place because I spoke only French and some German.

In late 1939 my parents split up again. My mother had boyfriends, my father had girlfriends, and they fought all the time. My mother put Ruth and me in a Protestant orphanage called Le Foyer des Enfants in Uccle (French; Ukkel in Flemish), a suburb of Brussels. Not everybody was an orphan; some children had been abandoned by their parents. We were further indoctrinated, this time in the Methodist religion. Twice a day the nurse, who was very nice, read a chapter or two from the New Testament, and we went to services on Sunday mornings. The directress was very nice, but she didn't really care much about what happened to the children or how vicious the people in charge of the children were. If we misbehaved, punishment was swift and quite violent. Because the orphanage didn't have its own school, we were allowed to leave daily to go to school. It was not a happy time because I didn't know whether I would ever see my parents again.

Our war started on May 10, 1940. We were asleep in the dormitory, which had big French windows. A sound like thunder woke us up. We quickly got dressed. Air raid sirens were blaring the frightening *whoo-whoo,* and then we heard what we thought was thunder, the ack-ack of the Belgian ground forces. We rushed outside, and the sky was full of German planes. Most of the Belgian air force was destroyed on the ground that day.

Shortly after that, on my regular morning trip to the bakery to get bread for the orphanage, I saw British soldiers. They had come to help the Belgian army, which was quickly disintegrating. The square, the *place,* where the bakery was located, was loaded with British soldiers and their lorries. They were leaving the next day. They gave the thumbs up sign to us, and we knew what it meant. After another few days they were all gone. The square was empty. The Belgian army had collapsed, the French army wasn't doing much better, and the British had decided to pull out. There was nothing else they could do.

On May 18, as I was returning with my load of bread, suddenly some German mounted soldiers came up the Chausée d'Alsemberg with swords at their side and pistols in hand. They were the vanguard of the German army, checking to see whether any snipers were hiding in the basements or anywhere else. Then the rest of the German army arrived. Almost from the day the Germans occupied Belgium, the color of the bread changed. Instead of being white bread, it was gray bread. As the war went on, the bread got to be worse and worse.

I was ten. I had become aware that I was Jewish because in the orphanage some of the children would taunt me about being a Jew. It didn't even make much of an impression. My main anguish at the time, since the war had started and the roads were filled with refugees, was that I didn't know where my parents were. I didn't see my mother again until August 1940, when I was sent on vacation to Boom, near Antwerp. Every year Antwerp's chief of police, who was a Methodist, took some children from the orphanage to stay there.

One day my mother showed up in a German staff car, surrounded by German officers. At the time she was working as a waitress in a restaurant in Brussels called the Café Rubens. She got good tips because she was pretty. German soldiers and officers frequented the place, and she spoke German fluently. I don't know whether they knew that she was Jewish and I don't think they cared very much. She was pretty, and she had a good attitude. You do a lot to survive.

She worked very, very late and had to walk all the way back to Jette after finishing work. One night she passed a bridge, and the German sentry there threatened to shoot her if she came by again after curfew. She repeated this to one of the officers at the Café Rubens, and he said, "Frieda, have no fear. We will drive you home." He was Franz Bauer, the personal chauffeur of Gen. Alexander von Falkenhausen, the military governor of Belgium. Bauer drove her back to Jette, where she was living with a school friend of hers, Bernard Horowitz, and his parents. Bernard and his family had fled Germany in the late 1930s. When he saw my mother arriving in a German staff car driven by German officers, he was very upset. The next day he told her, "You can't stay here any more." So she had to find another place to live.

When my mother came to see me in Boom, she told me that we would soon be together again. Our parents had gotten back together. Because my father was stateless, my mother had become stateless when she married him. Ruth and I were therefore born stateless. When you're a foreigner in a small country, it's difficult to work for anyone, so my father, to survive, found the black market, and he made a lot of money. Barges that had been sunk in the canals of Brussels, Bruges, and Antwerp had goods in them—food, tins of biscuits, cigarettes—and he salvaged whatever he could and sold it.

When we got back to the orphanage in Brussels, my mother came to get Ruth and me. We moved with our parents into an apartment in the heart of Brussels, above the Café Cambridge, which is still there. We started life together again in late 1940, after a fashion.

Every day we were exposed to German propaganda—posters, articles in newspapers and magazines, on the radio—about the Jews and how they were responsible for the war. There were always caricatures of the Wall Street Jews. I remember going to see a movie in early 1941 called *Jud Süss* (The Jew Sues). It was about a German Jew in the Middle Ages who had raped a girl and was caught. At the end of the movie he was hoisted in the village square in a cage with a sign that said "Jew." The bottom of the cage opened and he was hanged. I recall vividly how the people in the movie theater stood up, applauding and cheering wildly. I was petrified. In the audience were Belgian Blackshirts, with the swastika on their arm. I went out of the theater, onto the Place de Brouckere, and looked around. Everywhere around the square were huge panels of German propaganda. I ran home, got on my bed, and cried.

In March 1941 my father had a Russian passport, and Germany had a non-aggression pact with Russia. My mother very boldly went to the German *Kommandatur* and successfully demanded that she be given a two-month visa to visit her mother in Cologne. We took the almost-empty train. At the Belgian-German border German officers came through the cars. They took my mother's visa, looked at it, and said something about some of our Russian allies coming to visit Germany. So in we went.

When we got to our grandmother's home, we found Uncle Richard, who had married an American woman who had been born in Germany but had lived in Cleveland. They and our grandmother were confined to a small apartment. It was shocking for Ruth and me to see our grandmother, who had always been a very proud, strong, and wealthy woman, sitting all day with her face turned to the wall. She wouldn't talk any more.

During that visit Ruth and I got roller skates. Cologne was an unusual city in that it had macadam streets, which was very new to us. Brussels had only big Belgian cobblestones. We went skating through the streets of Cologne, and we spoke French to each other. One day about a half-dozen Hitler Youth, girls and boys, descended upon us. They came running up to us and asked, "Bist du Englisch?" They knew we spoke a foreign language. We said, "Nein, Franzosen." We didn't think they knew where Belgium was, so we told them we were from France.

Although we had a visa for two months, we left after about two weeks. That was the last time we ever saw any of my mother's family. They were never able to leave and were all deported. When we found out that Uncle Richard and his wife and baby had been taken, we sent packages to them through the Red Cross. My grandmother was transferred to Theresienstadt (Terezin) and after three months was sent to Auschwitz, where she was murdered. Uncle Richard and his wife were killed either in Łódź or in Auschwitz.

The persecution of the Jews in Belgium did not come up all of a sudden. It was gradual. Things we could live with. First there were curfews. We could live with that. Then came the *cartes d'identité,* the identity cards. We could live with that. Then we had to start wearing the yellow star. We were aware that once we started wearing it, the Germans could pick us up right in the street, and we would never be heard from again.

We had a lot of money by then. My father sold steel boot tips to the German army, millions of them. He had an army of shoemakers working all over Belgium, stamping out little steel boot tips. An odd direction for an interior decorator, but he was very resourceful. You have to survive.

Early in 1942 our mother took us back to the orphanage. She had arranged for us to be baptized as Methodists because we had taken religious instruction while we were there. That confused us, because we had had this slight Catholic indoctrination when we were seven or eight, and now we were baptized as Protestants. And still we had to hide. But the baptism didn't do any good because, according to the Germans, it was necessary to have been baptized through the third generation. By then my grandmother was in Theresienstadt, and all of my father's family had already died in Auschwitz. Nobody was left free, except the four of us, and we were hiding the fact that we were Jewish, but I wasn't Jewish. I was a Protestant.

My mother had befriended an SS colonel by the name of Eppstein, who was from the Cologne area. Because Eppstein was spelled with two *p*'s he was okay. He was not Jewish. I think he was my mother's lover. He told her what the Germans were doing to Jews in Poland. She related to me that once she was sitting in the apartment with him, and he was telling her about the slaughters in Poland and how they were killing Jews in the streets. He told her that in a few weeks he was going to start rounding up the Jews in the Brussels area, and we needed to make plans. My parents and their acquaintances, the Samuelses, planned to escape through Switzerland using false papers. My mother told Colonel Eppstein our plans. Eppstein said, "You'll probably make it—you, your husband, and your daughter—but the boy will never make it. He has Jewish ears."

That was the first time we had heard about "Jewish ears." In those days I was a pretty little eleven-year-old kid. I had a straight nose. I hadn't begun to have my grown-up features yet. He explained how the Gestapo and the SS had studied Semitic types, and they could recognize Jews from the back of the head by the shape of their ears. He explained that not all Jews have Jewish ears, and not all people who have Jewish ears are Jewish, but they just grabbed people in the street, and if they could prove they were not Jewish, good. If they couldn't, too bad.

After hearing that I had to have my Jewish ears taken care of, my parents found a Belgian doctor, Dr. Van Eyck, a member of the Belgian resistance, to perform the corrective surgery. The surgery consisted of removing cartilage from both sides of both ears and sewing the lobes of the ears to my cheek to eliminate the "Semitic trait." I went to a clinic, and in relatively primitive conditions, he operated on both ears with local anesthesia. It was a frightening experience. I don't recall any pain, but with the sound of the cutting and the ripping of the cartilage echoing inside my head, I became hysterical so they put me under completely. When I came to, it was night, and I was throwing up. The British were passing overhead. I remember the tracer shells of the German ack-ack going through the night. I went to the window to look at them and passed out again. Then I went back to my bed and fell back asleep.

Dr. Samuels, a very big surgeon from Cologne, his wife, and their daughter went to Switzerland ahead of us, the first to go with this particular passer (smuggler). We found out through the grapevine that they never made it. The passer turned them over to the Germans and also collected a reward from them. Mrs. Samuels and their daughter were killed at Auschwitz. Dr. Samuels stayed there for a long time, working as a surgeon until he too was killed. That's what I heard. These things leak out.

Shortly thereafter Colonel Eppstein told us that the time had come for us to disappear. If he saw us later, he would arrest us. Since we couldn't leave through Switzerland, my father looked for places to hide. My sister (now thirteen), our mother, and I (age eleven) had spent the previous summer in the small Ardennes village of Werpin, at the Pension Sovet. The people who owned it, M. and Mme Sovet, were very nice. They hid us, for free, no money at all. We stayed at the *pension de famille* (family boardinghouse) for about two or three months, until it became too dangerous. It was like a hotel, and people were in and out, so no one would notice another couple of kids. We had a daily routine there. After we got up, I had to pump water. Emil Sovet, the son, showed me at the beginning how to use the hand-operated water pump. My second chore was to get the eggs from the chickens. Most of the time, as far as I remember, I just went outside exploring with Emil. He showed me how to fire a gun. They had a couple of hidden weapons there.

The Sovets were wonderful. I went to visit them, probably thirty years later. I had business in Brussels and was driving near Liège, not far from the Ardennes, and found the tiny village of Werpin. I drove across the bridge, and it struck me how small everything was. In 1941, of course, I didn't drive, and we had to walk across the bridge, which was then a wooden *passerelle,* a footbridge. During the 1940 invasion Belgian troops had blown it up. I went to the *pension,* and there was Mme Sovet. I asked her, "Where can I find Monsieur Sovet?" They're very suspicious of strangers in the Ardennes, and she asked, "What do you want with him?" "I just want to speak to him." "You'll find him in the sawmill." I walked in, and he looked at me from afar, and said, "Qu'est ce que vous voulez?" What do you want? I started by saying, "Je m'appelle Rudy Rosenberg." He looked closer at me and he said, "Ro-dolphe! Ruth et Rodolphe! We were talking about you the other day, because we had hidden many people during the war but only two children. We were wondering if you had made it." We embraced. We had dinner, and we had a great time. The Sovets could really be called righteous ones.

We stayed in Werpin most of the summer of 1942. I don't know where my parents were at the time. My father was busy making money. He made millions in a very short time: paintings, furniture, carpets, jewelry, diamonds, gold. He managed to keep it hidden all those years. He was protected by the underground, to whom he paid some of the money he collected from the Germans. He was arrested once for black marketeering by the Belgian police but was released by the Germans, who regarded him as a valuable man. They didn't know he was Jewish; to them he was simply M. Hilaire.

One day Ghyslaine Fraiteur showed up at the Pension Sovet. I didn't know who she was. She had come to take Ruth and me back to Brussels. Her husband, Jacques, was in the Belgian army and was a prisoner of war in Germany. He never came back. I understand that he was killed by Russian troops who were liberating the camp and apparently did not recognize his uniform. Mme Fraiteur took us to her house in Uccle, where my father had already been hiding for several months. The big mansion, surrounded by a big garden, was inhabited by Ghyslaine Fraiteur; her mother, Mme Cuvelier; and Ghyslaine's German grandmother, who was senile and sometimes had nightmares. She was known to us only as *Grand-mère*.

Hiding with my father were M. and Mme Wolfe, an Austrian couple, busi-ness associates of his. M. Wolfe was a big man, very charming. He survived, but I don't know what happened to him afterward. The Wolfes had no money, so my father paid the Fraiteurs a lot of money for hiding us. It was brought to my father every few weeks by a young lady who was keeping his fortune at the time. When we went into hiding, he had given everything to M. and Mme Croisier to keep. They were gamblers he had met in the casino, and he trusted them. Now and then he arranged for something to be sold so that cash was available to pay the Fraiteurs and also to pay the people who were hiding my mother in Ixelles, another suburb of Brussels, in a private house next to the Gestapo. What Mme Fraiteur was charg-ing was considerably more than what my mother was paying the DeKnibbers for hiding her.

M. and Mme DeKnibber were retired Belgians in their seventies who had be-come Americans. They had emigrated to the United States, made some money in Philadelphia, and come back to Brussels, where they could live very nicely on their pension. However, as of December 1941 they could no longer collect their money from the United States, so they were without any means of survival.

They knew my mother from the Namur Casino, and the three had met again at a clandestine gambling casino. When the Germans invaded Belgium, they re-stricted access to the casinos to members of the Nazi Party, Blackshirts, and Ger-man military officers. Others had to find another place to gamble, so underground casinos sprang up. Now and then the Belgian resistance would burst into the casinos and confiscate everybody's money. M. DeKnibber had been caught at least twice in the gambling casino and had all of his money stolen.

At the casino M. and Mme DeKnibber got to talking with my mother. She needed a place to hide and they needed money, so they made an arrangement whereby my mother paid them a monthly fee for rent and food. For all practical purposes we had disappeared. We had no ration cards, no stamps, so the DeKnibbers had to buy food on the black market. That took care of my mother. There's a good side to gambling; if it weren't for gambling, I wouldn't be alive today.

My mother was feeling very insecure at the time. She was filled with anguish because she was in hiding alone and she knew that my father was hiding with Ruth and me. She asked that I come and hide with her, maybe because she was lonely. My father took me there late one night in March 1943. He had told Ghyslaine Fraiteur that I was joining my mother in Liège. We were supposedly going to the train station, but we actually went straight to where my mother was hiding in the basement. We opened up some stone slabs under the staircase of the basement, and my father and I filled two large lead pipes with jewelry, diamonds, gold, watches, and bracelets and poured candle wax on them so they wouldn't rattle. We buried them, covered them up again, and marked the top of the stone, and then my father returned to Uccle.

For a while Mme DeKnibber called my father every other week at the Fraiteur house. She pretended to be a telephone operator, and she would say, "There's a phone call, long distance, from Liège." Then either my mother or I got on the phone and talked to my father and Ruth. This was to convince the Fraiteurs that my mother and I had actually left for Liège. We stopped doing that after a few weeks, because we knew that the Germans were tapping telephone lines.

Until the end of the war I hid in the basement of the DeKnibbers's house with my mother, from March 1943 until September 4, 1944. The house next door was occupied by the Gestapo and the building on the left by the German women's army corps. The house in back of us was occupied by German labor forces, the Brownshirts, so on three sides we were surrounded by German military personnel. Because the DeKnibbers were so old, the Germans didn't bother them very much, even though they were, technically, American citizens and enemies.

We spent most of our time in the basement. A window looked halfway from the ground level up into a very small yard that led to the street. There were two ponds called Les Etangs d'Ixelles in front of the street. I could see part of the street and part of the ponds. I spent a lot of time there, looking just to see a bird, a bee, a rose.

Sometimes my mother and I slept in a room on the top floor. Then that became dangerous for us. The British and the Americans began to fly over a lot on their way to Germany. We never thought that they would bomb Brussels until the Americans did some daylight bombing. I watched B-25s carpet bombing all over the railroads and the marshaling (railroad) yards. They missed a lot. From then on my mother and I always stayed in the basement and never again ventured to the bedroom upstairs.

I guess the desire to see another day is what sustained me. There was nothing else to do. There was certainly no place to go. I read the dictionary, invented games, and made some puzzles. Then M. DeKnibber found some puzzles that had maybe sixteen or twenty pieces. I spent hours taking them apart and putting them back together. I imagined that each piece was a Pacific island being invaded by American troops. I developed a strategy for how best to invade each island.

In the winter of 1943–44 it snowed once. It doesn't snow in Brussels very often, and I wanted to touch the snow. At about midnight my mother and I opened the rear door leading to the little courtyard. Five or six steps led to the courtyard. I walked to the second step and gathered a handful of snow. I made a snowball out of it and quickly walked back into the basement again. I put the snowball into the sink and watched it melt. That was the only time I went out.

M. DeKnibber came down almost daily and played cards with me. I beat the pants off him, but he, being so much of a gambler, could not tolerate losing, so he cheated. I couldn't do anything and I couldn't say anything. This man was saving my life! Whenever he left, I fell into my mother's arms and cried bitterly because he was cheating. We grew to dislike M. DeKnibber and his wife, and they probably disliked us also. It was a strange relationship.

We were never really hungry. My mother did some cooking, and the DeKnibbers were able to get food for us. It wasn't scrumptious, mostly rutabagas, turnips, and herring. We slept twelve hours a day. We went to bed at midnight after we had listened to the last broadcast of the BBC on our little radio. We listened to Belgian radio broadcasts, which were controlled by the Germans, of course. We listened to Hitler's and Goebbels's speeches. We were fascinated by the vileness of these people, by the meanness directed at us and at other people.

We were like mice, hiding in the basement. We talked in whispers, and we had to cry softly too. Once, many years later, I was at a rehearsal of *The Diary of Anne Frank* on the North Shore of Long Island. I noticed that everybody in the play was walking around and talking at normal levels, but that's not what was done. There's only one thought that pervades you when you're hiding, and that is, "Am I going to get caught?" That was a constant fear. I don't think there was really a conscious moment when we said, "This is a beautiful day." It was just not there. It was one more day to get through and not do anything foolish in the meantime.

On June 6, 1944, M. DeKnibber came running downstairs into the basement. He said, "The Allies have landed!" He had heard the news in the Italian segment of the BBC. The next broadcast was going to be in German, so he wanted my mother to listen in. We listened, and, sure enough, there was the speech by General Eisenhower announcing that the liberation of Europe had begun. D-Day.

It was a happy time. From that moment on we no longer slept twelve hours a day, because every day we had something to hope for. Every morning at eight o'clock we listened to the news and followed the progress of the war on maps, the

Russians on one side of Europe and the Allies on the other. German propaganda gave glowing reports about how the Allies were being thrown back into the sea. We kept hoping. After a while even the Germans could not pretend that things were going well, and we began to realize that we might actually be freed.

One morning in late August 1944, after Paris was liberated, I was looking out my little window, and suddenly I saw three or four German soldiers enter our gate. I ran over to my mother, "The *Boches* are coming!" (We never called them Nazis. They were either Germans or *Boches*. I didn't really hear the term *Nazi* until I came to the United States, where it was a different story: there were good Germans; the Nazis were bad. To us, they were all the same, regardless of the color of their uniform.)

Mother and I ran to the back of the basement where the bathroom was. It was just a toilet. The door had a solid bottom, but the top was a piece of brownish frosted glass. We reached it just as they rang the bell. We heard the Germans come in and talk with M. DeKnibber. Suddenly, they opened the door to the short staircase, and they came into the basement. We were inside the bathroom with the lights turned off. We could see the shadows of people through the frosted window and hear their voices. My heart was beating so hard that it was hurting me. To this day I don't know how they didn't hear it. It was like a drum. I was petrified. Then they left. M. DeKnibber told us that because of the military situation, the Germans next door had come to see if they could tap the phone line in the DeKnibber house so that they could have an additional line in their house.

A few days later they came again. Same scenario. This time it was because the Allies were moving very quickly, and the Germans came to see if they could pierce the basement wall between our house and their house, and on to the next house, so that if there was house-to-house fighting, the troops could then run from one house to the other without having to go outside. After a few minutes they left again.

A couple of days before the liberation, we knew something was up. I could see through the window that the Germans were looting the building next door. They had three trucks that they loaded up with furniture, glassware, silverware, clothing, everything they could get their hands on from the house. Belgians were standing around the trucks watching them. The Germans got two trucks going, but they left the third one. The Belgians started to loot the truck. Then they went inside the house to demolish anything that was left, like mantelpieces, pieces of marble, anything at all.

We were liberated by the British on September 3, 1944, barely ninety days after the landing in Normandy. Three months. It's so short, but every day was an eternity. We lived each day for the liberation. At times we thought it would never come. Toward evening we began to hear noises far away. Now we knew that the time of our liberation had come. We went upstairs to the first floor, where the DeKnibbers lived. We wanted to see what was happening. Someone was yelling, "Put out the flags! The Allies are coming!" From every house around the avenue flags were coming out from windows and balconies—French, Belgian, British flags—not too many American flags because it's a complicated one to make. It had been dangerous to have a flag.

Dr. Van Eyck, the doctor who had operated on me, was wearing his Belgian resistance armband, and he was the one who was yelling from his motorcycle to put out the flags. Then suddenly another man rode by on a bicycle, and he yelled, "Pull in the flags! The Germans are coming!" Everybody started pulling in the flags, and suddenly a company of German soldiers came running down the street at half-time with their weapons at port arms. They didn't look left, they didn't look right, they didn't look up—they were just going as fast as they could.

I did not go out that September 3. It was too dangerous. There was a lot of fighting in the streets. The Germans were retreating on foot, with pushcarts, carriages, cars, bicycles, trying to get back to Germany. The partisans were firing and settling private scores. They were taking collaborators, beating them up, shooting them. I wasn't about to go out on the street and pick up a stray bullet.

The next day, September 4, I decided to go out and join the festivities downtown. I think I was wearing my slippers because I didn't have any shoes that fit. I got on a streetcar that was going to the Bourse. As I stepped onto the platform, a man inside the streetcar looked at me and yelled, "Hey, *youpin* (kike)! They did not get you!" Up to then my Jewishness had been dangerous. German propaganda made us very aware of the Wall Street Jews and the Zionists, who were supposed to be terrible people. But I had thought that with the Germans gone, this anti-Semitism, which I really had not known before the war, would be gone with them. I don't think I can really explain how it hit me. I was angry, I was ashamed. Here was a man who could tell just by looking at me that I was Jewish, and he called me a *youpin*. I looked at him and said, "What would you say if I called you a dirty Catholic?" I don't know who he was. I never knew his name, but he crippled me emotionally for the next twenty years.

From that day on I went back into hiding but a different kind of hiding, one where I totally refused to be Jewish. I denied that I was Jewish. I spent the next twenty years hiding my Jewishness, running away from it, ashamed of it. All I wanted to do was go to America, change my name, not be Jewish any more. I thought being Jewish was a disease. I had it, and I didn't like it.

I didn't find out until years later that the same thing had happened that day to my sister, my mother, and my mother's school friend, Solly Turin. As they walked into a restaurant in Brussels. some loudmouth said, "Hey! Look at the kikes! Look at the *youpins*! They're coming out of the woodwork." Solly turned around and ran out of the restaurant. Ruth looked for a place to hide. She was scared. My mother stared at the guy and pointed her finger at him, "Look, you. It's too late or too soon. Now you must keep your mouth shut." She was right. It was too late to be hunting Jews then and too soon for the new wave to come along.

I went back to school. There were six Jews in my class. Four were very religious and had been in a camp in Malines. There the Germans gathered captured Jews until they had enough to fill a convoy to Poland. The Jews in my class had been liberated by British troops just before the last convoy was supposed to leave. They looked upon it as an act of God, personally saving them. I had difficulty accepting that. They wouldn't come to school on Friday or Saturday, and this was all new to me. They took a tremendous amount of abuse from the teachers. There was a lot of anti-Semitism in school.

In mid-1946 I left school because we had no home life and because I had to earn a living. I worked for Lever Brothers, where I met Rosette, the girl I would marry seven years later. She was a Gentile, but that meant nothing to me at the time. Now, Unilever in England is a Jewish firm, but in Belgium it was totally Christian. The wife of one of the directors was Jewish, and she hired me. I was eventually fired for a lot of reasons. One was that they discovered that I was not Belgian. They had just assumed that, because I was born in Charleroi, I was a Belgian citizen, but I was stateless and I didn't have working papers. They could have suffered heavy fines for hiring an illegal alien. Also, I spent too much time running after the girls and doing Danny Kaye imitations on top of my desk. I worked there for nearly three years, until summer 1949. I was nineteen.

I eventually got my affidavit to come to the United States in 1949, thanks to Oncle Paul and Tante Lily Friedemann, my mother's brother and his wife. I left Belgium behind and came to America determined to be an American, determined never to be Jewish again. I wanted to call myself Rosemount or Mountrose. I figured that if Lord Battenberg could change his name to Lord Mountbatten, I could change my name too.

I left Europe through Rotterdam, on the SS *Tabinta* of the Holland-America Line, on September 1, 1949. After a long stormy crossing, we came into the Port of New York on September 12, 1949, a Sunday. I stood on the deck as we passed by the Statue of Liberty, and tears welled in my eyes. I had arrived in America. We landed that afternoon in Hoboken, New Jersey. I had always dreamed of kissing the ground, but there was no ground to kiss. We landed at a dock, and the floor was covered with huge steel plates that did not look inviting to my lips.

Paul and Lily Friedemann were there to welcome me. We took the Tube (a train running under the Hudson River) to downtown Manhattan, then the subway to Brooklyn, where they lived. The train stopped at Wall Street. I read the name on the station wall. I was filled with anticipation. Wall Street, the center of the world! The doors opened. I expected to see millionaires spilling into the subway car. A bum came in, unkempt, dirty, smelling. He sat in front of me and went to sleep.

I had arrived in the States at the beginning of the High Holidays, but I knew nothing about them. I went to work in a wholesale dry-goods store on Eldridge Street on the Lower East Side for a Russian Jew named Phillip Sirota, who adopted me like I was his own son. All our customers were Jewish, and we worked on Sunday and were closed on Saturday. This annoyed me no end. I didn't know how we could do that. To me, Sunday was Sunday; it was sacred.

Uncle Paul and Aunt Lily insisted that I go to their temple for the High Holidays. I didn't want to, but to please my aunt I went. The whole thing was a mistake. My aunt's brother Carl was standing next to me. He realized that I couldn't read Hebrew. Not only couldn't I read Hebrew, but I was belligerent about it. I'm Protestant, I don't want to have anything to do with that. Carl asked, "Weren't you ever bar mitzvahed?" This was the first time I had heard of bar mitzvah. "You mean when they cut a piece?" "No, no, no," he said. "When you're thirteen." "When I was thirteen," I said, "I was hiding." "You can have it done now." I had been circumcised, but I figured they were going to cut off another piece, so I said, "No, thank you. There's no rush." Little by little I began to learn what it is to be a Jew.

When the Korean War started, I joined the army, mostly because I wanted to get out from under Mr. Sirota's wing. I didn't want to work in the dry-goods store forever. I had also fallen in love with a young lady who was married. I felt I had to get away somehow. In the army I encountered severe anti-Semitism and couldn't understand it because I was a Protestant. My dog tags said I was Protestant. The whole thing was a mistake. When I first was in Fort Lee, Virginia, another soldier, Ishmael "Mayo" Sotel, sought me out when he joined our outfit. It was like being approached by a leper. I didn't want to have anything to do with him. We became friends, however, as long as he didn't discuss Judaism. He lives in California now, and I visited him most recently in April 2005.

I married Rosette Wauters, a Belgian national, in Brussels. I loved her very much, but I don't know if consciously or subconsciously I married her because it was again a way of hiding, of ending this lineage of mine. But I became more comfortable with being Jewish after twenty years. It was not a disease any more. I was like a leopard trying to deny its spots.

In 1978 I attended a scientific conference in Israel. I was by then reconciled to being Jewish; I was not going to hide it any more. When I landed in Tel Aviv, I had the strange feeling that I was coming home. I saw the desert vegetation on the hills around there, and I felt as if I had just been awakened. A few days later I went to visit the Western Wall (formerly called the Wailing Wall) in Jerusalem with a Vietnamese scientist friend who was living in Belgium. He was taking my picture. Suddenly, he asked, "Why do you look so sad?" I tried to explain it to him, but the words didn't come because I was choking. I began to cry. I was sobbing. It was uncontrollable. My friend asked, "Why are you crying?" I couldn't explain it to him, but I knew why. I was crying because for some reason I had been saved to go there. I thought about the millions of other Jews who never got to see the Western Wall. The million Jews who fled two thousand years ago. Anne Frank, my grandmother, my father's family, my uncle Richard and his wife, six million Jews who died, to whom it would have meant so much to be there. I was fortunate enough to be there, and it meant absolutely nothing to me to be a Jew.

I ran from that part of Jerusalem and went to the Muslim quarter. I found a Star of David that I purchased without even bothering to haggle about the price. I wanted to wear my Star of David. I was forty-eight years old. I thought that after forty-eight years I deserved it. Maybe the people of Israel deserved it. I was no longer ashamed of being a Jew. I was proud of my heritage. If I had to do it all over again, I wouldn't want to be anything else.

After leaving Israel, I had business appointments in Heidelberg and engagements with some German friends. I felt a little bit uneasy because I was wearing my star. I didn't want to hit them in the face with it. As it turned out, I wore a shirt and tie, and therefore the star didn't show. A few days later I went to Brussels to meet with my father, who was then seventy-six years old. He had remained in Belgium after the war and resumed work as an interior decorator. He picked me up at the airport. He took one look at my open shirt and the Star of David and said, "You shouldn't be wearing that. It's dangerous. If you wear it, you should wear it with a longer chain."

I guess he had a point. Living in New York, you tend to forget that there's a non-Jewish world out there. It also struck me that there was another reason. My father had lived in Belgium since 1920, but he was still very Jewish and spoke with a Polish Jewish accent. However, he still went by the name of M. Hilaire or M. Rose and lived in a fantasy world where he thought that nobody knew he was Jewish. It took a few more years before he joined me in accepting his Jewishness. In his later years he was very proud that he was Hillel and not Hilaire and that his name was Rosenberg and not Rose.

When I got back to New York, my wife, who is not Jewish, never mentioned anything about my star, never said a word about it, but for my next birthday she bought me a silver chain for it.

I went to California, and I saw my mother and sister. In 1952, while I was in the army, I had convinced them to come to the United States. They settled first in Brooklyn, then moved to California in the late 1950s and remained there. When my mother saw my star, she made a face. She said, "I don't like those things." I don't think my mother, who died in 2000, changed in the ninety-seven years that she was around. Ruth had about the same reaction, but she's changing. She understands me now, and I think she understands herself. She is still living north of San Diego and is retired from work at newspapers there. She is seldom in touch with our father in Brussels.

I have given testimony about my war experiences, my difficulties in the United States, some of the anti-Semitism, which is not confined to any one country. The first thing I did after I bought my house on Long Island was visit the attic. There's a little alcove in the attic, and my first thought was, "I can make a hiding place there."

Rosette and I have had our difficulties through the years. She has given me a son, whom I love dearly. Rudy Richard Rosenberg was born in 1957. He got his middle name from my murdered uncle. Rudy has two children, a daughter, Karen, born in 1981, and a son, Richard, born in 1984. I don't think they're aware that they are Jews. We never discuss it. I'm not sure whether my experiences in hiding affected the way I raised my son, but I don't think I was the best of fathers. One thing that I regret a lot is that I cannot talk to my son about this. He will not listen. I don't know why that is. Rudy will some day have to think of his own choices. I hope that he finds out more about it before I die.

I didn't see my father for eighteen years after I came to the United States, but fortunately we found each other again. We loved each other. I loved my mother. We said so all the time. It's so much easier to say "I hate you" than to say "I love you." When you say "I love you," you're naked. Whenever my father spoke to me about his youth and when he was hiding, I listened. I asked him again and he told me again. There was always a little extra detail that I was hungry for. We talked about many things. I really regret that I cannot do this with my son and my grandchildren.

I was in Paris with Rudy years ago. We went to a little shop that sold military uniforms and hats. I told the owner, M. Charlie Royer, that my son wanted a French railroad hat. Meanwhile, a customer had come into his shop, a gendarme. We went to the back room of the shop where we gave the owner our name and address, so he could send one, and on his card he wrote, "My name is Schildkraut." Then he turned to us very abruptly, and he put his finger to his lips. "Don't say anything." That was in 1980, more than thirty years after the end of the war, and this man in Paris was still afraid that someone might discover that he was Jewish. It impressed me. It impressed my son a whole lot. Maybe he understood a little bit of what was going on by then, but I never forgot M. Schildkraut.

One day I was visiting Brussels with my son. We stood outside the house where I was hidden during the war. Emotion overcame me and I began to weep. My son put his arm around my shoulder. I think that's probably the first time he understood me.

There are people, I know, who still don't like Jews. Sometimes I wonder if the Auschwitzes of tomorrow aren't being built already. Once, when I was a wedding photographer, some drunk made an anti-Semitic remark to me, and I laughed at him. A big bottle of wine was on the table. I said, "You're very lucky. Had you said that to me ten years ago, I would have broken this bottle on your head. But today if you want, have fun. It doesn't bother me at all."

I remember hearing about a rabbi in Warsaw during the ghetto uprising. He said, "All things considered, I'd rather be the oppressed than the oppressor." I think about that very often, and I wish so many good people were around to be with us.

And so I decided to attend the first International Gathering of Children Hidden During World War II in 1991, mostly because I wanted to be counted. I wanted people to know that I was here, that I have survived, and I intend to survive for a while. By coincidence, just before the conference started, I received a piece of hate mail at the office of my biochemical research firm. Twenty pages of the most hateful garbage that I've ever seen in my life, about Jews poisoning non-Jews. Things really haven't changed much in two or four thousand years. The big difference, though, is the way I received the hate mail. If I had received this forty years ago, I would have been shattered, ashamed. Today it saddens me that there are people as sick as whoever wrote this. I hope that the conference helped us understand these letters a little more and take them more in stride, knowing that we are survivors and that no amount of hate mail is going to change that.

My Red Chesterfield Coat

HILDE SCHERAGA
(b. 1930, Germany)

I do not like to admit that I was born in Frankfurt am Main, Germany, in 1930. After all these years I still feel very uncomfortable about having been born in that country. When people detect that I have a foreign accent and ask me where I come from, I often tell them that I was born in Europe. Incredibly enough, few question my response.

My family lived in a lovely apartment in an integrated neighborhood. My father was a businessman who came from a little town not far from Frankfurt called Büdensheim. My mother came from Grosszimmern, also not too far from Frankfurt. They were married in 1926 and moved to Frankfurt. My brother, Martin, was born in 1928 and I was born in 1930. My maternal grandmother lived with us. When Martin was two years old, he suffered from a middle ear infection (mastoid). His temperature skyrocketed, and he developed meningitis from which he never fully recovered. This illness left him mentally impaired for the rest of his life. He was not able to attend any type of formal schooling and had a private tutor who

127

Hilde and her brother, Martin,
in front of their apartment in
Frankfurt am Main, Germany,
1934.

came to the house every day. He learned to read and write and do some mathematics. The tutoring stopped forever after Kristallnacht on November 9–10, 1938.

Martin and I played on the street in front of our house with the children who lived near us. I recall many happy times of skipping rope and playing with our scooter, which had a pedal that we pumped up and down to give it momentum. It was red and I loved playing with it. My family was fairly religious. Every Saturday we went to synagogue, and we were not allowed to do any work on the Sabbath. We were members of the beautiful, imposing Boerneplatz synagogue, built in the middle of the nineteenth century. We walked there on the Sabbath, even though my family owned a car. We seemed to live a "normal" life in the early thirties, yet I always sensed that there were serious problems somewhere that were mysteries to

Hilde, Martin, and their
father in 1938 before Hilde
left Frankfurt for Belgium.

me. I was six years old before I realized that we, as Jews, were not leading normal
lives, even though at first I did not understand what was happening. My parents
never talked about anything serious in front of me or my brother. In those days
children were rarely, if ever, included in serious conversation.

I had started attending a private Jewish day school when I was five years old.
It never occurred to me that I was not allowed to attend a public school. Jewish
children were forbidden to mingle with the non-Jewish children, so we were not
allowed to attend public schools.

My life began to change rather drastically when I was six or seven years old.
My non-Jewish friends deserted me. From being happy to see me and play with me,
they now made it obvious that they would have nothing more to do with me. They
seemed to change overnight. It was not unusual for me to be insulted, to be called
awful names and laughed at, because I was Jewish. I vividly recall some of the horrible jingles with which they used to greet me when they saw me trying to play by
myself with my scooter.

Later, when I was seven or eight years old, I no longer dared to go outside to
play because my enemies had become violent and threw things at me that hurt. I
was once hit by a stone or a piece of glass, and I recall bleeding profusely from my
arm. I ran into the house screaming, telling my mother that I would never go outside again. That was the last time I played outside, something I loved to do. During
that same period I used to go out with my mother to shop. The stores now had their
display windows full of anti-Semitic graffiti, calling Jews all kinds of dirty words
and accusing us of being the cause of all the problems that Germany was experiencing. Many stores had large signs telling the Jews not to enter. Where were we to
shop?

Life for my family also began to change drastically on Kristallnacht, when
the synagogues of Germany and Austria were burned and desecrated, when the dis-

play windows of the stores still owned by Jews were smashed and the goods looted, when homes were broken into, and thirty-thousand Jewish men were arrested and sent to concentration camps or thrown into jail. Our home was invaded and my father was arrested. The next day was the last day that I attended school. When we entered our classroom, we were met by our teacher, who was in tears. She told us to go home, that this wonderful school would not reopen its doors. This was the last day that I attended school in Germany. Kristallnacht was the most frightening day of my life. My father's arrest terrified me. When would I see him again? What had he done? These questions were, of course, rhetorical. There were no answers.

Like most Jewish families in Germany, we had tried to obtain visas so all of us, including my two grandmothers, who were now living with us, could leave the country. The difficulties in obtaining these precious visas were beyond imagination. I know now that the Nazis were doing their best to force the Jews to leave Germany and Austria, but very few countries were willing to accept Jews. The Depression had not yet eased in most countries. While there were tortuous ways of leaving Germany and illegally entering countries where, it was believed, Jews could find safety and freedom, the reality was that most Jews wanted to go to the United States, Canada, or Great Britain. None of these countries was opening its arms to save Jewish lives. My own family was able to obtain one precious visa to the United States. My father was going to use that visa and then send for the rest of the family. Although he waited too long to leave, having that visa saved his life. When my mother found out where the Nazis had taken him, she immediately went to the authorities, visa in hand, and demanded his release. She succeeded. My father had to leave almost immediately, and he went to Italy, where he hoped to be able to get a ship to the United States. He had to wait a year before he was able to sail to America.

For us life in Germany became more and more difficult. My mother must have understood that the family still remaining in Germany was unlikely to get out. She now must have thought of the best way to save her children—my brother and me. The answer came when she learned that after Kristallnacht, Great Britain, France, Belgium, and Holland had offered to shelter Jewish children. She made the decision to send us away.

I remember vividly the preparation for our departure. Each of us was allowed to take only one suitcase. I got new clothes, a new toy, was allowed to take my beloved doll, and was very excited that I would be leaving on a train. At the age of eight I loved trains and railway stations. I was fascinated by the possibilities that train travel offered. I always wondered how far one could travel and what was to be found in the open spaces past our railway station, which I remember as being enormous and very majestic. I did not understand that this trip would be different from the short train trips that Martin and I had taken years earlier when visiting our paternal grandmother. How could I know that this trip was meant to save my life and place a concrete wall between me and my childhood?

The day arrived. I will never forget it. I will always see that railroad station as if it were yesterday. My mother accompanied us, and only at that point did I realize that our good-byes were not ordinary good-byes, that our lives had reached a watershed, that our lives, no matter what happened from that day on, would never be the same again, that my childhood had come to an end, and that from now on I was psychologically on my own and responsible for my six-year-old brother, who had no one else to protect him.

The train was full of children like me, lost in their own sorrow, lost in their memories of mother and father and home and childhood. Would this sense of security ever return? Was it stolen from us forever? Should my family have spoken to me about this day? Should we have been part of the discussion that led to this momentous decision about my life and that of my brother? Would the shock have been less and the sobs more subdued?

I remember the reception center. I only recently found out where this place was. I knew we had arrived in Belgium, but I had no idea which town I was in. Much later I searched for the name of this place. It was Wezembeek. Martin, who has an incredible memory, told me the name of the little town. I continued my research and finally found the documents that indeed mentioned Wezembeek as the reception center where we had passed the first few weeks of our arrival in Belgium.

I recall the enormous dormitories and the people in charge, who used to come at night and make sure we did not wet our beds. I also recall sitting around a long rectangular table with other children. I remember that I was always crying, hiding my head in my hands, leaning against the table, very ashamed of my tears. The highlight of my stay there came when we were allowed to ask for one item from our suitcase. I asked for a manicure set that I was extremely proud of. My mother had asked me what new toy I wanted to take with me, and I chose a manicure set.

We remained in Wezembeek for four or five weeks. Then Martin and I were picked up by a car one day and driven to a state orphanage in a suburb of Brussels. It was a very large institution with more than three hundred children, who were housed in several buildings. The orphanage was a very modern one, built in the 1930s. Incredibly enough, this Foyer des Orphelins de Molenbeek St. Jean was the first orphanage in the country to be run by a secular group and not by nuns or priests. My brother and I were sent to different divisions of the orphanage. However, since Martin had very special needs, he could not stay in this institution and was sent elsewhere in the country.

I was devastated when he left. My mother had asked me to look after him. I now had to break my promise to my mother. Furthermore, I was now all alone, separated from everyone I had known in my life so far. Little did I know that this place would be my home for the next eight years.

I was able to correspond with my mother for a while. When the Germans invaded Belgium in May 1940, I sent my mother a letter, begging her to allow me to come home. After all, the Germans were everywhere and what difference did it make whether I lived in Belgium or with my mother in Germany? My mother refused to allow me to come home. Of course, I was very disappointed, but I had no choice but to accept her decision. Today I know that her refusal saved our lives. I learned that my grandmothers had left for South America and that my mother was now alone in Germany. I learned later that she was forced to abandon her apartment and move into the Jewish ghetto. She was forced to work long hours every day and often had to walk back to the ghetto if she missed the last streetcar on which Jews were allowed to ride.

In 1942 I received a letter from my mother telling me that I would not be hearing from her for a while. I understood. Somehow I felt that she must have been arrested and sent away. Of course, I had no idea where she was, but I realized that her departure was not good, that she might be sent to a camp, and that her survival was a question mark. The orphanage never provided us with any information about the war. How did I learn that there were camps? I do not recall. I now felt truly alone in this orphanage. I did not feel that I was part of the orphanage family. I did not consider myself an orphan and wanted to believe that I had a real family and that we would be reunited.

With the invasion of Belgium by the Germans, my security and the security of the orphanage became problematic. All Jews were considered enemies, and those who protected them were as much the enemies of the Nazis as the Jews themselves. In fact, the Jewish children who were living in the orphanage when the Nazis invaded were sent to the south of France, which was considered "safe" territory. Six of us were forgotten as a result of a clerical error, and I was one of the six. Although the Jewish children could be protected in the orphanage because we were so few, nevertheless the danger that we would be denounced was real. The orphanage decided to take a chance and keep us. Fortunately, it occupied enormous grounds tucked away in the countryside. But the only school on the grounds was for children with learning disabilities. Most of the kids attended public school. In 1942 it was decided that it was too dangerous to send the Jewish children to school. Again my education came to an abrupt halt.

Little by little I began to blend into the orphanage family. Although all the other children were Catholic, I was never forced to attend church. But on special occasions, like Christmas, Easter, or a confirmation, I chose to go. I loved going to church. I loved the music and the quiet meditation that the setting of the church offered me. I never considered converting. I never forgot that I was Jewish, but being Jewish became less and less important to me. I missed my family terribly but gradually forgot what having a father and mother was like. I often wondered what it was like to live in a home with parents and extended family. My memories faded with the passing years, as I struggled to remember what my parents looked like (I had no photographs) or the sounds of their voices.

My ongoing concern was my own safety and that of the institution, for I was certainly aware of the danger that Jewish children presented for their rescuers. I was also very frightened that a German would come to the orphanage, see me, and ask me why I was not in school. Could I make believe that I could not understand him if he spoke to me in German? Would I be arrested? Would the institution be penalized? I was also very concerned about my future. As I grew older and reached the ages of twelve, thirteen, and fourteen, I wondered what my future would be. Would I be reunited with my parents and leave Belgium? Would I ever be able to catch up with my education, having lost years of schooling? Would I have a meaningful future without parents and without education?

Brussels was liberated in September 1944. It was one of the happiest days of my life. An enormous burden fell off my shoulders. My terror of being discovered vanished the moment the Allies, who were gods to all of us, liberated Brussels. I don't think I will ever again experience the elation and euphoria that overwhelmed us on that day. We, the children of the orphanage, were like a tidal wave and could not be contained. As soon as we heard the news, we ran for miles to witness the coming of the British soldiers, who entered Brussels on tanks, throwing chocolate, chewing gum, and oranges at us, things we had not seen in years.

I was now fourteen years old. I finally was free! I finally could resume my education. Though years behind my contemporaries, I was welcomed in the public school to which I was sent. The teacher, in fact, was delighted to have me as a student and gave me a very precious gift—something I had never had—a dictionary. But soon my thoughts focused on my future. What kind of a future could I have? Could I enter the adult world without family and without a proper education? I felt very keenly that I could never make up the lost years.

The Red Cross put me in touch with my father. The orphanage informed me that my brother was well and living in a little town called Geel. I started to correspond with my father. I had no way of getting in touch with my brother, and it would be another year before I had an opportunity to visit him.

On a bright Sunday morning in June 1945, some of us were invited to go swimming. These invitations were extended to the orphanage on rare occasions as a goodwill gesture from charitable organizations in Brussels. As we were returning to the orphanage, a group of children came to meet us, jumping and laughing, and indicating that something unusual was going on. Normally, no one met us. After all, we spent twenty-four hours a day together, so why would they now meet us and why focus all their attention on me? They took me by the hand and accompanied me for a few hundred yards. My mother was waiting for me.

She had survived two-and-a-half years in slave labor camps and the concentration camp of Stutthof. She was liberated by the Russians in January 1945 while being taken on a death march back to Germany. She came to Brussels because it was the only place for which she had an address where she hoped to find her children. It had taken her five months to make her way from the northwestern part of Poland to Belgium, walking, hitchhiking, knocking on doors, begging for food and shelter. Yet at that moment she was the richest person in the world, for she found out not only that I was alive but that my brother was well and that my father had been in touch with me.

I recognized her immediately, yet she looked so different to me. Poorly

HILDE SCHERAGA

dressed, with short hair that seemed so much lighter in color, she did not resemble
the mother I had last seen when I was eight years old. She was wearing a dress with
short sleeves, and I could see that her lower left arm was deformed. I was to learn
that she had been shot for an infraction of the rules, and the bullet had penetrated
her lower arm and exited from the other side. Nothing was done to heal the wound.
Later in the war she fell and broke the arm at that spot. She courageously talked her
bosses into letting her continue to work on the railway lines; her job was to blow
the whistle when a train was coming. She had some mobility in her fingers and refused to have the arm reset once we arrived in the United States.

I was now fifteen. I no longer spoke German. She, of course, did not speak
a word of French. I was a little child when I left home. I was now, or so I thought,
an adult who still looked like a child. Our inability to communicate did not really
matter at that moment.

Jewish welfare groups took care of my mother. I remained in the orphanage.
We saw each other every couple of weeks for a few hours. Once a month I was allowed to meet her in her room and stay with her overnight.

A year later, in the spring of 1946, my mother and I left for the United States
to be reunited with my father, whom I had not seen in eight years. I was now sixteen years old. My brother was not allowed to come with us because the United
States would not accept an individual who had a mental disability. My mother
and I visited him just before we left for the United States. Like a number of other
handicapped people, he was being well cared for by the townspeople. Later he was
moved to a wonderful government institution in Sint-Truiden, where he was a
woodworker for years. His caretakers are very good with him. He is able to shop in
town and has traveled around much of Western Europe. Now, however, he speaks
only Flemish. My husband and I visit him every year.

Little did I know that my first years in the United States would be the most
unhappy of my life. In Belgium I had dreamed of the day that I would arrive in this
land of freedom and opportunity. In the orphanage we adored President Roosevelt
and thought of the United States as a country where all our problems would be
solved. I conceived of our arrival in this country and the reunion with my father as
a beautiful fairy tale with a fabulous ending. Unfortunately, that was not the case.

Several relatives, as well as my father, met us at the boat. I immediately felt
uncomfortable. All these individuals were strangers, including my father. I had to
wear a red Chesterfield coat that my father had sent me so that he would know who
his daughter was. I resented that immensely. Why should my father not know who
his daughter was?

For the first few days we stayed with relatives in Bridgeport, Connecticut,
waiting for our flat to be ready. I immediately wanted to return to my orphanage.
I hated the way my relatives treated me. They did not like the clothes I wore, they
did not like my hairstyle (braids), they thought I should become Americanized
overnight and wear makeup, attend social events, join clubs, and become a regular American teenager. I was horrified. The only good memory I have of those first

days with our relatives was the food. I loved cornflakes, which I had never seen or heard of. I looked forward to breakfast every morning. We moved into a cold-water flat where the rent was $14 a month. We had no bathroom and no central heating. We shared a toilet in the hallway with the other tenants who lived on our floor. The three-room apartment, including the kitchen, was heated with the coal stove that we used for cooking.

Living with my parents was extraordinarily difficult. We were three individuals who came together as a family that had been irrevocably broken into three pieces. We seemed to come from three different planets. We did not speak to each other in any meaningful way. My father had been separated from my mother for six years. I do not believe that he could or wanted to understand the difficult life that she had experienced during the Holocaust. My father's life had not been easy, either. He had not made any money during the war years. He could barely provide for us when we arrived. My mother, who had been a model of strength and support and optimism for a group of younger Jewish survivors with whom she had been incarcerated, now seemed to collapse. She was often sick, very moody, and very unhappy. Yet as soon as we arrived in Bridgeport, she became a door-to-door salesperson for a company that sold cosmetics. Although she could speak no English, she went from house to house, showing and selling her products. She worked very hard. My father continued to sell garments, also from door to door.

As soon as I arrived in Bridgeport, I registered to become a student at Bassick High School. I was the first refugee to attend this school. I told the principal that I should be placed in the tenth grade. I had no documents to show him—no grades, no report cards. He simply accepted my word. I spent the remainder of the school year (from March to June 1946) going from one English class to another. No help was available for foreign students. I finished high school in two years, graduating when I was eighteen. My dream of not being seen as different from other students, of not standing out as that kid who is four years behind her contemporaries, came true. Much, much later I regretted my marathon race through high school. There were so many subjects that I never studied, such as American history. Much later, after I was married and had three children, I earned a bachelor of arts degree in French literature, followed by a master's degree in education. I later obtained my teaching certificate.

But in 1946 I was desperate to return to Belgium and to the orphanage that I regarded as my true home. After all, I had spent many happy years there and had grown to love the institution that had protected me and given me extraordinary strength of character. I felt so much more mature than my contemporaries, who seemed to know so little about life.

I had learned in the orphanage to be master of my own fate. I learned not to rely on others for my mental health. Relying on others proved too painful. In the orphanage children would leave without notice, making separation very painful if one had become emotionally attached to someone who left. I believed that my future lay in not needing anyone to love. I was very proud of this resolution. I believed that those youngsters who needed their parents and/or friends to be happy were deluding themselves, and I wanted no part of that scenario. In Belgium we never had the opportunity to meet boys and fall in love. Of course, some of the boys in the institution were my age, and I did have a crush on a couple of them. But in my judgment that did not invalidate my mental resolve to be independent.

Life with my parents did not get any better. My mother started to speak incessantly about her Holocaust experiences. I believed that she was the survivor in the family and that I was not a survivor, just a girl who had spent eight years in an orphanage. I felt guilty for not really loving my mother, who had suffered so much. We fought a lot. It never occurred to me that my stay in the orphanage had left open wounds in my soul. No one ever asked me what I experienced. The feeling was that as a child I had a bright future in front of me and I should take advantage of it. I agreed. Yet I felt that I also had a story to tell, even if it was not a real Holocaust story. I had not been in a camp or in a ghetto, and I had not been forced into slave labor. It would be many years before I learned that I was indeed a child survivor of the Holocaust.

I also had real problems with being Jewish. I had let my parents know that I would not marry a Jew, that I was against all religions. Religions only caused evil and suffering. Why should I adhere to any of them? Doing so would make me an accomplice to the miseries of the human condition. I felt that the world would be a much more humane place if all religions were abolished. Why should anyone suffer because of religious affiliations? I would eventually change my mind, but it took many years.

I married in 1953. My husband was Jewish. I believed that it was simply coincidence that I fell in love with a Jewish man. It was difficult not to meet a Jewish man in New York, where I was living at that time. In 1956 our daughter Judy was born, followed in 1960 by our daughter Debby, and in 1962 by Naomi. When Judy was eight, I nearly had a nervous breakdown. I felt that I was totally unable to be a mother once a child had reached the age that I was when I was sent away from home. I never spoke of my Holocaust life to anyone, including my husband. I was too busy raising children and taking university courses at night. I relived my mother's incredible courage to send her children away. Could I have done it? I consoled myself with the resolve that I would make my children very independent so that they could always find the inner strength to march through life, facing any difficulties that they might encounter. Now, when I think of what I expected of them, I realize that I was insane. When we spent a sabbatical year in Paris (my husband was a university professor of experimental psychology), I took Judy to the International School only once to show her the way, although it was some distance from our house. She had to take two different Métros and walk to school from the Métro stop. She then had to make the trip in reverse to come home. Although she spoke no French, she accomplished this task when she was just twelve years old.

My husband passed away in 1976. He had incurable cancer. We were devastated by his loss.

Hilde Scheraga, 1983.

Six years later I met and married my current husband, Mort Scheraga. I sold my house without any regrets. My friends could not understand how I could sell my house and move from Toronto, Canada, to Stamford, Connecticut, where Mort lived. I could not understand how anyone could put so much value on a piece of property and on a city. I had no concept of "home." I did not have a home. Germany was not my home. Belgium came as close to being a real home as anything I had from my childhood. I never really valued things more than human beings. My home was wherever I happened to live. To this day I have problems responding when someone asks me, "Where is your home?" I cannot go back and show my children where my home was. The concept does not exist in my mind.

In 1991 my life changed in an incredible way. I attended a conference, held in New York at the Marriott Marquis Hotel, for those of us who were children during the Holocaust. I was very nervous when I arrived there with my husband. I was frightened of what might transpire. For me, as well as the other twelve hundred child survivors, this was a real catharsis. We came together as strangers and parted as brothers and sisters. We were able to talk openly for the very first time about our experiences and our painful silence for so many years. It transformed my life.

Soon after the conference a group of child survivors, the Holocaust Child Survivors of Connecticut, was created and incorporated. I did not have the courage at first to become a member. It was at least two years before I thought that I could attend a gathering. Since then our group has bonded together, and we are like members of a close-knit family. We care for one another and understand one another. We have talked for years about our survival experiences and have learned to deal with our years of survival better than we could ever have imagined. The wounds have not healed; the wounds will most likely never heal. But we have learned in the years since the conference to deal with our pain and even, to some degree, find a better way of dealing with our past.

I have come full circle since coming to the United States. I am now very proud to be Jewish but only culturally. I like going to synagogue, because I like being with Jewish people, but I do not believe in God. I cannot believe that 1.5 million children died without any divine intervention. When reading the Mahsor (the High Holiday prayer book) during the High Holidays, I shudder whenever I come across the passage that states that the fate of every Jew is decided by God, who determines whether each has sinned and deserves to live or die. What crime could a child have committed? I have asked rabbis that question but have never received a good answer.

A Chance Encounter

ZAHAVA SZÁSZ STESSEL
(b. 1930, Hungary)

As members of the Jewish communities gathered in ghettos and camps, they met people whom they would otherwise never have encountered. This happened to me and my sister, Erzsike, in the cruelest of assemblies in Auschwitz-Birkenau.

We were there, in the second week after our arrival, two girls, thirteen and fourteen, suffering from the shock of separation from our parents and grandparents. Lost and lonely, we were holding on to each other. For a day or two we did not eat because as children we were easily pushed aside when people were fighting for survival.

After a few days we learned that our block was a special one that housed scarlet fever and typhus patients. In placing us in that barrack, the Germans were experimenting to see how many would develop typhus or scarlet fever during twenty-one days of exposure. We didn't work and were not allowed to leave the area of the barrack during the quarantine for the experiment. A medical committee headed by

Dr. Josef Mengele visited us from time to time. They were checking us and separating those who contracted the diseases.

One morning, not knowing what to do, we were waiting outside, in the area between two barracks. Some sat on the ground, others were moving around. We just stood there, in low spirits, when a lady approached us. She was a slender woman, about forty, with a gentle face and a congenial smile. She asked us where we came from. When we said Abaújszántó, she smiled and pointed confidently at Erzsike. "You are the daughter of Sándor Szász; you have his eyes and expression. I noticed it as we were standing in *Zahlappell* [roll call]."

We were stunned and shaken just by the mention of our father. "My name is Szerén," she continued. "I knew your father very well. I almost married him." As she talked with a slight twitch in her head, I recalled a story that Grandmother had told me. As a young teenager I was eager to hear about my father's boyhood adventures.

My father, Sándor Szász, was an only child under my grandmother's strong scrutiny and protection. Her task was not easy. Sándor was a gregarious, fun-loving bachelor of a well-to-do family. The girls liked his company, and Sándor had difficulty saying no to a girl without hurting her feelings. Among his friends was Szerén, for whom Sándor sincerely cared. She was a good-looking, delicate girl. Szerén received Grandmother's full approval, until one day she noticed a tremor in Szerén's face. The slight tic was indiscernible to anyone else, but for Grandmother it was a serious concern. She was satisfied when Szerén, who lived in another town, stopped visiting.

My mother, Margit-Mariska Markovics, was a pretty and intelligent city girl. She had dark brown hair and a light complexion. Her Hebrew name was Miriam, but everyone called her Mariska. She was from a family of five girls and four boys. Her parents owned a successful shoe store, located in the center of the city of Sátoraljaujhely. Mariska had calm manners and a pleasing, humble smile. My father met her when he went to her home to meet her older sister Rózsi, who had been recommended to him by a matchmaker. As Father entered the room and noticed Mariska, he ignored Rózsi, who was all dressed up for the occasion. Mariska was Father's real choice, but he had to wait till Rózsi found a suitable partner.

Marriage in those days was an important means for economic and social advancement. Because many professions, including the civil service and the academic world, were closed to Jews, a young marriageable man needed money so he could open a store or start a business of his own. Dowry was a major source of such funds. Customarily, before the wedding the bride presented the bridegroom with her dowry, which she had received from her father. It was common knowledge that a Jewish merchant was a credit risk while he was marrying off his daughters, for he required large sums for their dowries. A poor Jewish girl, regardless of how pretty she was, had a hard time finding a husband.

My parents were married after a three-year courtship and engagement. My mother kept their correspondence from those years in the linen closet, among her

Zahava's father, Sándor Szász, in Abaújszántó, Hungary, 1943.

precious embroidered doilies, pillow cases, and tablecloths. As teenagers my sister and I had discovered and secretly read some of the letters.

My grandparents were fond of the new bride, and Sándor settled down to be a devoted husband and, since January 19, 1930, a father. He good-naturedly accepted being kidded about having a daughter in a society where boys had more weight. The teasing increased as the second girl, Erzsike, was born on November 24, 1931. Erzsike, who resembled Father, became exceptionally pretty, to the pride of the family.

Being a joyful person, my father liked to entertain and make people smile. I remember how he teased the customers in our clothing store. One of his favorite tales was about neighbors over whom a train had passed. When the listeners were shocked, my father quickly added, "Don't worry. Nothing happened to them; they were under a bridge." In the 1930s simple jokes still delighted people in a small town, some of whom did not even have radios. Father kidded around even in the harshest of times. In 1943 our store window was painted with the word *arulok* (traitors). The term also means "I offer for sale" in Hungarian. Playing on that usage, my father completed the sentence by adding a list of the merchandise that he was offering for sale. Thus Sándor Szász used his sense of humor to turn an anti-Semitic insult into a joke, much to the amusement of passersby and local Jews.

Although my father was an easygoing person, the troubled times and the war left their marks on his spirit. I cared about his well-being and could read the distress on his face. His suffering grew as our economic conditions deteriorated due to multiplying anti-Jewish laws.

The concern for my father and the fear that he would be called for the army's forced labor battalion remained one of my most profound childhood memories. The sight of a mailman bringing special delivery letters made me suspend my most engaging play. I would follow the official with great anxiety to see whether he would enter our home.

The summons to report for duty finally came in 1942, and my father was stationed in Kér, a nearby village. Riding my bicycle, I delivered dinner and messages from home to him every day. As we sat together, he recalled events from World War I when he fought in the Hungarian army. He mentioned sadly the discrimination and the mistreatment by Hungarian army officers that he suffered as a Jew.

One day I found him overly worried and unusually quiet. In response to my probing, Father revealed his plan to place one of his legs under the wheels of a horse-drawn carriage to break it so he would not be transported abroad. This was overwhelming for me, a dainty twelve-year-old. I still tremble as I think and write about it. I do not know how I would have handled it if, soon after our conversation, Father and some others in his age group had not been released from service. Thus our conversation remained among the silent bonds between me and my father.

Looking back, I don't know whether forced labor would not have been better for Father than being in Auschwitz. The Jews in my town had no knowledge of Auschwitz, while they knew of the mistreatment in the army. My father's desperation was only one example of many crippling acts contemplated and committed by Hungarian Jewish men to avoid the dreaded forced labor.

My parents' love and profound devotion to one another were most pronounced during deportation. Once, while we were in the ghetto of Kosice, before we were transferred to Auschwitz, my mother was offered an opportunity to escape with false papers, brought to us by my aunts Rózsi and Hanni, my mother's sisters, who were living in Kosice. The documents consisted of identification as non-Jews for a woman and two girls. My aunt Hanni obtained them from a Christian family. Mother, without hesitation, decided against the offer and the escape. She wouldn't forsake my father and his elderly parents. Her sisters' persuasive reasoning was pale compared to the strength of my mother's loyalty and love for her husband and his

Zahava (the Hebrew name Katalin chose for herself in 1948) (*left*) and her younger sister, Erzsike (*right*), Haifa, 1948.

family. Mother perished and our aunts Rózsi and Hanni survived, using forged documents.

We liked Szerén instantly. She was kind and caring. We felt as if she was a special envoy from our father. We sat down, Szerén in the middle, and answered her many questions. She was interested in our lives and the fate of our parents during the war. While Szerén had never met my mother, she knew that she was pretty and a soft-spoken lady. We told her how our father was taken with us to the ghetto in Kosice and then to Auschwitz. There, my father and grandfather were sent to one line, while Grandmother held my mother's arm and walked together with me and my sister, Erzsike, until Mengele separated us.

"You will be with me now," Szerén said, hugging us warmly. "We will stay together in line and watch out for each other." Szerén told us about Miki, her only child, who was with his father on the men's side. Miki was a tall, handsome fifteen-year-old. "He will be happy to meet Erzsike. Maybe they will even get married some day." Szerén continued to spin the web of dreams, letting us almost forget where we were. We could not have known that Miki, her pride and precious child, was dead even as she spoke of him. As we learned after the war, both father and son were sent directly to the crematorium after they arrived in Auschwitz.

Szerén encouraged us to be brave and to trust that the war would end and the world would be a better place. Like a mother, she made sure that we ate the soup, even though it tasted like slimy water mixed with sand and grass.

We talked with Szerén about the good times and the delicious food at home. My sister and I liked the chocolate cake, the stuffed cabbage, and the pancake (*palacsinta*) that Szerén and our mother prepared in similar ways. Szerén even knew our favorite song, "Kis ablakok nyilnak" (Little Windows Open), which Mother sang for us. The song is short and has a beautiful, longing melody. I used it as a lullaby for my daughters and grandchildren.

Szerén's friendship eased much of the hardship of our life in Auschwitz. As we grew to cherish and respect Szerén, we painfully noticed that her health was deteriorating. Occasionally, when we found a slice of precious potato in our soup, we averted Szerén's attention and quickly put it on her plate.

Slowly, Szerén became weak, listless, and pale. To hide her worsening tic, we placed her in the middle of the five-person line. It obscured her for a while, but eventually she could not escape the penetrating eyes of the SS. In our experimental block the relentless scrutiny and search for signs of sickness by a team of Mengele's helpers made hiding more difficult. The day that Szerén was pointed at and told to step forward was one of the darkest in our camp life. Even today I see her startled face and desperate movements as she was led away. Rest in peace, sweet Szerén, our guardian. You are remembered, great lady.

Szerén's departure and her consequent sad fate left us downhearted and depressed. We lost hope in the future and of ever seeing our parents again. Life without them was not worth living, we concluded. Checking the ways to die, we decided to touch the electric wire of the fence. Holding hands, we left the immediate area of our barrack. It was strongly forbidden, but we had nothing to fear any more. As we approached the fence, a boy in striped prison uniform passed by. He looked at my sister and handed Erzsike a small round bread and an onion. "Take it—your father has sent it to you," he said. The boy supposedly recognized my sister from a photograph that Father had showed him.

The purported message from our father and our faith in his support provided the will to continue. We returned safely to our barrack and hid the bread. After that our spirits never fell so low again as to produce such suicidal thoughts.

Soon the quarantine of our block ended, and we were taken to C Lager (camp) in Birkenau and eventually transferred to Bergen-Belsen. There the terror of separation, which was the greatest horror that haunted us in the camp, became almost unbearable. After losing our parents, grandparents, and Szerén, my sister and I were holding on to each other, desperately, inseparably.

One day, during a special *Zahlappell*, it was announced that someone had cut a piece of canvas from our tent. This was serious sabotage, the Nazis said, and if the guilty person would not step forward, every tenth inmate would be shot. We stood there terrified, not because of the fear of death but of the possibility that one of us would have to live without the other. The voice over the loudspeaker repeated the crime and the detailed punishment over and over in German and in Hungarian. Unable to look at each other's frightened face, we just tightened the grip of our hands.

The minutes turned to long, terrified hours, as our minds were unable to produce even the smallest ray of hope. Then suddenly, after six hours of vacillating between thoughts of life and death, we were ordered to disperse. There was no explanation and we ran back to the tent, still holding hands. It took us some time to regain our composure, and these events left a permanent mark in our consciousness.

We survived Bergen-Belsen after Auschwitz and also Markkleeberg, a working camp in an airplane factory near Leipzig. On April 13, 1945, as the Allied forces advanced, the German guards set us on what is known today as a "death march." We endured fifteen days of indescribable hardship. In surviving it, we again felt a guardian hand over our fate and safety.

Trudging along on hidden side roads or deserted highways with very little rest, we learned to sleep, even to dream, while walking. One bright evening, with a beautiful array of stars overhead, I noticed a little house in the distance with its lighted windows, enticing my imagination and filling me with longing. Later in my sleepwalk I was home again, by the wood-burning fire. As my mother set the table for supper, my father entered with his relaxed manners and friendly smile. I was still studying his face and admiring his expression when I suddenly bumped into a stone on the road and awoke to cruel reality.

At the beginning of our forced march, the discipline was harsh. Urged on by the guards and their rifle blows, we walked in orderly lines, keeping up a steady pace. Later on, after several air attacks, one of which killed three inmates, the guards relaxed their vigilance.

Some girls took advantage of the situation and left the march. Because my sister and I were young, inexperienced, and could not speak German, we never tried to escape. We would continue the march till one of us fell and the other would wait; then we would both be shot, which was usually what happened to those who couldn't walk with the group.

After a night of walking we arrived at a crossroad in the forest where we were attacked again from the air. The planes descended to target us at close range, mistaking us for German troops in transit. All of us hurried to disperse to the trenches at the side of the road. There we lay, covering our heads for protection with the food bowls we carried.

Soon, as fate would have it, we fell asleep. When we awoke, we discovered that the group had left us behind. We were frightened, but soon two other lost inmates, a mother and her daughter, who was about our age, joined us. Then the four of us struggled to survive in a forest for eight days until we were liberated by the Russians. Destiny and Providence had thrust upon us the escape that we would never have dared to undertake on our own.

Walking along, we came upon a small wooden shed used by hunters. There we stayed, listening at night to the howls of the wolves nearby. In the daytime we begged for food in the nearby city. One morning we found the road crowded with German civilians who were escaping the advancing Russian army. They were carrying their belongings in small wagons, trying to reach the American zone. As we continued on the highway, we heard gunfire, saw wounded soldiers on the ground, and realized that we were at the front line. Then Russian soldiers appeared, and we understood that the war was over.

At the roadside we found a small hand wagon that we filled with clothing and food from one of the abandoned homes. In search of a railway station, we entered Dresden, Saxony's capital, on the banks of the Elbe River. After World War II it was famous as a city that was demolished by Allied bombing. Although all the houses had been reduced to piles of stones, we found the roads were clear, and we saw tidy streets with names clearly posted at the corners. We saw no dead people in the neatly organized destruction (so characteristic of German order), but the smell of decomposing bodies was considerable.

As we continued, we saw no movement in the eerie city. We did not know how to find our way, so we returned to our starting point after a week of walking in circles. Disoriented, tired, and hungry, we sat at the roadside. Then we heard the sound of an automobile. Soon a group of five or six Russian soldiers surrounded us. We were pleased to see them, but instead of extending the sympathy we expected, they looked at us with the eyes of men hungry for the company of women.

As we stood there, our apprehension growing, one of the soldiers quietly said something in Yiddish. Knowing only Hungarian, we were unable to answer him. The other soldiers stood back, waiting. Erzsike and I, scared and defenseless, heard ourselves pronouncing, as if on cue, "Shema Yisrael!" (Hear, O Israel), the prayer that reaffirms the tenets of Judaism. The soldier's face lit up with a smile of understanding. He spoke to his comrades, who made room for us in the truck, and we left our wagon behind. The two other inmates who were with us and had no Jewish education were in awe at the miracle of the Hebrew words. As for us, we felt that the sanctity of our home and the spirit of our parents and grandparents were helping us to survive.

In a short while we reached an army post where we had a sumptuous meal and were given food for the road. Then our soldier protector brought us to a refugee collection center. As he left, he hugged each of us, while we dried our eyes and sealed within our memory one of the profound moments of our return to humanity and faith.

Continuing toward home, we trusted, inexplicably, that our parents would be meeting us there. It seems that our minds could not accept a reality in which we would never again see the people dearest to us.

We traveled on dangerous roads and stood on top of crowded trains, facing again the danger of Russian soldiers, just to get home. In Budapest our hopes heightened as we read the name of Sándor Szász on a list of returnees. It never occurred to us that many others could have the same name.

In Abaújszántó we found no home and no one was waiting for us. Gradually,

Zahava with her husband, Meier, ca. 1958.

we realized that our mother and grandparents would never come back, but we did not give up hope for our father. Not knowing his fate and whereabouts haunted me all the years after liberation. We left Hungary, but the search for Father brought me back again and again.

While looking for surviving members of our family, I found someone we had known before the war, Ilonka Kohn, in Miskolc, Hungary. Ilonka was born in Abaújszántó. She had black hair and a white complexion, and she was still attractive at forty-five. She never had children and she had survived Auschwitz. Ilonka was fond of my father, and she was convinced that only her economic situation had prevented her from marrying him. "The dowry was very important in those days," she explained.

When I first visited her, Ilonka started to cry. "Poor Sándor," she said, "I saw him as we arrived in Auschwitz. He was in a striped prison uniform, his face ashen, digging with a shovel among a group of men. Hardly daring to raise his head, he was calling softly, 'Ilonka, have you seen someone of my family?' 'No, Sándor,' I answered. As he tried to say something more, the SS appeared. I still see his sad, large brown eyes giving me a last forlorn look." On my return visits I tape-recorded Ilonka's story five times, until her death in 1992.

After meeting Ilonka and Szerén, I wondered about the kind of love and

Zahava Szász Stessel.
Contemporary photograph.

esteem that my father was able to create. By that miracle of devotion Szerén had helped us in Auschwitz, and Ilonka had kindled my hope after the war.

But no one else from my town had seen my father. I have searched for him relentlessly for sixty years. Only recently, I received a Red Cross note stating that the organization could not find my father's name, even in newly released documents. Somehow, I feel that he did not survive the selection in Auschwitz. Yet I cannot accept the terrible fate of my beloved idealistic father, choking from lack of air as the gas penetrated that devilish room created by demonic minds.

My children, having had no grandfather, were deprived of his kind, warm personality. They never knew my father's love and inspiration, which accompanied me in Auschwitz and still guides my steps as I walk the sharp-edged stones on my road of life.

Although I could not learn my father's fate and whereabouts, I found his likeness in our children and grandchildren. My sister's son Amir Alexander, his first grandchild, who is named for him, looks like my father. Now, as Amir approaches his early fifties, which was Father's age when we lost him, the resemblance is both startling and comforting.

Characteristic features of my father appear in his other descendants. As I held my newborn granddaughter Rakefet, there were her tiny ears, formed clearly in the shape of her great-grandfather's.

Sándor Szász's tragic fate will probably be buried with the rest of the Holocaust's terrible secrets. But Father's legacy of spirit and the miracle of resemblance will live in my children and their descendants.

Editor's Note: In March 1946 the Szász sisters and other Hungarian orphans were brought to a DP camp in Bavaria. Nearly a year later they sailed to Haifa, but the British would not let them land and deported them to Cyprus. In August 1947 they were allowed to enter Palestine under a special quota. Two years later Zahava, formerly Katalin, married Meier Stessel, also a Hungarian survivor. In 1957 the Stessels came to the United States to study and never left. They had two daughters, and Zahava earned a BA from Brooklyn College, a master's in library science from Queens College, and later a PhD in history from New York University. She retired from the New York Public Library after fifteen years. Meier, who had studied the art of hand weaving in Hungary, cofounded Knitwaves, Inc., a company that specializes in children's sweaters. Erzsike, who married a sabra in 1953, studied nursing at Rambam Hospital in Haifa where today she is head nurse in the emergency room. The sisters remain close, talking each week by telephone and visiting at least once a year.

Betrayal and Heroism

IRENE FRISCH
(b. 1931, Poland)

I was a chubby, clumsy child, precocious and serious, and I wore glasses. I knew early on that I was not as beautiful as my tall long-legged sister, who had dark eyes and long thick braids. She was elegant and self-assured, the kind of child one enjoys showing off. Yet this never bothered me. I often hear tales of sibling rivalry, especially among sisters. Yet I was never jealous. I adored Pola, even bragged about her to others. When I grew older and went to school, my sentences would often begin: "My sister—" This was a standing joke among my friends.

My brother's name was Ludwik, but we called him Lusiek. The first born, the only boy, he was the family's favorite. He was tall and husky at a time when children were supposed to be chubby. He had thick black hair and dark eyes, was always ready with a joke or prank, and always had a candy or a little gift in his pocket for me. He was an ideal big brother. He would fight with my sister, Pola, but served as my protector, so that no one dared harm me. He played football and other sports but often took me along to watch his games. He dreamed of owning a bicycle, but

151

our parents, fearful he would injure himself, refused him this one privilege. And so he often borrowed a bike from a friend behind our parents' backs.

Pola, Lusiek, and I grew up in a small town in Poland called Drohobycz. Ours was an interesting town with an almost cosmopolitan flavor. Three nationalities lived there: Poles, Ukrainians, and Jews. The town's history contributed to its unique and diverse culture. In the mid-nineteenth century oil was discovered in Drohobycz. By 1872 the railroad had come through town, and Drohobycz became a Polish Klondike. People arrived in pursuit of work and money. By 1900 the population exceeded 20,000; by the time I was born in 1931, the town had more than 32,000 residents. At the start of World War II there were 45,000 people, 40 percent of whom were Jews.

The unexpected oil-related riches of Drohobycz led to some extravagant episodes. Men suddenly left their wives for younger, prettier women; older married women took handsome young boyfriends; people traveled abroad. Even today you can still see signs of the town's prewar wealth. Amid run-down neglected neighborhoods stand small palaces and large lavish apartment houses. Drohobycz also had a good deal of poverty in the 1930s.

My father prospered as a fur merchant and moved our family three times, each time to successively better quarters. Our last move was to a lavish custom-built single-family home. The entrance hall was larger than the living room, creating the grand style that my father loved. He was well traveled, spoke many languages, and was extremely self-assured. He told the most interesting stories, mostly from his own experiences, always captivating his audience. This talent may have saved his life during the war. At one point he escaped from a local work camp and hid in the woods. A Gentile peasant found him hiding among the trees. The peasant grew enchanted with my father's stories. He brought my father into his home and hid him for a time, without payment, sharing his family's scant food and resources. In exchange, Father entertained him with his many tales.

Mother was different. Tall, good-looking, and elegant, she was also quiet and modest. She never gossiped or told stories, and she had very few friends. She was charitable, in a modest, anonymous way, calling little attention to herself. For example, winters in Drohobycz were severe, and many people could not afford warm clothing. Each year our school appealed to affluent parents to donate heavy coats, sweaters, shoes, etc. for the needy. Teachers distributed the clothing to poorer children, while the rest of us looked on. Mother also clothed the needy but in a different way. She sent our nanny, Frania, to school with a bag of clothes and instructed her to find a needy child during recess. Then she was to discreetly dress the child in the bathroom so that others would not see. Later, when I saw other children, sometimes friends, wearing my dresses and coats, I pretended not to notice. In all, I spent my early childhood in Drohobycz, privileged and surrounded by a loving family and friends.

Frania was always a part of my family. One day long before my birth my mother, then a young housewife, took her baby son, Lusiek, for a walk in his stroller. On her way to the park she was stopped by a teenage peasant girl, who gushed over the baby and asked to play with him. The girl was about fifteen and had two long blond braids, smiling blue eyes, and a perky nose. She was barefoot; her only pair of shoes were tied together and hung over her shoulder, as shoes were to be saved and not worn. In her hand she carried a colorful kerchief tied around a bundle containing all her possessions. "My name is Frania," the girl explained. She had come to town in search of a job with a household. As she spoke with my mother, she shook Lusiek's rattle, made faces, and cooed at him. She was clearly smitten. Mother, generally not one to make hasty decisions, hired Frania as a nanny and took her home that day.

Mother soon learned that Frania had lost her father when she was five. Her mother, a poor farmer and widow, had been left with little land and many children. The children began working at an early age. Frania took her first job at the age of six, tending the geese of a wealthy farmer. She had no formal education but was observant, gifted with both natural intelligence and common sense. So she was a capable young woman, well equipped to deal with any situation.

Frania remained in our household for the arrival of my sister, Pola, and then me. Frania was always jolly, always ready for a joke or a laugh. She was completely absorbed with our household and had no desire to marry, have children of her own, or leave our home. We were her substitute children.

Mother was fond of Frania and, thinking of her best interests, eventually convinced Frania to marry. Mother was practical. She reminded Frania that we would eventually grow up and depart, leaving Frania alone and without a family of her own. Although Frania may not have been romantically inclined, she did not lack suitors. In fact, she was popular within her little social circle of housekeepers, nannies, and superintendents. She had a good steady job and substantial savings and was therefore a good catch. And so, in 1939, shortly before the war began, Frania married a nice, decent, hardworking man. Although I remember attending the wedding, I remember few details. It was a modest affair, with members of Frania's family and a few friends. After the wedding Frania moved out, and her younger sister, Marysia, took over her job of caring for us. Even so, Frania continued to visit us almost daily, to make sure that all was in order.

In 1939 the war began and our entire existence was altered. Father was drafted into the Polish army, our town was bombed, and our house was in danger. We moved in temporarily with relatives in a nearby town, farther from the fighting. One night in September 1939 Lusiek and Marysia went out to buy some cold cuts. After eating, they went to watch the German army enter our town. They were caught in the rain and returned soaked. Lusiek developed a fever, and we could not find a physician or proper medication.

By the time Father returned, the Germans had conquered Poland and had given our town to the Russians. The Russian army promptly confiscated Father's store, house, and money and most of our possessions, and ordered all Jews—now labeled "undesirable elements"—to leave town. But we stayed.

Irene's parents, Israel and Sara Bienstock, in Poland in 1939.

By the end of the month Lusiek was still sick but seemed to be improving. One doctor diagnosed food poisoning, another pneumonia. Pola and I returned to school, while Lusiek stayed home in bed. When I came home, Lusiek was in good spirits and even asked me to invite his friend over to talk about school. Marysia scrubbed the floor and joked with him. Suddenly, he said he did not feel well, and he was gone in a second. We never knew the precise cause of his death, but I suspect it was heart failure. It was October 1, 1939. Marysia summoned Mother from another room. I can still hear Mother screaming like a wounded animal, and I can still see Lusiek, thirteen and a half years old, wearing white pajamas with thin multicolored stripes. Within minutes our house was filled with people, including doctors. No one spoke. Pola and I were taken to a neighbor's home. Our world had fallen apart.

Pola and I did not attend the funeral. Our parents were devastated. Mother could not endure the loss, and no help was available, if indeed such help ever exists. Mother and Father often spoke of Lusiek, of the bicycle that they had denied him, of the education he would have completed, the profession he would have chosen. Pola and I quickly learned to hide our grief. I did not fully comprehend the permanence of death, and I would often run to the door, expecting Lusiek to return.

On my ninth birthday, shortly after Lusiek's death, I desperately wanted a party but did not dare tell my grieving parents. Pola solved my problem: she organized a party, serving refreshments to my friends and me through an open window while we played outside. Our mother never knew of this celebration.

In June 1941 the Germans occupied our town in place of the Russians. At first we were happy with the change. Father knew Germany, having traveled there often on business. He considered the Germans cultured and civilized, unlike the barbaric Russians. Our perception changed quickly, however, with the first pogrom. The Germans encouraged our Gentile friends and neighbors to wage an all-out attack on all Jews, to do with the Jews whatever they pleased. And the local Poles and Ukrainians complied. Within twenty-four hours friends and neighbors killed and maimed countless Jews and looted their houses. My family survived by seeking shelter at the home of an aunt's neighbor in a nearby town. We hid in her attic and, in exchange, my father paid her handsomely. Still, we were badly shaken.

When the pogrom subsided, we returned to Drohobycz. Our house was now empty. However, we were joined by three other Jewish families who had been forced by the Germans to evacuate their homes. Every day Germans and Ukrainians entered our home, removing possessions as they pleased. Every few months they rounded up Jews to work at menial jobs or to be killed.

In December 1942 there was a monthlong action, that is, an attack on the remaining Jews in Drohobycz. Many older people and children were killed. Father could work. Pola was tall and looked older than her age, so Father secured the necessary (that is, forged) work papers for her and found her a job. Therefore, they were not in imminent danger. However, Mother and I were at risk. Mother, who was in her early forties, had aged since Lusiek's death. I was young and looked my age. Appreciating our danger, Father hid us in the cellar of a building where he now worked. Despite his efforts, we were all caught after several weeks, and Mother was even injured by a Nazi bullet. Yet by some miracle the Gestapo set us free, and we returned to the Jewish ghetto of Drohobycz.

Near the end of December 1942, Frania came and took me to her apartment in a different section of town. Her husband had been drafted into the Russian army in 1941. I do not believe that she missed him, for her marriage seemed to have been more my mother's idea than hers. She never heard from her husband again.

Frania was poor, but she shared with me what little she had. Her apartment was small, one room and one small kitchen. It was originally part of a larger apartment that had been divided into two separate units. I lived with Frania for a few months, hiding alone, waiting for her to return after her long days at work to feed me and keep me company. This was a difficult time for me. I was afraid, I missed my family, and I worried about them. Even so, it never occurred to me to complain. I was a child, but children matured quickly at that time.

In the summer of 1943 the Jewish ghetto of Drohobycz was liquidated; Jews were killed or rounded up for concentration camps. In the confusion my parents

Franciszka Sobkowa
(Frania), the Christian
woman who saved
Irene's life.

and sister escaped. Somehow, my mother and Pola joined me in Frania's apartment. There was no space in Frania's small apartment for my father, so he hid in nearby woods. He was sheltered for some time by the peasant who enjoyed his interesting stories. Eventually, however, Father grew restless and wandered away from his safe haven for one night. He was immediately apprehended and taken from one concentration camp to another, posing and working as a gardener, an auto mechanic, a tailor, and in other trades.

Most of the time Pola and I hid under a bed. Since Frania worked every day, leaving her apartment early in the morning and returning late at night, we were not allowed to move, lest someone hear our movements while Frania was at work and suspect our presence. We were instructed to be quiet, like mice. And so we lay under the bed, whispering, without books, radio, or other distractions. Pola made up stories to entertain me. At night she slept with our mother, while Frania and I shared a bed.

In all, we lived with Frania for more than two years. We were scared. We knew or assumed that Father and most of our family and friends were dead and that we might join them at any moment. Now and then we heard of Jews who had been caught and killed along with their Gentile rescuers. This was done in public, in the middle of town, to warn other rescuers of their fate. Although she knew the risk that she took by harboring us, Frania's deep-rooted Catholic faith and her love for us compelled her to act on our behalf. I was too young at the time to realize it, but she must have been scared, as well as hungry, all the time. She assumed responsibility for three lives in addition to her own, and she shared with three others food intended for only one. Recently, someone heard my story and remarked that Frania was sent to us from heaven. This had never occurred to me before, but it must be true.

At the end of the war we were liberated by the Russian army. Mother, Pola, and I left the hiding place. Because of the political arrangements made at Yalta, we were evacuated from Drohobycz, which was transferred to Ukraine, and taken to Galicia, a part of Europe that had changed hands several times but was now part of Poland again. We traveled in a railway cattle car for several weeks. One morning I awoke on the train and saw my father standing at the entrance of the car. We had heard that he had been killed in a concentration camp, and so I thought I saw a ghost. I began to scream. People gathered around me, afraid that something had happened. I cannot describe our reunion. I recall only that after my initial shock, I asked him: "What did you bring me?" This silly, inappropriate question was a remembrance of our happy prewar days when he brought gifts for Lusiek, Pola, and me upon returning from his many business trips. Even now he produced blue raincoats for Pola and me. Somehow he had learned that we would be traveling on this train and had arranged to greet us that morning.

After a few days our train stopped in Legnica, an old German city known as the site of Frederick the Great's victory over the Austrians in 1760. We were given an apartment formerly occupied by Germans who had recently escaped and, before that, probably by Jews who had not survived the war. My parents made sure that Frania, who had come with us, had an apartment in the same building. Father tried to support us by working. In all, we tried to live a normal life. But what did we know about being normal? I was fourteen, but I had spent the last five years in abnormal, wretched conditions.

Pola and I resumed our studies. We were several years behind in school, so we began to study with various tutors. Eventually, I passed the entrance examination and started attending the local high school. There were only two or three other Jewish students, and most of the students and teachers hated Jews. Still, we persevered under these conditions, and in 1949 I finished high school.

After my graduation we emigrated to Israel. I fell in love with this country and was proud of being Jewish. Yet this was a difficult time. It was hard to find an apartment, to learn a new language, to make a new life. Father—a fur merchant by trade—could not earn a living in Israel's warm climate. Eventually, he moved to Germany to ply his trade in Frankfurt am Main, hoping to use his prewar connections there. Mother and I soon followed him. Pola had married in Israel and stayed there. She became a bacteriologist, and her Warsaw-born husband became an engineer. Again, I was faced with new surroundings, a new language, and the task of making a new life, this time in the land of our recent oppressors.

In 1955, sixteen years after my brother died, Mother became very sick. When a doctor asked what was wrong, she told him that she had lost a child who was too young to die. After so many years she had never experienced closure. She died soon after. Following Mother's death, I emigrated to the United States from Legnica and moved in with my sister, Pola, who had moved with her family to Atlanta some time before. Once again, I learned a new language and began a new life.

Although Frania remained in Poland after the war, we stayed in close contact. I wrote to her of my new life and my marriage and sent packages containing food, clothing, and money. She could not write, so others wrote for her. Father remained in Frankfurt but visited us in the States. He died in Frankfurt at the age of seventy-five.

I met Eugene Frisch in New York in 1960 and we married in 1961. He had spent the war in Russia and later earned a PhD in engineering in Italy.

We raised two children: Bertrand is a lawyer in the music publishing business in Manhattan, and Sharon, a part-time lawyer, is married to Paul Korman, who works in computers. Sharon and Paul have three children. They live in West Hartford, Connecticut, send their children to a Solomon Schechter school (Conservative Hebrew day school), and are active in a second-generation group. I earned a degree in library science and worked as a medical librarian.

Throughout this period I clung to two dreams: first, I must see Frania again. Second, I must return to Drohobycz. In the mid-1970s Pola and I convinced Frania to come to America, to my home in New Jersey and then to Pola's home in Georgia. Frania lived in Poland under Communist rule, and her trip required complicated arrangements and great efforts. Still, she came. At the airport we recognized each other immediately, although we had all changed drastically since our last meeting some twenty years earlier.

Frania brought gifts for my family, good humor and spirits, and her extraordinary cooking skills. I took her shopping despite her objections that I must not spend on her because I would deprive my family. After she cooked many of my favorite dishes and filled my freezer with provisions to last long after her departure, she embroidered a tablecloth for my home. Then she went to visit Pola in Atlanta. The highlight of her trip—aside from visiting Pola and me—was her visit to St. Patrick's Cathedral in New York City. Although the United States has many tourist attractions, Frania's desires and interests remained simple.

A short time later Frania's niece, Genia, who was living with Frania, wrote us of Frania's death and sent photographs of the wake and funeral. Frania's death left

Irene and Eugene Frisch on their twenty-fifth wedding anniversary, Teaneck, New Jersey, 1986.

a void in my life that I have attempted to fill by sending money and packages to Genia and her family.

Visiting Drohobycz and realizing my second dream was not so easy. Several years ago I traveled to Europe and stopped in Poland. I stood in line at the Russian consulate, hoping to gain a visa to visit Drohobycz. When my efforts failed, I left, disappointed.

In 2000 Genia invited me to her daughter's wedding. How time flies! I still remember Genia's father, Frania's brother, as a dashing young soldier in 1939. Without thinking, I quickly wrote to congratulate Genia and to accept her invitation. I had an ulterior motive: the wedding would take place in a town not far from Drohobycz. Since Drohobycz now belonged to Ukraine and unrestricted travel was possible, I saw before me an opportunity to visit my hometown.

I was excited but also scared to return there. I remembered the Gentiles' cruelty and had witnessed their hateful actions toward the Jews. So I asked that Genia or her husband accompany me on my visit to Drohobycz. Genia's next letter included detailed plans for the wedding, photographs of the young couple and both sets of parents, and her promise that she or her husband would take me to Drohobycz.

The next morning I stood in line at the Ukrainian consulate in New York, hoping to obtain a visa. I was surrounded by an assortment of people: Poles, Russians, and Ukrainians who wished to visit their families, and Hasidic Jews who wished to visit the graves of important rabbis. The clerk who asked me the reason for my visit to Drohobycz was puzzled by my answer. I could not provide the name of any person I wished to visit. When I explained that I had sentimental reasons, he repeated my story to a coworker. They both stared at me as if I were crazy. Nonetheless, they accepted my visa application and sent me home to wait for my papers.

My passport and visa arrived two weeks later. After years of insisting that he had no wish to travel to Poland, Eugene—who is also from Poland and also survived the war under horrific circumstances—suddenly decided to join me on my trip. He planned to attend the wedding and then tour Warsaw. But he would not travel to Drohobycz or to any area near his hometown, which was not far from Drohobycz. He had lost many relatives during the war and claimed that going back would break his heart.

Our first stop was Warsaw—Varsovia—the capital city of Poland. The last time I saw Warsaw was in 1949, just before my family moved to Israel. The city had been bombed and destroyed. One could walk for miles without seeing an intact building. Now we looked out upon a beautiful rebuilt city. As we toured the city, I recalled the exciting stories that my parents had told me after each visit to Warsaw before the war and the many stories that I had read about Jewish artists and writers from Warsaw.

One day, as my husband and I strolled through the city, we spotted a man selling small hand-carved wooden figurines. He was the proud artist. Physically, he was ugly. As we approached his stand, we saw that his collection consisted of ugly caricatures of Jewish characters: a shoemaker, a baker, a tailor, and so on, all displaying long hooked noses, oversized ears, large outstretched greedy hands. This was exactly how the Germans had depicted the Jews in *Der Stürmer,* a propaganda paper. I purchased a figurine of an ugly Jew holding a bag on which was printed a dollar sign. I then asked the man: "Where can one see a Jew like this?" Then I added: "Look at my husband—he is Jewish." Eugene is blond, blue-eyed, and has handsome, classic features. In fact, he is the Aryan prototype. The artist, without blinking an eye, answered: "Some Jews gave their family pictures to my parents to hide during the war and never returned to claim them. I have looked at those pictures, and this is how I saw the people." I saw no point in arguing.

After Warsaw we boarded a train to our next destination, the wedding in Legnica. Genia's husband, Peter, greeted us at the train station and took us directly to the church. I immediately recognized Genia. Genia and Peter were an attractive, nice couple with two beautiful daughters. They gave us a royal reception, included us in the wedding preparations, and invited us to numerous events. The ceremony took place in a beautiful old church, not far from where I completed high school in 1949. After the ceremony a caravan of cars left for a small town in the mountains. We took over an entire hotel for two days. Guests celebrated late into the night and awoke the next morning to the smell of pigs roasting, the sound of vodka flowing, and a sunny day. Music played nonstop for two days. Although Genia and probably some others knew of my connection to Frania and the circumstances of my survival during the war, that subject—in fact, the war itself—never came up during our entire visit.

After the wedding I began making preparations for my visit to Drohobycz. Peter and I would travel first by train, then by bus, while Eugene remained with Genia and her family. I traveled lightly, removing my jewelry and attempting to blend in with the local crowd. We arrived in Drohobycz at about noon on the second day of our trip. After checking in at our hotel, which was shabby and dirty, and freshening up, we hailed a taxi and headed for my childhood home, on Zupna Street.

The taxi stopped in front of a house, only it did not look like my family's home. This house was painted a dark shade; our little garden was gone, replaced by weeds; our red fence was missing; our beautiful entrance had been replaced with an ugly, plain door. When I went around to the back of this building, I saw two more doors, one with a terrace. The doors and terrace were not part of my family's home. In short, this house was not recognizable to me. An older man and a little boy, his grandson, came out of the house. I told them, in Ukrainian, that I had lived in this house as a child and would like to enter. The man informed me that his family had purchased the house from the city and now lived there. He was polite and admitted us into the house.

I saw that the house was now divided into three apartments. The beautiful, grand entrance hall that my father had been so proud of was now gone. None of the rooms looked like the rooms in my memory. I entered the room where my brother, Lusiek, had died more than sixty years before. I was bewildered at my detachment, that I felt nothing. As I walked from room to room, I continued to feel nothing.

I walked out of the house. The taxi was still there, and a small group of people was waiting outside. It is not every day that a taxi appears on Zupna Street. Peter was talking to the neighbors, probably telling them my story. For me it was like a dream. I inquired about long-ago neighbors. There was no one. The Russians have a way of relocating people, and all the current inhabitants had come from different parts of Ukraine in the fifties. At one time many years ago several houses had surrounded a large courtyard. It had all belonged to my grandfather, who lived in one multifamily house. The house where I was born and lived until I was about three was now dilapidated.

It was already afternoon. Peter and I inquired about a place to eat. The driver took us to a restaurant only two or three blocks away. It had once been an apartment house with two or three stories. My father and his friends had spent many afternoons in a beautiful garden there, playing cards in a gazebo. The place was very familiar to me, but now only one side wall was standing. It still had balconies, but I did not understand what happened to the rest. Now there was attached a long hall with a terrace and it housed a restaurant, very unusual and primitive.

After lunch we toured the city. Although more than half a century had passed since I left, I knew the city by heart. Here I found places where we used to live before moving to our house and places where my close friends lived, my school, Father's store, and, finally, without any hesitation, the building where Frania lived and where we had hidden. We went and left at night because Frania did not want her neighbors to know that she had been saving Jews. I looked at the window where I had so often stood behind a curtain, looking outside, envying the rabbits, cats, and dogs their freedom.

One of Frania's neighbors, an old maid during the war, had been in the habit of shaking out every part of her wardrobe. Since we had nothing else to do, we observed the habits of the neighbors from behind the curtain. We secretly gave the woman a nickname, The Shaker. As I stood in front of the house, the same window opened and a hand with a white rug appeared. Someone was shaking the white rug.

After this we drove to the outskirts of the town, to a small forest where the Germans had murdered and buried many Jews. The place is called Bronica. My cousin, who was one year older than I and who had the same first and last name, was killed and buried there with her mother. She was a lovely child, eleven or twelve at the time of her death. Many of my friends and neighbors are also buried there. I said a silent prayer for them.

About six years earlier survivors from my hometown had made a pilgrimage to that burial ground. They came from different parts of the world. Somebody dear to each of them was buried there. They put up a large monument, and the mayor gave a beautiful speech. Someone videotaped it, and I got a copy. Now the monument was desecrated, filled with garbage, and torn. I was heartbroken. I did not want to linger any longer in Drohobycz. We hired another taxi and left.

For years I could not speak openly of my experiences during the war, but I often dreamed of being pursued by Nazis: running, hiding, running out of hiding places, and other horrors. Recently, I have begun to talk and write short stories relating my experiences. At the same time I have noticed that my bad dreams occur less frequently. Perhaps my openness has had beneficial effects.

During the war I witnessed and experienced many of the atrocities that have come to be called the "Holocaust": the murders of people dear to me, the cruelty of German soldiers, and betrayal by good friends and neighbors. However, I also witnessed and experienced the kindness of a simple uneducated woman who risked her life in order to save mine. Frania was a member of our household for fourteen years. She was devoted to us and was convinced that we, her substitute children, were the smartest and the most special. A devout Catholic, she instilled in us her faith and fear of G-d, even though we did not share her precise faith. In her own simple way she taught us right from wrong. Her values were high and her code of ethics strong, supported by tales of her youth, and, more important, demonstrated by her selfless acts during the war.

The shelves of American libraries and bookstores are filled with books, movies, and articles about the Holocaust. There is no need for one more story of survival. Yet the story of Frania, the simple Catholic woman who saved our lives while risking her own, has not been written. Without this book her story would surely be forgotten.

Life, Death, and Angels

RENÉE GLASSNER
(b. 1931, Poland)

On the thirtieth of July 1948 I arrived in the United States. I was sixteen years old. On my back I carried a knapsack with my only possessions. With me were my parents, my older brother, Berel (Berko in Polish, Dov in Hebrew, later David), and younger brother, Itzek (later Irving). I considered myself very lucky to have survived the Holocaust with my immediate family intact.

As I was passing through customs and immigration in New York, an official asked me to open my knapsack so he could inspect the contents. Out came a stack of books, including Dante's *Divine Comedy* in Italian. "Is that all you have?" he asked. "Yes," I responded proudly. He waved me on and called out: "Welcome to America!"

I was born and raised in a small town called Łosice, in eastern Poland, about seventy-five miles east of Warsaw, between Siedlce and the Bug River. In 1939 Łosice had about eight thousand inhabitants, six thousand of whom were Jews.

Jews had lived there for more than four hundred years. My paternal grandfather, Shlomo, and his seven sons carried as their last name the name of the town, so my father was known as Yankel Łosice of Łosice. My mother also came from a large family—she had two sisters and five brothers. Three of the siblings and their families, as well as Grandpa Mendel Perelmuter, my maternal grandfather, and his second wife, lived in a big three-story house that Grandpa had built around 1912. On one side it faced the main square, where important events took place, such as the regular Wednesday market. Around the corner was the main entrance, which had wide cement steps and faced Polinowa Street. It had a big gate that opened to an inner yard in which were storage rooms, a cowshed, and outhouses. The house, like the others in town, had no running water. My immediate family—my mother, Anna (whose Yiddish name was Henia); father, Jacob (Yankel); brothers Berel and Itzek; and I, Rivkah (Rywka or Renia in Polish)—occupied an apartment on the second floor.

I enjoyed my large extended family of uncles, aunts, cousins, and grandparents. We didn't live far from each other and we visited each other often, especially on the Jewish holidays. I had lots of friends, both Jewish and Gentile, and was never lonely. I attended three schools: the Polish public school, the Yiddish school, and for a short time the local Beth Yaakov (a Hebrew religious school for girls). I liked all my schools and was a good student. Sometimes, however, it was a bit dangerous for us Jewish kids to venture outside the Jewish section of town because Gentile youths would throw stones at us, calling out "Żyd, Żyd" (Jew, Jew).

We learned very early in life about Polish anti-Semitism. The schools allowed corporal punishment at the time, for example, and somehow we Jewish children suffered more than the others. In spite of all that, I was proud of my Polish heritage and strived to be like my schoolmates. I also loved my Jewish studies and never lost track of my Jewish identity. For me the two cultures were not exclusive. I knew my place in each situation and functioned well.

The first seven years of my life in Łosice were happy indeed. I was fortunate to have a family of means. Dad dealt in grain and other agricultural products and was doing well, but he came from a poor family and had little education. When he was thirteen, he bought sacks of potatoes wholesale and hauled them on his back to the open market, where he sold them at retail. He had a pleasant disposition and was well liked by both Polish Gentiles and Jews. He would rather have owned farmland and been a farmer, but Jews were forbidden to own agricultural land. Few other Jews in town fared as well as we did. The town had lots of shoemakers, tailors, shopkeepers, seamstresses, and others who barely scraped together a living. There were even Jewish beggars going from house to house, asking for food and money. Yet nobody went hungry in my town. The Jews of Łosice looked out for each other.

This all changed on September 1, 1939, when Germany invaded Poland. It was indeed a blitzkrieg (German for "lightning war"). Łosice was burning. Our beautiful synagogue, the pride and joy of our Jewish community, was burned to the ground, and most of the damage was done in the Jewish section of the town. The Polish Catholic church, which was much more prominent, with its high steeple and cross, was never touched.

There was lots of confusion as to who was really going to occupy our town. At first we were occupied by the Germans, then the Soviet army arrived, and red flags were flying all over. Finally, the Germans came back and stayed. During those few weeks of uncertainty, people, especially Jews, were going back and forth across the Bug River, not far to the east. They couldn't decide which side was the lesser evil. Most Jews, however, including my immediate family, stayed on the German side.

At the end of September 1939, my older brother and I returned to the public school. But when we arrived there, the teachers yelled at us to run home. "No school for Jewish kids," they said. We ran home crying. Mother consoled us by saying that we would study at home with tutors, but soon we weren't even allowed to do that. We had to hide our books under the beds and lock the doors when we were doing our lessons. Once, when we rebelled against so much learning while many other Jewish kids seemed to enjoy a permanent vacation, she lectured us, saying, "Remember that some day the Germans might take everything away from you, but whatever is in your mind will remain."

In June 1941, when the Germans invaded the Soviet Union, a ghetto was formed in Łosice. The six thousand Jews were crammed into four blocks. In addition, about two thousand Jews from other towns were forced into our ghetto. At one point seventeen people lived in our three-room apartment. Living conditions worsened day by day. Many of the healthy young people had already been taken away to labor camps, to work assignments around town, or other places. Many never returned and were never heard from. The town was full of tattered beggars. Dead people were carried out to the cemetery daily. An epidemic of typhus broke out, and my little brother, Itzek, contracted the disease after he led a group of his hungry friends to a garbage dump to get food. We all feared the worst, but he miraculously survived.

There were selections, beatings, torture, and random shootings. One morning, as I was looking out from our living room window, I saw a lineup of men and boys in the town square. Armed German and unarmed Jewish guards kept watch. I noticed that my older brother, Berel (who was about thirteen), was in the group. I ran to my father and yelled to him to get Berel. Dad, startled and bewildered, ran down the stairs to the square and, like a maniac, began to pull Berel out of the lineup. For a while I watched as my father pulled his son in one direction while a German was dragging him the other way. Then, all of a sudden, the German let go of my brother's hand, and both my dad and brother ran home.

One night a number of elderly Jews, my grandpa Shlomo among them, were dragged out of their homes. They were beaten and their beards were pulled. They had to dig a deep ditch, perhaps eight feet long and five feet wide. First, the Germans teased and made sport of the victims; it was their evening's diversion. Then they let vicious dogs into the pit and forced the old men to jump over the open ditch one by one. Those who did not make it were horribly mauled. Grandpa made it, at least this time.

August 22, 1942. I woke up early that Saturday morning. I heard shots. I looked outside and saw dead bodies strewn about. German soldiers stood guard in the four corners of the square. Soon people in my building were in an uproar, running up and down the stairs between the cellar and the third-floor attic. Soon the whole town was yelling and screaming and calling to their dear ones. Germans with trained search dogs started running into the Jewish homes, ordering everyone out into the square. My parents ordered the three of us kids to crawl into the attic hiding place where, in happier days, we used to play hide-and-seek. But now twenty-seven people were piled into the attic, including the five members of my immediate family and the five members of my cousin Oscar's immediate family. Oscar Pinkus was about twenty, stalwart and brave. We kids especially looked up to him because of his relatively good education. He was one of the few Jews in town who believed the rumors of Nazi atrocities.

The attic hiding place was hot and cramped. Unsure what to do, some people ran in and out. But then Oscar took charge and said, "In or out and that's it." He locked the attic door and everyone was quiet. Outside the noise was slowly diminishing. Finally, the town fell silent. The Gentiles stayed still in their homes. It seemed as if all the gods all over the world had taken the day off. The Jewish community of Łosice, my beloved town for nearly eleven years, was no more.

We were now trapped in the heat and darkness of our cell. Several times Germans searched the house, but we were not discovered. Night fell and some people even fell asleep. But the next day we had to deal with basic human needs such as water, food, and lack of toilets. My mother and a few other brave individuals risked their lives, scouring the whole building for food and water, while German guards stood watch downstairs. When the Mordkowicz family of four left, they were all caught on the street, and the younger son was shot and left to die. We heard his groaning until he was killed by a German gendarme.

It was now the fourth day in hiding. We stared at each other, hollow-eyed, like ghosts. My mother decided that Berel and I, who were blond and looked Polish, had a good chance to sneak through the streets of Łosice. We cried and begged her not to send us out alone, but she was firm. She literally pushed us out through the small door, gave us some money, and said, "Go, get some water, water—"

Out on the street I held on to my big brother's hand. As our parents had instructed, we walked straight to the village of Swiniarów, to the home of a Polish peasant who was a good friend of my father's. When the peasant woman opened the door, she crossed herself and mumbled in astonishment, "You are alive? What are you doing here? Where are your parents?" "Water, water!" we cried and begged. She came out with a big pitcher of water, and we guzzled it down quickly. We told her that our parents were still hidden, that we needed temporary shelter, and that our parents would soon come to get us. She started yelling, "No, get away from here—run, fast!" Berel and I froze in horror. Then the woman said to me: "Rywka, you are not going to live anyway. Let me have your gold earrings." My brother grabbed my hand, and we ran toward the potato fields and hid there by stretching out on the ground.

When night fell, we started back to the ghetto. We stopped at a former teacher's home and begged him for shelter, but he refused us. One kind woman ran home and brought us a sandwich. Suddenly, a young Polish boy spotted us and started yelling "Jew and Jewess!" We started to run, then heard someone shout, "Stop or I'll shoot!" We stopped and put our hands up. When we turned around, we saw a Polish policeman pointing a rifle at us. We pleaded with him to let us go, but he led us to the Polish police station, where another policeman telephoned German headquarters and was told to take us to jail. We were then marched off with a revolver pointed at us from behind. I whispered to Berel that we should run in opposite directions so one of us might reach safety, but he rejected the idea and held my hand tightly.

We were led through the big iron gate of the jail and upstairs to a second-floor cell; the long steel bar outside the door was locked. We were doomed and we knew it. We both cried for Mommy and Daddy but agreed not to reveal their hiding place to anyone, even if the Germans tortured us. We spent two nights in jail. During the second night we awoke to approaching German voices and barking dogs. Downstairs the doors opened, and we heard people yelling, "We are not Jews, we are not Jews, they are upstairs, up, up." Two Polish kids, jailed for looting, were crying and begging as they were dragged outside by the Germans, who did not understand Polish. We heard two shots. The Germans and dogs left, and then there was silence. The two of us still stood at the door, numbed with disbelief.

Thursday morning, August 27. Three adult Jews were thrown into our cell. They told horror stories about the evacuation of the previous Saturday, but they also brought a glimmer of hope. Indeed, later that morning we were taken out of jail and marched to a newly formed small ghetto. There we found the Mordkowiczes, the family whose son had been shot while we were hiding in the attic. They had news about our parents and others: For a hefty bribe a Polish policeman—a friend of our father's—had led most of the group out of town the night that we had been thrown into jail. Berel and I were ecstatic. We now were sure that our parents would search until they found us. The sad news was that German guards had discovered two of our elderly aunts and an elderly uncle—Rabbi Yaakov Shejnkind—who were too feeble to venture out, and shot them inside the house.

Life in the small ghetto became routine. Of eight thousand Jews (including those from other towns), we were now a scant 150 or so. At first Polish or German guards were posted at each side of the ghetto block, but later on they left it unguarded because Jews had nowhere to run. No one wanted or dared to hide us. The Germans executed many who helped or hid a Jew. On the other hand, rarely could a German recognize a Jew outside the ghetto, unless someone denounced the Jew.

So days went by with most of us working at various chores in and outside the ghetto. One time I was working in a big warehouse, folding clothes that Jews had left behind, and I bent down to pick up some photographs. Suddenly, I felt a stinging pain on my thin legs. I looked up and a tall, red-faced German gendarme was facing me with a long whip. I felt outraged and humiliated. How could such a big brute pick on such a little, scrawny, defenseless child?

One morning a young man on a bicycle came to fetch me and Berel to take us to our parents and Itzek. He said that our father had been searching for us all over. At first I did not want to leave without Berel, who was working elsewhere, but Mrs. Mordkowicz convinced me to go. When we got to my family, hidden in a hayloft, there was lots of hugging and crying.

By the fall of 1942 we had firsthand accounts from people who had escaped from the death camp at Treblinka. They related the gruesome details of the mass murders. They said that few of our people from Łosice, perhaps five hundred, actually arrived at the camp. Most perished on the way to the train in Siedlce or in the hot wagons that lacked air or water. My uncle David was shot on the way to the railway station while he was trying to fetch water for his three-year-old daughter. Others were beaten to death, and some were taken to temporary forced labor such as clearing out dead bodies. The rest were gassed.

My father and my cousin Oscar became determined to find places for us to hide. This was no easy task. To our surprise, however, Jurek, the same policeman who had thrown me and my brother into jail, now agreed to take me into his home and hide me. My father gave him some money, and on November 9, 1942, my father walked me to Jurek's house. My dad pointed to the door and said, "Go." I obeyed and never looked back.

Marysia, the policeman's wife, received me in the kitchen. I went past the dining room, into the bedroom, and then into my place of hiding, a wooden wardrobe (armoire), a closetlike piece of furniture with two doors that opened from the middle outward. There I sat until nightfall, when the woman opened one door and said I could come out quietly into the bedroom, where she gave me a hot meal.

On November 17 most of the family went into hiding. Mother, Berel, and four members of the Pinkus family hid in a pit that they had dug under an animal shed. A poor farmer in the village of Koszelówka had agreed to a deal in which he would receive a large sum of money each month. Another farmer nearby, named Sylczuk, took Itzek in. He was to stay mostly outside the house, visible from their hiding place, in a haystack in the fields. This farmer helped out of the goodness of his heart and as a favor to a Jewish friend. He accepted only modest compensation. Manya, Oscar's older sister, was to work for another farmer and pose as a Christian. Father stayed on for a while longer in Łosice in order to gather money to pay for the underground shelter. He almost got deported on November 27 when the final liquidation of the small ghetto took place. Miraculously, he happened to be outside the ghetto when it was surrounded and was able to escape from town. He managed to reach the family's hideout.

But November 27, 1942, was not just another day of genocide for me. I had

Renée and her younger brother, Irving, in a potato field within the ghetto of Łosice, Poland, ca. July 1941. Note the barbed-wire fence between them and the farmhouses in the background.

survived liquidations in nearby Konstantinów in late September and Łosice in late August, but now I was hidden safely. In fact, my protector was out there, helping the SS round up the last Jews of Łosice. I peeked out a window and could see some people trying to escape by climbing over a high wooden fence. But very close to my window, hidden from his victims, was an infamous German gendarme who was so cruel that he was called sarcastically Sheyna Lea (Pretty Leah). He was carefully aiming his revolver at the people on the fence and picking them off with great enthusiasm. I still remember a woman in a long coat that he killed. Her coat snagged on the fence, but her lifeless body fell to the ground. I watched this horrible scene transfixed but numbed, utterly helpless. I was barely eleven years old.

For more than sixty years I have often had flashbacks to that dreadful experience but have kept it bottled up inside me. Unlike some other survivors, I have never felt guilty about surviving, but suddenly one night in September 2003, as I was revising this narrative, I had a terrible attack of guilt. I called my husband. He came immediately and I broke down completely. "I did nothing to stop him. I just stood there," I yelled. "I could have clubbed him, kicked him, something!" I cried and cried and my husband could not console me. "Oh, God! Oh, God! Why? Why?" I sat down on the bed and cried until there were no more tears. Later that night, alone, I pleaded silently with God to deliver that murderer to me so I might wring his neck.

Christmas Eve 1942 was a beautiful event for me. My protective "mother," Marysia, closed all the blinds and allowed me into the dining room. Dinner was a real feast. We ate and sang late into the night. For a while I allowed myself to get lost in a world of Christian fantasy. How nice it was to be part of a home, a real family, full of joy, laughter, and good food.

But January and February 1943 were cold and grim inside and outside the house. At night I heard the policeman talking to his wife about his possible transfer to another city. What should they do with me? Only one solution, they agreed. Jurek would take me out to the cemetery and shoot me. As the days passed, we talked very little. By now I was sleeping on a cot in their bedroom, and my ears were tuned to every whisper and murmur. I never revealed what I knew of their secret plan.

One morning I opened part of the hem of my sweater and took out a beautiful shiny gold ruble. Mother had told me to use it as needed, especially when my life was in danger. Certainly this was such an occasion. Silently, I walked into the kitchen as Marysia watched me. I placed the coin on the counter of the cabinet and quickly left the room without saying a word. In the evening I heard the couple deliberating heatedly in the kitchen. A few minutes later Marysia opened the door to the darkened bedroom. She pressed the coin back into my hand and left without uttering a word.

Days passed, months passed, the routine was now the same: three meals a day, keeping clean, daydreaming inside or out of the wardrobe, occasional chores in the kitchen. I was at the total mercy of one man and his wife. But late in April 1943 there was a knock on the door. It was Wacek Szpura, the "angel farmer" with a heart of gold. Since 1942 he had been risking his life to help Jews. Rarely did he accept remuneration except for minor expenses. He once carried Itzek on his back for about seventeen miles when we were escaping the Konstantinów deportation in September 1942. And here he was—my savior! He inquired about my well-being, and I told him that my life was in danger. The policeman also convinced him that I must leave. Wacek came back a week later with a horse and wagon, and I was off to my new home.

What a reunion! It was heaven. An underground heaven, to be sure, but still heaven. I had parents, my older brother, an uncle, an aunt, and two cousins—a girl and a boy. I was truly happy. I thought the shelter was a wonderful place to be in—a clever underground pit with benches, a table that at night was lowered to the

The farmer who saved the Łosice (Gewirtzman)-Pinkus family, with two of his three daughters, in front of the shed under which they were hidden for two years. Photograph taken in the early 1950s in Koszelówka, Poland. From *The House of Ashes* by Oscar Pinkus, 1990 edition. Used by permission.

level of the benches and thus formed part of the bedding system, a kerosene lamp, and a trap door that could be opened from inside and outside and was covered with straw and caked manure, as was the whole top of the shelter. The trap door was usually propped up with a stick to let in air from the animal shed. Only I, who stood about four feet, eight inches, could stand up with my head somewhat bent down. Above us were the cow, pigs, sheep, and lambs.

After a month or so the palatial aura of the place wore off. Like everyone else, I realized how hungry I was. The farmer, though well paid, starved us. Our diet consisted of a four-ounce piece of bread each and a cup of "coffee" made from burned grain for breakfast, a cup of hot soup with perhaps a potato for lunch, and the morning menu was repeated for the evening meal.

Hygiene was a real problem. We struggled with lice and bedbugs, and sometimes we had to fight off rats. Often we had to use our one cup of water or hot "coffee" for bathing or washing our hair. For my birthday in November I craved scrambled eggs. When the farmer, Stanisław Szczerbicki, heard of my wish, he only laughed. Then my dad and I agreed that I would surrender my golden baby earrings for this special event. Szczerbicki gladly obliged. It was the best birthday I ever had.

We passed the time by inventing stories and reading books and occasional newspapers. We played cards and chess. Berel took bets on insect races. Oscar, the oldest and best educated of the four cousins, taught us reading, writing, and some arithmetic. It was a very limited education for we had no school books and little paper. Most of the time, however, we sat and dreamed. But these dreams were often interrupted by terrible news about friends who were hiding in the forest. Groups of partisans of the Armja Krajowa (Polish Home Army, also called the AK) would often raid the forest shelters and shoot the Jewish occupants. We lived in fear of these partisans; they were more of a danger to our existence than the Germans.

In the late spring of 1944 the Russians were still moving too slowly to benefit us. We were emaciated and out of money. Szczerbicki wanted to kick us out of the shelter but then changed his mind when he saw us packing. We began seeing German troops retreating to the west. What a sight! German soldiers dragging along in ragged uniforms and dirty boots, begging for water. We heard explosions from a distance. Soon airplanes with red stars instead of swastikas were screeching over our farm. They were bombing the German convoys on the nearby highway.

On July 30, 1944, we heard the voices of Russian soldiers. We stood still in disbelief. The Germans were gone. At night Szczerbicki opened wide the gate of the shed and said, "You may go now—you are safe and free." For a while no one moved. Then Father told Oscar, "Let's go and get Itzek." They left and we waited for them to come back. When we were all together, we headed out for the main road. We were going home. The moon was shining bright. It was the most beautiful night of my life.

The Russians were kind and helpful. They spotted us on the highway and gave us a lift on their trucks to our home in Łosice. Strangers were occupying our apartment, but we allowed them to stay on for another two weeks.

At first food was a problem. All our cash was gone, and we had none of our other prewar assets. We had only the clothes we wore. But because my dad was still remembered fondly by some of the townsfolk, and especially by some of the surviving Polish noblemen with large estates, he soon managed to gather some money and goods that these people owed him from before the war. In addition, one kind Polish pharmacist, who knew and respected my dad, immediately offered him five hundred zlotys (roughly $20) for food and basic necessities. The pharmacist offered more as needed, but my dad soon managed to carry the burden on his own.

We now had all the food we desired. Even the Red Army was kind enough to feed us occasionally, if we volunteered to peel potatoes for the soldiers while they were marching toward Warsaw. I enjoyed laughing with them and singing their beautiful songs, and I learned Russian fast.

We were glad that some surviving Jewish stragglers from the surrounding area had joined us; their presence made us feel more comfortable and secure. We were about forty to fifty Jewish survivors in all, of whom only sixteen were natives of Łosice. At first we were all huddling around in the evenings, relating gruesome stories of our misfortunes and losses of our loved ones. After a while, though, we would gather at night in one apartment and sing, dance, and let loose our emotions. We had decided that we had to stop the mourning. It was time to build and rebuild. We became one big family and took care of each other.

Finally, school began again in September 1944. I was nearly thirteen and allowed to enter the third grade. I didn't care. I was thrilled. I knew that I would be a good student and would catch up quickly. I spoke Polish well and the teacher, Władysław Goląbek, was quite sympathetic to my family. I felt alive, and my brain was churning and my blood was flowing. The Gentile kids were amazed at my courage and watched me carefully. They had only heard about Jews from their parents and grandparents.

One day one girl was very sad and almost in tears. She told me that the tall female teacher of English and religion had told the students not to play with me because I was a Jew. The girl told me not to worry, that she would continue to be my friend. I went home crying and complained to my mother. Mom insisted that I go back to school the very next day. Now we are equals, she said, and we will fight back. She immediately reported the incident to the Soviet administrative officer. The next day he sent a secret agent to the school who arrested the teacher and sent her off to Siberia for reeducation.

The Soviets had no sympathy for such discrimination toward people victimized by the Nazis or Polish collaborators. Furthermore, many Russian soldiers were Jewish and empathized with us. Occasionally, one would throw out a clue such as *amcha,* a Hebrew word meaning "one belonging to your people," to signal that he was Jewish and on our side. The Red Army protected us for a while, but even with that we had rocks thrown through our apartment windows. The Poles did not want us there. We were an anomaly. In fact, they did a pretty good job of killing off most of the Jews who were hiding in the forests near us. In January 1945 Poles attacked us with guns and hand grenades. One grenade almost killed Oscar. Another attack by the AK at the end of March killed thirteen Jews in Mordy, the next town west of Łosice. The next morning all remaining Jews in Łosice left and moved westward behind the Red Army. All nine members of the Łosice and Pinkus families abandoned our home in Łosice for the last time and moved to Łódź, where many Jewish refugees had gathered.

Life in Łódź was heaven. There were Jews all over the city. I remember walking around the streets, searching for people I might recognize. One nice spring day I noticed a face I knew. I yelled "Avrumche!" and he turned around. It was my cousin Avram Shejnkind from Konstantinów, the eldest son of my uncle, Rabbi Yaakov Shejnkind, and my aunt Leah, who had been shot in our building two years earlier. Avram told us that his wife had died and his child was murdered in Auschwitz.

I seemed to be the scout of the family. I so very much wanted to find my friends and relatives. Children my age were especially scarce. In one refugee hall I heard someone call my name. I turned around and saw two girls with shaved heads staring at me. They were the sisters Esther and Chana from Konstantinów. Another miracle. The Pinkus family was especially delighted to find these cousins alive. But soon the sad news they brought from Auschwitz broke their hearts. Manya, the older daughter, had been gassed there.

I was now determined to go to a high school (gymnasium). This was quite an ambition for a refugee girl in Łódź with only three grades of elementary school. I went all over town, inquiring and searching, till I saw a sign for an accelerated school especially for people who had been deprived of a proper education because of the war. I was thrilled. But the secretary asked my age and demanded documents. I had no documents and I told her I was almost fourteen. No good, she said; one must be fifteen. I walked out in tears. The next day I bought high-heeled shoes and put them on, along with makeup and lipstick, and tried again. I was accepted. Not only was I now in high school, I had an identity card! I was a real person and a student.

My secret was that I really had very little knowledge of anything that normal thirteen-year-olds should know. I had an innate ability in languages, however, and was a good listener and thus absorbed some knowledge from adults. I made a good impression on my teachers. Furthermore, I passed all the exams and received a proper certificate stating that I had finished the first year of high school.

The idea of going to Palestine intrigued me immensely. My mother was an avid Zionist and often talked about going to Palestine some day. Father was less interested in going, especially before the war. His main interest was to provide a good living for the family, which he did. But anti-Semitism was still rampant in Poland, and a Communist regime was about to take over. We had *shlichim* (emissaries) from the Jewish Brigade, Palestinians who were soldiers of the British army, who developed plans for our escape from Poland. The plan was known as the Bricha (Hebrew for escape). In April 1945 Berel and our cousin Bela were selected to join a group of youngsters leaving for Italy to board ships for Palestine.

Father had gone to Łosice with Uncle Avram Pinkus to sell our building. While there, members of the AK were looking for them to kill them. My father and uncle miraculously survived, hiding in an attic while one kind Gentile woman told the attackers that the Jews had already left. They sold the house to one of the renters. This little money in American dollars was later very useful in our escape from Poland.

A young woman from the Bricha visited our apartment in Łódź. She said that we were about to leave Poland and join Berel in Italy. We were to travel as Greeks and were not allowed to carry any papers or identification that might betray our new identities. But what about my gymnasium certificate? I pleaded and argued with her. It was my very life, the only proof that I existed and was a normal young girl with some legitimate learning. She smiled and said soothingly, "Think of Palestine, of Jews dancing and singing, Hebrew schools, lots of gymnasiums, and your certificate will be waiting for you when you arrive in this land of milk and honey." I relinquished the certificate. I never saw it again.

In September 1945 the eight of us left Łódź for good. I remember leaving Poland with mixed feelings but never looked back. When we were crossing from Poland to Czechoslovakia, Soviet guards stopped us and searched my mother for gold and jewelry. They even stripped off her underwear but did not molest her. We were terrified. But when she came out of the guardhouse, she was fully dressed, a bit pale but with a faint smile on her face. "They didn't get it," she said. Before my mother died in 1993, she left me her diamond ring. She had smuggled it out of Poland by hiding it in a condom in her vagina.

I also found out later that my dad had salvaged another big diamond by having it implanted under the crown of a tooth by a dentist in Łódź. This beautiful stone was later set into an engagement ring that my brother Dave (Berel) presented to his bride-to-be, now his wife, Lillian.

In Czechoslovakia we stopped in Bratislava, where we were met by clerks from the Jewish Agency and the United Nations Relief and Rehabilitation Administration (UNRRA). In a big hall we were fumigated, clothes and all, and fed some soup and corn on the cob. I had never eaten corn before. In Poland only cattle and pigs ate such food, but we were hungry and devoured it anyway. Then we stretched out on the floor and fell asleep, exhausted. There were thousands of us.

Cousin Avram Shejnkind had made most of the travel arrangements. He had received instructions from the emissaries from Poland and the undercover soldiers from the Jewish Brigade. We crossed the Danube by rowboat with no significant incident and entered the beautiful city of Vienna. There we were treated royally.

Our next stop was a big displaced persons camp near Linz, Austria. Here we had to separate from Cousin Avram and his new wife, who were heading westward to reunite with her surviving sister in Germany. We spent a long cold month in Linz. It was the beginning of November and we were getting impatient to reach Italy. Oscar bravely traveled out of Poland on his own because, unlike me, he would not give up his graduation certificate. He also carried his original chronicle of the war and our survival, which he had written while underground.

Now Itzek and I and the four adults of our family and some other Jewish refugees from Linz were off to the Alps. We were packed into a railway cattle wagon and helped by various emissaries from Palestine and the Jewish Brigade. It was not a pleasant trip. After a while the train slowed down and stopped. The door swung open and the bright sunlight blinded us. But what a vision! In front of us was a Catholic priest, dressed in his immaculate black-and-white outfit, with a big sack of oranges. He looked at us and yelled out, "Benvenuti a Italia!" and started hurling oranges to us. We could not believe it!

The train moved on but now our railcar was partially open, and the fresh mountain air was exhilarating. What a sight Como with its beautiful lake was! Truly breathtaking. Romantic that I was, I fell instantly in love with Italy, its mountains, its people, the priest who threw us oranges.

Our reunion with Berel was euphoric. After a long separation we were a complete family again. We swore not to separate again. Berel led us to his residence in Ostia, also known as Lido di Roma, on the coast near Rome. There we also reunited with our cousin Bela and now formed a family unit of eight. Oscar was to join us soon from Germany. We settled into a house with other Holocaust survivors whose final destination was Palestine. We became a kibbutz nucleus, and our intention was to emigrate together to the Jewish homeland, even though it was risky and illegal.

Everyone knew that the British had forbidden Jews to enter Palestine, which was still under British control. Still, we were determined to do so against all odds. What did we have to lose? We had no country in Europe to call our own, we were stripped of our possessions and our psyches, and our morale was pretty low. The difference was that we now formed one large family with a purpose.

Our unit in Ostia was called "Behazit," the name we planned to give to our kibbutz. We all worked very hard to condition ourselves for that purpose. We elected a special council and we all had civic duties, but Itzek and I had very little to do. Children at the time were so rare that we were quite spoiled. I remember fighting for my right to do some chores. I was a true kibbutznik.

We spent more than a month in Behazit, this Italian Shangri-la. We were fed well, thanks to the Hebrew Immigrant Aid Society (HIAS), UNRRA, and other groups. We explored the beautiful surroundings of Rome, rode bikes, and swam in the warm waters of the Mediterranean. Then one dark night I was awakened by Berel, who told me that we were getting ready to depart. But the guides refused to take our parents and Itzek on such a dangerous expedition. Berel and I were heartbroken, but we were not going to leave our parents and younger brother. So most of the Behazit group left clandestinely by truck to board a ship waiting for them offshore, leaving us behind.

My parents rented a room with kitchen privileges from an Italian family. The Pinkus family moved to a nearby apartment. By now they were five, because Oscar was back and Bela's boyfriend had moved in with them. My father bought used clothes and other items and sold them in Vittoria Market in Rome. He hauled goods by train and bus and with practically no knowledge of Italian managed to supplement our income. I occasionally accompanied him to the market, where we both stood and yelled, "Pantaloni americani, comprate, comprate" (American pants, buy, buy). Mother was busy with shopping, cooking, sewing, etc. In the three years we lived in Italy, she never learned to cook Italian food.

Meanwhile, our thoughts turned to America. Father started talking about his younger brother, Noah, who lived there. He remembered that the city was Albany or New York, but he had no address. It was up to Berel to contact our uncle. He wrote the following postal card:

To: Albany, N.Y. To Jewish Centr, Comitee, U.S.A. [The text read:]
To the Jewish Centre Comiette. I bag from you to send me the address of my oncle who live in Albany. His name are: Losice Noah. He have a woman and a child. In the year 1938 he came in America from Poland. I bag to send me oncle my address. It is:
    Italia Łosice Dow Kibus "Bechazit" Lido di Roma (Ostia) Viadella Vittoria 13
    D. Łosice

As we found out later, someone at the Jewish Center recognized the last name of my uncle and notified him of the card from Italy. Emotional letters flew back and forth. We now had to decide where we would settle. Do we aim for our homeland in Palestine, or do we fulfill the desperate wish of the two remaining brothers out of the original seven to reunite the two families? Either way, we knew that it would be a long wait. Frankly, I did not mind staying in Italy. In the fall of 1946 I started school in Rome, learned the language, and blended into the society very fast. In addition, in sunny Italy my hair lightened, and the Italians declared me a blonde. Wow, Hitler should have heard that!

We children made plans to reclaim our lost years of education. Berel and I found a special school for refugees in Rome, an Italian Polish high school with an accelerated curriculum. We commuted daily by train from Ostia. Itzek was enrolled in an elementary school in Ostia where most of the teachers were Catholic. He was very well accepted by everyone. In fact, he soon became a star in soccer, and at the end of the first year he received a special commendation for excelling in the Italian language. Berel and I also passed our rigorous exams at the end of the school year in June 1947. He then enrolled at the University of Rome for engineering, and I started in the fall on the second level of studies at the Istituto Minghetti for a proper *maturità* (diploma). In addition, our parents hired tutors to help us with Italian and English.

Fall 1947. Uncle Noah finally shared with us the sad news about his youngest brother, Chaim Łosice, who had served in the Polish Army under Gen. Władysław Anders during the fighting in Normandy. Chaim was killed on August 9, 1944, in the battle of Falaise, about a month after we were liberated by the Soviet army. We were devastated. All during the war we kept hoping that Uncle Chaim might survive the war. He had escaped to Russia in 1939 but had volunteered to fight Germany. His armored unit had traveled through Palestine to England for training before joining the battle in France. In 1998 my husband and I visited his grave in the Langannerie Polish Military Cemetery near Falaise. It was very emotional for me. His tombstone, along with five others with Jewish stars, stood out among the six hundred crosses. I had a good cry, but I was proud of his daring feat and silently told him so. At least he fought back. He was a handsome, brave uncle, and I remembered him well from before the war. No, we'll never forget you!

Spring 1948. We were now registered at the American consulate in Naples to emigrate to the United States. We were told that the wait might be another three years. The Red Cross had issued all of us Polish identification papers. However, with the help of some clever friends, we acquired new passports from the Red Cross that showed our place of birth as Breslau, Germany, and our name as Gewirtzman, the maiden surname of my Aunt Yospe, Uncle Noah's wife. Her three brothers were wealthy enough to convince the U.S. government that they were willing and able to support our family of five. Somehow our old records were destroyed, and we registered anew under our new identities as Germans.

Before we left, two important events occurred. First, the State of Israel was established. We students celebrated in Rome. Some Jews ran to the Forum to walk under the Arch of Titus, which was forbidden according to Jewish tradition. Berel and I wanted to go to Israel to fight the Arabs when war broke out, but by then we already had visas for the United States, and our parents wouldn't hear of it.

Also, we were to leave before my final exams. More important, I now had a new identity but was still registered at the school office under my true name. I had worked too hard not to have any documentation of my studies. Two of my boyfriends marched me up to the secretary's office and told her that I needed a letter from the school to prove that I had finished the last year of high school in Rome. The secretary was so excited about my good fortune that she immediately typed out a letter containing my accomplishments, new identity, and date, signed by the principal and bearing the official stamp. I was stunned. I had a certificate under my new name. This piece of paper was later instrumental in my admittance to college.

On July 15, 1948, we left Naples on the ship *Marine Perch* and arrived in New York on July 30. The next morning our passports and belongings were checked and we were sent off with the greeting, "Welcome to America." Outside stood Uncle Noah and his nephew and my cousin Bel (formerly Bela). The hugs and kisses were swift, for we were all anxious to reach our new home in Albany.

In Albany Aunt Yospe had prepared a banquet lunch for us. We ate everything in sight—except the corn on the cob. Then Uncle Noah took us to our new fully furnished home, a five-room apartment on the second floor facing a busy urban street. What luxury! In Poland we had only three small rooms and a tiny kitchen. Downstairs was my uncle's furniture store, and only two blocks away was the apartment where he, Aunt Yospe, and their two children, Moshe and Chana, resided. My aunt insisted that we eat dinner with them for many months after our arrival. She was the kindest soul on Earth.

Father, who was now fifty-two, soon went to work in an upholstery factory. It was hard work. He had never before used a hammer or nails, but he made every effort to be independent and provide a living for his family. Mother worked in a glove factory for some time. Irving (formerly Itzek) and I entered high school, and Dave (formerly Berel) also worked at the upholstery factory. In January 1949 I enrolled at Albany State College for Teachers, thanks to my documentation from Italy. Dave had no such certificate under his new name, so he worked for two years to help the family finances, studied at night on his own, and earned a high school equivalency certificate. Later on both my brothers attended pharmacy school together in Albany and eventually became licensed pharmacists in New York.

While in college I was president of the Albany Chapter of the Intercollegiate Zionist Federation of America and often went to conferences at other colleges. During one of those meetings I met my husband, Marty Glassner. I graduated from college in 1952 and at twenty became a teacher of Spanish and French. Including English, I had learned three new languages within three years. Then I got a job in Germantown, New York, teaching the languages that I had just learned.

Toward the end of the 1952–53 school year, I came to a crossroad in my

The Gewirtzmans after becoming American citizens in the New York State Capitol in Albany, February 1954. *Left to right:* David, Irving, Governor Thomas E. Dewey, Renée, Jacob, and Anna. The man at left rear is an unidentified lawyer.

life. I knew that I could not spend the rest of my life in provincial Germantown. I moved to New York City, where I had good friends and relatives, and got a job in the Quaker Oats export department on Wall Street. I enjoyed the freedom of being single and financially independent, relished the cultural events and fun part of New York, and dated many nice young men.

Soon my good friend Marty reentered my life. This time I was able to get to know him better. What a surprise I had! I now found him to be serious and extremely intelligent. He always made me feel good, motivated my mind, and made me laugh. But he was doing graduate work in Wisconsin, and I was embarked on a master's program in the evening at New York University. I had a full schedule of school, work, and social life, but we kept in touch.

Meanwhile, my parents and I moved into a five-room apartment in Brooklyn, five flights up. I helped them financially until they somehow made a bare living by selling dry goods in a small store. How they did that was beyond me. They did not know the business, struggled with English, and in their late fifties hauled merchandise manually from factories on buses and subways. Their motivation was always their kids. Mom lived to be 92; Dad died at 102.

Marty started writing seriously to me from Wisconsin. A friend of his warned him that his absence from the New York area might cost him Renée (the name I'd chosen instead of Rivkah). At the end of 1954 he came to Brooklyn and proposed marriage to me. I was very much in love, and he charmed me to no end. He told me he had no assets, was still a poor student with no career goal, faced induction into the army—and I laughed. "Who cares!" I said. Two educated young people—we can do anything. Besides, I had $1,000 in the bank—and he had a collection of stamps.

Our wedding day was June 19, 1955. We got married in the Bronx, about halfway between Brooklyn, my home, and New Jersey, his home. My parents were elated and spent half their assets for the wedding. Marty was on leave after basic training in the army. After our brief honeymoon on Prince Edward Island, Canada, Marty went to his new post in Virginia and I to my job on Wall Street. After two weeks I joined him. Our first home was a one-room cabin at a motel outside Fort Belvoir.

Life in the army was great, except that we had no money, only a private's pay of about $100 a month. I got a clerk-typist job on the post, which doubled our income. And then I got pregnant. I had to resign from my job, and we moved to a two-room cabin in Lorton, Virginia. For once I was truly happy and enjoyed some peace. We were even able to enjoy a vacation in Cuba.

But I became very sensitive about my husband's military uniform and the explosions from the maneuvers on the army post. Noises from World War II reverberated in my head. I would sometimes wake up in a sweat in the middle of the night. I was dreaming of being chased by Germans. But the worst was the nightmare of Germans trying to take my baby away. I woke up screaming.

On April 24, 1956, a beautiful baby girl, Karen, arrived. By the end of 1956 we were pretty tired of army life. The plan now was that Marty would go back to school for a master's degree in community recreation at George Williams College in Chicago. So on New Year's Day 1957, after separation from the army, we loaded up our few belongings and said so long to Fort Belvoir.

Life in Chicago was no picnic. Marty studied full time and worked full time as a Boys' Club program director. Our apartment was cold, dust from the coal that was used for fuel penetrated every corner, and I found it all very depressing. So after two quarters at the college and a summer as a trip counselor at a boys' camp in Wisconsin, we returned to New Jersey. Marty worked in his parents' store until he got an assignment from the Foreign Service in April 1958. His parents were disappointed that he did not want to take over their store, but both of us dreamed of a more exciting life.

On September 26, 1958, our second daughter, Aleta, was born in Washington, D.C., while Marty was working at the Department of State. We were now a family of four in Arlington, Virginia, enjoying an adequate income.

While we were living in Virginia, two very important incidents occurred that affected me especially. While Marty was still in the army, he and I had driven to an inexpensive restaurant not far from Fort Belvoir. As we approached the restaurant, I noticed a big sign in the window: "Whites Only." I could not believe it—this was 1956—right near Washington, D.C., the capital of our democratic country, which I had idealized for years, especially after surviving the horrible experiences of the Holocaust. "What is this?" I cried to my husband. "Is this real? You call this a democracy, equality?" Echoes from the past—a past I was trying to forget. My heart and spirit were broken. Just as I had begun to idealize and have faith in the goodness of humanity and to rehabilitate my soul in this country, this sign shattered my dreams. Marty spent the night trying to "put things in perspective" for me. So, there is no perfect society, not even in the United States. What a shame.

The other incident occurred three years later in nearby Maryland. Chinese friends—a college professor, his wife, and two-year-old daughter—followed us to a widely advertised beach. We paid the entrance fee and were waved on, but our friends' car was barred from entering. The clerks told us that our friends were forbidden to enter because they were not Caucasians. "This is a private club," the clerks said. We yelled and argued, and I thought that my husband was going to punch somebody. I had never seen him this angry. I began to cry. We left the premises in disgust. We never did get to a beach that day. We had a private picnic in our backyard in Arlington, while the two children played in a small inflatable pool.

This time, however, we were determined to do something about it. Marty wrote a very good letter to the editor of the *Washington Post* about what had happened, and the Associated Press put it out on the wire. We received a lot of responses from around the world, including some local hate mail. It was a sensitive issue, because Marty was in the diplomatic service and the publicity might jeopardize his position. We discussed it and decided that we had to take the risk. Within a year the infamous "private" beach in Maryland was desegregated after the state adopted a public accommodations law. Several years later Marty failed to receive a promotion. We often wondered whether there was any connection. He was also one of only a few Jewish Foreign Service officers at the time.

In 1960, while I was pregnant with our third child, we were assigned to Jamaica. Cindy, our third girl, surprised us and arrived prematurely, on June 2, 1960, while we were still getting settled in our new home.

Cindy had a hard time. She weighed barely three pounds and the doctor gave her only a 20 percent chance to live. She was placed in the hospital's only incubator with another premature baby. At one point she stopped breathing, turned blue, and almost died. By chance a doctor visiting another patient heard the calls for help, massaged her heart, and revived her. I was traumatized and put on Valium. Cindy won her battle for life. She grew up to a normal size, graduated cum laude from the University of Pennsylvania, and is now a religious woman with eight beautiful children in Israel.

I had a second traumatic experience in Jamaica when the two older girls had to have their tonsils removed. The two kids walked into the operating room of an excellent clinic as brave troupers. Then, as the doctor administered some sort of tranquilizer to Karen, she started crying, "Mommy, Mommy." I could not take it; I fell apart. I sobbed without being able to stop. Aleta also started crying. Soon they were both quiet, but I was inconsolable. I had suddenly regressed to a horrible day during the Holocaust when I was hidden in the attic. At one point we had heard a faint cry—of a baby in a house in back of ours. Suddenly, we heard a rifle shot and the crying stopped. To this day, sometimes in the middle of the night, that terrible sound of an innocent infant's pleading for help comes back to me. I cannot erase it. It was my daughters' crying that brought back that image.

The rest of our stay was less eventful, except that I accepted a temporary interpreting job at the consulate, working with Cuban refugees who were fleeing Castro's regime. I was the only one who spoke fluent Spanish and other languages and was able to help the applicants for U.S. visas. As a former refugee myself, I could certainly sympathize with them.

Our big disappointment in the Foreign Service was that Marty was not recommended for promotion while in Jamaica. Subsequently, two of his other bosses gave him glorious recommendations for promotion, but it was too late. We did, however, accept another assignment.

During our two-month leave we drove to Seattle. The children took the cross-country trip in stride, and Marty loved it. But I could not feel such enthusiasm. The country was truly beautiful and friendly, but I was a stranger in this land, and I still felt as if I belonged somewhere else.

On September 14, 1962, we set sail on the Grace Line freighter *Santa Margarita* for our new home in Antofagasta, Chile, in the desert of Atacama, the driest place on Earth. Both Marty and I spoke Spanish well, so we felt prepared for our new adventure. Only one other American family lived there—the consul, his wife, and their three children. And, to my surprise, the wife was also from Poland.

We enrolled the two older girls in the Antofagasta British School, which was bilingual and quite adequate. Not only did they learn some Spanish there, but languages in general became very important in our family. Both our professions required linguistic and geographic proficiency. Besides, I carried a secret inner conviction that Jews must know many languages, for we never know when and where we must wander to. Our daughters got the message. They all learned Spanish, French, and Hebrew to various degrees of proficiency, and Karen became a bilingual teacher in Spanish and English.

We spent one year in Chile, more than a thousand miles north of Santiago, the capital. The Chileans were very friendly, cultured, and helpful. We explored the exotic Atacama Desert, where nothing grows at all, quite an adventure. A very touching scene was a small and lonely tree in the midst of this arid land. In front of the tree was a sign that said, "Riégame hoy—Mañana te daré sombra" (Irrigate me today—tomorrow I'll give you shade). Ha, begging for water, just like me when I was ten years old pleading "woda, woda" in Polish. We did pour some water around the tree and moved on.

In July 1963 we got ready to leave Chile and say good-bye to the Foreign Service. We had decided to go back to school and pursue academic careers. I was tired of moving around with the family. So we were two adults with three young children going back to school for advanced degrees with meager resources. Still young and full of energy, with some money from our sales in Chile, we settled down to a grueling but productive academic endeavor in Fullerton, California.

In January 1964 Marty started his program at Orange State College (now California State University at Fullerton) for a master's in social sciences. Unfortunately, Fullerton had no synagogue or organized Jewish community.

In the fall of 1964 Marty began a PhD program in international relations at the Claremont Graduate School while teaching part time in local colleges, and I began a master's program in Spanish and linguistics at Orange State. I felt like a young college student, yet I could not neglect my family, so I went only half time. We spent the summer of 1965 in Mexico City, taking courses at the University of the Americas, and we transferred the credits to our respective graduate schools. Our three kids even attended a local Spanish-language school.

In the fall of 1967, after I received my MA, I went back to teaching Spanish and French at a junior high school in Anaheim. Marty also taught full time while he was working on his dissertation. For once we had money. But we moved again, this time to Tacoma, Washington, where Marty taught political science at the University of Puget Sound. I taught Spanish and French at Stadium High School.

I have observed that in life one encounters "angels," who counteract the people of ill will. Both Marty and I ran into people who did not believe in our ability to achieve our goals. We sometimes had to persevere until a good Samaritan came along to help. Dr. Merrill Goodall, Marty's mentor at Claremont, and two people in the Foreign Service helped Martin. For me there were Mrs. Jacobs, from the Jewish Social Service in Albany, who convinced me that I could do college work, and especially Wacek Szpura, the Polish angel without whose help my family and I would not have survived the Nazi slaughter. For these worldly "angels" I do thank God.

Finally, Marty received his doctoral degree in June of 1968, our thirteenth anniversary. The future looked bright now. Our thoughts (at least mine) were beginning to turn toward the east, where our families were living and where we could find more active Jewish communities. So in the summer of 1968 we headed back east to a true and permanent home. We settled in the beautiful state of Connecticut, in Hamden. And the name of our street? Paradise Avenue.

We now immersed ourselves in our careers. Marty taught geography at Southern Connecticut State University, and I taught French and Spanish at North Haven High School. Our daughters were happily settled in the local schools and attended Hebrew and Sunday schools. This was heaven. A normal American family. Peace at last.

In the summer of 1969 we realized our big dream of visiting Israel. I breathed the sweet air of the land and touched the ground in Tel Aviv with great joy. Finally, our own country. If only my two young Zionist friends from Łosice could see it. After all, we had promised each other that we would someday fulfill this dream together. Alas, my two cherished friends had gone to the gas chambers of Treblinka.

My cousin Avram Shejnkind met us at the airport with great enthusiasm and joy. We made contact with all our relatives and friends in Israel. We traveled all over the country by car, bus, and plane. I had mixed feelings and trepidation, however, about the armed Jewish youngsters and adults who were protecting me and Israel. I thought it a pity to have to divert so much talent to security and preparation for possible war. No, life is not fair. After our ten-day stay in Israel, we determined to return with the family for a year, which we did in 1971.

Marty got a teaching position in the Haifa University Geography Department, filling in for a professor on sabbatical. We both took unpaid leaves of absence from our jobs so it worked out well—except financially. We rented a furnished apartment and placed the kids in the local schools. It was a wonderful experience, and we all felt at home there in spite of much bureaucratic nonsense.

One highlight of our sojourn in Israel was being invited to a betrothal celebration in the large village of Sakhnin by one of Marty's Arab students. Since I was the only female guest, I was seated with the men, while the women and children were seated on the floor in the kitchen. We discussed many topics, including the inequitable treatment of Israeli Arabs by the State of Israel. Life is unfair, really unfair, I thought.

Three other events made a strong impression on me during our stay in Israel. One was that our oldest daughter, Karen, had to join *gadna,* a premilitary training program, while she was attending Leo Baeck High School in Haifa. Like the Israeli kids, she went on maneuvers and was learning how to find and recognize bombs and various forms of booby traps. How ironic—to have survived a terrible war in Europe and now to fear for my own children's lives. However, Karen was proud to be with her Israeli peers and thought nothing of those activities.

Aleta also integrated well into her middle-school class in Haifa. She made lots of friends and learned Hebrew fast. In fact, she received first prize and honors in *dikduk*—Hebrew grammar—in her class. Our youngest daughter, Cindy, was struggling with her studies in the sixth grade. I spent hours helping her with Hebrew and hired a fantastic young tutor to help her with her homework. From then on, even in the United States, she was a model student.

Back in Connecticut, we finally settled down for good in our home and our community. Marty and I plunged into the regular routine in our old teaching jobs. We also resigned from the Reform synagogue, joined the local Conservative one, and participated in some of its activities and religious services.

Our most unusual summer occurred in 1976. Marty was in Nepal as an adviser to the Nepali government under the United Nations Development Programme, and I was in Poland with a group of graduate students on a study tour. Karen was studying in Bogotá, Colombia, and Aleta was visiting her. Cindy was studying in Dijon, France. What an international family! In our marriage I was the one who carried the baggage of fear most of the time, especially where the well-being of my children was concerned, perhaps a residue of the horrors of the Holocaust. Yet at the same time we tried to train our kids to become independent and self-reliant as early as possible. Our daughters tell us that we did a good job, and they enjoyed the freedom and independence that we encouraged in them.

I, frankly, wouldn't have had as much courage to embark on our extraordinary travels had it not been for my husband's steadfast manner and optimistic vision. I knew that he had a more secure footing because he was not a Holocaust survivor. Consequently, he often made it easier for me to deal with unpleasant and difficult issues because I could lean on him and his calm manner was very soothing. No wonder I never wanted to marry another Holocaust survivor!

But visiting Poland was my idea, perhaps a compulsion. I had waited long enough. My parents and brothers thought I was crazy, that it would devastate me, that it was even sacrilegious to go back to where there are only the ashes of our whole family and Jewish community. But for too many years after the war I ignored and even denied that I had lived through a horrible catastrophe. This time I was determined to face reality and see everything with my own eyes.

The study tour in Poland was interesting. I blended in well with the group and went to parties, sang Polish songs, and attended lectures about Polish history, politics, and culture. I even endured anti-Semitic remarks such as, "Let's do business the Jewish way." At the Jewish cemetery in Kraków, the guard said to me, "I hope there are no Jews in this group of students!" But nobody knew that my secret mission was to retrace the steps of my childhood. So one morning I notified my professor of my plan to break away for a full day in order to revisit my hometown, among other sites. I hired a taxi and two of my friends joined me, for which I was very grateful, for I can't deny that I was afraid.

We arrived at Koszelówka, the village of our rescuers. My heart was beating fast and my face was flushed—because I did not know what and whom I would find there. I had been told on the way that old man Szczerbicki, the farmer who hid us, was dead but that his wife was still alive. I entered the house alone. I faced the old lady for a minute and she stared at me as well. Then I threw my arms around her and cried profusely. "Who are you?" she cried. I was all choked up and blurted out, "Rywka, little Rywka, Yankel's daughter." We both hugged and kissed and cried. She could not believe her eyes and kept asking where I came from and where everyone else was. She kept crying about the awful times that we had lived through and how she was sure that we all, my family and hers, would be killed by the Germans sooner or later.

She still feared other Poles, even neighbors who might shun her and her family for helping Jews during the war. She related to me the sad fate of her husband,

Stanisław. It seems that years after liberation, some remaining troops of the Armja Krajowa beat him severely and took much of his money because he had helped Jews. He spent quite some time in a hospital but survived the ordeal.

Wacek of Dubicze, however, the true Polish "angel," was also brutally beaten at about the same time for the same reason, and he died of his injuries. I did not have time to visit Wacek's widow, who had remarried, but Stanisława promised to deliver a message to her. I wanted her to know that her late husband is remembered fondly as our great hero, a true righteous Gentile, honored as such at Yad Vashem in Israel.

The reunion was exhilarating. Everyone came to see me. The three Szczer-bicki daughters, Staśka, Janka, and Lodzia, and some of the grandchildren were there. (Staśka and Janka appear as children in the photograph with their father.) I established a special relationship with Janka's daughter Marianna, and we have been helping her and her family in various ways. Unfortunately, our time for the visit was rather limited. My friends and I had to rejoin our group. Besides, this was 1976 and the Communist government was not very kind to unauthorized travel-ers without special credentials. And no one could convince me to spend a night in a region where most of my kinsmen had been butchered by Germans and Polish anti-Semites and common bandits.

The taxi sped off to Łosice, my hometown. What emotion! My heart was pounding. I recognized the road, I felt the smell of the forest, I recognized the pas-tures and wheat fields. And then we arrived. There it was—the big town square, with more vegetation and trees but otherwise the same. And there in front of me on the corner of Międzyrżecka Street was the big house—my home. I started crying, and my friends and the taxi driver did not interfere. They understood.

Three of us entered the house. We got up to the second floor, but no one was around to let us in to my former apartment. Neither was anyone in the three other apartments that our family had occupied. We went up to the third floor, where the Pinkus family had lived. We were in luck. The lady was kind enough to let us in to see the apartment. She even showed me the attic that we had used as a hiding place. But when she noticed that I recognized a lot, she became suspicious and hurried us out. Still, I was satisfied. I had touched home. I indeed had had a happy childhood, albeit a short one. This gave me some comfort and peace.

After many inquiries we located the apartment of a former teacher. It was be-hind the house where I had hidden for five months in a wardrobe. More dreadful memories. But Władysław Gołąbek remembered me and my family. He especially talked about the brave woman—my mother—who risked her life by coming to the edge of the ghetto to receive books from him, an act forbidden by the Germans. He also apologized for not letting my brother and me hide in his home. He said he would have done so, but other Poles were observing us, and he was afraid that they would denounce us all.

And so we spent a nice afternoon with him. But he said he still could not understand why Jews were so different from Gentiles. He commented how he remembered that the Jews spent a lot of their time "counting money." How strange. This came from my teacher—supposedly more educated and compassionate than the average Pole. "What about my parents?" I asked. "Oh no," he said, "not yours, those with the beards." How ironic, I thought. Most of the bearded ones were rather poor and spent most of their time praying.

As we were taking some pictures, a Polish woman yelled after us: "So they are coming back and will take back our homes and our possessions." We ignored her and proceeded to two more sites that I wanted to see. One was the Jewish cemetery. Not a trace of it remained, just a nice wooded park where it had been. And so no trace remains in my town of the four-hundred-year Jewish presence. The other site was the town jail where my brother and I spent three days. Alas, in my anxious state I got very flustered and wandered around, fruitlessly trying to find it. Rather than ask more questions of suspicious bystanders, I gave up in despair, left the town, and headed toward Treblinka.

We arrived at Treblinka quite late, around 11 P.M. No one was there. Complete silence. The bright full moon and starry sky illuminated the stones of various sizes and shapes on which are inscribed the names of the towns whose Jewish citizens were annihilated. At last I saw it—my beloved hometown and my beloved people, symbolically buried under a large pointed rock with *Łosice* chiseled into it. I fell upon it and wept like a baby for a long, long time, till I was out of tears. I composed myself and looked up at the brightly shining moon, asking, "Why, why?"

Our group returned to the United States and we all resumed our daily routines. But within me brewed a fiery history, rekindled by my trip to Poland. I started talking to people openly about my Holocaust experiences without fearing retribution. When the chance came to give testimony to the Holocaust Video Archives at Yale University, I was the third one to volunteer for the project, in 1978. I was honest and fully shared with my interviewers many remote and recent memories of my incredible life. In fact, my recent experience in Poland helped me verify my earlier life. I also shared my photographs. I spoke passionately for more than two hours, unloading a heavy, painful burden that I had carried around for many years. It felt good to do so.

Two years before the Yale interview, I had another significant experience. In the spring of 1977 Cindy begged us to invite an exchange student to live with us during her senior year of high school. We agreed. What a shocking surprise—the student chosen for us was a fifteen-year-old girl from Germany.

I could not sleep. I grappled with the problem for days. One day I said to myself, "Why not?" The girl was born into a new society, and her parents were academics who never served in the war. I was also testing my own moral strength. Could I, a Holocaust survivor, overcome my negative feelings toward a new postwar Germany? I was willing to take a chance.

Luckily, it worked. Katie Hopf lived with us for a year like any normal teenager. Her parents, although also apprehensive at first when they found out that I was a Holocaust survivor, were later delighted with how well Katie fared that year.

Renée Glassner.
Contemporary photograph.

In fact, our families became good friends and have exchanged visits. Katie still calls us Mum and Dad and we communicate frequently.

But the biggest surprise came a few years ago, when I received a package from Friede, Katie's mother. In it were six copies of a book in German called *Aschenvolken*. It was her translation of my cousin Oscar's book, *The House of Ashes*. I was shocked and moved to tears. Friede had spent two years and considerable money on this project. She was in secret contact with Oscar, who now lives in New Mexico. She never recouped the expenses that she incurred in the translation and publication of the book in Germany. Friede, you are an angel. I salute you.

I made a second trip to Poland in 1988, when Marty attended a conference in Warsaw. This was a much less painful experience, because it was not new and I felt protected by his presence. He got a good feeling for the country of my birth and understood my background better. In fact, after that experience he became even more interested in the Holocaust.

Our oldest daughter, Karen, was married on August 30, 1981. It was the happiest time of our life. Karen graduated cum laude from Brandeis University in 1977 and is a bilingual (Spanish/English) elementary school teacher, while her husband, Richard, is in marketing. They have a boy and a girl, and all four are moderately observant Jews. Benjamin and Marisa graduated from a Solomon Shechter school (Conservative Hebrew day school) and have strong ties to Israel. Yes, we are making up for our losses in the Holocaust.

Our middle daughter, Aleta, graduated from Cornell University in 1980. Her main interests were history and theater, but because of some health problems she switched careers. She is now a recreational therapist in a mental health center.

In 1982 our youngest, Cindy, emigrated to Israel after graduating cum laude from the University of Pennsylvania. We applauded her wish to live in Israel, but we were dismayed by her strict orthodoxy. In Israel, however, she found her niche. She also found a mate with a similar background and they were married in July 1984. My mom in her wheelchair and my dad were there in Jerusalem to witness the joyful wedding of a second grandchild. Cindy and her husband have a boy and seven girls and live in a haredi (ultra-Orthodox) community near Jerusalem. Another defeat for Hitler!

People often ask me whether I am religious and go to synagogue. My answer is that I do not know what it means to be religious. I come from an Orthodox Jewish family and still enjoy the rituals and culture of Judaism. I am a faithful member of the Jewish community and a strong Zionist. I attend synagogue when the spirit moves me. As for prayers, yes, I often pray privately. Sometimes I stop what I am doing and silently converse with God.

In spite of some hardships in our family life, my husband and I have managed to use our talents and energies in a number of ways. We have been active in the Holocaust Child Survivors of Connecticut, have lived and worked in many countries, lectured on global affairs, written books and articles, and even taught folk dancing. We expect to continue these endeavors as long as we can, hoping to contribute to peace and understanding in the world. Are we naive? I think not.

My Story as I Remember It

NICHOLAS FRIEDMAN
(b. 1932, Hungary)

I was born on November 11, 1932, the eldest of four children. My sister Eva, born on April 1, 1934, was my only sibling to survive the war. She was followed on December 16, 1935, by my brother, Joseph, and the youngest, my baby sister Elizabeth, was born on June 16, 1937. We were all born in Hust, a town in the Carpathian Mountains that was at that time a part of Czechoslovakia.

My parents, Rose Schoen and Ludvik Friedman, were married in 1931. It was a second marriage for my father, whose first wife died in childbirth, and following Orthodox custom, he married my mother, the younger sister of his deceased wife. They were Orthodox Jews, and although they strictly observed the religious laws, my father, who did not wear a beard, graduated from a German university and carried on a somewhat modern lifestyle.

My father's family was quite prosperous. His relatives owned and operated several businesses. Their holdings included a sizeable block of real estate in the center of town, where they had a hotel, run by Father's brother Samuel, a cocktail bar run by brother Morris, and a hat factory run by their father. In addition, they owned a string of stores that they leased to other people. One of my uncles, Jeno, left the business to become a rabbi and run a heder (religious school).

My mother's parents were also quite well-to-do and as a wedding present gave my parents a flour mill, which my father ran with several employees. All the farmers from the region brought their wheat to the mill for processing into flour. The area was rich in sunflowers, and when they came to full bloom and ripened, the farmers brought the seeds to the mill, where the oil was squeezed out of them and the remaining pulp was pressed into discs to be fed to horses. We saw little of my father during the busy season, as he worked from sunup until late into the evening.

For the first four years of my life, we lived in an apartment in the block owned by my grandfather. Then we moved to a beautiful new house in a different part of town. I remember a beautiful rose garden at the front of the house and a wonderful backyard. At the rear of the yard was a magnificent large orchard, where we grew apples, plums, pears, peaches, and apricots. We also grew strawberries, various vegetables, including cucumbers for pickling, and, of course, an abundance of flowers. The perfume of that orchard is a cherished memory.

On Fridays, following tradition, we would buy a couple of chickens and take them to the *schochet* (chicken butcher), who would cut off their heads, and then my mother would cook the chickens for the Sabbath. Following Sabbath custom, she would also prepare a large pot of *cholent,* consisting of chunks of meat, beans, etc., which I took to the local baker to be put into a large brick oven. The *cholent* cooked overnight, then, after the Sabbath services, someone from each household came to the bakery to claim his pot. Our lunch consisted of chicken soup and boiled chicken followed by the *cholent.* It never varied. Perhaps that is why to this day I cannot eat boiled chicken.

My mother had two brothers and two sisters (one of whom, as I said, was my father's first wife). Her family lived in a small village, called Egres in Hungarian and Olesnik in Czech. The nearest town was Nagyszollos, where one of her brothers and his family lived. We didn't have a car, and to visit my grandparents we had to take a train from Hust to Nagyszollos, then switch to the narrow-gauge train that connected with Egres and some nearby villages. My maternal grandparents, Gizella and Joseph Schoen, spoke Yiddish, Hungarian, and Ukrainian. Because of the proximity of Egres to Ukraine (in fact it is now in Ukraine), Ukrainian was the only language of the local peasants, including all the help employed by my grandparents.

Both sets of grandparents were quite prosperous by local standards. The Schoens owned farmland, forests, pastureland, and fruit orchards. They lived in a big house overlooking a huge yard. A well at the center of the yard provided water for the horses and cows. Water for household use came from a separate well. Facing the yard was the housing for the mill hands and the farm help. At the far end of the yard, opposite the front of the house, stood the mill. It ran five days a week, and it generated electricity for the house during the day, but at night, when the mill fell silent, everyone had to use kerosene lamps for light, because the village had no electricity.

On Fridays my grandmother was very busy preparing for the Sabbath. With the help of my two half sisters (my father's daughters from his first marriage) and the maid, she baked enough fresh bread to last the entire week, using a brick oven outside the house. They also prepared a goose and a couple of chickens and of course the ever-present pot of *cholent*. My grandmother also served a couple of pieces of smoked meat that had been hanging in the smoke closet in the attic. Finally, they baked wonderful cakes to complete the meal. It was always a great feast. Every Friday my grandfather Schoen sent the coachman around the village to deliver food for the Sabbath to poor Jewish families in the area.

My life in Hust was pleasant and full of fun. I spent a lot of time outdoors, playing with friends. I swam in the Tisza River in summer and sledded down a nearby mountain during the long cold winter. But in 1939 my life began to change. The war had begun, and Hungary chose to become an ally of Germany, just as it had during the First World War. At the end of World War I, Germany and its allies having lost, parts of Hungary were ceded to its neighbors. Part of northern Hungary, where I was born, was given to Czechoslovakia, so I was born a Hungarian-speaking Czech citizen. In the southeast, Transylvania became part of Romania, and in the south some territory went to Yugoslavia. Because Hungary again allied itself with Germany in World War II, Hitler rewarded the country by returning all these territories.

I attended public school in Hust through part of the third grade. Gradually, dark clouds began to gather on the horizon. The police rounded up the Polish Jews living in Hungary and deported them to Poland. Hungarian Jews were ordered to turn in their shortwave radios, and so began the anti-Jewish laws.

In 1940 my parents divorced. The custody agreement stipulated that my mother would have the care of the two younger children, Joseph and Elizabeth, and my father would care for the two older children, my sister Eva (six) and me (eight). Mother was not really in a position to care for my younger siblings at the time so she sent them to Egres to be cared for by her parents. She then moved to Budapest to establish herself there. One of the anti-Jewish laws forbade Jews to own businesses; therefore my father's mill was confiscated and he was drafted into forced labor.

Until his discharge from the labor camp several months later, Eva and I lived with a family that he knew in Maramaros Sziget. When he returned in 1941, we moved into a furnished room in Hust. He realized, of course, that there were no business opportunities for him in Hust, so in January 1942 the three of us moved to a furnished room on the Pest side of the Danube in Budapest. There I was able to finish the third and fourth grades. In the meantime my father went into partnership with a Christian businessman who owned a powdered soap factory. It was the summer of 1943, and my father once again received a draft notice for forced labor.

Nicholas, 9, and his sister
Eva, 7, in Budapest.

He was not able to find a family willing to take Eva and me while he was away, so he placed us in the summerhouse of a children's home in a suburb of Budapest. We had fun, doing all the things kids like to do. In the fall we moved back to the city, to the main building of the children's home, and I entered the fifth grade.

Anti-Semitism, while always present, had grown stronger by this time. Many Hungarians were waiting for the Fascists to come to power. At school I was often harassed, called a dirty Jew, and sometimes beaten. In April of 1944, as the front moved closer to the city and bombings by Allied aircraft grew more frequent, all the schools closed. But March 19, 1944, was the darkest day of my life and of all Jews in Hungary. The German army entered and occupied the country. The next ten months seemed like an eternity. The constant fear of what awaited us next was horrifying. In short order Hungary passed a new spate of anti-Jewish laws.

In April Father came home for a short leave from labor camp. He must have sensed that this would be the last time that he would see us. He took us out of the children's home, which was about to close, and brought us to our mother. They both knew that she was the only one who cared enough to see us through this turbulent, horrible time in our lives. We, of course, were thrilled to be back with our beautiful mother and not in the care of strangers. My father gave his trusted Christian business associate, Vilmos Szekeres, a sum of money and instructions to give

Nicholas with his sister and father at the Budapest Zoo, spring 1943.

my mother a monthly allowance. In addition, he took us shopping for new clothes, shoes, underwear, and overcoats. All these clothes were placed in a large trunk and delivered for safekeeping to the soap powder factory. After finalizing all the details, our father bade us an emotional and, as it turned out, final good-bye before he reported back to his unit.

Within a couple of weeks Jews were ordered to move out of their apartments and into preselected houses, with one room allotted to each family. We moved into one room of an apartment owned by a Jewish family in Pest. The apartment consisted of three bedrooms, a kitchen, and a bathroom, so three families were forced to live there. A large yellow star was placed above the entrance to the building to denote that it was designated as a Jewish apartment building. Jews were given only one hour per day to do their shopping, and we children longed to go out and play in the street.

By this time we were hearing stories about German soldiers rounding up all the Jews in the provinces and transporting them to camps. This, of course, included the major part of my family. I never saw my little brother or sister or my grandparents again.

A distant relation through marriage, a very brave young man named Ludvik Wieder, managed through an elaborate scheme to be discharged from the labor force. Ludvik, whose sister was married to my mother's brother, came to Budapest, acquired forged identification documents, got a job at a defense plant, and lived as a Gentile. When he learned that Jews in his hometown were being rounded up and deported, he quickly boarded a train, determined to save them. He smuggled his parents out of the brick factory where they were being held, dressed them as peasants, and brought them to Budapest. There he managed to buy them used documents—and the key word is *used*—new was a dead giveaway—and set them up in an apartment. And so began his saga of saving as many Jews as he could.

Ludvik, who was very fond of his brother-in-law and his family, had grown quite close to my mother over the years, and he would visit us from time to time. One Sunday he was able to sneak me out of the house and take me hiking outside the city. The feeling was exhilarating. Unfortunately, it lasted for only a few hours, and at day's end he took me back to "prison."

Ludvik visited as often as he could, but one visit will stand out in my memory forever. He strongly urged Mother to take us and leave the building because he knew it was only a matter of time before the Jews in Budapest would also be deported to camps. As they were talking, we heard a sudden loud banging at the front door. German soldiers were hammering at the front door with rifle butts, screaming, "Open the door!" in German. Quickly, Ludvik asked where he could hide because he knew that if he were caught in a house meant only for Jews, the Germans would realize that his documents were false and would execute him. Of course, everyone was in extreme panic at that moment, and in our confusion no one could give him an answer. Two German soldiers burst into the apartment, screaming at the top of their voices and ordering everyone out of the house.

We were frantic and frightened as we rushed out, taking nothing with us: no belongings, no food. And of course we had no idea where we were going or for how long. We ran down the three flights of stairs onto the street with everyone else from the building, losing sight of Ludvik as we did so. We were formed into a long column and ordered to raise our arms above our heads. I had never known such fear. They ordered us to march, and as we were marching in the roadway, Hungarian spectators gathered along the sidewalk to watch the spectacle. Some stood there silently, while others hurled ugly insults at us.

We marched for two or three hours and then came to a halt in front of a building in another part of town. The Germans marched us into the courtyard, then ordered us to run down a flight of stairs into a large dark basement. Perhaps two or three hundred people were crammed into that basement. About midnight we were ordered out of the basement and into the street and told to start marching again. The street was pitch dark except for the bright headlights pointed at us from a Tiger tank. Some people whispered that we were being marched to the Danube River to be machine-gunned down into the river, which was a common practice at the time. The river often ran red. Others thought that we were being taken to the railroad station to be shipped like cattle to the death camps. Either way, we were going to die.

Finally, totally exhausted, we arrived at our destination. To our amazement we were halted at one of Budapest's grand synagogues, the Rombach Synagogue. After a short pause we were herded inside, where at long last—almost fifteen hours from the time we had begun—we were finally able to sit down on the hardwood floor. And this is where we spent the night, much too exhausted to even be hungry.

During the morning more people arrived, and we were packed so tightly that it became impossible to move. There was one toilet serving approximately two thousand people. Of course, it soon broke and conditions became horrendous. A small courtyard served as the only place for people to relieve themselves, in full view of everyone. We were given no food or water during the three days we were there. The gate was locked, preventing any movement in or out. This was truly a concentration camp.

On the afternoon of the fourth day the gate suddenly sprang open. A Hungarian policeman entered and made a surprising announcement. Everyone was to file out of the synagogue, and we were to line up with the people of the house from which we had come. We would then be escorted back to that house by the Hungarian police. We were astounded. We could not understand why we had been put through this agony, then returned to our homes. I was to learn why forty-seven years later.

A few days after our return Hungary passed a law requiring all Jewish women aged sixteen to sixty to report for forced labor. I was eleven, Eva was ten, and we were going to have to fend for ourselves, which was, of course, of great concern to our mother. Two days before she was to report for work, our guardian angel, Ludvik, reappeared. We were totally amazed. He told us that when the Germans had appeared at the door weeks before, he had had just enough time to run into the bathroom and hide behind a wash tub. Time had run out now, he told Mother. We had to make our move. He instructed her to leave the apartment house with the other women, walk with them toward the gathering place ordered by the authorities, and leave the rest to him.

On the designated morning my mother did as instructed. Suddenly, she was grabbed from behind and pulled into a narrow alley. Ludvik put his hand over her mouth until she realized who it was. He waited until all the women had passed the alley, and then he tore the yellow Star of David from her jacket. They took a streetcar to another neighborhood, where a Gentile friend of his, a former Hungarian army officer, had a small furniture store that was temporarily closed for business. Ludvik opened the door with a key that the officer had given him and told her to hide among the furniture temporarily. Then he locked the door and left. My very frightened mother spent the night there in the dark.

By this time the city was being bombed twice daily. At midday the American bombers flew overhead, liberally discharging their bombs on the city, and at night the British repeated the performance. As luck would have it, there was a terrible bombing raid in the vicinity of the furniture store. A bomb landed across the street, completely demolishing the apartment house that had stood there. The concussion blew out the store window and smashed most of the furniture. By some miracle Mother was unhurt.

During the German occupation Regent Miklos Horthy had begun armistice negotiations with the Allies, but in October 1944 he was forced to resign. In his place the Nazis installed Ferenc Szalasi, a bloodthirsty Fascist and anti-Semite, to head a new puppet regime. Szalasi organized young thugs who wore armbands with an arrow cross and roamed the city armed with guns. They arrested any Jews they found in hiding or carrying false papers, took them to the thugs' headquarters, and shot them.

So it was a very terrified Rose whom Ludvik found in the store the next morning. He handed her a counterfeit document that identified her as a Christian, and they took a streetcar across the bridge to Buda, where he had rented a furnished room for her. He also arranged for a Jewish friend who had false papers to fetch me and my sister at the house and take us to our mother at the furnished room. The man told us who he was and where he was taking us. We were so young that being in the outside world and riding a streetcar to Buda with a stranger was very frightening to us, but we managed to make it to our mother without incident.

By mid-October we had been living in the furnished room for about a week when yet another frightening incident occurred. My mother had hidden a few of our old photographs, birth certificates, and other documents in what she thought was a safe place in the bathroom. On Sunday morning, while looking around the bathroom, the landlady discovered our papers and immediately went to the telephone and called the Fascist Arrow Cross. Fortunately for us, my mother overheard the conversation. She burst into our room, grabbed us and some belongings, and we ran out the door, down the stairs, and into the street before the landlady realized that we were gone.

We roamed the streets all day, because we didn't know what to do or where to go. Mother happened to know the address of the maid who worked at that apartment. She was a sweet, kind person in her early twenties, and we decided to ask her to put us up for the night. Despite the danger, she allowed us to stay in her apartment for just one night. After sleeping on the floor that night and thanking the maid profusely for her kindness, we left early in the morning.

Once again we were wandering the streets of Buda with no place to go and no one to turn to. At last Mother recalled a shoemaker who used to repair her shoes. He and his wife were a very poor young couple, living in one small room in an attached house a block from our old apartment. From her many discussions with this lovely couple, she gathered that they were extremely anti-Fascist. It was growing dark, and we were getting colder and more desperate with each passing minute. We had to do something. Finally, we approached the house where they lived. They agreed to let us stay with them, and we slept there overnight, five people huddled together in that small room.

Early the next morning our hosts went to work in a defense plant, and our mother left to look for a permanent hiding place for us. Eva and I were terribly frightened to be left alone. It was a great relief to see everyone return at the end of the day. Finally, we were able to move around and whisper a few words. The following morning this routine was repeated. At nightfall Mother came back with good news. She had met Vilmos Szekeres, our father's business associate, who agreed to have the three of us move in with him and his wife, Elizabeth. It was such a great relief to know that in this mad world of war, hatred, and persecution, good-hearted people were willing to risk their lives to help us.

The Szekereses rented a three-bedroom apartment on the second floor of a two-story building. One bedroom was rented to an elderly couple, but the Szekereses were able to let us have the spare bedroom by explaining that my mother was Elizabeth's sister, a refugee from the countryside escaping from the advancing Red Army.

It was now late October 1944. Almost all of Budapest's Jews had either been herded into a ghetto, where they were starving or dying of disease, or they had been deported to a concentration camp. Although we lived with constant fear and rarely left the house, afraid of being recognized by former acquaintances, we were better off than most Jews. We managed to buy food and other necessities with the money that Father had given to Mr. Szekeres for just such circumstances.

Elizabeth Szekeres did have a sister who was living in Kiskunhalas, a town southeast of Budapest that had already been taken by the Russian army, and Mrs. Szekeres provided my mother with a document in her sister's name. With this paper Mother went to the authorities and told them that she was a refugee from the advancing Russian army. She claimed that she had left everything behind, including her identification card and food ration cards. Mother had always been a good actress and had no trouble convincing them. In addition, she was a very pretty twenty-nine-year-old—tall, slim, with gray-blue eyes, and no so-called Jewish features—so they had no reason to suspect her of being a Jew and replaced her ID card.

The new ID card soon served its purpose. Every apartment building had a political overseer whose job it was to report any suspicious residents. The overseer in our building ordered all residents to report to her office and present their documents to her. During the process she questioned all the people about their background, and our mother acted quite naturally during the interrogation. The overseer accepted without question Mother's story about being Elizabeth's sister and a refugee.

At this time the Russians were on the outskirts of Budapest, and the artillery shelling became increasingly heavy. But this did not prevent the Arrow Cross thugs from looking for Jews in hiding. One morning the doorbell rang and Mother happened to be there to open the door. Facing her were two young members of the Arrow Cross, and one pointed a pistol at her and screamed, "You are a Jew, come with us right now." Mother had the unbelievable presence of mind to show no fear. On the contrary, she went on the attack. She started screaming back at them, "How dare you accuse me of being a Jew? My husband is on the front fighting the Russians, and he is probably dead by now! You punks are safely away from the fighting, and you dare to accuse me of being a Jew?" They were so taken aback by her outpouring of hysteria that they quickly apologized for their mistake and said they were looking for a couple named Bayer. They knew the Bayers lived there and insisted on seeing them, so she had no choice but to show them the couple's room. The Bayers were taken away and shot the same day. That was what we all lived with during those horrible days.

About a week before Christmas the shelling and bombing became unbearable. Houses were being struck all around us, and finally the residents of the house decided to move into the basement. It was not a secure place because only the lower half was below ground. The upper half was separated from the outside world by a thin wall. We slept in bunk beds and survived on dried beans cooked with snow brought in from outside. The snow was also the only drinking water available to us. During heavy shelling the steel door leading to the basement was kept shut, depriving us of fresh air. At times we could not light the candles because of the lack of oxygen.

Once, during a lull in the shelling and bombing, I decided to venture outside. As I stood in the backyard, I saw four Russian fighter planes flying toward me at very low altitude. I noticed that flashes of light were coming from the front of the planes, but I didn't realize that it was machine-gun fire. As I stood near the door to the basement, I heard a sudden loud explosion and was enveloped in dust. In absolute panic I ran to safety in the basement. After my mother finished spanking and scolding me for venturing out during the siege, I realized how close I had come to being killed, and I did not dare go out again.

We had another close call a few nights later. I was sleeping in my bunk bed, when I heard a loud thud coming from the wall next to me. In the morning a couple of the men went outside to find out what had caused such a loud noise. To their amazement a huge artillery shell was lying on the ground next to the wall. They theorized that the shell fell without exploding after it had lost most of its velocity. Had it exploded, I would not be here today.

Finally, we were liberated on January 15, 1945, when we heard rifle butts hitting the steel door late in the day and someone yelling in a foreign language. When one of our men opened the door, six soldiers in Romanian army uniforms entered our shelter. Although most people in our basement home were overjoyed to see them, the three of us knew unmatched elation and relief. No longer did we need to fear that we would be killed because we were Jews. No longer would we have to hide our identity or be afraid of saying the wrong thing. We were free. What a beautiful word—*free*!

Two of the women who had been living with us were originally from Transylvania, so they knew both Hungarian and Romanian and could converse with the soldiers. A couple of our men volunteered to lead the soldiers to a nearby house, where they believed they would find a doctor who could treat a wounded comrade. But the Germans were still holed up across the street, and bullets were flying everywhere.

Because there was still street fighting, we all stayed in our shelter, and the following morning Russian soldiers came in. Everyone was frightened of them and expecting to be harmed because Hungarians were the enemy fighting alongside the Germans. Because my mother had been raised in Egres, she spoke fluent Ukrainian, a language almost identical to Russian. She took a chance and told the officer in command that she and her two children were Jewish. She also assured the officer that the residents of this building were not Fascists and welcomed them with open arms. He ordered his men not to harm anyone, and because we looked so starved, they shared some food with us.

When the front line moved west of us, we finally moved back upstairs to the Szekereses' apartment. We were lucky for once because most buildings in the city were at least partially destroyed, whereas our house sustained only minor shrapnel pock marks from a bomb that had exploded in front of it.

We had spent a month in the basement with almost no water to wash and no change of clothing, so we were all covered with head and body lice, and our first task was to delouse ourselves. We poured vinegar on our heads to kill the head lice, then threw our clothing into boiling water to get rid of the body lice. It was great to take a bath and put on clean clothes. We had only one change of underwear and one set of outer clothes, because that was all we had been able to grab when we ran out of the furnished room in Buda. Suddenly, we recalled the clothes that Father had bought for us just before he reported for forced labor that last time—and everything was stored in the soap powder factory. As I look back now, I am amazed that he had the foresight to do what he did.

Mom decided it was worth the risk to go downtown to retrieve the trunk. She had to walk several miles, skirting the ruins of bombed-out buildings, and made her way to the factory. Father's business partner was there and acknowledged that he had the trunk, but he refused to relinquish it. He was aware that the new clothing in the trunk was quite valuable, and Mother could not make him release the trunk to her. She was not going to be outdone by this man! She recalled seeing a Russian army truck parked around the corner with several soldiers in it. She walked over to the soldiers and told them of her problem in Russian.

Hearing about a mean Hungarian from an attractive young woman who spoke Russian made the soldiers angry. They told her to hop into the truck, and they drove over to the factory. They went right to the man and never had to say a word. He took them directly to the trunk and begged them to take it if they would just spare his life. The young soldiers loaded the trunk onto their truck and drove it and my mother to our building, then hauled it up the stairs and into the apartment. For good measure they left us small sacks of sugar and flour, which was truly a treasure.

As the situation began to normalize, anti-Fascists took control of the city and soon began to round up known Fascists. My mother told the authorities that the former political overseer in our building was responsible for the murder of the elderly Jewish couple who had shared our apartment. Two policemen showed up and removed her. Shortly thereafter we moved into an apartment vacated by a Hungarian Fascist family that had run west with the retreating Germans.

Miraculously, two cousins, the sons of my father's rabbi brother, survived the Auschwitz death camp and managed to find us in Pest, where we were living in our new apartment. They told us that they had seen Father in the camp and that he had survived until liberation, but he had died shortly thereafter from typhus.

As we came to accept that no other relatives had survived the Holocaust, Mother decided to leave Hungary, which really didn't want us, and move on. There had to be a better life somewhere. She quit her job as an interpreter in a Russian-operated factory, placed Eva and me in Dror Habonim, a Zionist children's camp (I was about thirteen now and Eva about eleven), and traveled by train to Czechoslovakia to investigate the possibility of moving there. She returned about three weeks later, in early November 1945. She took us out of the camp, packed whatever we had, and the three of us boarded a train for Karlovy Vary, formerly Karlsbad, an exquisite spa resort in the Sudetenland. We were permitted to settle there because they considered us Czech citizens.

The Sudetenland had been part of Czechoslovakia until March 1939, when Nazi Germany annexed the territory. At the end of the war it reverted to Czechoslovakia. The predominantly German-speaking population was ordered to wear yellow armbands, had to observe a nighttime curfew, was issued ration cards for less food than the Czechs got, and faced other restrictions. The authorities systematically put them on trains and deported them to Germany. As their apartments became available, officials assigned them to Czechs arriving from other parts of the country. Thus we moved into a completely furnished apartment formerly occupied by a German family. Since Mother spoke fluent Czech, she was able to get a secretarial job with a large food distributor. Eva and I, who spoke no Czech, attended public school.

Life was difficult for us. Mother's salary was meager, and we lived in relative poverty. Something had to be done to improve our living conditions. Mom made inquiries and learned that getting a visa to the United States could take several years. She was advised to move to Germany, then emigrate from there as a refugee.

A member of the local Jewish community gave her an address in a border town from where we would be taken illegally across the border into Germany. So once again we packed our bags, and in May of 1946 we moved on without telling anyone. We took the train from Karlovy Vary to Ash and reported at the address given to us. We were met by a group of young Jewish men from Palestine, whose mission it was to help smuggle Jews into Germany or Italy and from there by ship illegally into what was then British-controlled Palestine. By midnight enough people had gathered to attempt the border crossing. All the belongings of the group were loaded onto a truck along with all the children and elderly. Both the truck and the adults on foot crossed into Germany without a hitch.

In Hof, Germany, we were taken to the railroad station and told to take the train to Munich. Once in Munich we were to go to Funk Kaserne, a former German army camp now being used as a gathering site for refugees pouring into Germany. When Mother told our guide that she didn't have the train fare, he reached into his pocket and gave her a handful of money, more than enough for the trip.

We found our way to Funk Kaserne. We were issued DP (displaced person) ID cards and food coupons and were each assigned to a bunk bed. We received three warm meals a day, served army-style in a mess hall. One day a truckload of used clothing arrived from the United States. We all dug into it, trying to find something that would fit. I was lucky to find a pair of summer shorts and a jacket that fit me.

Within about three weeks the camp was filled to capacity. To make room for the new arrivals, several hundred of us Jews were driven in a long truck convoy to a permanent camp in southern Bavaria in the town of Bad Reichenhall. Our camp had about a dozen large two-story cement buildings with small rooms that opened onto long corridors. The three of us shared one room with another family. We divided the room equally and then hung blankets between us for privacy, à la Claudette Colbert and Clark Gable in *It Happened One Night*. Later the blankets were replaced by a floor-to-ceiling wooden wall that made us feel as though we were in the lap of luxury. We slept on army cots under army blankets and ate army food at the mess hall. Everything was army surplus, left over from the war—just like us.

We tried to settle into some kind of normal life while waiting for transport to the United States. When Yiddish newspapers appeared, I learned the language quickly. A grade school was started, and the Organization for Rehabilitation through Training (ORT) operated a trade school that offered instruction in several trades. Zionist organizations sprang up with a full spectrum of ideologies, ranging from the extreme left to the extreme right, including moderately to extremely religious parties. When elections for the camp council were held, rivalries were fierce. But with it all we always managed to have some fun. Jews have always been natural performers, so people also formed theater groups that traveled among the camps. We kids always managed to sneak in to see a show without paying. Some things never change.

Bad Reichenhall was a pretty Bavarian spa resort town with a scenic view of the Alps. I enjoyed hiking in the woods and climbing nearby mountains with friends. Every other Saturday a large part of the camp population proceeded to the town soccer field to watch our home team play a visiting team. And on alternate Saturdays we went to the town cinema to see an American, British, or German movie. The local Germans used the soccer field and movie theater on Sundays.

Most people in the camp were Polish Jews who had escaped from the occupying Germans and spent the war years in Russia. Many fought the Germans alongside the Russians in a Polish brigade. They had no desire to return to Poland at war's end and chose instead to travel to camps in Germany to await an opportunity to emigrate to a new country.

As time went on, Mother grew frustrated, seeing us with so much idle time. She enrolled Eva at the Yavneh (religious Zionists) school, where she was taught Hebrew, Jewish history, math, and other subjects. She registered me at the ORT school, where I chose to study to become a machinist. It had a well-equipped machine shop left behind by the Germans. At first we learned to use hand tools. After becoming competent with them, we were instructed in operating a lathe, a milling machine, a surface grinder, and other machines. We were also given instruction in general math, geometry, physics, and technical and freehand drawing. Our instructors were fellow camp residents who taught us in Yiddish, the universal language of the camp.

In time most of the camp residents grew tired of eating army-style food in the mess hall. The camp management then was kind enough to give us a choice between eating at the mess hall or cooking for ourselves on makeshift stoves in our own rooms. Nearly everyone wanted to cook, and we were given a variety of foods and provisions by the United Nations Relief and Rehabilitation Administration (UNRRA). Our rations were supplemented with additional food from "the Joint"—the American Jewish Joint Distribution Committee. These rations included American cigarettes. Mother smoked some of them and sold the rest to the Germans on the black market. One pack of those cherished cigarettes could buy five movie tickets.

At the camp Mother met a very nice Polish man named Henry Gartner. When the Germans invaded Poland, he escaped to Russia, where he joined the Polish Brigade and fought with it from Russia all the way to Berlin. When he was discharged, he remained in Germany and wound up in our camp. Henry and my mother both worked as switchboard operators at the camp telephone exchange, for which they each received some spending money. They dated for a while and then married. Henry, of course, moved into our cramped room, but somehow we all managed to get along quite well.

Shortly after my graduation from the ORT school, I applied to the new ORT Teacher Training Institute in Anieres, a suburb of Geneva, Switzerland. After passing a battery of tests at the ORT headquarters in Munich, I was chosen as one of the six applicants from Germany to attend the institute. On March 8, 1949, when I was sixteen, an ORT representative took me and my fellow students from Munich by train to our school in Anieres. After all the destruction and horror that we had been living with for so many years, beautiful, undamaged Geneva looked like a dream. Seeing a city without devastated buildings, once again tasting a banana, savoring the sweet aroma of an open orange, biting into a Swiss chocolate bar—these and so much more were experiences I will never forget.

The students at the school came from Europe, Africa, Asia, and Latin America. Its purpose was to train future instructors for ORT schools throughout the world, enabling them to be self-supporting in a world that was becoming more and more industrialized. All instruction was in French, a language of which I knew not one word. But I was young, and after intensive training I understood almost every word spoken in the classroom. The courses were college level and included hands-on training. Regretfully, I was unable to complete the course because my mother sent word that we were finally going to the United States and I was to return immediately for processing. To our great disappointment, our celebration turned out to be premature because of another delay by the American immigration authorities.

During this time we learned that my mother's sister, Aunt Regina, and her two daughters had survived Auschwitz and were living in Belgium. The sad news was that her husband and young son had perished. We also learned that our wonderful savior, Ludvik Wieder, had also survived the war and was living in Italy, with his wife and son. Eventually, both Ludvik and my aunt emigrated to the United States.

By now many of the camp's residents had emigrated, either to Israel or the United States, and as the population of the camps shrank, the authorities began to close some of them and consolidate the remaining ones. Our camp was among those closed, and we were taken to a camp in Aschau, where we stayed for another year until we were finally told to report to Funk Kaserne in Munich once again. Usually, people had their physical examinations and political interviews there, and, if all went well, within ten days they were on a train to Bremerhaven, bound for an American troopship. Why this was not happening for us we never knew. While we were waiting to go to the United States, Mother gave birth on October 11, 1950, to my little sister Hedy, who now has two grown children of her own. I had too much time on my hands and decided to go back to the ORT school in Munich.

At last, after waiting more than a year in Munich, we were cleared to proceed to Bremerhaven in August 1951. There we boarded the troopship *General Sturgis* and off we sailed for the United States of America. Eva and I slept in bunk beds three levels high with hundreds of other people. Since it was an American troopship, it had many bathrooms, and we were able to shower and keep clean for the seven days we were on the ship. Because Mother and Henry had a baby, they were assigned a private cabin. Onboard everyone was given a job, either cleaning, working in the kitchen, or painting.

We arrived at New York on August 17, 1951, a glorious, hot, humid day. We had never experienced such humidity and felt as though we had been hit with a wet wash cloth—but we had made it, we were in America. From the ship we could see the skyline of downtown Manhattan and the never-ending movement of cars on the West Side Highway. In that moment we experienced a joy beyond description. This was the opening page of our new life, and it was wonderful.

At the dock we were met by a representative of the Hebrew Immigrant Aid Society (HIAS) who drove us to the organization's building on Lafayette Street in Manhattan. Eva and I were fed and given sleeping quarters there, while Mother and Henry, because of the baby, were driven to a nearby hotel for a little comfort. Eva and I went with them to see the hotel, which was rather old and certainly not fancy.

For once we were lucky to be Jewish. We had HIAS to help us and smooth the way for our new life. The HIAS people were wonderful. They helped us find an apartment in the East Bronx, gave us financial assistance until we were capable of supporting ourselves, and because of my ORT training they were able to help me find my first job in a machine shop. Since I was young—nineteen—and spoke English quite well—I had taught myself while we were waiting in Germany—I adjusted to my new surroundings quite easily. I did well at my job and advanced fairly rapidly.

In 1951 the Korean War was still raging. As a permanent resident, I was required to register for the draft six months after I arrived. A year later, in February 1953, I was drafted into the American army. My employer pleaded with me to let him get an exemption for me because our machine shop did defense work. I refused his offer because I was proud to serve the United States in any way that I could.

Before starting my basic training at Fort Dix, New Jersey, I was given a battery of tests. I passed them all and was given an opportunity to enroll in Officer Candidate School. I chose not to, because it meant staying in the army for an additional year. Instead I was trained as a military policeman. At the conclusion of my basic training, I was assigned to a military police unit at Fort Devens, Massachusetts, while half my training company was sent directly to Korea. At Fort Devens I became an American citizen without waiting the usual five years. Serving in the army gave me an opportunity to meet Americans from every part of the country, improve my English, and get to know the thinking, customs, and behavior of Americans my own age.

In January 1954 I was shipped to Japan, where I was assigned to a military police company at the U.S. Army Far East Headquarters at Camp Zama. It was almost impossible for me to comprehend all the changes and moves that had occurred in my short life. As a small child in a little town in Hungary before the war, I would never have imagined in my wildest dreams that I would be in mysterious, far-off Japan. But here I was, and I wasn't dreaming.

The camp was not far from Tokyo and Yokohama, and on days when I was not patrolling the camp and surrounding countryside in a patrol car, I would hop an army bus headed for either of those cities. I was very proud of being an American soldier serving overseas, but I also had a great time traveling and enjoying the culture of Japan. I also took and passed a high school equivalency test while I was there. Although I was able to complete only the fifth grade in Europe, I had no trouble passing the test.

In February 1955, after two years of service, the army sent me home and discharged me with the rank of corporal. Shortly thereafter my family moved to the West Bronx near Kingsbridge Road. I had no problem finding a job, and I started seriously dating a Hungarian girl from Spring Valley, New York, to whom I subsequently became engaged. I moved to Spring Valley to be near her, but in time we realized that it would not work out, and we broke off the engagement.

I moved back to the Bronx and had no trouble finding a new job. This time it was in Manhattan on Mott Street in Little Italy, a very colorful old section of the city. The machine shop, which employed only five people, was in a smelly, dusty loft building. In retrospect, I don't know why I stayed there, but fate moves in mysterious ways. I had no way of knowing it then, but this job turned out to be my last move.

Orders for machined parts were dropping off as the Korean War concluded. My boss took on a new partner, a young man with a new idea: machining technical ceramics instead of metals. Technical ceramics are not made of clay but of various composites that can be machined to close tolerances and fired at very high temperatures. We were able to sell the idea to manufacturers of electronic components for use as tools in the high-temperature production of transistors and diodes. We provided samples to potential customers who required very precise parts that proved superior to the graphite tools that they had used previously. Although we were not a large company, we became quite well known in the business because of the quality of our work, and I can say with some pride that its success was largely a result of my knowledge and my guidance of the plant over the years. As the company grew, I grew with it. I moved from the plant to the office and eventually became president of the company.

At about the time I joined the company, I also decided to take advantage of the GI Bill and get a college education. I went to school at night for many years and eventually earned a degree in mechanical engineering. I also developed a social life, and on weekends I dated and went to parties. Then, in August 1959, I decided to take a vacation at a singles resort in Wingdale, New York. There I met my future wife, Judy Lee. We were seated at the same table for meals and immediately took a fancy to one another. Spending all that time together for one week was equal to months of dating. We fell in love and became engaged in October. On a cold, crisp Sunday afternoon in January 1960, one day after a snowstorm, we were married.

As the company grew, our little space on Mott Street became inadequate, and the company moved to New Jersey just about the time that we got married, so that is where Judy and I made our first home. The business moved to Palisades Park, and we moved into an apartment in nearby Leonia. In December 1960 our son, Michael, was born; in September 1963, after we had moved into our house in River Edge, New Jersey, our daughter, Erika, was born.

In October 1990, after thirty-five years with the company, I retired at the relatively young age of fifty-seven. Retirement has permitted me to pursue my favorite hobbies of tennis, golf, and hiking.

In 1997 Judy and I moved into a beautiful new house in Norwalk, Connecticut, to be near our daughter, her husband, David Yarmoff, and our three beautiful grandchildren, all of whom are being raised as active Jews. In fact, as I write this, one is studying to become a bar mitzvah. We have made some great new friends and are only an hour away from our old friends in River Edge. Michael is a broadcast meteorologist in Hartford, and we have the pleasure of seeing him regularly on television.

There is no doubt that the Second World War completely changed the course of my life. I never got the chance to really know my father. He was only forty-one when he died in the concentration camp. My little brother and sister were snatched from us before they even had a chance at life. Except for my very early years, I didn't experience the warmth of family life with grandparents, aunts, uncles, and cousins. But I have lived the American dream. I succeeded at my work, I have been happily married for more than forty-two years, and we have wonderful children and grandchildren and through them a great extended family, and many friends. I can never make up for what I lost, and although I am no longer Orthodox, I thank G-d for the blessings that he has bestowed upon me since I arrived in the United States.

Afterword

While visiting the Holocaust Museum in Washington, D.C., several years ago, I saw a film that included an interview of a Hungarian woman. I was totally amazed at what I heard. She related that in late 1944 the Swedish diplomat Raoul Wallenberg had learned that a large group of Jews had been rounded up for deportation to a concentration camp. He had gone immediately to the German commander of Budapest and demanded that the order be rescinded, falsely stating that he had spoken to Adolph Eichmann, who told him that the order for deportation had been rescinded. The commander then told Wallenberg that he had no authority to rescind the order unless Eichmann personally told him to do so, and Eichmann was then out of town. Wallenberg told the commander that unless he reversed the order, he would be among the first ones that the Russians would hang as a war criminal in the square below when they arrived in the city. That warning apparently had the desired effect, because the commander then assured Wallenberg that he would order those people sent home.

At last I knew why we were released from the Rombach Synagogue after being held there for three days.

Commentary on Group 2

ROBERT KRELL

The accounts of child survivors born primarily in the early 1930s are informed by memory that is both more accurate and less fragmented than the recollections of the youngest survivors. The greater sophistication of language skills and capacity for abstract thought in these youngsters does not obviate the possibility of their suppressing, or having "amnesia" for, events too horrible to allow into their consciousness. It is in this age group that the foundations of identity are formed, and all had become aware of being Jewish, either through the family's traditions or through the experience of anti-Semitism.

Hilde Scheraga and Renée Glassner, for example, report limited experience with anti-Semitism before the war, but Nicholas Friedman was subjected to more intense discrimination in Hungary even before the Germans invaded the country in March 1944. After the war both Rudy Rosenberg and Renée Glassner were driven into different forms of hiding by virulent anti-Semitism, and Rosenberg was emotionally scarred by it for two decades. He came to America in 1949, assisted by his aunt and uncle, who attempted to reintroduce him to Judaism. But he had learned that being a Jew had brought him only persecution and fear. The gap between Jews who had spent the war years safely outside Europe and the European Jews who had survived was so great that most survivors decided not to speak of what they had seen or done.

Children separated from their parents and siblings—whether voluntarily to increase their chances of survival or forcibly by the Germans and their allies—typically suffered deep emotional scars, sometimes for the rest of their lives, even if they were eventually reunited. Such reunions were not always happy occasions, as Hilde Scheraga's story illustrates. Everyone had changed too much. She sums up the situation succinctly: "We were three individuals who came together as a family that had been irrevocably broken into three pieces."

Nearly all the child survivors in this book, even some of the oldest ones, felt compelled to achieve as much as possible intellectually after their liberation. They strived to begin, resume, or complete their formal education, often under most stressful conditions. Scheraga, for example, finished high school in two years, after being unable to attend school for eight years, and went on to obtain a master's degree in French literature. Although we have no studies to substantiate this observation, there appears to be an overrepresentation of professionals in the child-adolescent survivor group. Because they had been deprived of education, their appetite for it was insatiable, as was their need to appear to be "normal," which they associated with achieving professional status.

The theme of return runs throughout these accounts. After more than fifty years, the emotional weight of carrying unverified bits of memory proved too great a burden. The visits to former places of hiding and survival, and particularly reunions with hider families, have allowed child survivors a degree of reintegration and healing. Because memory is an important part of identity, the sense one makes of oneself is aided by verifying one's memories. In the older group of young survivors, issues involving identity and memory are not quite as profound, for they had had an opportunity to experience intact family life.

Rudy Rosenberg, Irene Frisch, and Renée Glassner all describe in considerable detail their return to their European homes and hiding places and the profound influence that these visits have had on their own understanding of their prewar and wartime lives. Sometimes these visits bring closure; that is, simply verifying their often vague or garbled memories can satisfy the survivor's emotional needs. In other cases survivors and their hiders or rescuers and their descendants develop warm relationships. Such visits have become commonplace for those who can afford to return to the sites where their memory was formed. Because such trips can be highly emotional, child survivors tend to travel with family members, frequently their adult children. They also wish their children to see the places that inform the stories the parents are finally sharing so many years later.

Another theme running through the stories of adolescent survivors is the courage and selflessness of individual hiders and rescuers. Few as they were, they represent the best qualities of human beings, regardless of nationality, religion, age, gender, or any other characteristic. Frisch writes eloquently of Frania's devotion to the family for fourteen years. Glassner pays homage to Wacek, her "worldly angel," who rescued other Jews as well as her own family and for his efforts was murdered by Poles after the war. Friedman writes of Ludvik, a Jew who appears unexpectedly several times at crucial moments to help the family. Zahava Szász Stessel tells us of the love and inspiration that she and her sister received from Szerén, a friend of their father's, even in the hell that was Auschwitz. Almost every story of a child survivor has an angel, for children simply could not survive without help. Such people represent the only redemptive aspect of humanity during that bleak and murderous time.

Most child survivors have remained somewhat uncomfortable about revealing themselves as Jews. The perception of exposure to danger lingers and perhaps for good reason. But the driving dynamic relates to their concealment in Christianity. For most child survivors, their decision to practice Judaism to some degree has been a gradual process, seldom marked by one or another definitive experience. The fanaticism behind the killing of Jewish children did not require that they identify themselves as Jews. That definition was imposed by their oppressors. Recovering and redefining a satisfactory sense of Jewishness has remained a lifelong preoccupation.

GROUP 3: SURVIVORS BORN BEFORE 1930

Two Saved by Schindler

KUBA AND HELEN BECK*
(b. 1922, 1925, Poland)

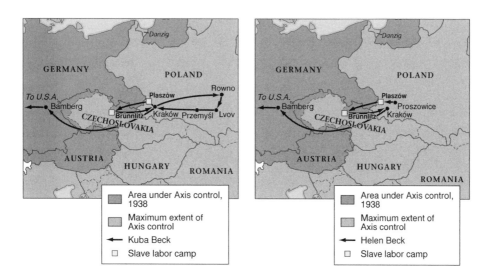

Kuba's Story

I was born on August 31, 1922, in Kraków, Poland, a city of about a quarter million people, about sixty thousand of whom were Jews. Most Jews lived on the west bank of the Wisła (Vistula) River, in the heart of the city, but my family lived in a mixed neighborhood called Podgorze on the outskirts of the city. My parents had a paint and hardware store nearby. I attended a Polish public school and then a private Hebrew high school. I had both Jewish and Gentile friends, and we played together and got along together very well. My main sport then was soccer, and during the winter I ice skated quite a bit.

I went to the private Hebrew high school, where the emphasis was on commercial subjects, because my father's plan was to take me into his business, and I

---

*No. 611 and No. 8, respectively, on Schindler's list.

really enjoyed working in the store. We learned bookkeeping and other business subjects as well as Hebrew and Jewish subjects and about Palestine.

My brother Emmanuel was two years older than I. After he graduated from high school, he went to work as a bookkeeper. My other brother, Isadore, was seven years younger than I. I graduated from high school in June 1939 and entered my father's business, which was very successful. Everything was going along quite well until September 1, 1939, when the Germans invaded Poland.

My parents were observant Jews. The business was closed on Saturday, and my two brothers and I attended synagogue services with our father. We were tutored in Hebrew at home, where we prepared for our bar mitzvah ceremonies. There was definitely quite a bit of anti-Semitism in Poland before the war, but I personally did not experience any special problem until I was a teenager. When Jewish friends went for a walk together, we had to be careful in the parks and certain other places, because we never knew when a group of anti-Semites would attack us for no other reason than that we were Jewish. Usually when that happened we didn't try to fight back. We just ran away or avoided trouble altogether.

In the business we had many non-Jewish customers. We were very, very friendly. For example, at Christmas my parents always prepared some gifts for their non-Jewish customers and friends. We lived in a thirteen-family apartment house that my parents owned, and the tenants were both Jewish and non-Jewish. Kraków had no special restrictions on Jews at that time. We could own land and there were some Jewish farmers outside the city. However, the universities had Jewish quotas. For example, some Jews had to go to Austria or other countries to study medicine, law, and so forth. High schools, both public and private, were open to everyone. At home we spoke Polish. I didn't learn Yiddish until much later, when I was in the camps. My parents spoke Yiddish to each other when they didn't want us kids to understand them. I had a very normal and happy life.

My mother had a very close girlfriend who moved to the United States. When I graduated from public school, she invited me to the United States to get an education and so forth, but my mother said, "Never mind. I don't want to part with my children. We have a wonderful life here." We had a beautiful apartment. My mother had only one brother; he had children, and they didn't live in Kraków, but we had some family and many friends there.

During my mother's childhood Austria occupied part of Poland, so she wrote and spoke German perfectly and loved the Austrian people. Whenever she had free time, she would go to Vienna, to the opera and so forth.

When the war broke out, the Polish government broadcast an announcement that the Germans planned to send young people, especially Jews like me and my brother Emmanuel—he was nineteen and I was seventeen——to the front lines to be killed. The government advised us to leave our homes and go as far east as we could. Emmanuel and I did leave and started walking eastward. It took us about two weeks to reach Rowno, near the Russian border, on a Sunday.

That day a radio announcement said that the Russians would be entering Poland to help the Poles fight the German army. At about two in the afternoon the first Russian tank arrived in Rowno. You should have seen how happy everybody was. They jumped on the tank, they kissed the Russian soldiers. However, things turned out quite differently. A few days later the Russians announced that the Polish army had to bring all its arms into one square and deposit them there. The Russian army disarmed the Polish army and began the Russian occupation of eastern Poland, up to the River San. Przemyśl was actually on the border.

We were in Rowno for a few weeks while things stabilized. We decided to go by train to our uncle's home in Lvov, and he took us in. We were in contact with our parents by mail and through people who were traveling. In December 1939 I told my brother that I was homesick and wanted to go home, but he could stay in Lvov with our uncle. I went to Przemyśl and hired a Polish man to take me over the San River at night. From there I took a train to Kraków. By this time Jews on the German side were already required to wear armbands with the Jewish star, but on the train no one questioned me about not wearing one. Emmanuel made the same trip home four months later, in March 1940. Now we were all together again, and we still had our business.

One day in June 1940 a German man came into the store and presented my father with a document. The German said, "I'm taking over your business. From today on you have to work here but this business is mine, all the money and everything." At this time many German civilians had come to Poland to take over Jewish businesses; among them was Oskar Schindler.

The German did not want me in the business and chased me out. I had to find something to do, or I would be taken to a forced labor camp, so I got a job in a metal factory and started to learn how to be a toolmaker. Meanwhile, the German was not paying my father anything to run the store for him, but luckily my father had money put away, and we didn't need any from the German. But in 1941, when the ghetto was created, the store was inside the ghetto, and the German had to liquidate the business.

The factory where I worked was outside the ghetto, and I had a pass that allowed me to go out to work every morning, but I had to come home every night. Working outside the ghetto gave me an opportunity to smuggle some food in once in a while. Anyone caught smuggling food was shot on the spot, but I took the risk to help my parents. I brought in a few potatoes, some bread, a piece of cheese. It was very little but it helped.

In early 1942 the Germans made the first "selection." They said that the ghetto was too crowded, there wasn't enough food, and so on, and they were going to create a labor camp outside Kraków so some ghetto residents could live and work there, and they would be well taken care of. Everyone in the ghetto had to have an identification card, and a Nazi decided who would have his card stamped to permit him to remain in the ghetto and who would be "resettled." I got the stamp but my parents and my brothers did not. Afterward, I was sitting with my parents and suggested that maybe I could sneak in with them to be resettled so we could be together. But my parents said I should stay, because I still had contact with non-Jewish people outside. They would give me some money and some jewels, and later, when I found out where they were, I could help them if necessary. So I listened to my parents. They were sent to Belzec in the first transport in March 1942, and I never saw them again.

There was another transport in October 1942, and the liquidation of most of the remaining Jews took place on March 13, 1943. I had been taken by foot with some others to Plaszów, a new slave labor camp about five miles away. The rest, at least a thousand people, including my wife's parents, were machine-gunned to death in the square in Kraków called Plac Zgody.

Plaszów had a number of factories and shops for metal goods, woodworking, making uniforms, etc. I was there until September 1943 when I was selected with about four hundred other young men to go to Schindler's factory, called Emalia, on the outskirts of Kraków. I don't know why I was chosen, perhaps because while I was in high school, which required that we get practical experience in business, I spent a month one summer in a big textile factory as an apprentice to Itzhak Stern, who later became Schindler's bookkeeper and adviser. Stern was very intelligent, a very nice man, very religious. He may have recognized my name.

The Steven Spielberg film *Schindler's List* was generally very accurate. Some Hollywood scenes were added that were not accurate. For example, there was no wedding there, no one blessed the bread on Friday night, there were no selections of naked women, no German soldiers were present when Schindler addressed us the night of May 8, just before the war ended, and so on. But it was not intended to be a documentary, and it was very good. Incidentally, I was working right next to the fellow in the film who was making hinges.

Men and women worked together in the factories but otherwise were separated, both in Plaszów and later in Czechoslovakia. Men's barracks were guarded by SS men and women's by SS women. Plaszów was a hell, where people were constantly harassed and often killed at random. But in Schindler's enamelware factory things were much better. The workers were housed in a satellite camp on the factory grounds, not in a concentration camp. Even the food was a little better. The soup was a little thicker, and sometimes we were given a spoonful of margarine or sugar. Maybe they'd throw some beans in. But we were constantly hungry, even working under Schindler.

As the Russians came closer to Kraków, Schindler had to move the munitions department of his factory from Poland to Czechoslovakia. He produced only munitions in Brünnlitz, a subcamp of Gross-Rosen. Meanwhile, the three hundred selected women who worked at Emalia were accidentally sent to Auschwitz, Plaszów's main camp, until Schindler managed to get them sent to Brünnlitz weeks later.

Schindler did all he could to find extra food for us. His men combed the neighborhood, buying food on the black market. He even had a dead horse that had been found in a field dragged back to Brünnlitz so we could have a little meat.

Living conditions were terrible. In the morning a few faucets had cold water, but that was all, and the lice were eating us alive. A few Jews told Schindler of this and were given permission to set up a delousing room.

Another incident not in the film occurred in January 1945. Word came to Schindler that cattle cars with people in them were just sitting on a siding nearby. They contained about three hundred Jews from Auschwitz, who had been working in a quarry in Golleschau and were evacuated as the Soviets approached. Now they were abandoned in Zwittau (Svitavy) near Brünnlitz. Schindler went to Zwittau with trucks to rescue the survivors. He took a crew, including me, to pry the doors of the cattle cars open. Many Jews inside were skeletons but still alive. At the risk of his own life Schindler brought most of them back to the barracks and, with his wife, nursed many of them back to life. Schindler made sure that those who had died were buried properly in a cemetery. We almost died ourselves from the cold. The only clothes I had were a shirt, pants, and wooden clogs, not even underwear or socks. But in addition to the thousand workers in his factory, Oskar Schindler had saved another hundred to two hundred Jews.

Near the end of the war the commandant of the Brünnlitz factory, Liopold, prepared a mass grave for the Jews, whom he intended to murder. But Schindler managed to have him sent away before he could carry out his plan. As the Soviets neared Brünnlitz and we learned of Germany's surrender, the Germans disappeared from the factory. During his tearful good-bye, Schindler told us that we were now free but advised us to remain there for a while because there were still Nazi soldiers out there who would recognize our prison uniforms and shoot to kill. We watched him leave with an escort of a few Jews, headed for the American lines and, he hoped, safety, after the Jews explained to the Americans who he was and what he had done. We did take his advice and waited until the Soviets arrived.

Helen's Story

I was born Hela Brzeska on May 10, 1925, in Proszowice, about fifteen miles northeast of Kraków, Poland, the third of ten children born to my parents—six girls and four boys. My father was a grain merchant, and he also gradually bought farmland and grew grains and so on.

The Germans came in September 1939, and we suffered from the same restrictions as all Jews in the occupied countries. One night in the spring of 1940 we were awakened by loud knocking on our door by Jewish policemen from the Judenrat (Jewish council of the ghetto) and SS men. They wanted two people for work and took my sister Cecilia (Cela) and me. They took us outside the city to the Zablocie factory, which made bricks and roof tiles. It had been owned by a Jew but the Nazis had confiscated it. We were among several hundred Jews forced to work there. Cela and I would never see our parents or our brothers again.

Cela was younger than I. I was fourteen, and she was born on December 24,

1926, which made her not quite thirteen when we were sent to the factory. Both of us found the work very hard. We had to carry heavy loads of clay from the pits to the factory. Luckily, a little while later the Nazi owner of the factory chose me to be an assistant to the maid in his house. Living conditions were much better there, and I was able to help my sister with extra food and other things. I did the cleaning, laundry, and other jobs. It was interesting to observe the dual behavior of the Nazis. At home they were quite nice, but when they put on their uniforms and boots and went outside, they became beasts.

Cela and I worked at the brick factory until the summer of 1941. Then we were sent to the Plaszów slave labor camp, which was just being built on the site of an old Jewish cemetery. We helped to build the barracks and also a road made from Jewish tombstones. We worked in the quarry at Plaszów until March 1943, right after the liquidation of the Kraków ghetto. Then we were selected to go to Schindler's factory. I have no idea why we were selected. We were in a group of women that seemed to have been chosen at random.

Schindler built a subcamp, complete with barbed wire and watchtowers, a few miles from Plaszów, the main camp. The barracks were smaller than those in Plaszów, and the sanitary facilities were a little better. The food was much better. Everything was much better in Schindler's factory. But the most important ingredient was seeing Schindler almost daily. When he was walking through the factory where we were working, we felt we were seeing a godlike person walking by.

When the Germans occupied Poland, a whole army of Nazis came to Poland to seek their fortunes, and Schindler was one of them. He took over a Jewish factory that had been producing pots and pans. This was a good item for the black market. He did have advice from some Jewish professionals, people who knew the business. He also made enameled pots and pans for the German army.

I was a painter. I dipped the pots into a vat of paint and then shook off the excess paint. It wasn't bad work, but we were constantly watched by the Nazis. They always tried to reduce us, to make us look like we were not human.

One Sunday they announced that we would not be working that day. Immediately, we suspected that something horrible was going to happen. However, the Nazis brought truckloads of striped uniforms to the factory that day. We had to exchange all our clothing for these uniforms. For the women it was a one-piece dress, a one-size-fits-all. I was still a teenager, very petite. Borrowing scissors from this one, a needle from that one, I made my dress shorter and added a waistline and fitted sleeves. I just wanted to look human. At the evening roll call the SS woman noticed me. She began beating me and I was thrown into isolation. According to this woman, I was supposed to be brought the next morning to the main camp in Plaszów for execution. I was in shock.

During the evening, somehow, word reached Schindler. He accomplished the impossible. That very night a *Kapo* came to me with an order to go straight to the barrack and to undo as much as I could of what I had done to the dress. In the morning I went back to work, and that woman never looked or said anything to me again. I survived only because of Schindler. Beyond any doubt, he saved my life that time.

Schindler had opened a munitions department in his factory. He was very smart. He kept asking for more and more workers. In midsummer of 1944, when the Russians were advancing on Kraków, the Germans were liquidating most of their smaller camps and sending the prisoners to Auschwitz and the other death camps. We were put on trucks and brought back to Plaszów from the subcamp. A group of men had to disassemble the machines from the munitions department. The machines were sent by train to Brünnlitz, Czechoslovakia, and Schindler ordered the reopening of the munitions factory there.

In Plaszów the Nazis were shipping as many prisoners as they could to the death camps. They also ordered all the mass graves in Plaszów to be reopened so they could erase the evidence of what had happened there. I was in the group selected to carry the remains to a certain square and then pour gasoline on those bodies and turn them into ashes. It was horrible. I was thinking maybe this is the mass grave where my parents are buried. So again we lived in such fear. We didn't have time to think. We followed orders.

After being in Plaszów for a few weeks, witnessing the most horrible things, Cela and I heard from somewhere that we were on the list of people going to Brünnlitz to work in Schindler's factory and that the three hundred women chosen would bypass Auschwitz. The famous list was supposed to be of those Jews who had worked for Schindler, but he tried to squeeze in as many Jews as he could. Some Jews, who were close enough to Schindler to influence the list, crossed off some names and added the names of their relatives or friends, even a few who had never seen Schindler or his factory. Maybe God watched over me, for my name was not removed.

We started for Brünnlitz but arrived in Auschwitz. Auschwitz will forever remain the most horrible nightmare. But since we all had names on a list, the Nazis did not know what to do with us. They put us in front of the ovens in Birkenau for hours, standing and waiting. I remember watching the chimneys, the heavy black smoke going into the skies, and the flames and the stench of burning flesh.

After the war we found out how hard Schindler had worked to get his three hundred women. He sent people with fortunes, with diamonds and gold, to get us. Finally, after several weeks the Nazis decided to release us. We got a little extra food and then were packed into cattle cars, a hundred women in each one. It was horrible. It was late fall and very cold.

In Brünnlitz the men were already setting up the machines. When we arrived, Schindler greeted us at the door. He looked at us, and the first thing we heard from him was, "You don't have to worry any more. You are with me again." You have no idea how, after that terrible experience, our hope was lifted by what Schindler had said. Cela and I worked for Schindler in Brünnlitz, operating heavy machinery, until our liberation by the Soviets on May 10, 1945.

The Becks' Story (Narrated by Kuba)

The three of us—Kuba Beck and Hela and Cecilia Brzeska—returned to Kraków after liberation. We had a difficult time dealing with freedom. There was no fanfare, no family to return to, no country to speak for us. We thought people would embrace us, help us recover. Instead, people looked at us with disbelief, told us that we were exaggerating, that we lied.

We found temporary housing in a former Jewish orphanage, now a camp for displaced persons, that had been set up by other refugees. Hela and I had seen each other in Schindler's factories but were not allowed to talk, so we only got acquainted at the former orphanage and we started to date.

All our parents and brothers were dead. We learned that one of Hela's sisters had been killed by the Armja Krajowa (the Polish Home Army, also called AK) six weeks before liberation. Another sister and her husband had been hidden on a farm for four-and-a-half years by a family who had been friends of the Brzeska family before the war and refused to take any money for hiding them. After the war the farm family told them not to tell anyone who had saved them. They were afraid of retribution by the AK.

One day in June 1945 Hela was in the Kraków railway station, waiting to take a train to visit her sister, when she noticed a bundle under a bench on the railway platform begin to move. She went over to look and found it was her sister Mila—another miracle!

Later in 1945 Cela and Mila went to the British zone in Germany where the Bricha, the clandestine project to resettle displaced survivors in Palestine, arranged for them to go to Palestine legally under a special quota for Jewish refugee children. Now there are three sisters living in Israel. In 1946, after attacks on our camp by hooligans or the AK (we're not sure which), we went to a displaced persons camp in Bamberg, Germany, where we were married on December 1.

In Bamberg I worked first for the United Nations Relief and Rehabilitation Administration and then for the International Refugee Organization and was paid in food and cigarettes. Since neither of us smoked, I sold the cigarettes or traded them for more food or other things we needed. We also had free shelter. Our first son, Robert, was born there in 1948.

We were registered to go to Palestine, but after we were married the Haganah (the major Jewish underground military organization in Palestine) no longer wanted us. So we also registered to go to Canada, Australia, the United States, and other countries. I was registered with the American Jewish Joint Distribution Committee as a tool-and-die maker. In 1949 President Harry Truman signed a law establishing a special quota for displaced persons and that opened the door to the United States for us. Six weeks later we were on a ship to the United States, the *General McCray.*

We had no relatives and only a few friends in the United States. We were sponsored by the Jewish Community Center of Lynn, Massachusetts. I had studied

English in high school, and we both took English courses in Germany, and we both spoke some German. Hela then changed her name to Helen.

When we arrived in New York, the Joint (as the committee was known) gave us train tickets to Boston and arranged to have people from Lynn meet us there and take us to Lynn by car. It was very difficult to get an apartment at that time so they put us in a hotel for a couple of weeks. Then they found a Jewish family that let the three of us use a room and have kitchen privileges. We were there for a while until they found us a one-bedroom apartment. We moved later to a larger apartment. Our second son, Arthur, was born in 1952. I worked in Lynn as a tool-and-die maker for six years, two years with one company, then four with another. When we became citizens, I applied for a job with IBM. I was accepted and assigned, in 1955, to its facility in Poughkeepsie, New York.

I began taking courses in engineering. I got my associate's degree in mechanical engineering in 1959 and continued working for IBM for thirty-two more years. I retired as an advisory engineer in 1988.

In Poughkeepsie we have all been active in Jewish affairs. We belong to a Conservative synagogue, Beth El, where I was vice president, and Helen was very active also. The children were both president of United Synagogue Youth and became *b'nai mitzvah* (the collective term for bar and bat mitzvahs). Both are now lawyers, one in White Plains, New York, and one in Milwaukee. Robert has two daughters, and Arthur has a daughter and a son.

When Holocaust deniers became prominent, both of us, especially Helen, became active in speaking to colleges and other groups about our experiences in the Holocaust. We have spoken in many places, not only in this area but in Mississippi, North Carolina, and other places. We will continue to do so. We have not suffered any bad psychological effects, nor have any of our survivor friends.

We went through hell and it's a miracle that we are here. We will never forget. However, life has to go on and you have to live a normal life. We went from ashes to life. There's nothing we can do about the past, but we have to do our best to teach the young generation and other people that we have to learn to live together and respect each other. Now our children are speaking to groups about our experiences, but they don't live it every day.

Do Not Go Gentle

CHARLES GELMAN
(b. 1922, Poland)

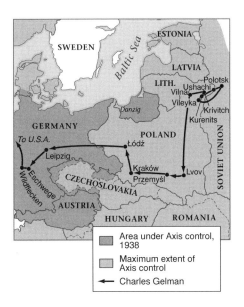

July 1941. We were huddling in the backyard of our neighbor, Mote-Leyb, sitting on the ground, our backs against the wall, and talking in whispers. The German army had arrived in town barely one week earlier. We met there daily just to stay out of the way of the police and the Germans, to exchange the latest rumors, and to kill time. Our former routine of living had been broken, most likely forever.

We lived in the eastern part of Poland, in Kurenits (sometimes pronounced, but never written, *Kurnits;* in Polish, *Kurzéniec;* in Russian, *Kurenéts*). When the Soviets occupied it on September 17, 1939, they promptly divided the population into politically "acceptable" and "unacceptable" segments. Anyone who didn't have his passport stamped with the designation "worker" or "peasant" could expect trouble from the authorities eventually. Because a large segment of the shtetl Jews made their living before 1939 by buying and selling, they had been designated "businessmen." Many were just peddlers and small merchants; they earned barely enough to survive. Nevertheless, they received the negative designation.

Throughout the period of Russian administration there were Jews living in our region who had come from the western part of Poland, which had been occupied by the Germans in September 1939. The stories they told were not pleasant, but we heard nothing of outright shootings. When the Russians offered them a chance to return, many signed up to be transported back to the German part of Poland. Of course, the Russians never intended to honor their offer; instead, they shipped these transportees east to Siberia. In so doing the Russians unintentionally saved the lives of thousands of Jews.

I was not quite eighteen then and lived with my parents, Yitskhok and Feyge, and four older sisters. My oldest sister, Sarah, was married and lived in Volozin. My youngest sister, Dina, who was about four years older than I, was also married and lived deep inside Russia, out of reach of the Germans. Also living at home were my two middle sisters, Ethel and Minn. Minya was in the last stages of pregnancy. Her husband, Sam Spektor, had received permission to visit his brother in Kharkov in Russia. When war broke out, he couldn't get back. He remained there throughout the war and survived.

One day an official order of the German commandant was posted in the public square. In German and Polish it demanded that all Jewish males between fourteen and sixty-five years of age assemble in the square at 2 P.M. the next day. Failure to comply, it stated, was punishable by death. About eight hundred men showed up and were made to stand in the hot summer sun until the commandant finally came out. He told us not to worry. He wished to have a Judenrat (Jewish council) appointed. Then and there he selected an Austrian Jew named Schatz to be the Judenrat leader. Then the commandant dismissed the entire group.

We didn't appreciate how lucky we were until a month or so later, when we found out that in the town of Vileyka, less than five miles away, all Jewish males had been assembled in the same way at about the same time, but all of them—about two thousand men—had been taken away, vanishing without a trace. They had in fact been shot the same day. Their place of execution was not discovered until after the war.

Toward the end of July I was among the 150 Jewish young people sent to the state farm of Lubanye for three days of work in the fields. Then we were relieved by another group of the same size. Each of us had to work there about once every two weeks. The rest of the time we worked in or around town. On Simchas Torah in 1941 I was at Lubanye for the spring potato harvesting. I recognized two young men from Kurenits, now policemen, who were approaching us with guns drawn. They began and kept up a diatribe, accusing us Jews of helping the Soviets. It became clear that what motivated them was a need for revenge—not for something we had done but for something the Soviets had done. What a convenient punching bag the Jews made under the Germans! No one was punished for injuring or even killing a Jew.

A group of armed German soldiers let us pass. At close range their uniforms and insignia looked different. They were, as we found out later, SS Einsatzkommandos (members of the SS Emergency Strike Force), who specialized in massacring supposed enemies of the German Reich within conquered territories: communists, Jews, Gypsies, and others. Something horrible was happening in Kurenits. In the previous thirty-six hours the SS had killed fifty-three Jews, more than half of them women and children.

Now I was sent to work in Vileyka. Before the war it had been an unpretentious, middle-sized town of about fifteen thousand inhabitants, four thousand of whom were Jews. Late in October 1941 it became the seat of the provincial government. The provincial governor (*Gebietskommissar*), along with scores of officials, both military and civilian, took up residence in Vileyka. Dozens of German businessmen also settled there in order to appropriate as much grain, cattle, and clothing as possible for the population back home. The military did their own requisitioning. All these people, with their staffs and secretariats, constituted quite a sizeable number of Germans in need of living quarters and office space.

All that was left of the Jewish population of Vileyka at this time were women, children, and a few old men. Many houses and offices of Jews were empty and abandoned; some had been partially destroyed by looters. The Germans needed these places restored quickly for their own use, so they ordered a number of skilled workers to be sent from Kurenits to work in Vileyka. I joined the four painters working for the *Gebietskommissar*.

After the governor's house was finished, we had to paint the houses and offices of lesser officials. We also repainted their theater. What I remember most, however, was working on the house of the chief of the local Sicherheitsdienst (SD). The SD, the Security Service, was part of the SS, and its sole mission was murdering Jews and Gypsies and all others the SD considered undesirable. The number of Germans in these local SD units was not great—perhaps about thirty in all—but in less than two years they were responsible for obliterating about 85 percent of all the Jews in the province under their jurisdiction.

The Germans couldn't accomplish this all by themselves. They were assisted by special volunteers recruited in Latvia, Lithuania, and Ukraine, countries known for their widespread anti-Semitism. These volunteers were part of the SD units and wore the same uniforms as the Germans did, with the same skull insignia on their hats. They were zealous and efficient and did most of the actual killing, while the Germans supervised. These volunteers all seemed to be selected for their size: they stood at least six feet tall and weighed at least 200 pounds.

It took us about three weeks to complete the paint job to the SD chief's satisfaction. The distinctive smell of burning human flesh assaulted our nostrils most of the time that we were working on the chief's house. Dozens of human beings were being shot in Vileyka every day, then thrown into a huge pit near the old courthouse, and burned. The fire burned day and night for as long as the SD was there, that is, approximately three years. People were continually brought into the old courthouse to be interrogated, tortured, and incarcerated. Sooner or later most of them wound up in the pit.

We couldn't celebrate Purim in 1942 in any really traditional way, of course. In the evening I read the Megillah (Book of Esther) to a few neighbors. Except for its being Purim, this was an evening like any other. The pattern was that most German *Aktionen* (roundups ending in mass murder) against Jews were carried out on Jewish holy days or, in order to confuse us, a few days before or after a holy day. Soviet Russian holidays could also trigger these *Aktionen*. Thus around three in the morning I was suddenly awakened by a loud banging on the front door. When we opened it, we were facing three huge men in SD uniforms, carrying submachine guns. They led us out the back door and into the yard. There we were confronted by three more SD men. There were seven of us, two women and the five of us painters. The SD men marched us out of the yard and into a truck; they lowered the canvas flaps at the back and on the sides. Then the truck started moving. We couldn't tell what direction it was going in, but it did not really matter. We said good-bye to each other.

About ten minutes later the truck stopped. As we got off one by one, I recognized the interior of the SD compound—it included the jail, the courthouse, and a garage. Once inside the garage we were put in a corner and told to wait with about three hundred other people. Trucks arrived, bringing more and more people, who were then driven into the garage. This continued all through the night and most of the following day.

Many of the Jews who had been rounded up were originally from Kurenits, and a large number were young women working at menial jobs in Vileyka. I recognized the chief of the SD as he walked up to one of the smaller groups. He talked to the people there and after each conversation motioned with his hand for the person to join the large group. When the chief finally got to one of us painters, the answer to his question was, "I'm a painter and I work for the *Gebietskommissar.*" This time the finger didn't move. "Have you the certificate to prove it?" the chief asked. We each took out the certificates that stated we were working for the *Gebietskommissar* as painters. The SD chief glanced at the certificates and told the five of us to stand apart from the others.

Presently, we were led into a small side room; there we joined eleven other people who had been picked out of earlier truckloads. Later we were joined by one more couple. Besides the five of us, two others, carpenters, were from Kurenits. The rest were from Vileyka: two saddlers with their wives and one twelve-year-old son, one candle maker, and, I believe, one printer and his wife. We began to hear shooting outside and saw a reddish light coming through the small barred window high up near the ceiling. What I saw through the window was two SD men, each of whom was leading a group of three people toward the fire in the infamous pit. The shooting continued throughout the rest of the night and most of the next day.

No food or water was brought to us, but worry and tension depressed our appetites anyway and nobody felt hungry. Early in the evening the door finally opened and an officer came in. He announced that we were going to be released. I'm not certain of the exact number that perished in this *Aktion,* but it could have been as many as two thousand, including the fifty Jews from Kurenits. The SD spared only eighteen people out of two thousand.

That night was the longest I can remember. Sleep was out of the question. About eleven in the morning the door finally opened again and an officer called us out into the garage. This time it was really empty. They took us to a place on the outskirts of Vileyka where the Germans had created a second ghetto. Sixty families had been brought in from Kurenits, all headed by *Spezialisten* (skilled workers): tailors, shoemakers, carpenters, blacksmiths, sheet-metal workers, glaziers, and others whose skills the Germans needed. All were allowed to bring along their wives and their children younger than fifteen. These workers and their families were quite happy to move to Vileyka because working for the *Gebietskommissar* afforded a measure of protection for the immediate future.

One day in the early spring, when I came home from work and walked into our room, I noticed that all conversation among the ten people present had come to an abrupt halt. My questions were answered in a vague and offhand manner. Something must have happened to my family in Kurenits. I decided to go there and find out for myself what was up. So the next morning I left the place I was working, with the other painters covering for me. I could sense that something disastrous must have happened, but I could not imagine the extent of it. In Zalman Mandl's house I found my mother holding little Shimshon, Minya's son, on her lap. Mother burst out crying when she saw me, and we cried in each other's arms for a long time.

The disaster had struck two days earlier. Without warning two Polish policemen, both drunk, had barged into our house. They ordered everybody except Mother out into the backyard—my father, my sister Ethel, and my sister Minn, with the baby in her arms. Then they shot Father and Minn dead. The baby fell from Minn's lifeless arms into the snow. Ethel tried to run away, but one of the policemen shot her dead too. Mother was standing by the kitchen window and saw everything. These policemen were not only accustomed to cruelty, they positively reveled in it. In addition to my sisters and father, the pair had murdered twenty-nine other Jews in Kurenits, a total of thirty-two.

If there is any consolation, it is in the knowledge that some measure of justice came down on the killers. One, a native of Kurenits, was killed four months later by partisans. Then one day during the summer of 1942 the other one decided to settle a few private accounts of his own with some of the other townsfolk. He went out and shot eighteen of them, all non-Jews, since no Jews were left in Kostenevich. He apparently saw little difference between killing Jews and non-Jews. The Germans, however, did make the distinction. They picked him up, put a bullet in his neck, and tossed him into the pit.

By the summer of 1942 the population of the newer Vileyka ghetto had swelled from the original sixty families to about 240 people. This was an open ghetto in that it had no fences around it and, most important, no guards. However, if you were stopped in the street, you had to explain your absence from the ghetto.

Consequently, only workers were able to move around certain streets with relative ease.

The survival rate among the Jews of Kurenits, relative to that of surrounding towns, was greater because their destruction came comparatively late, three days before Rosh Hashanah in 1942, giving people more time to prepare for the inevitable and to devise or construct hiding places, some of them quite ingenious. We called such a place a *malina* (hiding place) or a *skhron* (shelter). The most popular kind of hiding place was constructed under the floor of a room of a house. Another was a false wall several feet out from an existing one. People constructed other kinds of shelters too. They dug holes in their backyards and camouflaged them as best they could. In the end, however, relatively few were able to escape the Poles and Germans who were hunting them.

In September 1942 the long-expected thunderbolt struck. Kurenits's turn had finally come. The Kurenits Jews were being destroyed. The news electrified and stunned the entire ghetto. Almost everybody had family members who were being massacred at that very moment. One day details of the Kurenits *Aktion* began to trickle in. It began before dawn. SD troops and police surrounded Kurenits and began to flush out as many Jews as they could from homes and hiding places. Then the whole collection of some fifteen hundred Jews was herded outside of town where they were driven into a large barn. The barn doors were closed and a wooden bar set in place. The structure was then torched. Those who managed to break out were shot down by the SD and police who surrounded the building. The cold ashes of victims were eventually spread over the field on which the barn had stood and plowed under.

Now, if there was any chance at all of surviving, it would have to be outside German control. For us in Vileyka that meant just once place: the forest. I became an organizer of an escape from the ghetto. While our families were still alive in Kurenits, we had felt constrained to postpone such an undertaking, lest we put their lives in jeopardy. With that last constraint removed we started to plan our move systematically.

Several days after the Kurenits *Aktion* we got word that some Kurenits families had escaped and were living in a forest outside town. We also got word that partisans lived in the forest. That would explain why the Germans and the police had not hunted down the Jews who escaped. Of course, none of us really had any idea at all of how to keep warm and dry in the woods, and that realization tended to restrain even the most enthusiastic among us. We also came to understand that the great majority of the ghetto residents were simply not ready to abandon "home," and that they were also adamant about preventing anyone else from leaving, thinking it would jeopardize the position of those who stayed behind. From then on we communicated with each other secretly.

Five of us, the hard core, were ready to go at any time. We were just waiting for final preparations to be completed and for the best time. Another ten or twelve were undecided. We tried to sway them into coming with us. Simple as it may sound, leaving was actually quite complicated. To begin with, you had to know where to go to find either partisans or at least other Jews who could initiate you into forest living. Otherwise, you could wander around for weeks without finding a safe place. In reality, there were many different woods and very few partisans, and those few were constantly moving from one place to another, so running into partisans in the woods by chance was unlikely.

October of 1942 was drawing to a close. Unless we moved out soon, I thought, we'd be stuck here for good or at least over the winter. Yet we seemed simply unable to follow a preconceived and organized plan. The escape, when it came, would have to be spontaneous— and that would require some sort of catalyst. It came in the form of a major tragedy on November 7, the anniversary of the Russian Revolution. At about ten in the morning a Gentile woman who lived across the street from the old ghetto of Vileyka appeared with the terrible news that the entire population of the old ghetto had been wiped out during the night.

I happened to be in the workshop building when this news reached us, and it caused an uproar. But I could already hear people questioning the validity of the news: "Don't listen to her. She must be an anti-Semite." The same old story. People don't want to hear bad news, and they mistrust and dislike the messenger who brings it. I brashly volunteered to go there and check out the situation. I saw with my own eyes the absence of life there only hours after the residents' lives had been extinguished. Ten minutes later I was back at the workshops, giving the people there the report of my harrowing experience. Now no one could question the truth of what the Gentile woman had told us.

Sixteen of us were ready and willing to go, fourteen men and two women, all of us young and unmarried. Our plan was to walk through town singly or in pairs, starting at four in the afternoon. The day was cold but dry and we were grateful for that. By the time we met up again, the sun would be setting, and the Germans and the police were known to dislike going into any woods after sundown. I wanted to dress as warmly as I could, so I put on an extra pair of pants, a double shirt, and a wool sports jacket—all the clothes I owned. None of us ran into any difficulty getting across town. We reassembled near the woods and counted all sixteen of us present. Then we discarded the yellow Stars of David that we had had to wear. The sun was quite low in the sky—it was less than half an hour to nightfall.

We had the name and location of a partisan contact, a woman we had known before the war as a Soviet activist. I asked for two volunteers to come with me to get our bearings. It was dusk by this time. To our surprise, on our return we found nobody where we thought the group would be waiting for us. We were learning the first lesson in forest living: it's easy to get lost among the trees, especially after dark. We had no choice but to keep going on our own. Around midnight we came to the village and found the right house. The woman instructed us to go on to another village, a little more than a mile further on, to the local shoemaker. We found the village and the house easily. The shoemaker was already up and at work.

We were quite happy to find a Jew from Kurenits there, Iche Fiedler. The village was right at the edge of the forest. Jews felt somewhat safer lingering here than in more distant villages. Iche said he usually walked all night, going through several villages, knocking on doors and asking for food. Usually, such a night of collecting would bring in enough food to last a family several days. Then he would repeat the process, this time in different villages so as not to overburden the same households. Nearly two hundred people lived in the forest, he said, and they all gathered food the same way.

The Germans and the police rarely visited the nearby villages, but partisans did so occasionally and forest Jews quite often. Some villagers gave food to the Jews out of compassion; most, however, gave because they didn't want to offend the authorities, the partisans, or the Jews, whom they assumed to be under partisan protection. The true state of affairs between partisans and forest Jews was somewhat different, however. Partisans would sometimes help feed the Jews, but their concern for the welfare of the forest Jews hardly ever went beyond that. And most of the time no partisans were around. But the myth of partisan protection certainly helped the forest Jews, and the Jews did what they could to foster it.

It was time for us to take leave of the shoemaker and his hospitality and go into the forest. Before long we reached the camp we were looking for. Each family had gathered around its own fire. Sometimes the remnants of two or more families came together as one unit around a single fire. People were already digging bunker-like winter homes, I was told. Nonetheless, some families spent the whole winter above ground, no small feat, considering the harshness of Russian winters in general and the exceptional cold of that winter in particular. Only the fire, which they always kept burning, prevented them from freezing.

The second day after my arrival at the camp I was introduced to a mother, her twenty-year-old daughter, the daughter's fiancé, and the woman's son, who was a partisan. The son and his friend, also a partisan, had just returned from visiting another partisan friend. The two partisans were armed with rifles and grenades, and my eyes popped when I saw them. These were the first partisans I had ever laid eyes on, and one was even a Jew. In the ghetto my dream had been to be armed the way these men were and become a partisan to fight the Germans. Regrettably, the two men could not help me make my dream come true.

A couple of days later I met a small group of young people. Slowly, the idea emerged of going somewhere safer for the winter. We decided to go north to a particular wooded area, build a *zemlyanka* (dugout or underground shelter), and stock it with enough food to last the winter. In our group Motl Varfman owned a sawed-off rifle, a sorry piece of armament, and only three rounds of ammunition. Another man in our group had fashioned what could pass for a revolver from a tree root.

The closer we got to the area where we planned to settle, the shakier our original plan became. We had counted on finding an area free of the enemy as well as of partisans. Instead, the farther north we went, the more partisans we ran into. At first we were glad, hoping they would let us join them, but none would accept us. We finally stopped at a village called Charnitse, where a whole *otryad* (company) of partisans was stationed. I was impressed by how they moved freely in and between the villages during the day and how they stayed in one village for a long period of time.

To be accepted into a partisan unit you needed to bring your own weapon, a rifle or a handgun. But these items were very hard for Jews to come by. Our group split up. Some managed to buy several hand grenades from a farmer whom they had known, and they were accepted into the partisan unit stationed in Charnitse. Motl and I undertook a dangerous thirty-mile hike into German-held territory to see a farmer, who Motl believed could obtain a rifle or two for him. However, Motl's confidence was entirely misplaced. We returned empty-handed. Motl's foot was sore so I decided to stay with him until he was ready to travel. We set out a day later, and for the next two weeks we kept finding that we'd taken the same route that two other men from our group had taken.

As Motl and I continued eastward, we entered a corridor under partisan control. That meant that we could go through villages in broad daylight and keep walking as long as we had light to see by. Because this was partisan country, neither the Germans nor the police dared set foot in it. Later we found out that this corridor was a full sixty miles long—extending all the way to the city of Polotsk—and about twenty-five miles wide. It was almost like a separate state; the partisans even collected taxes from the peasants in the form of food and clothing.

We reached the town of Ushachi. Before the war it had counted about eight thousand inhabitants and had been the seat of county administration. Now the population was about a third of what it had been. Most men of military age had retreated with the Russians, while most of the others had left to join the partisans. There was something depressing about Ushachi. The atmosphere was different from what it was in the smaller villages, where people generally were more pleasant and friendly.

After trying without success to get into a number of partisan units, I was finally accepted into the Utkin Brigade, stationed in a village less than four miles from Polotsk. I went to the village and reported for duty. The commanding officer was a young Red Army lieutenant, a former prisoner of war. The unit also had a political officer *(komissar otryada),* equal in command authority to the military officer, just like the Red Army. Our company consisted of 350 fighters. Most were younger men, but there were a few middle-aged men among us. Of the 350 no more than about a dozen had noncombat, or support, duties such as preparing food, managing food supplies, making and repairing boots, etc.

The real threat that we posed to the Germans lay in our hit-and-run tactics, and for this our light armaments were quite adequate. What we overran by dark of night, we usually abandoned in the morning. If the enemy decided to take back a lost position and brought in artillery and tanks, we simply faded into the landscape and hit him again the next night, either in the same place or elsewhere. After a few such experiences, the Germans were sometimes persuaded to abandon certain garrisons altogether.

Psychologically, the winter of 1943 was not easy for us. Guard duty in inclement weather was draining, while being cooped up indoors the rest of the time was stressful for young men. By the end of April, however, spring was in the air. At nine o'clock one morning a messenger on horseback burst out of the woods and galloped up to the commanding officer's quarters. The Germans were bearing down on the base in force from the northwest. As expected, they were taking the road across which the partisans had felled trees, a few of them mined, and into which they had dug pits, also mined. We took our assigned places on the perimeter of the base, some in trenches that had been dug during the previous year and outfitted with heavy machine guns. The mortars and light machine guns took their places. The people of the village evacuated their houses and fled into the woods. Twenty minutes after the first alert, the village was empty, and all our men were at the ready.

Two hours passed. Scouts now brought in reports from which we estimated the enemy force to be at least eight hundred men, with four tanks and many trucks. One partisan had hidden under branches in a depression right by the side of the road. Then he leaped up and tossed an antitank grenade at the lead tank. That attack was our cue. We opened fire with our rifles and machine guns. The grenade hit the rear of the tank. A tremendous explosion shook the ground under us. Stunned, we paused just a moment in our firing. Then we started firing as quickly as loading and aiming permitted. It was almost unbelievable that so much could happen in such a short time. Barely a minute had passed since the first explosion. The Germans recovered from the shock and initial confusion of our attack and began to return our fire in a more confident and organized manner. Then the two tanks that remained also opened fire. The tide of battle had definitely turned. The order was given and we melted away into the forest. A few days later partisan intelligence reported that we had killed twenty-seven Germans and wounded thirty-two.

It had been a long, hard, tiring day for all of us, especially for a novice like me. I had marked many firsts this day: my first time under fire, the first time I saw people killed, and the first time I saw the hated enemy as mere mortals like everyone else. Yes, the Germans died like ordinary folk when bullets hit them or fire burned them. With a gun in my hand I was on an equal footing with them. For me the master-slave relationship died on the battlefield that April day.

This was also my first opportunity to begin to even the score with the Germans for the deaths of my family and of so many others. This day's action constituted the down payment. I would use the rest of my service with the partisans doing my best to discharge the debt in full.

The political officer of my company, an obvious anti-Semite, was the exception rather than the rule. The rest of my company did not exhibit any direct feelings of anti-Semitism toward me, other than an occasional subtle dig about the fighting ability of the Jews. After a reasonable time, however, when I and the few other Jews in our brigade had the chance to prove our worth in battle, we were fully accepted.

One warm sunny afternoon the brigade commander and a party of officers from brigade headquarters paid us a visit. They needed nine volunteers for a special assignment, and I was among those chosen. This mission had been ordered all the way from the Soviet Union, and it was as ambitious as it was dangerous. Russian pilots sent to fly over the city of Polotsk had noted how strong the city's antiaircraft defenses were. Our task was to go to a village on the outskirts of Polotsk and penetrate a garrison that housed all German personnel operating the city's antiaircraft defenses. We were to kill or disable as many as possible and cripple these defenses.

When I reached my target house, I took out three grenades, armed each in turn, and heaved one through each window. All this took no more than a few seconds. I started back at a run toward the yard we had started from. The first explosion went off when I was just one house away from my target. Explosions two and three followed closely. I heard other explosions, some near, some far, and then some rifle shots. So far, we had gotten hardly any response from the Germans. We had taken them by surprise. Intelligence a few days later reported five Germans dead and twelve wounded, but later they reported that the final effect of our raid was almost nil.

Summer 1943. An elite company was being organized, the Komsomolski company. It would consist of a hundred or so fighters drawn from our brigade and from others. We were to concentrate on demolition missions, like blowing up bridges, trains, and railroad tracks. All members of the new unit were expected to be young and to excel in demolition. I qualified on both counts and so was transferred into it. We operated mostly on special assignments for which were assembled ad hoc units of squad or platoon size.

I was becoming quite adept with explosives, and on a mission it was usually my task to select the kinds of explosives or mines to be used and to assemble and prepare them. This was a demanding job; it required the most extreme care at every stage of preparation, from assembling through the final placement. The explosive we used most often was called, in Russian, *tol*. It looked somewhat like soap but was harder in consistency. We used *tol* explosives on bridges, small factories, captured food or materiel that would be awkward to burn or cart away, enemy bunkers, and other strongholds. When the partisans first began blowing up railroads, they used *tol* almost exclusively and with much success. They derailed many locomotives and cars, killing many Germans and destroying great quantities of war materiel.

My first operation took us nearly two weeks to bring off. On our fourth try we succeeded in planting a mine between two ties of a railroad line. Three stood lookout while the fourth man and I did the actual work. Soon we saw a very long train traveling very fast, and it was getting close to where we had planted our mine. Obviously, its two locomotives were hauling something heavy and important. I remember thinking quite clearly that I was not going to let myself miss the timing on this one. I gave a jerk on the rope just as the front wheels of the first locomotive ran over the mine. Nearly twenty-two pounds of *tol* went off in an ear-shattering explosion. The front end of the locomotive danced up into the air and then returned to Earth on the slope of the embankment next to the tracks. The cars behind the second locomotive followed it down the embankment. Then there was a second explosion, and a fireball began to expand right in front of me, while debris spewed up into the orange air along with what looked like huge metal drums.

Before the day ended, we had reports from a number of sources. They all agreed that two locomotives and eighteen to twenty cars had been utterly destroyed. Traffic on the line was halted for at least a full day, while the salvage crews cleared away the debris and restored the damaged track. It took us another two days to get back to our village, where a heroes' welcome awaited us.

The Germans were determined to keep open this most important lifeline to their armies on the eastern front and so were obliged to take still further countermeasures. By 1944 no trains passed through partisan-controlled territory after sundown. During the day foot patrols often preceded a train, and the Germans trained dogs to sniff out concealed explosives. Sometimes they pushed an empty flatbed car ahead of a train to take the brunt of any explosion. Eventually, these countermeasures put us out of the demolition business, at least in areas near Ushachi County— but at a cost. Thousands of German troops were tied up working as railroad guards and patrols. Rail shipments to the front were slowed enormously. Thus the partisan effort was taking its toll, even when the primary business of demolition was no longer possible.

We then moved our operations still farther to the west, into an area that had belonged to Poland in 1939, before the war. Through the remainder of 1943 we operated with a certain degree of success, chalking up twelve derailed trains that were carrying large quantities of war materiel, including some heavy guns and a whole trainload of new tanks.

Toward the end of 1943 we planned a colossal, one-night attack on the railroads that was to extend close to 1,250 miles. The plan was to damage more track than the Germans could replace from reserves at hand. They would have to send to the west for replacements, thus tying up their lines even further. Our attack was also planned to coincide with a big Red Army offensive to the east. The operation that night went off smoothly, and I had the added satisfaction of knowing that all the explosives that my company set off caused the maximum damage planned. Except for repair crews, there was no traffic on this line for a full two weeks.

During the winter of 1943–44 we kept up our operations against the railroads and managed to derail two more trains farther to the west. Closer to home, we often mined a section of heavily traveled highway between Lepel and the town of Kamen, and over several months we blew up a number of trucks. German countermeasures, however, soon made our ambushes costly and impractical.

Another winter was coming to an end. Our morale was high as news of more and more German defeats reached us. Even though the front line was still far to the east, we could now contemplate the German retreat through our area. Evidently, the Germans also gave some thought to that eventuality. They assembled seven divisions of their own and, together with sizeable units of police, prepared a systematic assault on the whole Ushachi County area, which was occupied by as many as sixty thousand partisans. They had wrested it from German rule, village by village, and then had held off the Germans for more than two years.

There were continual skirmishes along the perimeter. This time, however, the German assault was mounted simultaneously from every side. My company was sent to the front line with the others and given a sector to defend. The enemy forces far exceeded our own. It was estimated that some 100,000 Germans and police took part in the "blockade," as it was called. Yet for the first two weeks our resistance was strong. We clung to every hill and village and gave up very little territory. During daylight we were often bombarded by artillery and heavy mortar fire—and twice by planes—and we had to give up positions. Then at night we usually counterattacked and regained the ground we had lost during the day. But lack of sleep and irregular and inadequate meals left us haggard and worn out, and there was no relief in sight. The main German push was apparently coming from the north and east, and by the middle of the fifth week of fighting, the partisan-controlled area had shrunk to about twelve by six miles in size and was still shrinking.

The next day the order came to abandon all our positions after sundown and to do it as quietly as possible. Survival called for a concentrated breakout as soon as possible. We started off and marched all night. Thousands of partisans were streaming in from all directions to a central area that was little bigger than four square miles. The roads were primitive and narrow and could accommodate horse-and-wagon traffic in only one direction. Within twenty-four hours we had abandoned all the horses and wagons.

By morning we had settled down in the woods at the edge of a large clearing. Around noon enemy planes subjected us to a lengthy aerial bombardment. At dusk about a thousand of us set out single file. But after a couple of hours it became apparent that I was part of a short trailing segment that had broken off from the main column. There were about thirty-five to forty of us with no leader and no idea where we should be heading. We sat down on the ground, dejected.

Then we heard the first shots. Machine-gun fire was coming from the garrison to our right, followed by mortars. Luckily, we reconnected with the main group again at the edge of the forest. Our objective was to reach the almost impenetrable bog just beyond the clearing. We would be safe there, as no Germans or police would risk entering a bog that stretched for many miles. I was just coming out at the far end of a neck of dry land in the bog when the first burst of artillery landed behind me. I pushed myself to the limit and dashed across to the other side. There I joined about eighty partisans who had already made it to safety. Then a barrage of artillery fire closed the neck behind us, and nobody else could get through.

There were several more skirmishes over the next month of moving through western Poland. We marched eastward all day. One afternoon we met the first unit of the Red Army that was coming in the opposite direction, a company of foot soldiers led by a captain riding a bicycle. He stopped to talk a minute. I was shocked by the appearance of our liberators; they looked so tired, so haggard, and so small.

We were the first partisans the captain had met. Apparently, he was as fascinated by us as we were in meeting the liberating Red Army.

Our destination turned out not to be the town of Ushachi but a village some distance from it. We pulled in a couple of days later, and there we found assembled just about the whole Utkin Brigade, approximately 90 percent of the original force. We were told that the brigade was going to be disbanded the next day and the men would simultaneously be drafted into the Red Army. Only twenty-two partisans out of the entire brigade were exempted and I was one of them, thanks to the political officer of my company. When the partisan leaders walked by me, standing in formation with the others, I heard the political officer say, "Let's leave this young man here. We'll need him to help build the county back up again. He had a good education and will make a fine teacher." I did not fully appreciate then that with those few words he had saved my life.

Within six or seven weeks few of the men from the Utkin Brigade who were mobilized into the Red Army were still alive. They were all sent into battle without adequate preparation or any further training. Of the nine or ten Jewish men in the old Utkin Brigade, I know of only one who survived, and he was badly wounded and had to spend six months in a hospital. When the twenty-two of us who had been exempted from induction were discharged, we each received a certificate attesting to our length of service with the Utkin Brigade and describing our accomplishments. My certificate also noted that I'd been nominated for the Red Star medal.

So I left Ushachi and started back to Kurenits. I hitchhiked and got rides on trucks, about the only means of transportation for civilians. I soon found that Eli Spektor and his family were living in one of the vacant Jewish houses in Kurenits. Their old house, on the town square, had been burned down. They welcomed me and let me stay with them whenever I was in town. They brought me up to date on everything that had happened in the forest. In all, out of a Jewish population of about two thousand in Kurenits before the Holocaust, only about 220 had survived.

The center of town had been destroyed. All but a couple of the houses on the square had burned down, including ours. This had been a farewell present from the local police just before they fled. Only the thick masonry walls of our house remained standing. Strangely, this sight did not provoke any unhappiness in me. On the contrary, I felt relieved. It would make it easier for me to break with the town altogether. I spent nearly three weeks in Kurenits. I walked through every part of the town, as if searching for something. Maybe I was trying to understand why it had all happened. I knew many Gentiles there and I had gone to school with their children. Interestingly enough, though, none of them, not one, approached me with any expression of sympathy or regret for what had taken place so recently.

I heard much, from the surviving Jews, of a righteous Gentile by the name of Bakacz, who lived on Vileyka Street. He had managed to save a Torah scroll from one of the burning synagogues, exposing himself to reprisals from the police and to ridicule, or worse, from the bystanders. He guarded the scroll through the remainder of the occupation and handed it over to the first Jews who returned to Kurenits. It was also said that he helped, as much as he could, with food and in other ways.

I went to pay a visit to this extraordinary man and to thank him for all he had done. He said he didn't feel he had done anything out of the ordinary. He said any decent human being would have done just what he did. True, I thought, true. He had meant only to express a sense of modesty but had managed in that one sentence to expose the cause of our predicament. How many more people like him were there, willing and ready to think and act like him? Unfortunately, too few.

A modest monument marks the place where a Jewish community was cruelly wiped out three days before Rosh Hashanah in 1942; it keeps its lonely vigil unadorned by flags or flowers. The inscription on the monument proclaims in Russian: "Here lie 1,040 people of Jewish nationality brutally murdered by the Fascist occupiers on September 7, 1942." It is one of the rare instances where the Soviets permitted the victims to be identified as Jews and not merely as "Soviet citizens."

From Kurenits I often made the trip to Vileyka, the regional capital, to see what jobs might be available but without much success. I had definitely decided not to settle down in Kurenits. Finally, I landed a decent office job in the town of Krivitch.

In 1945 the governments of Poland and the Soviet Union reached an agreement that allowed everyone who had been a citizen of Poland before the war but was now living in Russia to return to Poland if he or she so desired. For Jews, returning to Poland rarely indicated a desire to settle there. It was first a means of getting out of Russia and, after that, a springboard for emigration to Palestine or one of the Western countries, preferably outside Europe. In 1945 and 1946 more than 80 percent of the Jewish survivors who could do so chose to leave the Soviet Union, a country whose borders had been hermetically sealed until then. Only two Jews, both of them old men, chose to remain in Kurenits.

I was fully qualified to apply for permission to return to Poland. However, because I had become an investigator in the office of the county attorney, an important position, my application would have been denied and my freedom jeopardized. The only option open to me was to leave illegally.

It was midnight in the large, crowded Vilna station. The train for Lvov was still not ready for boarding, but such delays were common. This was February 1946, and transportation, along with all government agencies, was in shambles because of the long, bitter war.

Soon the train for Lvov was ready and I boarded. It started moving and gathering speed. Now it was safe to enter the lavatory. I carefully locked the door behind me and began to work rapidly, mixing bits of lead from a special type of pencil with water from a small bottle to make a perfectly usable ink solution. I added "Lvov" next to "Vilna" on the destination line of my travel permit.

We arrived at the Lvov station. The clock showed that it was a few minutes after 8 A.M. I inquired about the train to Przemyśl, Poland. "You missed it by a half hour," replied the clerk, and I would have to wait until 7:30 the following morning, as only one train a day went to Przemyśl.

Few people were in the streets, and I walked around the ruins for a few hours. The time had come to switch identities. I was excited, but I forced myself to work methodically. I had planned every detail so that I could make the switch in the shortest time possible. I changed from head to toe into clothes worn by soldiers of the Red Army, including a soldier's epaulets and an army brass star on the front of my sheepskin hat. In less than ten minutes I had transformed myself into a private who was being transferred to an army outpost north of the Polish city of Łódź. I took the travel orders and other documents necessary to support this new identity out of concealment and put them into a front pocket, ready to be produced instantly if needed. My old clothes and identification went into my duffel bag.

The street was still empty. The option of taking the 6 P.M. local train now became more attractive. Although I would have to spend the night at a small station about two miles from the border, I hoped this would pose no problems. The moment I stepped on this train, I knew I would have to rely on improvisation and expediency. By traveling on a train headed for the border, I had effectively severed the last connection with my legitimate past in the USSR. After a short while I threw my old papers and clothing from the rear platform of the moving train.

Most of the passengers in my car and probably also in the rest of the train were peasants from villages along the route. One villager seemed to be in good spirits and quite talkative. My ears perked up instantly when I heard him mention that he was getting off at the last stop. I asked him if I could stay the night in his house. I was pleasantly surprised to hear the man agree with my request. By the time the train reached its last stop, the villager and I were the only two passengers left in our car. He, however, had obviously had a change of heart. I felt let down, to put it mildly. Somewhat later, I would realize how truly lucky I'd been.

Four military men—a second lieutenant and three soldiers—also stepped off the train. They too were headed for Poland, where they would join their unit at some Soviet garrison. We entered the station, which consisted of one small room, now dark and deserted. I soon got into a comradely conversation with my new-found fellow travelers and felt that it was good to be traveling with a group.

A train soon pulled into the station and stopped. I went outside to investigate. A freight train was returning to Poland after delivering a load of Polish coal. I rushed back into the station to wake up the lieutenant. We woke the rest of the group, grabbed our gear, and ran to the train. Both the lieutenant and I understood the opportunity at hand and were anxious not to miss it.

Riding freight trains was an accepted practice in postwar Soviet Union. It helped relieve pressure on the chronically congested passenger train lines and also often saved time and money. After ten minutes or so the train began to roll. Some of my companions, if not all, were already asleep. Soon the train arrived at the border. The sound of approaching footsteps soon stopped at our door. A flashlight beam danced around the interior of our car, finally settling on our stretched-out bodies on the floor. I heard a man's voice demanding to be shown identification papers. I gathered that he was addressing the lieutenant, who, being in charge of his group, had all the needed papers in his possession. After no more than a minute I heard him pronounce "khorosho"—okay. Rubbing my eyes and acting as if I were still half-asleep, I responded to his demand for my papers. I handed him the *komandirovka*—travel orders. "The soldier's booklet," he demanded after a while. This booklet, approximately three inches by four inches in size, contained all the pertinent information about its owner. Every soldier in the Red Army was supposed to carry such a booklet on his person at all times. I handed the booklet to him. I had been assured in Vilna by the man who obtained it for me that it was all a traveling soldier needed. I fervently hoped and prayed he was right. Finally, after what seemed ages, he handed both documents back to me and wordlessly walked out of the car.

It was daylight when we arrived at Przemyśl. My next destination was Kraków, Poland's ancient capital. From there I would continue to my final destination in Poland—Łódź. Łódź, according to my information, was an unofficial way station for many Jews coming into Poland from the Soviet Union. Their objective was to reach a Western country outside the Soviet orbit. I joined the lieutenant's group, which was also going to Kraków, in a freight car. The cars were filling up fast with Polish civilians. As soon as the later arrivals noticed our group of Russian soldiers, they moved to an already congested area. Their hostility seemed to be based on deep-seated hatred of the Soviet Union. We arrived at Kraków about 7 P.M. without incident. I immediately took leave of the lieutenant and his group.

The train for Łódź was not due to leave until seven o'clock in the morning. After a while a middle-aged couple caught my attention as they passed by me. They were speaking Yiddish. I followed them out of the station and engaged them in conversation. They were both survivors of concentration camps and were now living outside Kraków. Within a month or two they'd be leaving Poland for the West. They urged me to consider defecting from the Soviet army and handed me the address of the Jewish Committee in Łódź. I pocketed the address without giving any intimation that I intended to use it.

In the morning I was on my way to Łódź. By 11 A.M. we were approaching the city, and I felt my heart beat faster as I neared the end of my journey. However, the end to my tribulations hadn't quite arrived yet. Two Soviet MPs were checking the documents of all Soviet military personnel passing through the station. I got back into the train and quickly tore the epaulets from my coat and shirt and removed the star from my hat, transforming myself back to a civilian. I joined the line of people moving slowly toward the station, but I could see no way of getting by the MPs unobserved.

A solution suddenly presented itself at the very last moment. Two railroad men from our train who had been walking ahead of me suddenly veered to their left and continued at an angle toward the chain-link fence about 150 feet away. I fell in behind them, and soon a hole large enough for a man to climb through became visible. Within seconds I found myself in the street outside the station. A streetcar had just stopped nearby. I sprinted over and got on it just as it was pulling away.

My nightmare was now finally coming to an end. Only half an hour later I was sitting in the office of the Jewish Committee. Soon I was reunited with friends from Kurenits. The next day I was helped to acquire civilian clothing, and the committee also provided me with a card stating that I was a duly registered member of the Jewish community in Łódź.

I found life in Poland different in many ways from the life I had known in Russia. The political climate was somewhat more relaxed, at least at the grassroots level. The leaders knew that Poles were overwhelmingly opposed to Communist ideology in general and to Russian domination specifically. Of equal, if not greater, importance was the role of the Roman Catholic Church. Despite all this, however, Poland was now a firmly established totalitarian country ruled by the Communist Party. What had not changed in Poland was the scourge of anti-Semitism that for centuries had emanated openly from the pulpit and the classroom. This hatred of Jews resulted in a full-blown pogrom in July 1946 in the city of Kielce, when forty-two Jewish Holocaust survivors were murdered by a Polish mob with the assistance of some Polish military officers. It marked a turning point in the postwar history of Polish Jewry.

One week after arriving in Łódź, I met a young man called Lolek who was an active member of the Bricha, a project of the Jewish Brigade of the British army that was dedicated to helping Jews cross the borders of Europe with the aim of settling illegally in Palestine. He was a native of Poland, twenty-one, and blessed with many attributes rarely possessed by a man so young. He had survived the war by his wits, posing as a Pole. He was now in charge of the Polish section of a new illegal route to the West across the Oder River, which marked the border between Poland and Germany. Lolek was now ready to open the new route by sending out the first group, twenty-two young and middle-aged people, including me.

The next morning two documents, typed on Red Cross stationery and most likely forged, were handed to the group. Each paper served half the group and was designed to give us a measure of at least superficial legality. These papers contained a plea to anyone in authority along our lengthy and arduous journey to facilitate the travel of the "homeward-bound Greek Jews" named in the document who were survivors of German concentration camps. Around noon a canvas-covered truck—our transport—drove up. The trip to the border lasted several hours. To counteract the creeping feeling of boredom, I tried to sort out my inner feelings, wondering how I would react upon entering German territory for the first time. I had lost my entire family to the Nazi killers and had witnessed countless other atrocities perpetrated for the glorification of the German nation and Aryan supremacy. This experience had fostered a deep and smoldering hatred for the people who had spawned, nurtured, and supported such false ideals and bestial philosophy. I was filled with a burning desire for revenge.

Around midnight Lolek brought us news that was both heartening and disquieting. The border crossing was on, but the two bribed Polish policemen would not take us over the bridge. However, they assured us that they would get us across in a rowboat that they had hidden for just such an occasion. We walked behind the policemen to the bank of the river, but the boat was nowhere in sight. Curses and recriminations began flying back and forth between the pair, making all of us nervous. Where did it leave us but stranded with two unfriendly and unpredictable policemen?

After an hour's search they found a small rowboat about a half-mile down-stream, in an advanced state of disrepair. The Oder here was about 350 feet wide and its waters flowed turbulently here, unlike the placid waters upstream. Before long the first group of four reached the opposite bank, and the boat was pulled back with an attached rope. Several more crossings were accomplished. Then I entered the boat with three others, and we too crossed without incident.

However, the boat capsized while carrying the next group and was carried away. We counted sixteen people on our side of the river: seven of the original group, including a pregnant woman, remained stranded on the other side with the policemen. We could do nothing for them and had to move on. The town where we were supposed to board the train for Leipzig was only a few miles away, accord-ing to the road sign. Suddenly, I realized that the Red Cross document covering the group of eleven to which I belonged was still on the Polish side of the river. Four of us from our group, now on German soil, were without any documentation what-soever.

As we approached a bend in the road, a policeman on a bicycle asked for our documents. We were arrested and ordered to accompany him to the police station in town. One person in our group had traveled twice before from Poland to west-ern Germany. The Germans, with the well-deserved burden of guilt pressing down on them, were usually lenient with all refugees moving across their territory, espe-cially Jews, he said. I considered myself much more vulnerable, however, than my companions. Most of all, I feared falling into the hands of the Soviets. Presently, we were ushered into the police station, and the arresting officer reported to his su-pervisors. Half an hour later two policemen escorted us to the public baths, where we got a thorough and sorely needed scrubbing, followed by mandatory delousing. The chief then informed us with a smile that we were free to continue on our way to Leipzig.

Before long we boarded our train, settled into a couple of empty compart-ments, and waited for the train to leave. Two Soviet officers went by. They turned out to be security officers who, unbeknown to us, were keeping us under surveil-lance. When our train stopped at the next station, the same two officers, with two others, presented themselves in front of our compartments. Expecting an unevent-ful ride to Leipzig, I had closed my eyes just a few moments earlier, luxuriating in a feeling of relaxation. Suddenly, I was looking at my worst nightmare come to life. My companions were gaping in disbelief. Our situation was now collapsing.

They escorted us unceremoniously into a building near the station, hustling us into a small room and locking the door behind us. The "Red Cross" document, without my name on it, was taken away. We were under detention again, this time by none other than agents of the notorious KGB. I expected our interrogations to begin around midnight, the time of choice for the Soviet secret police. By then the detainee was usually overcome with fatigue and desire to sleep, and his resistance would be low.

At 11:30 P.M. a guard entered and motioned for me to pick up my rucksack and follow him. The suddenness of the summons gave me no time to prepare myself emotionally for the coming ordeal. He led me into a room where I faced a lieutenant behind a desk. "Search him and his belongings," the lieutenant told the guard in Russian. Disappointment clearly registered on the lieutenant's face when the guard found nothing incriminating. Dismissing the guard, the lieutenant told me to get dressed. I spoke up in German, telling him that I didn't understand Russian. Another officer, who spoke passable German, took over the interrogation. Despite being utterly fatigued, I parried his questions satisfactorily. My ordeal lasted forty minutes and I felt cautious optimism. We were released the following morning and put aboard the train to Leipzig a full day after we had been taken off. The Red Cross document was returned to us without comment.

We reached Leipzig around four in the afternoon and found our hotel without difficulty. It was a small, run-down hotel on a side street, but it was clean. Ration coupons had been left for us at the hotel desk with instructions to use them at a small nearby restaurant. We lost no time in doing so. We were exhausted and famished because we had eaten little for the past two days. Most of us, if not all, turned in for the night right after the meal.

As in Poland, an organization like the Bricha couldn't function legally in Leipzig, of course, nor could anyone living in eastern Germany—citizen or alien—represent it. It was all done secretly and quietly. We would be moving on, whether or not the missing members of our group reached Leipzig in time. Our destination this time was a *Durchgangslager,* a transit camp about ten miles from where three zones of occupation—Soviet, British, and American—converged. Later that same afternoon the stranded remnant of our group showed up. They had somehow avoided falling into the hands of either the German police or Russian security. The next day, after a two-hour ride by truck, we all arrived at the transit camp.

On the third day we began wondering why no arrangements were being made for our departure to the American Zone. By the fifth day we were hearing rumors that Soviet security forces would be scrutinizing German repatriates from Poland and their papers before they'd be allowed to leave eastern Germany. This, if true, would complicate our situation and expose us to danger all over again.

I struck up a conversation with the camp's friendly German electrician, and after a while I felt confident he could be trusted. I asked him, "Could I leave camp on my own and make it to the American Zone on foot?" He assured me that it would be easy to do. He agreed to carry my rucksack out of the camp and gave me directions. I reported this to three of my old friends, who agreed to join me. Late in the afternoon the electrician came by my tent to pick up my rucksack and was surprised to find four people instead of one waiting to leave. We followed a short distance behind him, acting as if we were on a leisurely after-dinner stroll. At the edge of the camp he repeated which routes we should take and mentioned that once we reached a certain railroad station, we would be safely inside the American Zone. We tipped him nicely, picked up our gear, and started off.

We left camp without food and with scant knowledge of the roads ahead and conditions facing us. After three hours of walking we entered a fairly large town. I could not recall that the electrician had ever mentioned it in his instructions. Despite our search, we found no markers to point us in the right direction. A lone bicycle rider was coming our way. I asked him for directions to the railroad station, and he reluctantly complied. Soon we were out of town. After we rested for several hours in a village, our marching pace picked up considerably. Suddenly, a sign appeared on the road—"You are entering the American Zone."

Soon we were on a train through the American Zone, which was sprinkled with a fairly large number of displaced persons (DP) camps, but we knew neither their locations nor what advantages one camp might have over another. Two of my friends knew of a certain camp near Munich that had been their goal since leaving Poland. Because this was the only camp we had heard of, my other friend and I tagged along. However, at the next station we learned of a newly organized DP camp nearby at Eschwege.

A man boarding our car drew our attention. From the moment we'd laid eyes on each other, a sense of kinship seemed to flow between us and the new arrival. Something about us marked us—more to each other than to outsiders. The tragedy of the Holocaust seemed to have etched itself permanently in our faces, close to the surface of our every thought and action. It reflected our lack of inner peace and the lack of a sense of belonging.

"Amkho?" the stranger inquired. We nodded. It was the first time I had heard this expression, but its meaning was quite clear. The word *amkho*, which means "your nation" and comes from the Hebrew daily prayer book, was broadly interpreted as "one of ours." Our newfound friend was a resident of the Eschwege DP camp, and he recommended it highly. When we got there, I was happy to discover several friends and distant cousins. My search for a suitable camp was now over.

Eschwege was located at a former German military airfield less than a mile from the town from which it took its name. The airfield lay in ruins, but the barracks that had housed airfield personnel—about ten or twelve in all—were now housing hundreds of Jewish refugees, mainly from eastern Europe. It was administered by an official from the United Nations Relief and Rehabilitation Administration (UNRRA) with the assistance of an elected committee called the Komitet. The camp also had its own police department, a medical clinic staffed by a doctor and a nurse, a Hebrew day school for children, and a night school for adults. Courses in driving, auto mechanics, drafting, and sewing were also available. Before long a weekly Yiddish newspaper was started. In time we had a strong football (soccer) team, the pride of the camp.

The population consisted of Jews from various parts of Europe, thrown together under one label, "refugees," and facing the agony of patching together our fractured lives. All of us had been saddled with tragic memories, carrying with us the souls of those who had perished. We were still tormented, each in his own way and to different degrees, by our horrible experiences. To go on with life after such a crushing tragedy was the greatest test of faith. Deep down, the survivors knew healing would come, but it wasn't that simple. Throughout the immediate postwar years, the dreadful experience hung like a pall over everything. Many of us were the only survivors of large families. Rare indeed was the family that had survived fully intact. But one trait, common to most of us, was definitely evident—a determination not to give in to despair and to rise to the challenges of a new life.

I had decided early on to apply for emigration to the United States, where, I knew, an aunt and cousins lived somewhere in Brooklyn, New York. It took several months to locate them with the help of a friend who was one of the few lucky ones to land in the United States early. He had placed an ad in a Jewish newspaper offering information about survivors of Krivitch and Kurenits—his and my towns, respectively.

At the end of 1946 I faced a major health problem. A small spot was discovered on one of my lungs, signifying a tuberculosis lesion. Although it appeared to be old, the doctor advised further observation and a rest period in a sanitarium. The experiences of the war years had left some of us with more than just emotional scars. The wear and tear of terror, the inadequate diet and unsanitary conditions, capped by the rugged and vagabond existence in the forests and villages, had weakened the resistance of some of us to various diseases. I was sent to the Merkshausen Sanitarium, which was administered by UNRRA. After three months the doctor at Merkshausen pronounced me fully healed.

In the autumn of 1947 I replaced the camp bookkeeper, who was leaving for Palestine. I had learned the basics before the war by working for several months with a bookkeeper. I held the position for more than a year and was then promoted to deputy UNRRA director of the camp. Barely two months later the position of acting director became vacant and I was chosen for the job. By then the camp was only a shell. Most of the camp's population, which had been four thousand residents at its height, had already left for the countries of their choice. I was officially notified by the UNRRA district office in Kassel that the camp would be closed in the early spring of 1949. The camp's atmosphere had changed dramatically. Most social activities had been disrupted. Many of our friends, old and new, were gone by now, leaving our social lives fractured. Conversations all too often turned to emigration.

When the camp closed in early May 1949, its population had shrunk to fewer than five hundred. It was a busy time. In addition, the last days at the camp were

Charles Gelman in a part of his partisan uniform with a young Polish friend at the displaced persons camp in Eschwege in the American zone of Germany.

blessed with a bountiful crop of visas to the United States and other countries. My own emigration process began at the end of May 1949 with a letter from an American consul instructing me to appear at his offices in Butzbach near Frankfurt am Main. At the end of July 1949 we were moved again, this time to a Polish DP camp near the village of Wildflecken. The camp was way past its heyday. About two weeks later I was notified, finally, that I had been granted my long-awaited entry "number" to the United States. It was the equivalent of a visa. But it took two and a half months more before I was actually scheduled to leave Germany.

Several weeks before leaving Germany, I took the train to Berchtesgaden. One unaccomplished task gnawed at my mind and had to be dealt with: a visit to the "Eagle's Nest," Hitler's favorite home aside from Berlin. I was now ready to see where much of the evil and darkness had been discussed and planned. It was as if I expected to confront Hitler's ghost there and taunt him with my physical presence. I found the entrance to the building barricaded and was thoroughly disappointed with its unimpressive exterior. The mountain and the view, however, remained unaltered and in full natural beauty. It occurred to me that Hitler might have stood at this very spot, enjoying the same view just a few years ago. Not only did I triumph over him just by surviving, but I was here!

Under the sponsorship of the American Jewish Joint Distribution Committee, I left Bremerhaven on the fourteenth of September 1949, on the American army troop transport *General Ballou*, which was filled with more than one thousand refugees. It was a stormy crossing, so most passengers were seasick the whole time. Early in the morning of October 5, 1949, our ship passed the Statue of Liberty. The day was beautiful and sunny and exceptionally warm for this time of year. It seemed as if the city, the country, and even nature itself were extending us a warm welcome. October 5, 1949, has remained forever ingrained in my mind as the day I finally reached shore—emotionally as well as physically.

I stayed with my aunt in Brooklyn until the spring of 1950. I also had a cousin in New Haven, Connecticut, Eli Zimmerman. He and his wife, Anna, had advertised in a newspaper, seeking information about any relatives who might have survived the Holocaust. A rabbi in Providence, Rhode Island, saw the notice and was instrumental in getting Eli and me together. I moved to New Haven and stayed with the Zimmermans until 1955, when I married Sydonie Tanenbaum on March 27. She was also from Poland but had been spared the hideous persecution of the Germans. In 1955, a memorable year, I also became an American citizen.

I held a variety of jobs in New Haven, including working in a printing shop, the Walker-Rackli Company, and for the Disken Shoe Company, a wholesaler. Meanwhile, I was taking singing lessons and studying and, finally, in 1962 I became the cantor at Temple Beth Sholom in Hamden, Connecticut. At the same time I was selling insurance. I retired from the insurance business in 1982 and from Temple Beth Sholom in 1987. We bought a second home in Boca Raton, Florida, and now spend about half the year in New Haven and half in Boca Raton.

Our son, Irwin, is head of the microbiology unit at Rosewell Cancer Institute in Buffalo and has two daughters. He is also a fourth-generation cantor. He began singing the liturgy when he was fourteen and has served every Shabbat and holiday at the Conservative Synagogue of Fifth Avenue in Manhattan for about twenty years, mostly while he was working at Mount Sinai Hospital. Our daughter, Phyllis Kukin, is a speech pathologist in Englewood, New Jersey. She is married to a cardiologist at Mount Sinai and has two girls and a boy. She was an interviewer for Steven Spielberg's video testimony project. Both children are active in second-generation groups.

Looking back at my sojourn in the United States, I can honestly say that I have never had any psychological problems deriving from my Holocaust experience. For me and for other survivors this experience prepared us for survival in a new country. We went through the "college of life."

Both Sydonie and I had learned English fairly well in Europe, but we still had problems of acceptance here because we were considered Europeans for a while. People simply could not understand the hardships that I had endured in Europe.

At first I was too busy making a living and adjusting to life here to tell my story in detail. When I did try to relate something about it, people did not want to hear about it. I put my story in a cabinet with the doors closed. Eventually, after I retired, I wrote out my entire story in detail, and the first part of it was published in 1989. Like most naturalized citizens, I feel a fierce sense of loyalty, patriotism, and gratitude to the United States, the land of liberty and opportunity.

From Prague to Theresienstadt and Back

EVA BENDA
(b. 1924, Germany)

It is more than sixty years now since the war in Europe ended and the Holocaust in its full dimension of horror became public knowledge. I carry its stigma around with me and hide it like a character fault. I will not volunteer that I am a survivor, that I was in a concentration camp. I try to pretend that it didn't happen, that it doesn't matter any more. But it is seared into my soul.

Only recently did it finally dawn on me why I was so petrified in 1961, when my husband and I were flying to Portugal with our children, Peter and Susi, then aged six and five. In midair I became anxious, convinced that they were at risk. I kept repeating that we had no right to expose them to the danger of this flight, that they had a right to their lives. Actually, I was reliving the events of twenty years earlier, when a five-year-old boy and six-year-old girl shared our cattle car, on their

Eva Bloch at age 3,
Berlin, 1927.

way to a certain death in Auschwitz. My memory of them has been indelible; it has never left me.

I understand why Bruno Bettelheim and Primo Levy committed suicide after long lives of professional achievement. As Rabbi Weiss of the Yale chapter of Hillel once said to me: "On the other side of belief there is despair." If you cannot believe, then all that is left is despair. But I don't believe. Is that what makes life so hard?

I remember so little—was my childhood so painful that I have banned all memories? My father, Martin Bloch, died in 1929, when I was four years old; that event I do not remember. I do not know what I was told or whether I was told anything at all. Now there is nobody left to ask.

In Berlin, where I was born in 1924, we had school six days a week, from 8 A.M. to 1 P.M. On Saturdays Aunt Becca's maid would pick me up from school, and I would go to her house for the weekend. My great-aunt Becca, a substitute grandmother to me, was a short, round, lively woman who seemed to be always on the go. Aunt Hedwig, her daughter, lived with her. She was petite, elegant, and charming. She raised canaries, about forty of them, in two big cages. On warm sunny days the two cages were taken to the balcony, and we would feed the chicks hard-boiled eggs with toothpicks. Since I usually spent Saturday night at their house, I had my bed and my toothbrush at Aunt Becca's.

On Sunday my mother would come for dinner and then take me home. There were no trees on our street and no balconies with growing plants. My home was dark and cold, very different from Aunt Becca's. Was it my mother's presence that made it appear that way? I know she was there, but I don't remember her.

When I was eight, my mother and I moved from Berlin to Prague, her hometown. Although my mother always provided for me, she did not show me any affection. I was never again to have the love and acceptance that I had experienced at my aunts' houses. I was orphaned for the second time; it was the end of my childhood.

While we were living in Germany, we always went to Czechoslovakia for our vacations. I remember once coming back to Berlin from visiting with my aunt Ana Kratochvil in Susice in southern Bohemia. I had become proficient in Czech during that summer. But Aunt Becca pronounced Czech a nonlanguage and encouraged me to forget it. I followed her advice. As a result, when we moved to Prague in 1932, I did not speak Czech sufficiently well to attend a Czech school and was placed in the third grade of the local public German primary school. Prague had public German schools, including a German university. So much for the "oppression" of the *Volksdeutsche* (German-speaking minority), claimed later by Hitler.

In Czechoslovakia parents had to decide whether their children would continue their schooling in the public high school for the next four years, with its vocational curriculum, or take entrance examinations for the eight-year gymnasium. The gymnasium consisted of strenuous academic schooling that culminated in the *Abitur*, a final examination on all thirteen subjects taught during the preceding eight years. (The education received at a gymnasium is considered equivalent to that of an American junior college.) Liberal arts education was considered completed with the *Abitur*. Universities were professional schools and were free of charge.

By the time I was to take the entrance examination, I was equally proficient in Czech and German. The question was whether I should attend a German- or a Czech-language school, and Mother consulted her brother, Jirka. Jirka, who had a Viennese wife, suggested that German literature was much richer than Czech literature and I should therefore go to a German gymnasium. My mother, who thought that education was not very important for a girl, nonetheless decided to send me to a private gymnasium, where French and English were taught rather than classical languages.

On the day I was to take my entrance examinations, my mother walked me to school. The examinations normally took four hours so she returned home. How-

Eva on the first day of school, Berlin, 1930.

ever, I was taken out of the classroom and subjected to a short oral test that seemed very pro forma, even to an eleven-year-old. I was then told that I was accepted in the school on the recommendation of my grade-school teacher. When I explained to Mother the circumstances of my early return, she did not express any pleasure in my success. She just nodded acceptance.

School turned out to be very enjoyable for me. I learned easily. I excelled in mathematics, especially in algebra, and did very well in physics. A spinster who sported a swastika on her ample bosom taught history and geography. A dislike of history and geography remained with me for a long time. I did my homework during the ten-minute breaks between classes or under my desk. My mother never mentioned or wondered that I had no homework. Above all, I had a group of girl-friends in school, a sociable and pleasant surrounding for me, an excellent antidote to my lonely existence at home.

My mother's indifference continued right through school. She never asked how I did in my classes and never asked to see any of my work. That attitude did not encourage me to do my best. I always held back slightly so I could tell myself that whenever I did not fully succeed, I could have if I had really tried. I gained that insight many years later and only in this country, after I had finished my inter-rupted education.

Mother certainly was an excellent manager. Although she had been left alone with a small child and virtually no income, she never seemed short of money and I was never deprived of anything. We lived modestly, but I was always indulged in material ways. I now understand that Mother, who had never received much love or caring herself, was unable to give it to me.

During those years Mother always seemed to be crying, and she often talked about suicide. She had frequent sore throats and walked around the house with a scarf around her neck. One night she really felt miserable and was sure she was dying. She would not let me leave her bedside to call a doctor. I was thoroughly scared. The next morning she got up and cleaned the house. I never forgave her and learned never to take anybody's illness seriously, not my husband's and not my children's.

Once my mother decided that I didn't need a babysitter any longer, I was alone at home in a dark and still apartment almost every evening. My mother had caught the bridge bug. As a result, I became a voracious reader. To this day I read obsessively, unwilling to put a book down. Books still are a solace and a refuge.

When I was eleven, I had a boyfriend, Bobby, who was thirteen. We had met on a school skiing vacation. This skiing vacation looms large in my memory. It turned out to be the most exciting and romantic time of my life. Bobby and I were inseparable. He was the most gifted person I have ever known. He was a straight-A student in his demanding classical gymnasium, a musician, an athlete, an artist, and—above all—in love with me. He wrote me a booklet of poetry, white engraving on black paper, folded like an accordion, including pictures that are still vivid in my mind. I carried that little package—it was only one and a half by two inches—on my person—right into Auschwitz.

I continued to avoid home and my mother as much as I could. Mother never inquired what I did in my free time or who my friends were. However, she did know about Bobby and approved of this relationship, since she was well aware that Bobby came from a well-to-do family.

March 15, 1939, was a sleety, unpleasant morning. My mother, obviously unaware of what was happening that day, sent me to the main post office on one of the principal thoroughfares of Prague. I was fourteen. There I stood, in front of the post office, watching the German tanks roll into Prague. I saw a German soldier climb out of a tank, push the Czech policeman aside, and start to direct traffic while the Czech policeman stood by helplessly. Little did I know the implications of that event for my tranquil life. German Jewish refugees had passed through Czechoslovakia before, and we had known some of them. We were aware of what was going on in Germany, but, secure behind *our* fortifications and *our* army, we were sure that what was happening in Germany was not going to happen here.

At the time of the Munich Pact in 1938, there had been a general mobilization of the Czech army. I remember that on the evening of that mobilization a friend of my mother's from the Yugoslav embassy stormed in and said, "Mrs. Bloch, you have to emigrate. Where do you want to go? I'll get you a visa for anywhere." The next day my mother went to consult with her sister. Her sister asked, "Where would you go? Nobody is going to hurt a widow with a child." And my mother took her sister's advice.

It is easy now to see the foolishness of it. But it has to be remembered that my mother felt Czech to the bone. She grew up in the Czech countryside, with a tenant farmer's daughter as her best girlfriend. To think of emigrating must have appeared outrageous to her. Where would she go and what would she do there? And, above all, why?

Soon after the Germans arrived, the Germans began to enforce the Nuremberg anti-Jewish laws in Czechoslovakia. The first order the Germans issued was that we had to hand over all radios. Then we had to hand in all valuables—jewelry and silver. Then one day Jewish children were expelled from public schools. Soon afterward we were no longer allowed into restaurants, hotels, trains, streetcars, or public parks. I had a group of classmates and friends from other schools, five girls and seven boys, all aged thirteen to fifteen. At first we would meet in each other's homes or we would take the streetcar to the end of the line and go swimming in an old abandoned quarry. When streetcars became forbidden to us, we would meet in the now-famous fifteenth-century Jewish cemetery in the center of town. This was the only place still open to us.

My mother took me out of public school, even before we were expelled. She sent me to a private language school in Karlin, a suburb of Prague, where I would have two hours of English and two of French each day plus one hour of conversation in each language.

My mother's brother, Josef, a lawyer, had been imprisoned by the Gestapo and was very anxious to emigrate. He managed to get a visa to Venezuela, one of the last countries still willing to sell visas for several thousand dollars. Before he was ready to use that visa, the Germans closed the borders airtight and nobody got out any more. Early in the occupation Jewish stores, offices, factories, and other enterprises were confiscated. Men lost their property and their livelihood. Josef, whom we called Pepa, lost his practice. He and his wife and daughters were evicted from their apartment by the Germans. My mother's sister Ida and her husband lost their shoe store. The two families decided to move together into a summer home that Uncle Pepa owned in Revnice, a village not far from Prague. Later, another sister, Mizza, and her husband, also a lawyer, joined them there.

Finally, the youngest sister, Anka, joined them there as well. According to the Nuremberg Laws, since Anka co-owned a house and pharmacy with her Gentile husband, the property would be confiscated unless her husband divorced her, so they agreed on what they thought would be a pro forma divorce. Aunt Anka's divorce was perfectly legal, however, and since she was no longer married to a Christian, she was murdered in Auschwitz.

It is still a wonderful old house, on the main square of Susice, a small town in the Sumava Mountains of southern Bohemia. I spent many a summer there. Even then the house was protected by the Czech government as a historical building.

The Germans decided to make the countryside Judenrein (free of Jews) before they even started on the cities. My mother's siblings went into "transport," which meant that early in 1942 they were "evacuated" to Poland in sealed cattle cars. These trips often took many days. The trainloads of condemned Jews were considered very low priority and often stood on rail sidings for several days.

The last anti-Jewish edict forced us to wear the yellow star. It was very, very embarrassing. I often tried to hide my star with a handbag. It felt as if we were being branded, and in a way we were. We were property of the Germans now, to do with as they pleased. After the Nuremberg Laws were extended to private schools, I was expelled from the language school. Now my mother arranged an apprenticeship for me in a leather handbag factory. I was to learn a trade to prepare us for emigration. From the windows of this workshop we watched transports as they left for the fairgrounds, the assembly area.

By this time we had been evicted from our apartment. We left all our belongings behind, including my grandparents' furniture and my mother's beloved grand piano, and moved with our suitcases into an assigned room in somebody else's home. My mother had not strictly obeyed the order to deliver all valuables to the German authorities, and we packed a lot of our silver, china, and oriental rugs and our bank books and took them for safekeeping to Christian friends.

One day I was no longer allowed to work in the leather goods workshop. The owners were told that they had to provide separate toilet facilities for their Jewish employees. In a workshop of eight people, that was clearly an impossibility. Now my mother found me a job as a telephone operator with the Jewish Community

Center. Although we didn't know it when I took the job, this employment was to protect us from transport for two crucial years.

Finally, in October 1942, after many transports had left Prague, our luck ran out. The expected and dreaded call-up notice arrived by mail. It informed us that we had to present ourselves for resettlement at the fairgrounds on October 9. We should bring only one suitcase, which we should be able to carry by ourselves. Though the wording itself seemed innocuous, we knew what it meant. We carefully packed our suitcases with warm clothes and essential supplies and put in as much food as possible. We were not told where we were going or how long the trip could be.

We duly presented ourselves at the fairgrounds and were left there, sitting on our suitcases, for two days. On the day we went there, I was menstruating. My period cut off that night and I did not menstruate again until October 1945. Neither did any of the other women, though that did not seem to protect them from becoming pregnant. After two days at the fairgrounds we were marched, all two thousand of us, to the train station. I don't remember the train ride. To our vast relief we ended up in Theresienstadt (Terezin), only thirty miles north of Prague.

Theresienstadt had originally been a small, walled-in garrison town. Now it was a Jewish settlement run by the Judenrat, the Council of Jewish Elders, under SS direction. We seldom saw any Germans, although they were guarding the outer perimeter of the camp. But we knew about the adjoining Gestapo prison, Kleine Festung Theresienstadt, from which no Jew ever escaped. Its very proximity made us fearful.

Within the secure walls of the town we were free to move around during the day, though a nightly curfew was in place at all times. Occasionally, we could see a cluster of German SS officers going about their business. Gauleiters, SS officers, were administrators in the occupied countries. Each was assigned special duties, one of which was to see that Jews were evacuated to Poland.

On our arrival we were taken to a small house that probably in normal times had been the home of a small family. The room we were assigned was approximately thirteen by twenty feet. Roughly twenty-four mattresses were spread out on the floor. Families were separated. Men were housed in the barracks that had once held soldiers. We were issued ration cards and told when and where meals would be served. Cooked food was handed out at lunchtime in the yard. I remember dumplings and gravy but do not remember whether there was anything else. In the morning there was black coffee or what they called coffee. I don't remember what there was for supper. Our water supply was a pump in the courtyard.

There were roughly 128 women in the house. For all of us there were only two toilets, which were often out of commission. Diarrhea was rampant, and almost every night some elderly woman got lost before finding the toilet and ended up near or on somebody else's bunk. The ensuing commotion did not contribute to restful nights. The other thing that made sleep practically impossible was the number of bedbugs. I finally gave up the fight against them and carried my mattress out into the courtyard every evening. I slept there all summer. In the fall the authorities finally fumigated the house.

On July 24, 1944, a Swedish Red Cross commission came to inspect this "Jewish settlement." Before the commission arrived, the two ground-floor rooms were emptied of the thirty-two women who had lived in them, and the women were sent east, to their deaths. A married couple was put there instead. I saw the Red Cross delegates walk past our house. They were flanked by SS officers and nobody could approach them.

When we arrived, we did not know that Theresienstadt was only for transshipment to Auschwitz. For that matter, we didn't know that Auschwitz existed. However, we soon found out that periodically transports left Theresienstadt and that, as newcomers, we would be the first ones chosen for transport. Fortunately, I developed scarlet fever and was put into an isolation ward. This protected us from the first few transports. In an effort to protect us from further transports, after my release I volunteered for a tonsillectomy, as had been recommended by the attending physician. It was performed without anesthesia. Although there were lots of competent surgeons in Theresienstadt, medical supplies were nearly nonexistent. However, I had miscalculated the timing, and I was out of the hospital by the time another transport was ready to leave.

My having scarlet fever saved our lives once more. In the hospital I had learned from another patient that transports were organized by pulling cards from a file. She knew somebody who worked in the office where this was done. My mother had smuggled some money into camp, and she suggested to me that we should pay somebody for protecting our cards. Through an intermediary the woman in the catalogue room agreed to accept the money. When the next transport was called up, we were very scared, not knowing whether the deal would work. It worked! We were not called up.

After this my mother managed to get both of us protected employment, which meant that we were not subject to being called up for transport. She worked in a factory where they were splitting mica, and I became a telephone operator for the Council of Jewish Elders and the German *Kommandatur* (the SS officers who administered Theresienstadt). Thus I was a small cog in the wheels that made it possible for the Germans to be in charge without being involved. Now, in retrospect, I have become very uneasy. Does this make me a collaborator? To the extent that it saved us from transport, it certainly did. Was I aware of the implications of our seeking to save ourselves? No, I was not.

For two blissfully innocent years we lived in relative safety and comfort. That is, for two years we did not feel that we were in any personal danger and did not worry about being included in the next transport. We still had our own clothes and didn't go hungry. We were allowed to write fifteen-word postcards once every six months to anybody we wanted to. We wrote to the ex-husband of Aunt Anka and received from him two precious food parcels in two years. Being young, healthy, and having extra food not only made life more comfortable for us but also gave us a privileged position.

But every morning open wooden carts pulled by two men would come around, and the naked corpses were then unceremoniously dumped into the carts. I never found out whether these bodies were buried or what happened to them. Only rarely did a family member accompany them. After the war we learned that the Germans kept meticulous records and knew exactly who had died and when.

With all this going on around us, daily life in Theresienstadt was still really quite tolerable for me and actually in some ways enjoyable. After the restrictions we had suffered in Prague for the previous two years, life in Theresienstadt was much freer. In 1942 I was eighteen, and being able to spend time with friends and away from my depressed mother was a big relief. Every evening I would lie in bed and relive the good events of the day: encounters with friends, concerts, theater performances, and other pleasant times. This probably was useful as an antidote to the generally desolate atmosphere of Theresienstadt.

In October 1943 another transport was called up by the Judenrat. This was the first time parents were called up without their children, in an effort to save the young and gifted ones. Bobby's parents and his sister were called up, but he was spared. He volunteered to accompany his parents. This happened in many families then living in Theresienstadt, so this transport took all the gifted and professional people, among them, Bobby and his family and most of my other friends. After that Theresienstadt was an old-age home.

In October 1944 our luck once again ran out. We were called up for transport but only as a "reserve." We were told that we might not have to go. We still knew nothing of the death camps or gas chambers. However, we seemed to know enough to dread the transport. I talked my mother into hiding out. While the people who were going were being assembled, we hid in a bathroom. When the reserves were finally called up, my mother lacked the courage to defy the call, and we duly presented ourselves for transport. The result of my failure to communicate with my mother was especially tragic since we later learned that this was the last transport to leave Theresienstadt.

My mother and I were the last ones to get into that train with its infamous cattle cars. About thirty-five men, children, and women were already in our car. I do not remember how long we were on the way. Often the train would be standing on a siding for hours, only suddenly to move on again. In all that time not once were the doors opened, nor did anybody check whether we were alive or dead. We could not see out of the small high windows and had no idea where we were or where we were going. Our guess was that we were going east. East to us meant away from civilization, away from the way we had lived and all we knew.

Unexpectedly, late one night the train came to a grinding halt. I later learned that the trains were always unloaded at night to keep people disoriented and helpless. When the doors opened, we could see long lines of barbed wire illuminated by searchlights. I thought at first that we had landed in a mining area. But the doors of the train were opened for us by prisoners in their striped uniforms, and the first words we heard at Auschwitz were "Raus, schneller, schneller!" (Out, faster, faster). To this day these German words still sound ominous to me. The English translation does not carry the same power.

There were many SS men in uniforms around, many more than we had ever seen before. We were told to leave our suitcases behind, that we would get them later, and all of us were hurried down the platform, past an SS officer in uniform. He was telling people to go left or right and wanted to separate my mother and me. We had no idea what that meant. My mother in her fluent German said, "Leave us together; we are mother and daughter." He considered for a moment and then with a nod of his head sent us off to the left. We walked toward a building and found ourselves in a large hall with two hundred young women from our transport, which had consisted of 2,576 people. (I knew the exact number because we were in the last carriage and people were being counted off on entering the train.) Why were we chosen and not the others?

As soon as we were out from under the direct supervision of the SS, longtime prisoners appeared, as if from nowhere. They lost no time in telling us that whoever was not in the room with us was now being gassed. My mother started crying, saying, "This is the end of us," and started to embrace me. I shook her off. I couldn't bear her despair.

That night we were held in a large room with a cement floor and several bathrooms, with tiled floors, toilets, and washbasins. I did not realize what a rarity that was, and I would not see another real bathroom for a long time. These were being used for sexual encounters between some of the *Kapos* and some of the new young women. I was no party to this; I didn't even quite understand what was going on.

The next morning we were marched, eight abreast, to a room where we were told to undress. We were then lined up and slowly, a few at a time, were made to walk naked into the next room. From where I stood, I could see that the women ahead of me were getting their heads shaved by other female inmates. There was a lot of nervous giggling, but not until it was my turn did I realize that they were also shaving all body hair.

We were marched out of the room through a different door than the one by which we had entered. We never saw our clothes or any of our belongings again. I asked an attendant whether I could go back and get the little souvenir book of my boyfriend. She just shook her head. We were issued old rayon dresses, an old woolen overcoat, wooden clogs, and nothing else—no underwear, no socks, no scarves for our naked heads. That same day we were marched through the endless mud to Birkenau, always with the "schneller, schneller" pushing us on. It was difficult not to lose the wooden clogs in the mud and to keep up with the group. Finally, we arrived at the place that was to be our home while in Auschwitz.

Since the crematoria were in operation, a curfew was imposed on the whole camp. The talk was always about crematoria, never about gas chambers. It seemed to be easier to think of burning bodies, rather than about the process of killing people. The whole time I was in Auschwitz, we didn't see or hear anything about what was going on outside our barrack, although acrid smoke was hanging over us.

Roll calls were a nightmare. The weather in late October in Poland is cold and rainy. Every morning, while it was still dark, we would be rushed out for roll call, and we would stand there, eight abreast, way past daybreak. This would be repeated from midafternoon till after dark. We had no underwear, and it was always freezing. We had torn linings from our coats to cover our naked heads and were holding onto each other for warmth and support. We would take turns standing on the outside of the line, where exposure to the weather was the worst. Anybody lacking community support did not survive very long.

The latrines were out in the back. They consisted of two long boards set up over a ditch. I found the lack of privacy more difficult than the smell. Sometimes lime was spread over the ditch. We were allowed to go to the latrines only in the morning and once in the evening. There were two buckets for five hundred or more people to use at all other times. There was enough drinking water.

Before daybreak one morning, a week after our arrival, the two hundred of us from my transport were marched to another part of the camp and sent into a shower room. We had neither soap nor towels, and after the shower we stood outside, our insufficient clothing clinging to our wet bodies. That day we stood from before daybreak till well after dark. I thought that my back would break and I was just going to fall. If I had fallen, that would have been my death warrant. While we were standing there, one of our women told the *Kapo* in charge that we had had nothing to eat all week. The woman shook her head; evidently, somebody had stolen our bread rations. She got us a barrel of cabbage soup. I still remember the sand in that soup.

Somewhere in the course of that day we learned that we were going on transport to a labor camp. We didn't know whether this was good news or bad news. Wasn't anything better than Auschwitz? What would that work be? We knew that sometimes work was used as a means of exhausting and killing people. Late in the day two *Kapos* joined our ranks. Their long hair told us that they had been in Auschwitz a long time, most likely several years. They assured us that they had chosen to go on this transport and that we were going to a good place. I didn't quite believe them.

Before embarking on the train that evening, we were each given a small loaf of bread, a piece of margarine, and some unwrapped meat paste. I didn't know how to preserve it and ate the margarine and the meat there and then. When we finally got to the train, two soldiers in full uniform were in each carriage, each with a rifle. They were Wehrmacht—regular army, not SS—young boys, conscripts.

This time we were forty-eight women in each carriage. We took turns standing and sitting. It was now November 1944 and we were freezing. At the next stop the soldiers called to the guards outside to close the shutters. It was cold for them with their greatcoats, but for us it was a matter of life and death. Only because the soldiers accompanied us were we allowed to empty the buckets and get fresh water whenever the train stopped. By their presence and helpfulness on that interminable trip back to Germany, those two soldiers certainly saved our sanity, possibly our lives.

After perhaps four or five days the doors finally opened and we were told to get out. We found ourselves on a railway siding outside a small town, which we later learned was Oederan, near Dresden. To guard us dangerous criminals, soldiers were lined up along the way, from the railway siding to the factory where we were to live. The guards were fourteen- to sixteen-year-old youngsters and old men, all in military uniforms. Even though I was not in a frame of mind to appreciate the irony of it, I could not be unaware of how pathetic the situation was, both because the Germans felt the need to guard us helpless prisoners and because that was all the manpower they could muster.

Our new home was part of a textile complex that was being converted into a munitions factory. It was separated by a courtyard from the factory building itself. When we arrived, roll call in the courtyard was mercifully short. A building had been prepared for us. Each of us had a clean, individual bunk, with a new straw-filled mattress and a blanket on top of each mattress. Never mind that they were just horse blankets—they were clean. We had real bathrooms, and the dormitory was heated by pipes from the factory. Imagine, we had heat and towels! We did nothing but sleep and revel in our new comforts for a few days. We felt as if we had arrived in paradise.

When we arrived, three hundred women were already there. They were young girls who had mostly come from a Polish ghetto to Auschwitz. Their dormitories were next to ours, and they assured us that the place was as good as it looked. Though we kept ourselves largely separate, I befriended some of them. Within the first few days we were issued underwear. We also got the solid, heavy cotton prison uniform, wonderful protection from the elements, much better than our flimsy rayon dresses. I borrowed scissors, needle, and thread from my Polish friends, cut off the bottom part of the undershirt, and fashioned a bra for myself.

For the first few weeks in Oederan we received a daily ration of one thick slice of dark, nourishing German bread, and at lunchtime there was a thick soup with potatoes and vegetables. Twice a week we received a quarter-pound of margarine and a few ounces of some kind of sausage. This was good food, an undreamed-of luxury. My first helping of soup did nothing to still my hunger so I lined up for a second helping. Although I was not entitled to two helpings of soup, the camp ethic allowed you to "organize" (the preferred word for stealing in all camps) something from the kitchen or administration. Some women from my group saw me lining up a second time, but apart from some whispers nobody commented.

A few days later, when Edith, our *Kapo,* was giving out job assignments, she gave me a choice position, working on the road crew. I was given a pick and was supposed to help build a road. It was a complete joke. I could not even lift the pick. It was a good job. One day a couple of German women from the nearby town walked past where we were working; our supervisor was some distance away. Very surreptitiously, I asked them for food. We were not supposed to talk to Germans—or anybody else, for that matter. For many weeks one of them often brought me a small sandwich. When I was watching her, she would put it behind a rock on the side of the road. I always kept half for my mother and left it on her bed. She would find it there when she came home from her work in the factory.

In the meantime, as the war progressed, food became increasingly short in Germany, and our rations suffered accordingly. My memory for dates deserts me. I only know that one day our margarine and salami rations abruptly stopped. In the late winter there was suddenly no more bread. The once-a-day soup, our only food ration by now, became increasingly thinner. In February 1945 our soup started to consist mostly of squash. In the spring we learned that the soup for five hundred prisoners was made from fifty pounds of potatoes. Mostly, we would end up with some hot colored water. At the same time, my German woman had stopped coming. I believe that the Germans had no bread, either, or at least not enough to share. I would have been happy with a cooked potato, but I never had a chance to tell her.

From our windows we watched Dresden burning only a short distance away. For us it was an exhilarating sight. The whole horizon was aflame, and our dormitory was lit as if by daylight, except the light was red. We knew that the Allies had bombed Dresden. We stood at the windows all night, delighting in the spectacle. To us it was proof that the end of the war and liberation could not be far off.

It was April 1945, and the railway tracks in Germany had been disrupted by now. We were supposed to be sent to Mauthausen, and we were panicky about going to this large infamous camp. We knew that in any camp, we as newcomers would be at a disadvantage. We would be given the hardest jobs and would be the first ones to go if another *Selektion* was to take place, or maybe we would just plain be herded right into a gas chamber.

We were loaded, forty-five women each, into open freight cars. These cars had no roof; they had been meant for bulk freight, coal or gravel, perhaps. This time no soldiers were on the train with us. The SS women from Oederan did allow us to empty buckets of urine and get water whenever we were standing still. Sometimes the train moved, but for most of a week it was standing on different sidings. Providence was merciful; it never rained that whole week. And the train couldn't make it to Mauthausen. After one week on the train, with no rumor to warn us, we found ourselves getting out of those freight cars in Theresienstadt. We had arrived exactly where our journey had begun.

The Swedish Red Cross had by now taken over Theresienstadt, and it was now very different from the place we had left. Tens of thousands of former prisoners were in Theresienstadt now. I had not seen any of those walking skeletons up to that day. It was a scary experience to walk around among these barely human-looking people and consider ourselves one of those survivors. I found a friend of Bobby's. More correctly, he found me; I would not have recognized him. I immediately asked after Bobby. He rolled his eyes skyward as an answer.

Only later did I learn the fate of the transport that had included the elite of our young people who had volunteered to accompany their parents. For six months they were allowed to live together as families, carrying the label "SB," which meant *Sonderbehandlung* (special treatment). I was told that when they were waiting to be herded into gas chambers they sang "Hatikvah," the Zionist anthem, and the Czech anthem.

The former prisoners, who had come from all parts of the German Reich, had brought typhoid and cholera to Theresienstadt, and it was now quarantined by the Czech authorities and guarded by Czech gendarmes (state police). With Prague so close, we were impatient to leave. We had received a Red Cross parcel that included cigarettes. I went to the next available gendarme and sold him two packs of cigarettes for enough money for two train tickets to Prague.

Since we could not get permission to leave Theresienstadt, we left illegally, on May 5, pushing a cart used by the laundry located outside the walls and then walking to the railway station. At the Red Cross office at the railway station in Prague we received identification papers, important for the next few years, and were offered a hotel at the other end of the city. Because of the continuing fighting, no streetcars were running, and we were in no shape to walk that far. After some discussion the Red Cross gave us a hotel closer by, Hotel Beranek. Ironically, when I took my children to see Prague in 1986, the tourist office directed us to that same hotel!

We made our way to the hotel, presented our authorization slips, and were given a room with two beds. They were the first beds we had had to sleep in since October 1942. The room also had a washbasin, with hot and cold running water. It was heaven on Earth. For us the war was finally over.

In a reaction to all that had happened, now that we were both safe, my mother and I became sick. We were running fevers of about 102 degrees Fahrenheit. While we were lying in bed, the fighting continued, no shops were open, and no streetcars were operating. We had no food and no money. This was May 7 to 9, 1945. On May 13, I would be twenty-one years old, and I therefore think of freedom as my coming-of-age birthday present.

At this point it seems worthwhile to say that although my chronological age in 1945 was twenty-one, my emotional age was at best fifteen. The five to six years under German occupation and in German camps were not conducive to emotional growth. We had no chance to make any decisions for ourselves. It was a strictly circumscribed life. We lived day by day, waiting for what the next day would bring. As a matter of fact, I had to relearn some social behaviors, like modesty, that had no place in camps. I remember vividly being at dinner with some friends and lifting my skirt to adjust my garters. On another occasion, on a trip with friends, a married couple, I did not understand why I could not share their room.

As soon as the streetcars started operating again, I borrowed carfare from the chambermaid and, in spite of my fever, set out to find Mother's friends at the Yugoslav embassy. The embassy was still there and so were Mother's friends. They not only welcomed me but also gave me Holland Rusk Zweiback, tea, and a little money. With these riches I returned to the hotel. I repaid my debt to the chambermaid and she made us tea. The mere fact that I still remember all these details, some sixty years later, testifies to their being monumental events.

When we recovered, we went to our old apartment house and visited that simple woman with whom we had hidden our china, silver, and bank savings books. She alone, of all people, returned everything we had left with her. The next urgent step was to find a place to live. A Czech family was living in our old apartment now, and we had no way of getting that apartment back. The Germans who had come to Prague with the occupation forces had now fled, and their apartments were vacant. My mother, with her usual knack for communicating with Christian Czechs, soon found a concierge who told her of a small vacant apartment in his building. We went to the local Communist cell, the de facto government, and were given permission to move in. Since Prague had a severe housing shortage, we considered ourselves lucky to get an apartment at all. It was sparsely furnished but had all the essentials. Some dresses were hanging in the closet and they fit me. Evidently, the Germans had left in a great hurry and had not been able to take all their possessions with them. Though it did not nearly compensate us for all we had lost, the thought that the Germans had to flee and that we occupied their place was a source of satisfaction for us.

Worse than the lost possessions was having to accept the fact that none of my mother's family had survived, nor had Bobby. Only one boy from my youth group of thirteen returned. Because we had survived, we had assumed that some other family members and friends would also return. For years afterward I tried to learn the final fate of my mother's siblings and their families. Finally, in 1989, in a final act of desperation, I wrote a letter that I addressed to "The Jewish Community, Prague," not knowing whether such a thing existed. By return mail I received documents with the exact dates of their arrival in Auschwitz and Treblinka. These documents are now officially considered their death certificates. To this day I grieve for my boyfriend and my two young cousins who were like sisters to me.

All through the war years we had lived with one thought in mind: When the war is over we are going back to Prague and to our old lifestyle. This now turned out to have been an illusion. The prewar city, with its lively Jewish community, did not exist any longer. In this respect Hitler had succeeded: Prague was Judenrein. Although a few individuals were now slowly returning to Prague, it was only a handful from a prewar community of forty thousand. When I visited Prague in 1972, the Jewish community amounted to approximately six hundred elderly people. There was no Jewish life left.

Next we tried to collect some of our other possessions that we had stored with various trusted Christian friends. A relative by marriage did return my clothes, which were badly worn and not very presentable. A prosperous lawyer, a friend of Josef's, returned only an empty suitcase. He denied having received anything else, while my uncle's painting was hanging on the wall in the office in which we were sitting. The house in Revnice, from where my mother's siblings had left for transport, had been taken over by the caretaker. His married daughters were now living there. They claimed that my uncle had given them the house. My mother went to collect some oriental rugs from another storage place in Revnice, but the woman who had them claimed that they had been given to her, and the Communist cell officer said that he had no reason to doubt her word.

Before the war anti-Semitism had not existed in the Czechoslovak Republic. However, the Czechs, who did hate the Germans, had been only too willing to accept their anti-Semitism. We had not known that anti-Semitism was part of the Communist credo, and it hit us very hard. It was an exceedingly painful and disillusioning time for us. Although we had not denied being Jewish, we had always considered ourselves Czechs. I remember that Uncle Josef was very upset when I joined the Maccabi gymnastics club. "We are Czechs," he said. He didn't want us to have anything to do with Zionism. None of my family was religious or had any religious affiliation. At Hanukkah I would go to services with my girlfriend in order to get some candy, but my mother refused to set foot in a temple. I regret now that I never asked her why she felt so negatively about organized religion. We never celebrated any Jewish holidays, and I felt cheated by the lack of holiday spirit in our house.

My first job was as a secretary in an import-export firm, and I went back to school to get my *Abitur*. The Czech government had made special arrangements for anybody who had been excluded from the public school system to take this exam.

Then we set about establishing contact with whatever family we had left overseas. In 1946 my mother managed to find my cousin Ursel. She was now married to Fred Lennhoff, another refugee, and they had a little girl, Marion. Ursel had emigrated to England before the war, and they now lived in London. A little later we found Mother's half brother, Jirka Steiner. Jirka and his wife, Helli, had emigrated to New Zealand in 1939. Helli's parents, the Kaufers, were in Los Angeles. When we wanted to emigrate, the Kaufers sent us an Affidavit of Support and encouraged us to come to California. But we were told that the quota was filled for the foreseeable future and that we had no chance of getting a visa for America. I learned only much later that the American State Department was as anti-Semitic as the Communist government.

I had a wonderful time in England. To be away from my mother was in itself a vacation for me. I was now twenty-two years old. I asked for and was given permission to join an English shorthand class. I did well and have used the shorthand I learned there all my life. After I finished the school term, Ursel and Fred tried to talk me into staying in England. But London in the winter of 1946 was not a very hospitable city. They had no central heating, food was severely rationed, and the weather was dreadful, the worst in many years. In Prague our apartments had central heating, and the food supply was much better than in London. I never considered staying in England. I was both committed to my mother and still dependent on her and could not see leaving her.

At this time Czechoslovakia had a truly democratic government. There had been elections in 1946 and, though the Communists had gained 36 percent of the vote, I still trusted the democratic process there and had no misgivings about going back home. After my return to Czechoslovakia in early 1947, I found a well-paying position with the American Jewish Joint Distribution Committee (the Joint). I was secretary to the director and was very proud of being able to do the English correspondence for the organization. We had given up the thought of emigrating to America.

I had a new boyfriend, Honza Musil, whom I had known before the war. He had survived three years in Auschwitz, where his brother died. He had worked in a hospital there. We got engaged and life seemed to settle down.

But I got engaged only because it gave me license for a sexual relationship. In Prague, even before the war, once a young couple was engaged, this was tacitly accepted behavior. I was not in love with this man and had no intention of marrying him but liked being engaged. I had not thought about sex in the camps. First comes survival and safety, then food, and sex is way down the list. Now I was in a hurry to make up for lost years, to live life, and being engaged seemed a step in the right direction.

New elections were called for February 1948. My mother and I went to vote. When the functionaries collected the ballots we had not used, I became thoroughly frightened. The next day the Communist Party announced that it had won 97 percent of the votes. The first glow of victory and idealism that communism had engendered had worn off. That same week we received the Landing Permit that Jirka (now called George) had sent us from New Zealand. It seemed a sign of Providence to me. I did not care whether Czechoslovakia had an authoritarian regime of the left or the right; I wanted no part of it, and from that day on I started aggressively pursuing documents for our emigration.

By this time the Communists had put almost as many restrictions in the path of any would-be emigrant as the Germans had done a mere ten years before. Since we could claim the hardships of concentration camps and that we had no family left in Czechoslovakia, we were allowed to apply for an exit permit. Equally important, the Joint, where I worked, was willing to pay for our trip in dollars, and we could reimburse the organization in Czech crowns.

It stands to my mother's eternal credit that she did not object to my plan to emigrate. On the contrary, she supported my efforts. At one of the last steps in my six-month odyssey of getting all the necessary papers together, I found myself completely stymied. I finally asked my mother for help. She went to the appropriate office and succeeded in removing the last obstacle to our departure. I don't know how she managed that.

Honza had already left. He had crossed the border illegally on foot. Because he was of military age, he would never have received an exit permit. He went to Paris and was waiting there for permission to emigrate to America. Mother and I took the train to Paris and I looked forward to meeting Honza there. He was planning to send for me from America.

From Paris we went by train to Genoa and from there by ship to Australia. It had been a hospital ship during the war and was now run by the Italian government. The trip took five weeks and was incredibly boring. I was once asked to play bridge with the captain. I did not really know how to play, but I won and was never asked again. We were in first class, but I always went down to the tourist class, where there were more young people.

We arrived in Australia in November, and since all of Australia and New Zealand goes on vacation at Christmastime, their summer, we could not get a reservation to go on to New Zealand. In Sydney the Jewish community housed us with a widow. I had a great time in Sydney. During the day I did some secretarial work at the Jewish Community Center. I fell in with a group of Jewish White Russian emigrants, found a new boyfriend, and enjoyed going swimming and hiking in the bush. It was wonderful to be free, to feel free and in a group of Jewish youngsters, as I had been before the war. But when a passage to New Zealand became available, we left.

To this day I remember how shocked I was on arrival in Wellington. After Sydney it looked like and proved to be a small provincial town. To this day I can think of no redeeming feature of Wellington. The weather was abominable. It rarely hit 70 degrees and then only in February. It rained every day. And New Zealanders, like the English, didn't believe in heating. The offices were heated—everybody knew that you can't work in a cold place—but the homes were not. To warm up I would go for a walk.

Mother's family greeted us warmly and gave us the best room in their modest home. Helli and Jirka (George) had two boys, then nine and sixteen, and we were part of the family. Once we started working, I again in an office and my mother as a seamstress in another refugee's workshop, we paid them a modest rent, which my aunt saved for us to use when we would start housekeeping. Housing was very scarce, but we were anxious to be on our own, and when my uncle found us an apartment, my mother and I moved. One of the first things I did after arriving in New Zealand was to sign up at Victoria University College. I enjoyed taking classes and did very well. I still remember the A that I got on my first paper in political science.

The New Zealand refugee community was small, and we soon met everybody. Actually, Harry Benda had heard that a girl from Prague had arrived and asked a friend to invite me to her party. Thus I met Harry within four weeks of arriving in Wellington. We started seeing each other, and after our third date he asked me to marry him. We hadn't even kissed! Things moved more slowly in those days. I laughed in his face. I was seeing other men and was generally having a good time and didn't feel any desire to commit myself to anybody. But Harry was persistent. After he wrote me a furious letter, I decided he really loved me, and on New Year's

Eve 1950 Harry Benda and I got engaged. That same week my Prague fiancé, Honza Musil, sent me a ticket for America. At his expense I cabled back my rejection and broke up with him. Once I got engaged to Harry, I expected to spend the rest of my life in New Zealand. In 1973, when I met Honza in the United States, I apologized to him for my behavior.

Harry came from Prague. He had emigrated to the Dutch East Indies in early 1939, just weeks before the German occupation, and ended up in a Japanese internment camp. He came to New Zealand in 1946, sent there by the Red Cross for R&R, and decided to stay. When I met him, he had his bachelor's degree and was finishing his master's. He looked forward to teaching in New Zealand. However, he was told that, because he had not been born British, he would need an advanced degree, although the teaching staff at Wellington University had only master's degrees.

On April 13, 1950, we were married in a synagogue but only because there was no civil marriage in Wellington. I stopped my studies and devoted myself to working as a secretary and to housekeeping. In 1951 Harry applied for admission and a scholarship to Cornell University, the only American university that had a program in Southeast Asian studies. He was accepted and received a scholarship of $1,000 per annum, and a Fulbright travel grant to Cornell.

We borrowed money for my fare from a refugee friend, and in September 1952 we sailed for America, fully intending to return within two years. We arrived in Ithaca with no money to our name. Fortunately, some friends in New Zealand, members of the Baha'i faith, had managed to get us an apartment for $35 a month. It was not quite the glamorous, modern apartment that I had anticipated but some rather primitive student digs.

Now we had another problem. Harry had a student visa, and I had a visitor's visa that prohibited me from working, but Cornell employed me as a native instructor in Czech in the Modern Language Department. Harry worked very hard. For his doctoral dissertation he received original research materials from a friend in Indonesia and completed his degree (including dissertation) in three years. His degree was in political science and Southeast Asian studies. It was one of the warmest and most caring academic institutions we were ever to experience. The years in Ithaca were the happiest years of our married life, perhaps the happiest years of our lives.

But because Harry had finished his studies, he was expected to leave the country. Cornell again came to our rescue. Though the university had a stringent policy of never hiring its own graduates, Cornell gave Harry a part-time temporary position. In 1955 he got an offer from the University of Rochester to be an assistant professor at the magnificent salary of $4,200, which we gladly accepted. We moved to Rochester in September 1955, and in December 1955, our son, Peter, was born. In March 1957, fifteen months later, we had a daughter, Susan. The next four years were very hard. My mother, who had had a heart attack before Harry and I left New Zealand, joined us in Rochester in September 1957.

Harry had no time. He had a full teaching load and taught summer school and night school to supplement his meager salary. Although the department head assured Harry that Rochester valued his work, and he was a very popular and effective teacher, he never received any promotion or a meaningful increase in salary. These were hard and lonely years. We had no family or community support and were constantly short of money. In 1959 Harry was offered an associate professorship at Yale and a salary almost double what he was earning at Rochester. He was happy to resign his position at Rochester.

We moved to New Haven in September 1959, Mother followed us, and Harry started teaching. I had asked him in Rochester whether he was a bit apprehensive about coming to such a big university and department. (Rochester's had eight teaching members and Yale's had a teaching staff of sixty-three.) He vehemently denied any anxiety. However, in December 1959, just three months after we arrived in New Haven, he became seriously depressed. Our financial problems were by no means over, and when our VW Bug needed a $600 repair, we simply did not have the money. Harry stayed in bed all through the Christmas vacation, and when he was supposed to go back to teaching, he could not do it. He went to see our doctor, who promptly hospitalized him for suicidal depression.

Harry was the first person in his department—and, for all I know, in all of Yale—to suffer from depression. Yale continued his salary and that was certainly all one could expect. There I stood, alone and on my own. The children were four and two and a half years old. Again, we had no family to rush in with emotional or physical support, which I certainly needed at that moment.

In due course Harry recovered and took up his teaching duties again, and our marriage, which had suffered under the stress of the Rochester years, mended. In 1961 he became chairman of the history department, and in 1962 he was appointed tenured full professor at Yale. In the meantime his only brother, who had survived the war in Italy and was still living there, died of a heart attack at forty-eight. Harry took this further loss very hard. Although he became depressed, he remained functional. Anyone who has not lived with a seriously depressed person cannot appreciate how hard it is.

Harry was very successful professionally. The Southeast Asia Program grew and he became Mr. Southeast Asia. In 1967 he was invited to go to Singapore and set up the Research Center for Southeast Asian Studies for the government of Singapore. Yale gave him a leave of absence and we moved to Singapore in June of 1968. We were given a government house, a big old barn that was so isolated that we could not see our neighbors.

The children started school at Raffles, a local government school, where the language of instruction was English. In September we decided to send them both to an international school, which was very expensive. We really could not afford it. Fortunately, the Ford Foundation came to our rescue. We also found an Orthodox rabbi who prepared Peter to become a bar mitzvah. We all ended up having a very good year. We made friends, and one of Peter's Singapore classmates came to his wedding in 1999. Singapore remains a warm spot in my memory.

In 1968 we returned to New Haven and to the house we had bought before leaving for our year away. Harry found that the Southeast Asia Program, like other area studies programs at Yale, had been severely cut. There was a lot of stress on him.

Mother had several angina attacks in 1968 and 1969 and refused to go to a hospital. On January 17, 1970, she got up, got dressed, and died as she sat in her favorite chair. I am grateful for her easy death. She is buried in New Haven.

In October 1971 Harry suffered a heart attack in his office. He was rushed to the hospital. In those days they could not do much for heart attacks. He remained in the hospital for three weeks and was released on a Tuesday. On October 26, exactly one week after his return home, I went to wake him at seven thirty in the morning. His body was already getting cold.

What followed was a nightmare. According to Jewish law, his funeral had to be within twenty-four hours. Students and colleagues from all over the States rushed to attend. There must have been three hundred people at the funeral. There I stood, with two teenage children, no profession, no income. Harry's salary would stop at the end of November. One of Harry's publishers had offered me money, but few friends remained at my side. What hurt most was not that the academic community did not rush to my aid but that some of my closest personal friends also suddenly had no time for me. That remained a hurt for a long time and still hurts as I write about it today.

The children reacted very strongly to their father's death, of course. Susi was more open about it, while Peter was hiding his feelings. I regret that that first year after his death I was not able to tune in to their needs. I found out only much later how hard that time had been for them and how much they suffered.

Although the chairman of Harry's department wrote a few letters for me, the personnel office at Yale did not find me a job. We lived on Social Security. After a year I wrote a furious letter to the Personnel Department and a week later had a job at the Association for Oriental Studies.

In the meantime Peter had gone off to Swarthmore College and had chosen to do his junior year at Chicago. In December 1976, when he was twenty-one, he came home from Chicago for the Christmas recess. He had lost twenty-five pounds. He sat in the kitchen and cried. He felt so terrible. The next day I rushed him to my doctor, who immediately diagnosed diabetes and gave him his first shot of insulin. Next, a nutritionist explained how Peter would have to live from then on. This time it was my turn to sit there and cry. To live with diabetes is something only a person familiar with the disease can appreciate. Peter had a terrible time with it, but he never complained. I don't carry his diabetes manfully; it has been a burden for me all these years.

One year after Peter left for college, Susi went off to McGill University in Montreal. It was the right choice for her. She made many friends and those friendships have weathered the test of time. However, I was alone in the house, only three years after my husband's death.

While working for the Oriental Association at Yale, I started studying for my bachelor's degree in an extension program of the University of Vermont. I received it in 1974 and then got a master's in psychology at the University of New Haven.

In 1979 I started working in an outpatient clinic for the town of North Haven and also had a small private practice. In 1981 I secured a position as a psychiatric social worker at the High Meadows Treatment Center, a residential facility for children. I retired from there in 1989 at sixty-five. Although I had planned to return to private practice on retirement, I found I did not have the energy or the desire to take on that responsibility.

Peter graduated from Swarthmore with highest honors, but he had been severely traumatized during those years. He was admitted into doctoral programs at Chicago and Princeton but left, with his dissertation unfinished, for a teaching position at the University of Virginia. He loved his two years there. However, since he had only a limited contract, he followed a siren call to Swarthmore. He found work with a small foundation, then with the Pew Charitable Trusts. Then he was at the New School for Social Research in New York for six years.

In 1999 Peter married Helena Jareb, now a licensed psychologist in Maryland. They have two sons, Aaron, born in 1999, and Jacob, born in 2001. Though Helena is a Quaker, the boys are being brought up Jewish. They have a small house in Silver Spring, Maryland. Peter works in the Academic Exchange Program of the State Department, and he now seems happier than I can ever remember. It is a joy for me to visit them and watch them in their busy lives.

Susi graduated from McGill with a double major in political science and Asian studies. She accepted a stipend to go to China and to continue her Chinese.

Upon her return, she went to Washington to look for a job. She got a position with the American Civil Liberties Union, whose director became her mentor and her fan. They are friends to this day. She went to Georgetown Law School evenings, and for three and a half years she both worked and studied. She graduated magna cum laude. After that she accepted a clerkship with a federal judge in Brooklyn.

She had met a Jewish Israeli, a son of Czech Holocaust survivors, at the New York State Bar exam, which she passed superbly. Next, she went to Washington, D.C., where a job with a law firm was waiting for her. She hated the work and the affair with the boyfriend ended. Then she accepted a position with the National Democratic Institute for International Affairs. She enjoyed her work, including worldwide travel, and was professionally very well regarded.

In 1997, when she was thirty-nine, Susi's son—my first grandchild, Elias Daniel—was born. We celebrate the Jewish holidays together. Susi is now working for the State Department in the legal adviser's office.

The 1999 candle-lighting ceremony at the State Capitol, Hartford, Connecticut, for Yom Hashoah (Holocaust Memorial Day).

The memories of my Holocaust experience are still with me daily. I begrudge the Germans their intact families, their uninterrupted lives in their homes and in their own country, and not least their prosperity. But however bad the times we had, and to some extent still are having, I have never wished that I were not Jewish. I am proud of being Jewish and believe that Judaism is the only truly humanistic and tolerant religion. Since Harry's death I have been attending services on the major Jewish holidays at Yale University, where services are open to the community. My son's wife, who is not Jewish, said at the time of their wedding that she wanted their children to be brought up Jewish. I need hardly say how much I appreciate this.

As for my own life, I remain retired, even though I occasionally flirt with the possibility of part-time employment. My time is mostly devoted to my Holocaust work, including writing a newsletter for my group. For several years I have been doing a lot of lecturing on the Holocaust, mostly in public schools but also to civic groups. I have been told that I succeed in leaving an impression with the children that they are not likely to forget. I know that I can now do this only because I became a member of the Holocaust Child Survivors of Connecticut and have gained strength from this group.

Most importantly, I have a circle of friends, good health, and financial independence and value all of it. Moreover, I derive my greatest satisfaction from watching my children in their successful careers and rich family lives and also from watching my grandchildren, who are a joy and give meaning to my life.

Latvian Nightmare

SARA MUNIC
(b. 1926, Latvia)

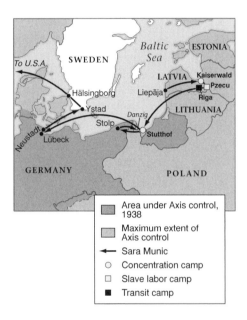

Area under Axis control, 1938

Maximum extent of Axis control

→ Sara Munic

○ Concentration camp

□ Slave labor camp

■ Transit camp

I was born to Yitzhak and Raule Levenberg on January 14, 1926, in Liepāja, also known as Libau in German, the second-largest city in Latvia. My father's family had lived in Liepāja since leaving Bauska, Latvia, soon after he was born in 1895, one of four brothers and two sisters. My mother's mother came from Cologne, Germany. Her maiden name was Johanna Hertsenberg, and her married name was Berelowitch. After her marriage she lived in Pāvilosta, Latvia, also on the Baltic Sea but further north. Her family had four girls and one boy. Her brother was an engineer, and he came to Latvia to work on some kind of building project. My great-uncle died when he was quite a young man, and he didn't have a family, so my grandmother was the only one left. My mother was very close to her cousins the Hertsenbergs, and we saw each other quite often.

My father's mother passed away when I was about three and my father's father when I was about eleven, so my memory of them is very vague. My paternal grandfather, Shmuel, lived with his youngest daughter, Zlate. Passover was a family tradition, and we all went to the seder at their house. He liked to conduct the seder with his children and grandchildren around him. Passover was my favorite holiday. I well remember how the house had to be turned upside down and cleaned, and even the outside furniture had to be cleaned and scrubbed. It was quite an undertaking but it was very nice.

I was the oldest of three sisters. The second was Ella, whom we called Ellie. She was two years younger than I. Henie was eleven months younger than Ellie. We lived in a mixed neighborhood in Liepāja. I don't think we had a strictly Jewish neighborhood there. We lived in a good-sized apartment with five big rooms. In addition to my parents and the three girls, my aunt from Pāvilosta lived with us. I remember we had a big round dining room table where everybody sat for meals and conversations.

Before the war there was a great deal of anti-Semitism in Latvia. The government was a dictatorship, and hating Jews was inbred in them, so to speak. When we were kids, we always had to watch out because there was always a bully or two when you went from school to home or anywhere else. It wasn't pleasant, but you just lived with it like a bad habit.

I went to a Yiddish school called Sholom Aleichem and then went two years to another Jewish school. We had a lot of Jewish and especially Zionist groups and activities. The three of us girls belonged to Maccabi, and we were into sports quite a bit. We also had meetings and talked about life in Palestine and on the kibbutzim and other interesting things. In the summer we had what was called Mahane, a camp with tents and other simple facilities. One year I went to the shore. I must have been about thirteen. It was very nice to have young people from all over the country together. At that time I was not an ardent Zionist. I wanted to get an education and that meant staying home.

Then in 1940 the Russians came. At that time I was in the hospital with scarlet fever. I remember that it was so funny to me: when I went in it was Latvia and when I came out it was Russia. Not much really changed for me, however. I was still going to school. Of course, there was a lot of excitement with the Russian army and other people all over the city, and they had concerts for the population. But otherwise not much changed. We stayed in the same apartment. My father, who was in the building business, was very busy because he did a lot of work for the Latvian army, and when the Russians came he worked for them too. There were shortages of this or that at times, because even though Latvia was an agricultural country, much of our production was sent to Russia. But everyone survived.

We were aware, in general terms, about the German attacks on Poland and other countries and about persecution of Jews and so on. But this information was mostly in the Jewish newspapers. My parents and many others were very upset about all this, of course, but nobody imagined what the consequences would be. No one thought it could happen in Liepāja. Because of his work with the Russians, my father could have taken us to Russia, but he couldn't leave the rest of his family in Liepāja, and perhaps he was scared for no reason. So we just stayed.

All of a sudden, on the night of June 24, 1941, we were bombed by German planes. Fires burned all over the city. Some residential areas were bombed, but mostly it was the harbor and factories and so on. Liepāja was a port city that stored a lot of grain. They bombed that, and you have no idea how terrible it is when grain is burned. It is just unbelievable. I think the fires burned all week until the Germans entered the city around July 1. Liepāja was one of the last Latvian cities they occupied. The Russians ran away and the Germans took many Russian POWs. It was terrible the way the Germans treated them.

We had no idea that this could happen to us. We couldn't even imagine it. No sooner had the Germans arrived than they began issuing proclamations. Jews had to turn in their jewelry, gold, money, radios, bicycles, even copper pots. I remember we had quite a collection of copper pots, and they took them. Later on we got them back in bullets.

People were then made to go to work for the Germans. They were gathered in an area they called the *Umschlagplatz*. Trucks took the men to work in the morning wherever they were needed and brought them back. Quite a bit later we learned that the Germans shot them all one day with the help of Latvians.

Proclamations were posted all over the city like bulletins. We were so naive about all this. After all, the law was the law and you followed the law. When they said come here to go to work, you went because you couldn't go anywhere else to work. You were basically cut off from society. You couldn't even walk on the sidewalk. You had to wear a yellow patch beginning in the summer of 1941, sometimes a star but mostly a yellow patch. No one really enforced this rule but everyone followed it.

This went on all through the summer and fall of 1941. Little by little they emptied the city of Jewish men. Then, in the middle of December, they had what they called an *Aktion*. A proclamation said that no Jew was allowed to leave his home. Then they went from house to house and told us we could take only one suitcase and then kicked us out. Both Germans and Latvians took people to jail and from there to the forest, and they killed them there. That is where my father's sister and her family died, I think on December 15. My father's sister was married to my mother's brother, and they had three children, and my mother's sister also lived with them, and they were all killed at that time. A few people managed to escape. This is how we found out what had happened.

We were lucky in a way that my father worked for the German navy. One of the people he worked for found out what was happening, and he went to the jail and looked for my father. One of the Jewish men there heard him calling, "Where is my Levenberg?" Of course, he couldn't find us because they hadn't come to our house yet, so the Jewish man said, if you let me out I will take you to Levenberg. So the German arranged for this fellow and his family to leave the jail. The German was a navy officer who worked in the hospital. When all kinds of wounded people were brought in, they found they needed all kinds of stuff for different wounds. My father helped them build some of the equipment they needed.

I remember it was such a horrible day. It was very cold with rain and sleet and snow. They came to our house to look for my father, sliding along and holding on to each other. It was the strangest sight: this German officer and a Jew holding on to each other to get somewhere! My father had a permit from the SS that said that they needed my father for work that they were doing and that he and his family should not be touched. So when the SS came, they just looked at the permit and went away.

We stayed in our home through that extremely cold winter. The Germans were hunting Jews all winter long. They would go out in the middle of the night, with Latvians pointing out where some Jews were still living. The Germans went into the houses and took them out, and their fate was the same as everyone else's. Nobody ever came back. We actually had a Jewish acquaintance, a shoemaker by trade, who worked for the German police. He used to take care of their boots after they came in from a night's killing. He had to clean the blood off the Germans' boots, the Jewish blood. He noticed that they had a certain routine when they went out at night, so he spread the word when they were on the prowl.

I remember when we spent one night in the wash house on the first floor of our apartment building, a separate area for doing laundry. We had a superintendent who lived on the second floor. He kept a pig in back of the building, but one night we went into the wash house and the pig was there. We went someplace else every so often because we never knew who might come for us or if they would honor my father's permit.

The Latvians in our neighborhood could not have been more pleased about what was happening to the Jews. A neighbor just down the hall from us had no children of her own, but she was raising a nephew, in his teens at that point. One day I went out to throw out some rubbish, and there he was—in uniform with full regalia and a gun. He scared me to death. He was in the Latvian militia. They were very eager to get rid of the Jews, and I think that really they were the ones who did a great deal of the killing.

We had no plans to escape because there was no place to go. We were surrounded by the Germans except for the Baltic Sea. We could only hide. In the summer of 1942 they started enclosing us in a ghetto. We were surrounded by barbed wire. The Judenrat (Jewish Council) assigned people to their new homes. Space was very limited. At that time we were eight people in our family, and we were given only two small rooms and a kitchen that we shared with another family. We were allowed to bring with us only basic furniture: bed, table, and chairs.

At that time there were only 832 of us all told. After the ghetto was established, we would go outside to work and come back at night. The ghetto was closed at night, and we had to be inspected by guards when we came back. Food was very scarce. We had a nanny named Milda. We gave her whatever clothing and other things we still had, and she sold it and bought food for us. After a while she got scared and stopped doing that. I don't blame her; it wasn't easy.

Everybody had to work, even my sister who was only twelve. She worked in a place where they cut wood into small pieces that were used to fuel trucks. They were short of oil so they used wood. Poor thing, many times her fingers were cut in the chopping machine. I was sent to the port and did different things. At first we unloaded all kinds of wood from railcars. We had to move from one rail system to another, so we were always outside and my hands and feet were bleeding from the cold. In the summer I was able to get into a unit that cleaned the officers' apartments, and that was a little better. My mother worked in the ghetto garden. She enjoyed that, and sometimes she was able to get some extra tomatoes or cucumbers or cabbages or whatever. My father continued to work for the Germans. None of us got paid.

The Judenrat had a store in the ghetto. With the coupons they gave us, we were able to get bread and milk and sometimes a little meat or fish. We were able to survive with this food and what we could get illegally outside the ghetto. But that was dangerous. If anyone looked suspicious coming back into the ghetto, he was searched and told to empty even his secret pockets of potatoes. The German guards were not always too strict. Actually, we were quite lucky because the commandant was a halfway decent man compared with those in other places. He didn't go around killing people.

In September 1943 the Germans dissolved the ghetto. We were to be taken somewhere else to work, and we were allowed to take a suitcase with personal clothes. Latvians and Germans guarded us all the way to the railway station. We were packed in cattle cars for a couple of days. We had no food, no water, no sanitation facilities. It was just horrible.

We finally arrived at Kaiserwald, a concentration camp outside Riga. As soon as we arrived, our suitcases were taken from us, and the men and women were separated. Then we had to take off all our clothes and take showers. We were allowed to keep our own shoes but were issued dresses after the showers. We just got whatever dress happened to be on top of the pile. So big women often got tiny dresses and small women got big dresses. We looked like clowns. It was another way to dehumanize us. The women handing out the clothes had been sent there from the Vilna ghetto after it was liquidated.

Early every morning we had an *Appell,* or roll call, outside the barracks, sometimes lasting for hours. During one *Appell* a couple of weeks after we arrived, some men in uniform came to us. We didn't know who they were, but they said they needed people for work. For some reason—I still don't know why—I stepped out. Then my mother, my aunt, and my sisters and others stepped out. They also took 120 men, mostly from the ghetto in Liepāja. By luck my father was one of us.

They sent us in buses to Pzecu, a labor camp near Riga. The men and women were separated again by barbed wire. Once in a while they let us go to the wire and talk so we were able to see my father, who was still working for the Germans. My

281

mother washed his clothes for him. She actually became a housekeeper for one of the German officers and took care of his garden. He was kind of nice to her. He didn't abuse her.

They trained us on all kinds of machinery for the *Reichsbahn* (railways). A lot of their train cars and engines were lost or damaged by bombing and explosions. They brought them there and we repaired them. The factory was outside the camp. We walked there in the morning and walked back at night. We worked maybe ten hours a day. Every day all we had to eat was soup and a slice of bread and sometimes a bit of margarine, just enough to keep us alive to do the work they wanted us to do.

At night all we could talk about and dream about was food. Imagine: a whole loaf of bread that you don't have to share with anybody! This would have been ecstasy. I never realized the importance of food. Hunger is a terrible thing. We talked about recipes and about what our mothers cooked and baked before the war. We were always talking about food.

The German and Latvian guards just guarded us. They did not hit us or anything like that. Until July 27, 1943. In the middle of the night, all of a sudden we heard, *"Raus! Raus!* Everybody out!" We got out of the barracks, and we were taken to one of the big locomotive sheds. They had emptied it and now they put us in there. They told us to strip, men on one side and women on the other. When we were naked, we had to go through a commission. That meant we were inspected by doctors and SS officers. If you were young and still had the strength to work, you were sent to one side. The older ones were sent to the other side and taken away, including my mother and father. Both of them looked older than they really were, and my father had lost a lot of weight. We learned later that they were all taken to Auschwitz, and they died there along with millions of others.

Of my family, only my mother's youngest sister, Mary, and my two sisters and I were left. Those who survived the selection had their heads shaved and were given new striped uniforms with numbers on them. We remained there working until about the third week in August. By this time the Russians were coming closer. So the Germans started to prepare railway cars so they could take us along the line wherever we were needed to fix other cars. They put bunk beds for us in some of the cars and tools and machinery in others. Now we worked day and night.

All of a sudden the Russians got so close we could hear the guns. I couldn't wait for them to arrive, but we were not that lucky. The Germans took us to Riga harbor and put us on a ship. On the ship were many other Jews, many from Estonian camps. The conditions on the ship were terrible. We were packed like sardines in a can, and we had very little food. By shifts we were able to go up on deck and get some air. This continued for three days and then we arrived at Danzig. From there we were taken, mostly on barges, then on foot, to Stutthof, in what had been the Free City of Danzig, now in Poland.

Stutthof was a big camp where they had selections and a crematorium. You could smell the burning bodies and see the smoke from the chimney. There were

Jews there from Hungary, Romania, and other countries, even Italy. There was a German named Max. He walked around in boots and a leather coat with a couple of dogs and a whip. He was a monster. It was a terrible place. Some of us had to sleep on the floor. We just prayed from day to day for survival. We were there about a month, and then they took us by train to Stolp to work on the railway.

We were put on a regular train with hard benches in cars separate from the local population. We were crowded, but by now we were so skinny we didn't need much space. Stolp was then in Pomerania and is now in Poland and known as Słupsk. We were put into a gymnasium that had been converted into living quarters for the women. The bunks were in tiers of three, and each of us had a bunk. They deloused us with all kinds of chemicals but we still had lice. That was a great occupation, killing lice every night. They ate more than we did. They ate us.

From September 1944 to March 1945 we worked there. We took down a hill with just shovels and laid railway tracks. Jewish men were working there also, the same ones who came from Riga and elsewhere, but they were separated from the women. We were always looking for food. One day a railway car burned. It was full of cheese. The cheese melted, and the guys dug out pieces of cheese, and we were able to give the cheese to some people, a piece here, a piece there. Another time they discovered a railway car that was sealed, probably an army or air force car. They broke the seal and found that the car was full of cigarettes. They took some of the cigarettes to the barracks. Before long the Germans discovered what had happened and searched the barracks. They found the cigarettes and took away the six or eight guys that took them. I knew two of them who were from Liepāja. One was named Aronson. The Germans hanged him, and we all had to walk around and watch.

In March, when the Russians got close, the Germans took us outside the city, but instead of working on the railway, they made us dig trenches to stop the Russian tanks. I don't know if the trenches would have done any good, but we did that for a week or so. Then they put us on another train and took us to another camp named Burgraben, near Danzig, which was almost empty. They just dumped us there. I was lucky to be picked to work in the kitchen, so I could hide a few potatoes and carrots here and there. I even managed to get some straw so my sisters, my aunt, and I did not have to sleep on the bare floor.

In April 1945 the Germans took us back to Stutthof in buses. Most of the camp was empty. Only some Norwegian and Russian POWs, Gypsies, and a few Jews were there. The guards were not Germans but Ukrainians, both men and women. Then the Germans again put us on barges and took us downriver through Danzig and out to sea. Besides us Latvians there were Norwegian POWs and some others but not the Gypsies. The guards now were SS men. There were three or four barges and conditions on all of them were terrible. We were sitting but did not have enough room to stretch out our legs. The only sanitary facility we had was a pail. We were given no food at all.

One night they took us off the barges onto an island that had been bombed to smithereens. Parts of cows and horses and dogs and people were all over the place. They took us to an open space and dumped us there overnight. The following morning we went back on the barges. We were just roaming the sea, for about ten days altogether.

One day the barges stopped at Lübeck, Germany. A German officer came onto one barge and got very angry at the condition of the people. He went into town and made some stores open. He came back with cans of ham or whatever it was and just threw them into the barges. I was lucky enough to catch one. It was very fatty, and we licked it just like you lick ice cream. The officer left and went on his way, and we continued on to the north.

One morning we found ourselves sitting not too far from shore, and the Germans had all disappeared. As luck would have it, the Norwegian POWs got suspicious, and they discovered the Germans had mined the barges. They disconnected the explosives and then tried to get us close to the shore. None of us had the strength to jump off the barges and walk to the shore. The Norwegians managed to get to shore, found some ropes, and tied the barges to trees. Then they helped us get off them.

Almost everybody was off when the SS men returned, wearing navy uniforms. They started shooting at us. My sister Ellie was already quite sick, and we tried to hide her. Little by little the guards got us all together and started walking us through the town of Neustadt. That was quite a walk, especially for people who had not eaten for ten days. They walked us to a naval officers' training school and marched us all to the soccer field. Later on we were told that we were taken there to be placed on the ship *Cap Arcona*.

While we were on the soccer field, we saw the *Cap Arcona* being bombed by English planes. They didn't know, of course, that the ship was filled with refugees—Jews, Poles, and others. Many died there. Years later bodies from the ship were still washing up on shore. We were too far away to see the ship actually explode, but we heard the explosion and saw the smoke and fire.

On May 3, 1945, five days before the Germans capitulated, we heard this terrible noise. It came from tanks coming down the road. At first we didn't realize they were British. Then we laughed and cried. The British unfortunately did not know how to treat us. We hadn't eaten for such a long time that our insides were all dried up. They fed us the same food that they had, and many got so sick that they actually died. My aunt was already sick with typhoid fever, and she died three days later. My sister Ellie was so sick that when an ambulance came to take her to a hospital, she screamed, "Please don't touch me!" She was in pain all over and passed away in the hospital on May 11.

Henie was now sixteen and so terribly sick. But God was with her in the hospital and she managed to survive. She wanted to live so she could come back to me. I was now nineteen and also very sick. I knew we had to get some food. Everybody who could walk was roaming the town, looking for food. I went into a warehouse and found some sugar, of all things. I took some and licked it. Henie and I stayed in Neustadt, Germany, until July 27, 1945.

I wanted to go back to Latvia to continue my education, but Henie insisted that we were not going back there. She was right. She had more sense than I did at the time. We had no reason to go back. So we did what everybody else was trying to do: find relatives in the United States, England, Australia, wherever. Everybody tried to get out of Germany. I wanted to go anywhere except Germany.

The United Nations Relief and Rehabilitation Administration (UNRRA) was run at the time by Count Folke Bernadotte, a cousin of the Swedish king. In late July an UNRRA commission came and examined my sister Henie and me and arranged for us to be sent to Sweden. On July 27 we were taken to Ystad, a town on the Kattegat. We were quarantined, of course, but everybody was fabulous to us. Because of her lung and other problems, Henie was sent to a sanitarium in Borås, farther north, and she was there for quite a while. I stayed in Ystad for a short time. Then I went to Hälsingborg and got a job with the Bunsteins. Mrs. Bunstein was a diabetic and had bad vision, and she needed companionship and help. I lived with them for quite a while. I even met my husband, Abe, there. He and his sister were from a town near Vilna and survived the war. He came looking for an apartment for them and found a wife. We were married on December 25, 1947, in Malmö because there was no rabbi in Hälsingborg. My husband was a bricklayer in Poland and served in the Polish army. He continued to work as a bricklayer in Sweden and later in the United States.

Our first son, Chaim Yitzhak, was born in Sweden in September 1948. I was working in a big factory that made boots and shoes and went back to work there six months later. The factory had a good day care center. They were very good to workers with small children. I continued working there until we three came to the United States in January 1951. My husband had family in Hartford, Connecticut, and they made out the papers for us. That is why we came to Hartford immediately. I went to night school here for a couple of years. Then I had three more children and could not go to school any more. The children were Rachelle, Miriam, and Jerry. I now have seven grandchildren. In 1954 we brought my sister Henie and her husband and daughter here, and she now lives in New York and Florida.

When we moved to West Hartford in 1967, I decided I needed to get out of the house, so I took a job with an insurance company and stayed with them for twenty-one years. I started out as a filing clerk, and then I became a supervisor in Agency Accounting. I did auditing and accounting for them and retired in June 1988. Meanwhile, Abe developed heart problems and died of heart failure on August 25, 1987.

Looking back on my wartime persecution, I think the most dehumanizing and horrible experience was the time we were all taken to a big shed and stripped naked in more ways than one. It was not just a matter of taking your clothes off. You are stripped naked as a human being. You don't amount to anything, you are nothing. And when they cut your hair off and everyone is bald, that was just terrible. To top the whole thing off, I lost my parents at that time. But the whole experience was horrible. I don't know how I got through it. Maybe God was with me.

Sara and her grandsons at the bar mitzvah celebration of the youngest, New Orleans, February 1998.

The whole experience is not something one can forget. I'm on Prozac now. It helps a little, but now that I live alone, it's even harder. When I was working and had a husband and children at home, I was so busy with day-to-day living that I didn't think much about it. But in bed at night I'd wake up in a sweat because everything came back. You never know when this is going to happen. Sometimes I have to lie down during the day because I can't sleep at night. I have several other health problems and take medications.

But I am still a believer. My family in Latvia was quite religious. My father did not have *payot* (side locks hanging in front of or behind the ears) but we were Orthodox Jews, and religion was quite important in our lives, including Shabbat and holidays and kashrut (dietary laws). That has not changed. I'm not as observant as I was when my parents were alive, because I belong to a Conservative synagogue now, and I do ride on Shabbat.

I have not been back to Latvia since I left and have no intention of going back. I have nothing to go back to. I don't want to see those people. I don't want to look at their faces. I have no contact with anyone in Latvia, but I belong to an organization of Latvian Jews in New York. Some of them go back, even to Liepāja, and the situation there is very grim. Why should I go back? It would only bring back all the old wounds and hurts that have never quite healed. Even my children are not interested in going.

I hope that everyone, especially my children and grandchildren, will never forget what happened to me and my husband, and I hope that nobody ever has to go through anything like that. I'm glad that I am here to be able to tell the story.

Growing Up Jewish in Italy

GIORGINA VITALE
(b. 1926, Italy)

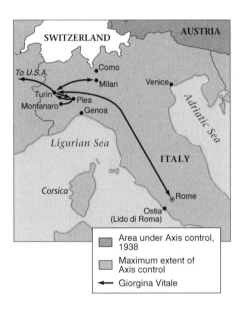

Italy is the only land outside Palestine where the settlement of Jews has been continuous from remote times to the present. From the times of the Maccabees (161 BCE), Jews sent ambassadors to Rome to establish friendly relations. Later on, the record of Jews in Rome and Italy is unbroken for more than twenty-one hundred years. After the destruction of the Second Temple by the Romans (70 CE), many Jews were brought to Rome as slaves, but they were not slaves for long. Their fellow Jews ransomed them. In 1492, with the expulsion from Spain, many Jews settled in Italy.

Italy was, until a little over 150 years ago, divided and under the dominion of various kings, popes, dukes, princes, and, later, mercantile cities. As the conditions in one place were better than in others, Jews sometimes moved from one part of the country to another. Perhaps the worst times started in 1555, when the ghetto period began and Jews lived under the most repressive conditions; this lasted until 1821. At this time Italy was in ferment, trying to shake off the yoke of the German and Austrian rulers. With great enthusiasm Jews joined the struggle to free their country and to win equality for themselves. In 1848 the wars against Austria started the Italian movement of national unity and liberation, called Risorgimento.

Piemontese Jews, more than others, felt deeply involved in the history of the state that had united Italy under the House of Savoy. They helped put Cavour, the famous statesman, in the Piemontese parliament and financed his wars through the great Jewish banks. They sheltered Giuseppe Mazzini, the Risorgimento hero, and volunteered to fight with Garibaldi. My father's family was part of this great patriotic tradition. Two of my father's brothers were named Attilio and Emilio after the heroic Bandiera brothers. Attilio's only child was named Italia.

By 1870, after the unification of Italy, the Jews were accepted as equal members of the Italian people. They could live wherever they wanted, although many continued to live in what was previously the ghetto. Jews became prominent in public life. Rome had a Jewish mayor; there were Jewish generals, admirals, cabinet ministers. The involvement of Jews in the political life of Italy continued up to 1938. Mussolini himself had numerous Jewish advisers, particularly in the field of finance. Although Jews comprised only one tenth of 1 percent of the population of Italy, an unbelievably high percentage of Jewish university professors, scientists, doctors, lawyers, writers, and social scientists enriched the life of the nation.

I was born in Turin on February 11, 1926, the second daughter of two very special people who complemented each other perfectly. My father, Giorgio de Leon, was the youngest of four brothers, born into a family of modest means and with recent memories of the ghetto. His father, Isacco (Isaac) de Leon, had been born in the ghetto of Venice and was a shoemaker. His mother, Michelina Ovazza, was born in the ghetto of Turin and was a tailor. One thing that I was told and that I will never forget is that my grandmother sewed well into the night and, to be able to see with the small lightbulbs available at that time, she would put her chair on the kitchen table, to be near the source of light.

My mother, Emma Segrè, was the youngest of three sisters, born into a middle-class family. Her father, Mario Segrè, was originally from Trieste but moved to Piombino, a small town in Tuscany across from the Isle of Elba. Piombino was known for the steel mills where railroad tracks were manufactured and where my grandfather was an executive. There he met my grandmother, Emilia Jona, who was born in the ghetto of Turin (as was my paternal grandmother), a member of a large family of merchants and scholars.

In 1912, my father, who was then only thirteen, and his eldest brother opened a small store and repair shop for electric and hydraulic systems and supplies, and while they took care of repairs, their father tended the store. Between 1915 and 1921, one by one the brothers were called to arms in the First World War, and they had to close the business.

Life after the war was a struggle. Within a few years three of the brothers married two sisters and their first cousin and, with their unmarried brother, opened a workshop for repair and installation of electrical parts for cars, for which they coined the name *Elettrauto*. It was one of the first in Turin and it prospered.

A new generation came into the world. When I was born in 1926, my sister, Lina, was only fifteen months old. Life must have been difficult for my mother, living in a cold-water flat with a toddler and a premature newborn, but she had a great deal of family support to lighten the burden. The brothers did well in the business, added a retail store on one of the main streets of the city, and became well known for the quality of their products and service.

At the time my memories begin, we lived in a lovely Turin apartment with all the conveniences. I remember when our first telephone was installed and when we got our first radio. My early years, as I remember them, were so regular and carefree that it is difficult to say what was so different about growing up under Mussolini's Fascist regime. Fascism was the only way of existence. There was no way to compare it to other political systems. The youth organization to which I belonged—the Piccole Italiane—was part of the school system. It was not a matter of choice, and it was mostly concerned with gymnastics, not ideas.

Jews enjoyed complete freedom and equality and assimilated willingly into the mainstream of Italian life. I have wonderful memories of my childhood in a large family that included grandparents, aunts and uncles, and cousins, all living within blocks of each other, near the Jewish community, which included the synagogue, the Talmud Torah, the Jewish Home for the Aged, and the orphanage, which was near our fathers' store and the park where we played after school.

Very few families were Orthodox, and kashrut (dietary laws) was hardly observed. However, enthusiastic celebration of the traditions was particularly evident during the High Holidays (Rosh Hashanah and Yom Kippur) and the ceremonies connected with the rites of passage: circumcision, bar/bat mitzvahs, weddings, and funerals. We practiced our Judaism within the walls of our homes, while we lived in harmony and equality with our Catholic neighbors. Jews tended to marry Jews.

I remember evenings at home when relatives would come for dinner. After dinner, while we were still sitting at the table, we would sing a variety of songs in Italian, Hebrew, and the Piemontese dialect. We went on Sunday outings with family and on summer vacations with aunts and cousins. While we spoke only Italian, no Yiddish or Ladino, our parents spoke a mixture of dialect and Hebrew whenever they wanted to exclude us children from the conversation.

The holiday I remember the most is Pesach (Passover). Weeks in advance, all families would order from the synagogue two kinds of matzoh, one for eating and the other for cooking, and *shmurah* flour to make the traditional sweets that we called *matzoh nasirot*. All the women of the community would go to the synagogue's kitchen to prepare and bake those wonderful cookies. They would fill up sacks with them and share them with all the relatives, friends, schoolteachers, and Christian neighbors. Then, early one morning, my mother would get us out of bed and start cleaning the house from top to bottom.

The seder was held at my grandparents' home as long as my grandmother lived, and I remember the three daughters-in-law joining my grandmother in the kitchen to help with the cooking. Some of the traditional food included hard-boiled eggs served with a delicious green sauce and goose salami as appetizer; *day-enu*, which is chicken broth with pieces of matzoh cooked in it; roast lamb with new potatoes; turkey breast and sauteed spinach; and, for dessert, fruit compote and *matzoh nasirot.*

We celebrated Yom Kippur with family dinners before and after the fast, breaking the fast with a wonderful concoction called *bruscadela,* which is challah soaked in sweet wine and cinnamon. Most Italian Jewish food was inspired by Italian regional cooking, with substitutions to conform to rules of kashrut. In the synagogue the customs were Sephardic Orthodox, with happy melodies and a highly dignified service. When a man was called to read the Torah, his family would stand up. When the rabbi gave the benediction, the children, boys and girls alike, joined their father, who would cover them with his tallith and bless them. On Friday nights some families lit an oil Shabbat lamp rather than candles.

We children lived an idyllic life, shielded from all cares. During the school year we went to the Talmud Torah, then to the park to play together after school, and visited our grandparents and all the great-aunts and -uncles in turn once a week. But the best memories are of the long, lazy summers at the seashore, where we would spend two glorious months in a *pensione* with our mothers, finding the same friends year after year and making new ones, playing endless games of marbles, volleyball, and ping-pong on the beach, swimming and cavorting in the water for hours, and going to outdoor movies at night. Or we might go for a walk, culminating in the enjoyment of an ice cream cone or a cool slice of watermelon from a street vendor.

Unfortunately, our fathers were left in the city and came only once or twice during the summer. Our parents deemed these holidays essential for our health, worth the sacrifice of separation. At the end of August, before school started, we would spend a week or ten days in the country for the grape harvest at our grandparents' small summer house, again a big sacrifice for our mothers, who were forced to cook in a tiny kitchen on a wood stove, but wonderful for the children, who could run in the fields all day long, pick fruits from the trees and vines, and play together in total abandon.

In 1935 the business continued to expand and prosper; it now included a factory that produced its own brand of electric supplies for cars. The brothers decided to open stores in Rome and Milan. The oldest brother, Attilio, was in charge of the factory, Arturo of the store in Turin. Emilio moved to Rome with his family to manage that store, and we moved to Milan, where my father ran that store. Separating the family was difficult, especially for the older generation. But Milan is only about eighty miles from Turin, and we drove back every other weekend to visit our grandparents and the rest of the family.

Again, we rented an apartment close to the store and to the Talmud Torah, where I attended the fifth and last grade of elementary school, while my older sister, Lina, started going to public school, also within walking distance. We still spent the holidays together with the rest of the family in Turin and summers in the summer home, at least for a short time. But in 1936 my grandmother died, and the center of the family shifted to our home in Milan.

In September 1938 the whole family was gathered, as was customary, in our grandfather's summer house to celebrate his birthday and enjoy the grape harvest. I was twelve and it had been such a happy year. I had celebrated becoming a bat mitzvah in May with a great family gathering, and in July, my sister Emilia was born, bringing much joy to our home. On September 8, while we were at the dinner table, one of my uncles opened the newspaper and showed us the headlines announcing that all Jews were excluded from school as of the start of the academic year. It came as a blow without warning, and I was totally stunned. The Nuremberg Laws against the Jews were promulgated that day, bringing severe restrictions.

Today, as I think of those years, I ask myself how we could have been so blind to the events that were already taking place all around us. How could we feel so secure, despite being aware of being different from our schoolmates and being exempted from attending religious classes with them? Perhaps it can be explained by the fact that we children lived a life of our own. We did not share in grown-ups' conversation, we did not read newspapers, except for the Sunday comics, or listen to the news on the radio. Children were supposed to be seen but not heard.

My uncle Arturo decided to leave the country to avoid discrimination and humiliation, and my father started commuting to Turin to take his place in the business. In Milan the Jewish community worked together to enlarge the day school to accommodate every Jewish student up to college level. That school became my inspiration and my haven. What it lacked in space it made up in the quality of teachers and students. For the first time I was introduced to Zionism, and I embraced it with the fervor of a young pioneer. We learned modern Hebrew, we sang the songs of the *halutzim* (pioneers), and we dreamed about our return to Zion.

The public reaction was mixed. Our Christian friends and neighbors did not change their attitude toward us, and faithful employees continued working for my father. The firm was incorporated, and the family name did not appear any more. Fascist propaganda filled billboards, movie screens, and newspapers. A new magazine, the *Defense of the Race,* found its way onto newsstands for the sole purpose of inciting hate against the Jews. Some stores, cafes, and restaurants had signs on the door saying that dogs and Jews were not welcome or proclaiming that their store was "Aryan."

With the entry of Italy into the European war in 1940 as an ally of Germany, restrictions were intensified: radios were confiscated, Jews were expelled from areas near military bases, young people were forced to go to the Department of Public Works every day after school to be assigned to jobs on streets, parks, hospital grounds. In addition, together with our Christian neighbors, we lived through countless nights in shelters, while the whole world seemed to collapse around us. The hardships of war multiplied as time went on. There was no fuel, and people heated their homes with small stoves using whatever little wood they could find.

The de Leon family, Piemonte, Italy, June 1940. *Left to right:* Giorgina, Giorgio, Emilia, Emma, and Michelina.

Cars were converted to methane gas and could be used only for work pertaining to the war effort. Food was rationed and of poor quality. Some food items were not available at all.

As the continual air raids of the Allied forces made life difficult in the city, schools were closed. In 1941 my father brought us back to Turin, and we went to live in the summer villa, located in the hills at the outskirts of the city. Many families had abandoned their homes in the cities and found refuge in surrounding small towns. Men (and working women) went by train or bus to the city to work and returned to the country at night. In our house we had made a makeshift dormitory for employees who could not join their families at night. Two consecutive air raids destroyed the factory.

My father and his faithful employees searched in the ruins for whatever they could salvage and traveled across Piemonte in search of a site suitable for the factory. He found an old theater in a small town, and whatever they had found among the ruins was brought back into use. He purchased a van to transport the workers from the city, and the new factory was in operation within three months. Again,

Attilio took charge of the factory, while my father returned to work in the central store. Both Lina and I went to work in the business at that time, she in the store and I in the factory. During another air raid the store in Milan and the synagogues of Milan and Turin were destroyed.

I needed only a semester to finish my senior year of high school, and my parents decided that I should finish my schooling. They sent me to Rome to live with my uncle and his family, and I was accepted as an auditor in a Catholic school that my cousins were also attending. I spent the last semester there and then went back to join my family.

Slowly, history was made. Mussolini was replaced by Marshal Badoglio in July of 1943, and on September 8 Italy surrendered to the Allies and there was jubilation all over the country. But within a few hours the Germans, with extreme efficiency, were marching on the streets of most Italian cities and occupying the country.

That was the day we left our home and started our life in hiding. Thanks to a friend at city hall, my father had been able to secure false identity cards and had made plans for our escape. I was seventeen and my two sisters eighteen and five. We arrived late at night in a rural hamlet called Piea, near Asti, only about twenty-eight miles from Turin, and, with our new name, we started a new life. "It will only be for a few weeks," my father said confidently. The Allies were already fighting their way from Sicily to Naples, and they were expected to land somewhere in the Gulf of Genoa. Unfortunately, the landing did not take place, and our weeks in hiding turned into two years.

I had attended a *scuòla magistrate,* or normal school, that would permit me to teach elementary grades after I had taken proper exams. The exams were given in September, when we were already in hiding. On the day of the exams I took the bus to Turin and went to the school. I showed my regular papers stamped with "of the Jewish race." The instructors were confused and didn't know what to do. They looked at each other and . . . they gave me the exams, written and oral, and then I took the bus and went back to Piea. Eventually, I got my diploma.

In December 1943 the Jews were declared public enemies of the country, and news of roundups and deportations reached us. Our hiding place did not seem safe enough, so we decided to separate to be less conspicuous. My grandfather remained in Piea at the house of the priest. My mother and father returned to our apartment in the city, where a Christian family was now living, having lost their home and belongings in an air raid. My two sisters and I went to another little village, Montanaro, changed names again, and moved into a room used to store furniture that we had removed from the city because of the air raids. It was difficult to explain to our little sister the reasons for all our changes. When told of her new name, she curiously inquired: "Our name in Torino was de Leon; when we went to Piea, we became De Giorgis; now we are the Alpozzos. If we went to Venice, what would our name be?"

We spent two months in Montanaro. It was a brutally cold winter, with no heat in that room except for the small wood stove that we used for cooking. The water pump was across the street and the outhouse in the courtyard. Those were the harshest days of our long ordeal. Besides the physical discomforts, we didn't know whether we would ever see the rest of the family again. In February 1944 we decided to take our chances and return to Piea, so we would all be together again.

Days and weeks went by while we listened hopefully every night on our shortwave radio to the BBC with the somber news of the painfully slow advance of the Allied forces from the south. We became part of the rural life of the little town, working side by side with the farmers, who became our friends. Partisans were hiding in the woods all around the town, and the Germans were never far away. Almost weekly they came in search of young people and guns and went from house to house, at times rounding up the whole population in the square while the search went on. During one of the searches the Germans saw a patch of freshly dug ground in our vegetable garden. With machine guns pointed at my father, they made him dig so they could see what was buried there. It was our dog, which had died just days before.

The German armies retreated, still fighting and destroying in a frenzy of desperation. Finally, on April 29, 1945, the unconditional surrender of the German armies in Italy put an end to our nightmare. The Jewish Brigade, part of the British army, reopened the synagogues in town after town and gathered the remnants of each community. My father, with a group of young people from Piea, went to Turin and rushed to put the Italian flag on the balcony of our apartment and at our place of business, while the Germans were still there. He came back to Piea the next day in a state of euphoria, and we made plans to go back home.

The losses were great—six thousand to eight thousand Italian Jews had been obliterated—but the tragedy would have been much greater if not for the exceptional role of the Italian people in saving Jews. Countless Italians, individuals and organizations, refused to participate or cooperate in the German attempt to slaughter a whole people, putting their own lives at risk. While 80 percent of European Jews perished, 80 percent of Italy's Jews were saved. Only after the liberation did we find out that the people of the village of Piea knew all along that we were Jewish, yet they never made mention of it during the two years that we lived among them. We owe our lives to the people of Piea.

During all this time my older sister had been engaged to a young man who had joined the partisans and whose family was in hiding not far from where we were. After liberation they finally were able to marry. Theirs was the first wedding performed after the war in the Turin Synagogue, almost an empty shell because it had been completely gutted during an air raid. There wasn't a dry eye that day, with the chuppah (wedding canopy) standing among the ruins and with everyone present showing signs of the tragedy that they had survived. It seemed to signify the rebirth of a people almost reduced to ashes by the evil schemes of a world gone mad.

When we returned to our apartment in Turin, we lived with the family that had been living there during the war, until that family was able to find an apartment. My sister Lina and her husband settled in Milan in our old apartment and managed the store, which had been moved to new quarters after the air raids. I started working in my father's store, where I had worked on and off throughout the years during vacations. I went to night school to learn English, typing, and shorthand. We stayed close to the family members who had experienced losses and mourned with them. One night at the movies, in a newsreel of the liberation of Dachau, we saw my uncle Attilio. We had that frame reproduced and tried to find him through the Red Cross, the Jewish Agency, and the Vatican, but he never returned.

We counted the losses in the community, we compared experiences with our family and friends who had returned, we rebuilt what was destroyed and went back to a semblance of normality. My father employed in his business several young men from Piea who wanted to leave the country for the city, and we kept our ties to those wonderful people who had befriended us in our hour of need. We put our memories of the recent past in the back of our minds.

Emilia, who had been tutored at home for the past few years, went back to school. During her high school years she met a young man from the Jewish community of Turin, Elio Schlichter, whose parents had immigrated from Germany. When she became nineteen, they married and subsequently had four children. They lived near our parents, who were delighted to enjoy the proximity of their grandchildren. Elio had a brother living on a moshav in Israel, and first David, Elio and Emilia's older son, and then Lea, their older daughter, went to spend a summer in Israel. Lea especially fell in love with the ancestral land and wanted to go and live there. After careful consideration Elio and Emilia decided to make aliyah as a family, to the dismay of our parents, who enjoyed the present closeness. Elio and Emilia settled in Rehovot. Emilia learned Hebrew incredibly fast, settled the children in the appropriate schools, went back to school herself, and became a registered nurse. Elio was trying to make a living by continuing to represent an old and well-known Italian Jewish philatelic company, Bolaffi, in Israel.

Sadly, Emilia developed cancer and, after a valiant five-year battle, died at forty-six. She had been an outstanding wife, mother, and nurse, loved by everybody. Her children are grown now, all married in Israel and with twelve children among them. Recently, their father died too, and I feel the need to go to Israel often to see them, being, with my sister Lina, the closest family they have.

In 1946 my sister Lina had a baby girl, Paola, the focus of all our affection. Family ties were more important than ever. We resumed our family lunches, which, as in the past, would last into the late afternoon, with conversation, sewing, and knitting. My mother was an exceptional cook, and those meals were very important, especially for some of the older people living on very modest means.

I remember especially my grandmother's sister, Gemma, who had lost her only daughter in the last air raid of the war. Our home and our all-embracing love carried her through the pain of her loss. A cousin, Raffaella, who had lost her parents at Auschwitz (the rabbi of Pisa, Augusto Hasda, and his wife, Bettina) also found comfort in those long afternoons. One day she told us that her dear aunt Letizia, her mother's sister, was coming from the United States with her son Luciano to see all the relatives and take possession again of all that they had left when they had gone to the United States in 1940.

I remember one day, while I was working in the store, Aunt Letizia and Luciano came to pick up Raffaella's husband, Mario, an accountant in the business, and I met them. Luciano and I took to each other right away, and soon he was coming to meet me and often walked me home. Before emigrating to the United States, the Vitale family had lived in Milan while we did, and my mother and Luciano's mother were acquainted with each other. Mother invited them for dinner at our house. Then, when they went to Milan to see the apartment house that they had left behind, I went too and stayed with Lina. Luciano and I met for coffee under the Galleria, went to La Scala to see *La Traviata,* spent a great deal of time together, and made plans for the future.

After Luciano went back to the States, we corresponded for almost a year, while I went on with my life of work, school, and family. He came back to Italy then but still couldn't decide whether he could really take me away from my family for a life in a new and different land, and he left again. A few weeks later his mother arrived, bringing me a letter from Luciano and a proposal of marriage! We were married in Turin in November 1948, in the same synagogue where my sister had married. By now it had been refurbished, if not to its original splendor, at least in a good state of repair.

Luciano's family suffered many losses in the Holocaust. Besides his mother's sister and her husband, an entire family of cousins from Genoa, the last people they had seen when they sailed for the States, was taken, as were many other relatives. No family came through those years unscathed.

And now I have been in the United States for nearly sixty years. Luciano and I had a wonderful life together; we had four lovely daughters and taught them to be proud of their Italian Jewish heritage. In the beginning I never spoke of what happened during those terrible years. I didn't think people would be interested. I never spoke of those experiences, even to my husband or daughters or to people at large who could not even understand how we could be Italian and Jewish. Then, all of a sudden, as has happened to most of the survivors, I realized that, unless I spoke of what happened, those years would be lost and forgotten, just as if nothing had ever occurred. So I started to tell the story, and the more I talked, the more people were eager to know.

In 1963 Luciano and I brought our four daughters to Italy and visited Piea. I was eager to show them where we lived and all the wonderful friends who had helped us. We went from house to house, enjoying the wine from their vineyards and the home-baked goods. They were very proud to show us the electric installations put in by my father where there had been no electricity and to tell my husband and children about those years: when they had called me to come to their yard

Michelina de Leon Treves (*left*) and Giorgina de Leon Vitale (*right*), Ottawa, June 2000.

and talk to the German soldiers who were setting up camp, so that their sons, hearing the German voices while in hiding, would not come out. Or, when I had helped a cow in a difficult birth or the long winter nights that we spent in their barn, the only warm spot, spinning and knitting and telling stories. It was wonderful for me to share that part of my life with my family.

I observed another important milestone in 1988, when I went to Milan to celebrate the fiftieth anniversary of the establishment of the Hebrew Day School. Speaker after speaker spoke of the influence that school had had on them, of the incredible teachers and the schoolmates who had shared those difficult years with them, and I marveled at the realization that it had not been my unique experience but one that had been shared by all. I cherish the memories of those years, when I earned an elementary school teacher's diploma from the Scuòla Magistrate Domenico Uberti in 1943. Much later, in 1986, I received a bachelor's degree in comparative literature from Southern Connecticut State University in New Haven.

Now my daughters rush to Italy with their children, to recapture with them a past that will soon be extinct. They were lucky enough to visit their grandparents, their aunts, uncles, and cousins, the cities they had heard about and the cemeteries, looking for familiar names. They sense the passage of time and the urgency of the pilgrimage home. And I rejoice in their discovery of our rich heritage.

I am at times invited to speak to schoolchildren about my experience in Italy

Giorgina and her daughters, celebrating the birthday of Elizabeth (*seated*) in Branford, Connecticut, January 2001. *Standing, left to right:* Loretta Vitale Saks, Jean Vitale, Miriam Vitale, and Giorgina Vitale.

during the war, as part of their Holocaust studies, and I am happy to do so, trying to impress on those eager minds what it was like for a young teen, just like them, to live through those years. I will continue to do so as long as I am able and I am asked.

Luciano was taken from us much too early by a dreadful disease, amytrophic lateral sclerosis (ALS—Lou Gehrig's disease), in 1972, and a day doesn't go by that we don't think of him. He was a loving husband and father and had a great influence upon his girls. But he never had the joy of holding a grandchild in his arms, and the grandchildren were never blessed by his presence. Whenever we gather for any occasion, though, we speak of him and keep him alive in our memory. Even though he and his family had escaped the tragedy of the war years, he was extremely sensitive to any trace of anti-Semitism and never let an occasion go by without responding to it in letters to the editor, personal correspondence, or open discussions. He was a wise and just man.

We who have survived the Holocaust will always feel the absence of those who perished, of the unborn generations with their unlived future, and of the thousands of extinct communities where Jewish life had been so vital. But from that darkness rose the reality of Israel and the rebirth of a people restored to dignity and life after being marked for destruction.

The SS *St. Louis* and Afterward

JULES WALLERSTEIN
(b. 1927, Germany)

My introduction into the world happened on March 21, 1927, in Fürth, Bavaria, Germany. My given name was Julius Wallerstein. (When I came to the United States, I changed my first name to Jules.) My mother was Paula (née Rau) Wallerstein. She lived in Forchheim, twenty miles north of Fürth. She attended Heidelberg University before she got married. My father was Anton Wallerstein. He worked as a bookkeeper in Frankfurt am Main. My parents were introduced to one another by relatives.

My mother was twenty and my father thirty when they were married in 1926. The marriage ceremony was held in the Haupt Synagogue in Fürth. During their honeymoon my father's father passed away, and my father returned home immediately to Fürth. He then took over his father's jewelry store. My sister, Edith, arrived on February 11, 1932. It was nice having a baby in the family. However, since there was five years' difference in our ages, I really did not pay too much attention to her.

We lived in a six-room apartment with my father's mother. My mother took us visiting to various places, such as Marienbad and Karlsbad in Czechoslovakia. My mother's mother lived in Forchheim by herself after her husband's death in 1932. I visited my grandparents in Forchheim many times. I did many things with my grandfather. One thing I remember quite vividly: I drove with him in his horse and carriage many times to different towns. Two months before Kristallnacht my grandmother from Forchheim came to live with us.

My mother had a brother named Louis Rau. In 1932 he had to flee Germany for France because someone falsely accused him of wearing a Nazi uniform. Later he became a French citizen.

I attended the Jüdishe Realschule in Fürth. I was active in sports and competed in many sports events. My family belonged to the Haupt Synagogue, a Liberal (Reform) institution, and we had a kosher home. My father closed the store every Saturday and on the Jewish holidays. My friends were Jewish and non-Jewish. We played soldiers, went to each other's homes, and made fun of some of the Nazi leaders. My non-Jewish friends never called me foul names or called me a dirty Jew. However, after Kristallnacht everything changed, and we no longer saw one another.

On Kristallnacht, November 9, 1938, we were awakened by a banging on the door. My father answered the door and before him stood two Nazi Brownshirt officers. They told my father to get dressed, bring the keys to the store, and come with them. The store was around the corner from where we lived. We heard the shattering of glass. We did not hear from my father until the next day. He came home unharmed but had been forced to turn the store over to the Nazi Party. My mother was "asked" to go down to the store and clean up the shattered glass from the sidewalk. I went with her and tried to help clean up the glass. While we were doing this, a gang of people came and insulted us with anti-Semitic remarks and tried to beat us in front of a Brownshirt officer who was guarding the jewelry store. He did not come to our rescue. An elderly neighbor chased the mob away and told us to go back home. It broke my heart to see what had happened to my father's store and to see how badly my mother was treated by other people. I was eleven and did not fully comprehend what was happening to us just because we were Jews.

The same day as Kristallnacht we found out that four synagogues in the Schulhof compound, as well as the rabbi's home, had been completely destroyed by fire. The fire department was not allowed to extinguish the flames. One synagogue was not burned; that was in the orphanage. When the Nazis wanted to burn the synagogue, all the tenants around the orphanage came out of their homes to protest and urge the Nazis not to start a fire, because in doing so they would destroy the nearby homes.

Many days later I went back to school, always worried about being attacked by the German public. We always traveled in groups. It was always dangerous walk-

Jules Wallerstein, 10, and his sister, Edith, 5, in Fürth, Germany, in the summer of 1937.

The Wallerstein family boarding the SS *St. Louis* in Hamburg, May 13, 1939. *Right to left:* Jules, Edith, Paula, and Anton.

ing on the streets. Most stores displayed signs reading, "We do not sell to Jews." My parents went shopping for groceries late at night. Also, one of my parents' friends, a Christian, would come to our apartment and sell us groceries. We had to empty the store and bring everything to our apartment. Under the supervision of two police officers and an auditor, everything was itemized and a value was assigned to each item. This took a long time, and after everything was itemized, the two officers took all items away. Much later we were compensated with a small sum of money. My father was forced to close down his jewelry store.

My father knew that it was time for us to leave Germany. He had applied for a U.S. visa a few years before 1938, but the quota was limited. The next best thing we could do was to have my uncle Leo Wallerstein secure a visa for us to go to Cuba and then possibly to the United States. We were not rushed to leave Germany, and we were able to book passage to Cuba on May 13, 1939 on the ship SS *St. Louis.*

We were to depart from Hamburg on the Hamburg-America Line. On the voyage were 937 passengers. I was happy to leave the hated Germans and begin a new life in a strange country. I was a little scared about how we would survive in our new environment. Before we left for Cuba, a person from the customs office took inventory of everything that was packed. We could take all the clothes with us but were allowed only one place setting of silverware for each person. The value of all our articles was specified, and we had to pay a tax on everything that we had packed, and the suitcases were sealed. We were allowed to take with us ten marks ($6) per person.

The owners of the *St. Louis* knew even before the ship sailed that its passengers might have trouble disembarking in Cuba. The passengers did not know that eight days before the ship sailed, Cuba's president, Laredo Bru, had issued a decree invalidating landing certificates. When the *St. Louis* arrived in Havana Harbor on May 27, 1939, only twenty-eight passengers were allowed to land. They had been notified before departure that they had to buy another entry visa. Aboard the ship was a Nazi official who was to land in Havana, meet with a German spy, and take secret information back to Germany. That was accomplished by giving the crew shore leave to go to Havana. Cuban officials wanted an additional $500 per passenger (bribe money) or the passengers would not be allowed to disembark. Negotiations were under way with the American Jewish Joint Distribution Committee (known as the Joint), but no commitment had been made.

On June 2 President Bru ordered the ship to leave Cuban waters. On June 5, 1939, the *St. Louis* headed back toward Europe. On June 6–8 the ship sailed back and forth along the coast of Florida. We could see the lights of Miami. The U.S. Coast Guard prevented the ship from getting too close to Florida. Pleading by passengers with the U.S. State Department and telegrams from passengers to world leaders urging them to support entry of the ship were all to no avail. People aboard the ship were so panicky that there was a suicide watch day and night. German Propaganda Minister Joseph Goebbels announced to the world: "If nobody will take the Jews, we will take them." He did not say that they would be sent to a concentration camp.

My father took me aside and told me in a shaking voice, "It was decided if the ship has to turn back to Germany, all the passengers aboard the ship will commit suicide." That was the shock of my life. I was so young—only twelve—must my life end so soon? Who will remember me? I won't be able to marry and raise a family. The captain was determined not to bring his ship back to Germany and have nine hundred Jews slaughtered by the Nazis. His intention was to have a fire aboard the ship and then ram the ship on the coast of England. While crossing the Atlantic, passengers sent telegrams to world leaders for admittance anywhere.

Just before we reached Great Britain, an agreement was reached between Jewish organizations and representatives of Great Britain, France, Belgium, and the Netherlands that those countries would admit the *St. Louis* passengers. We docked at Antwerp, Belgium, on June 17, 1939. We disembarked and were sent to Brussels, but we were granted only temporary asylum. We applied for U.S. visas, patiently waiting for our immigration number to be called.

In Brussels I attended public school, where I had to learn French and Flemish. We received an allotment from the Joint so that we would not be a burden to the Belgian government. We lived in a one-room apartment and made new friends. We were free to worship and live in freedom. To me, this had all been like an adventure. Being on the ship was scary because we did not know where we would end up, but coming to Brussels was a challenge to me. It took time, but I feel I adjusted quickly. In April 1940 I became a bar mitzvah, the ceremony attended only by friends, in the main synagogue in Brussels. Had it been in Germany, I know I would have had a big celebration with my relatives. This was sad.

Germany invaded Belgium on May 10, 1940. The next day my father went to the bank to withdraw all our savings. On his way home the Belgian police arrested him because he had a residence slip that showed he was a German. We did not know where he was or where he was being sent. He had all our money. Later we found out that he was sent to France and interned at Gurs with other Jewish men.

As the Germans were advancing, we tried to flee Brussels with thousands of other refugees going south to France. The highways were blocked by the refugees and by Allied troops. We made no headway, and we had to return to Brussels, hoping that my father would contact us. The western war ended in thirty-five days and Brussels was occupied. Having no money, my mother was forced to beg for money and food from the German soldiers, who were kind to us. One soldier knew we were Jewish, and, when he was going home on furlough, he asked for my grandmother's address in Fürth. He promised he would return with money. The soldier did return and gave us money from my grandmother.

School opened up again and food rationing was introduced. I stood in many food lines that did not require food stamps. Many times I stood in line from 1 A.M. until the store opened up at 9 A.M. I joined a youth group to harass the German soldiers. We entered the red light district and threw stink bombs in the stores. Brussels was run as it had been before the war, but German soldiers roamed the streets. As Jews, when we saw an SS officer, we went the other way.

Gurs was in Vichy France near the border with Spain and was not occupied by the Germans. My father again applied for a visa to the United States, but he could obtain one only if the rest of the family was in unoccupied France. We found a woman in Brussels who illegally smuggled people into Vichy France. The price per person was $1,000, which my uncle Leo sent us in traveler's checks.

We were in a group of about forty people. The trip took five days. On the way the smuggler bribed German soldiers and French civilians at various checkpoints. We arrived in Marseille in February 1941. Since we had entered France illegally, my mother, my sister, and I were interned at the Hotel Terminus in Marseille. This was an open camp for mothers and their children younger than fourteen. Many German soldiers visited Marseille. A female friend from the Hotel Terminus and I traveled as brother and sister, asking the Germans for money and food. The soldiers always asked us how come we spoke German. Our story was that we were from Alsace-Lorraine, where both French and German are spoken.

We stopped one German officer on the street. He agreed to give us what we asked for, but first he wanted to go to the famous church of Notre Dame de la Garde in Marseille. He went to confession, while we just waited inside the church.

We told him we were Lutherans. Before we left, he went to the priest and paid for special medallions that were blessed by the priest, and each of us received one. This is now my good luck charm.

We did not receive a visa to the United States, and my father was transferred to Les Milles, a concentration camp near Marseille. On December 11, 1941, Germany declared war against the United States, and we were afraid that the Germans would occupy Vichy France, but they did not. Finally, we all got our visas.

We booked passage on a Portuguese ship, the SS *Guinee,* which left from Casablanca, Morocco, for New York. We left Marseille on December 14, 1941, by ship to Oran, Algeria, then went by train to Casablanca. A few days later we boarded the ship and arrived in New York on January 20, 1942.

I was overwhelmed by the tall buildings and the many people on the streets in the city. My sister Edith and I—she was ten and I was fifteen—were boarded with a family in Manhattan. My recollection of that is very vague. Three weeks later a family on Staten Island took us in. It was all arranged by Leo Wallerstein, my uncle. My parents were placed in an apartment in Manhattan, and we saw them on weekends.

This was not my dream—to be separated from my parents, especially since we had come this far together, but I did realize that my parents had a language barrier, and they had no means of earning a living at that time. I could not believe the availability of food and the freedom of expression. In Germany you could only whisper and shush; in the United States you could openly argue and speak freely. All my new friends were excited to hear my story and took me under their wing. I graduated from PS 29 and Curtis High School on Staten Island. My dream was to go to engineering school and attend college in New York.

I was drafted into the U.S. Army on August 22, 1945—three months after VE Day—and had basic training at Fort Knox, Kentucky. In the meantime Edith returned to live with our parents. After basic training I was sent to Germany, attached to the Counter Intelligence Corps as an investigator stationed in Frankfurt am Main. I was sent to Dachau to interview Ilsa Koch, "the Bitch of Buchenwald," who was noted for killing men who had elaborate tattoos and for making lamp shades from their skin. The impression she left on me was one of hate for what she did.

I also went to Fürth and visited some of my friends who had returned from concentration camps. It left me sick at heart to learn what they had gone through. I also visited the parents of non-Jewish friends to ask of their whereabouts. The answer was always the same: either they had been killed in action or were still missing from the Russian front. I felt sick that my former friends were not alive, but here was I, a Jew, consoling the parents of my old Christian friends.

I was sent back to the United States and discharged on February 11, 1947, my sister's birthday. I returned to my parents' home in Washington Heights, New York. I was excited that we were united as a family again, and we became reacquainted with each other. My grandmother, Gertrude Rau, and my aunts were all murdered at Auschwitz. It was sad indeed that so many of my family had perished.

After I had settled in to civilian life again, I worked during the day at various electronics companies. In the evening I continued my education in electronics. While I was living in Washington Heights, I never thought about the Holocaust. My family never spoke about it. My mother always spoke about the good times in Germany and what she left behind, but she suffered very badly from depression and melancholy.

I met my dream girl, Helen, through mutual friends on a blind date in 1952. After dating six months, we became engaged and we were married on May 31, 1953. We lived in Washington Heights and had two daughters fourteen months apart. My dream of a family was fulfilled.

In 1967 I was offered a position at the Perkin-Elmer Company in Norwalk, Connecticut. My family and I moved to this community, where life was new for all of us. We joined the Conservative synagogue and became active in various organizations. Since I was a new member of the community, the story of my life during the war became a subject of interest. I found myself telling my life story more openly, and the Holocaust became alive to me again. Not that I ever forgot, but now I spoke about it. After the book *The Voyage of the Damned* came out, and later the movie, schools, colleges, organizations, churches, and synagogues asked me to tell my story. No one could believe the atrocities that the Nazis had perpetrated against the Jews and how I escaped with my family from Germany. I appreciated the audiences who came to hear my story, and I became overwhelmed that I was able to relate my story to others. My family shared my views and supported me.

Time has moved on now. My grandchildren are being taught about the Holocaust. They are amazed at the atrocities that occurred during the Second World War and how life could change in such a short time. I am of the last generation to express these feelings and hope to convey them to the public during the rest of my lifetime. All the things that happened to my family and me taught me how precious life is and what we had to do to survive. My childhood was stolen. My greatest fear as a family man was that I would not be able to provide for my family. My inner thoughts were that my family should never have to go through wars of any kind.

My family and I have gone to several reunions of people from my hometown, Fürth. Frank Harris, who works in Norwalk, Connecticut, started the reunions in 1972. All those who are from Fürth or from Nuremberg are invited for this event. Everybody has a different story of how he or she left Germany. They come to this reunion from all parts of the world. At a recent reunion I met a childhood friend who I thought had perished in the war. Frank Harris called Walter Haas to the stage, and there we embraced after fifty-five years and rekindled a friendship that we both thought we had lost.

The *St. Louis* survivors have also had reunions, including one on November 5, 2000. The invitation came from Watchmen for the Nations, an organization of Canadian Christians. David Demian is the director. He is an Egyptian who now resides with his wife and five children in Richmond, British Columbia. He gave up a medical career and is now following the healing of the world through God. The people of Canada contributed $250,000 so the survivors of the *St. Louis* could attend this reunion, which was held in Ottawa. Twenty-eight survivors and their spouses attended, and we were treated like kings and queens.

Before the gala dinner in our honor, we were brought into the ballroom to the sound of the shofar (the ram's-horn trumpet used on the High Holidays), which moved me to tears. The applause sounded like it came from a thousand people, but there were only 360. It made me feel humble and overwhelmed. Priests, rabbis, ministers, bishops, Indians, an archbishop, and many other religious leaders from several countries were there. Each one cried and asked for forgiveness for not allowing the *St. Louis* to dock on the shores of her or his country. It was a moment I will never forget. At the dinner the survivors were called to the stage, and each of us was presented with a glass image of the Star of David. Inserted in the star was the *St. Louis,* lifted from the water by a pair of hands mounted on the Canadian maple leaf. What a gift—so much thought went into it. It gave me the feeling that people cared about what happened and they were sorry that their country did not help.

My wife, Helen, and I also made a trip to Florida with forty-five survivors from the *St. Louis* and their spouses, on June 3–5, 2001, sponsored by the Convocation of the Americas. This is an interdenominational Christian charitable organization headquartered in Jerusalem. I had been quite ill at the time and in the hospital, and Helen called Rosemarie Schindler, the coordinator, in California to say that we would be unable to attend. Rosemarie said that her organization would pray for me and I would be able to go. My health did improve, and my doctor gave me permission to go.

It was a wonderful gathering of shipmates. We visited the area where the ship sailed along the coast. We said kaddish (the prayer for the dead) and threw roses into the waters to memorialize those who never made it to freedom but perished at the hands of the Nazis. All these trips have united the survivors of the *St. Louis* and have helped us to realize how precious our lives are, now that we have reached our twilight years.

The next trip for the *St. Louis* survivors was again sponsored by the Convocation of the Americas from March 15 to March 25, 2002. The organization paid all our expenses for two days in Hamburg, then eight days in Israel. Traveling was not very attractive at the time because of 9/11, and Israel was being hit every day with acts of terrorism, but we wanted to show our allegiance to Israel and to show we were not afraid. Only twelve survivors of the *St. Louis* and their spouses went. In Hamburg the Germans were most polite and went out of their way to make us feel welcome and comfortable. They humbled themselves at our feet and asked forgiveness for the sins of Hitler and what he did to the Jewish people. We were taken to dock No. 76, where the *St. Louis* left for Havana. A plaque there tells the story of the *St. Louis* and memorializes those who perished. We also visited the grave of Gustav Schroeder, the captain of the ship. We found out that the Christian communities of

Jules and his wife, Helen, at a bar mitzvah celebration, Long Island, New York, October 1, 2004.

Hamburg and Berlin had paid for part of our trip.

When we left Germany, a few of the German members of the Convocation of the Americas joined us for the trip to Israel. What a trip it was! The convocation took us everywhere. One of our *St. Louis* survivors lives in Israel, and he was so pleased that we came to Israel. We went to Yad Vashem, where all twelve survivors gave their testimony. That was a very moving aspect of our trip. We saw Captain Schroeder's name on a tablet on the Avenue of the Righteous Gentiles. We spent a night in a kibbutz (Nof Ginosar), where Helen and I had stayed in 1976. Our final night was in Tel Aviv. The survivors received a plaque reading, "Your Ship Has Come Home, Israel 2002." The highlight was the celebration of my seventy-fifth birthday at the King David Hotel in Jerusalem in a country I love so much. Helen and I felt very special and honored that these Christians have tried in a small way to give us back something of what was taken away from us. These are young people dedicating their lives to create a better world without anti-Semitism.

Helen and I also accepted an invitation to be guests of the city of Fürth from June 3 to 11, 2002. I was astonished at how Fürth has changed. Many foreigners now live there. Five survivors and their guests were invited. Oddly, we all lived on the same street. We went to the old Jewish cemetery. Three-quarters of the headstones were missing, but the new cemetery was in good shape and contains a memorial to the 680 Jewish people who were deported to concentration camps and never returned, among them, my maternal grandmother, Gertrude Rau. The highlight was a Jewish wedding at the only synagogue (Waisenhaus), the first in forty years. Instead of breaking a glass with his foot, in Fürth the groom threw it against the wall, which has a large block used only for such an occasion. I did not meet any old-timers; they are all dead. And I could not find any of my old Christian friends. The people we met did not know much about the Nazi atrocities. There was always silence. We visited a high school, where we told students of our escapes from Germany. They were shocked. They knew very little about the Holocaust. Their parents and their grandparents did not talk about the Nazi regime. That is in the past.

The most recent, and perhaps the last, *St. Louis* reunion was also sponsored by the Convocation of the Americas, but the organization is having increasing difficulty raising funds. Since participants had to pay their own expenses for travel to Miami and their hotel expenses in Havana, only twelve or thirteen survivors and their spouses attended. Nevertheless, our hosts treated us extremely well as we commemorated the sixty-fifth anniversary of the voyage of the *St. Louis* during the weekend of May 13, 2004.

Belonging to the Holocaust Child Survivors of Connecticut has inspired me to continue telling my story about the Holocaust and has opened the door to many new friends whom I never would have met otherwise. We have a support system that helps us and keeps us connected. This connection cannot be made with any other group, because we are survivors and have gone through similar experiences firsthand.

Editor's Note: According to the Jewish Virtual Library, "Accounts often mention that U.S. Coast Guard ships were following the St. Louis *to prevent it from landing, but those ships had actually been sent at the request of Treasury Secretary Henry Morgenthau, Jr., because the location of the ship was unknown and he wanted to keep track of it in case a change in policy would allow it to land." See "The Tragedy of the SS* St. Louis*" at http://www.jewishvirtuallibrary.org/jsource/Holocaust/stlouis.html (accessed May 5, 2005).*

And Life Is Changed Forever

MADELEINE SWIDLER SCOTT
(b. 1928, France)

My father, Eloucha (Eli) Swidler, was born in Russia in 1897. His life was one of tragedy and hardship from the very beginning. His mother died when he was four years old. Because life was very hard, and Grandpa needed a wife to take care of his three sons and one daughter, he remarried. Soon his wife had another child and now the household had five children. Soon after, he became ill and died. Shortly after his death, his young widow took her child and went home to her parents. The other children were left on their own.

For the next few years the "orphans," as they were called (no one used their names), would wander from home to home for the bare necessities of life—something to eat and a place to sleep. When my father, the middle child, was nine years old, the boys were apprenticed to tailors in different places. My father was placed with an uncle. By learning a trade so young and working hard at it, he was a man

313

of substance by his teens. He owned and operated his own little tailor shop.

My mother was born in 1901 in Russia. She was the third child but the first daughter of my grandparents. Her father greatly loved life, and to celebrate her arrival, he had the whole neighborhood in for food and drinks. His tiny wife, my grandma Anna, was always prepared, for she never knew when he would feel a party was in order. But the family also knew sorrow. One of my mother's brothers had died in 1915 at the front in the First World War. This news caused my grandfather to have two heart attacks, and he died at the age of forty. He left behind a sick wife. Another son and daughter died young. My mother, as the oldest of the daughters, took upon herself the responsibility of making some sort of a living to help her family.

In 1915 my father rented space from my mother's family. Living conditions were very bad in Evpatoria (Yevpatoriya) in the Crimea before the Russian Revolution, but my father's rent payments made life a little easier for my mother's family. My father was twenty and my mother was sixteen when they were married. He was a kind and loving man and took my mother's whole family in to live with him. He was now responsible for a large household. A year later my sister Fira was born.

When the Communists took over in 1917, shop owners and Jews, such as my father, were in danger. To escape from a world in which they felt unable to live during a revolution was not easy. Taking only what they could carry, my parents and their families boarded an overcrowded small boat to Bulgaria. These were mostly small-town people who had never gone farther than the surrounding villages. After many long days at sea, hungry and exhausted, they were picked up by kind people as they lay helpless on a Bulgarian beach.

For two years my father worked in Bulgaria as a tailor and tried to make a good life for the family. But somehow they were not happy there. In 1920 they went to Turkey, where they settled in Constantinople. My brother, Jacques, was born there. Now life was even harder for my parents, and they decided to leave Turkey. But this time my father and his brothers, who had been together up to that point, decided to separate. My father's older brother, Lova, decided to stay in Turkey; the youngest brother, Sam, went to America; my father opted for France.

It was 1923 when my parents and their children, Fira and Jacques, arrived in Paris and settled in. As usual, Father and Mother could always find work. Grandmother Anna and Aunt Zina joined us in Paris. They lived and worked with my parents for a short time. When Aunt Zina married, she and her husband and my grandmother moved out to start their own household. I was born in Paris in 1928 into this courageous and hard-working family. Four years later my lovely little sister Paulette was born.

From that time on, life was harder for me. I felt unwanted, unloved, and insecure, with an overpowering feeling of jealousy. I loved and hated everyone in the family. Being the third child is not easy. For this reason I have always been more sensitive to other people's moods than is really necessary.

At first we had an apartment where we not only lived but worked, on the sewing machines set up in the living room. As we prospered, my father moved us into a larger apartment that he split in half. The front part was the tailor shop, and the back was our living quarters. We became more prosperous and moved to our own apartment. Finally, my parents had their own tailor shop around the corner. Father was an excellent tailor, and as his reputation grew, our lives became better and better.

My father's store was very nice, and he was very proud of it. His French was not very good, but no one seemed to care much about that. In 1937 we started to go away as a family to the seashore. Father would come during the two weeks that the store was closed. These were great times for us.

In 1939 my brother, Jacques, was searching for a career for himself. A Mr. Georges owned a beauty parlor in a small fishing village in Brittany called Quiberon. Jacques could serve as an apprentice there, but he didn't like it and it didn't last very long. However, that year, since we all wanted to be with him, we spent our summer in Quiberon. It was on a peninsula, and it was beautiful. The men would go out to fish for sardines and bring them back to the canneries in town, where most of the inhabitants were employed. During the summer there was some tourism, but few foreigners went there.

In the summer of 1939 the air was heavy with apprehension and fear because of Hitler's actions. Everybody felt that war would be declared, and on September 2 it was. At the end of the summer it was time to go back to Paris. Because of the uncertain future, however, our parents decided that only Father would return to Paris to work, and the rest of us would stay in Quiberon. From September to November of 1939 my mother and Jacques worked in a sardine cannery. Every night they came home exhausted and full of oil. Their tiredness was mostly from the emotional struggles that they were going through. Paulette and I started school, but we felt strange and could not understand this break in our usual routine. However, as long as we were with our mother and brother, we just did what we were told and, though we were uneasy, we didn't ask questions. We just tried to lead a normal life in this village.

One day it was decided that Jacques would join our father and Fira, who had remained in Paris, so he left Quiberon. Now it was just the three of us in our apartment: Mother, Paulette, and me. Many people in the village knew that we were Jews and were aware of our predicament. My mother spent many hours talking and trying to find a solution to our problems. In Mr. Georges's beauty salon, where Jacques was apprenticed, my mother met a young woman named Simone Le Bourhis. From the moment they met a very special energy passed between them, and they became friends. One day my mother asked her to stop by. She did so, and since we children were home, we met Simone for the first time. Thereafter, Simone would stop often at our home to talk to our mother and to bring us candy or something special.

And then the war came. Our parents decided that we were not to return to Paris. My mother stopped working in the sardine cannery and set up a sewing

Madeleine (*right*) with her younger sister, Paulette, and their Christian hider, Simone Le Bourhis, in Quiberon, Brittany, France, 1940.

shop in our little apartment. She had a few clients and did fairly well. In November 1939, when Paulette was eight and I was eleven, we were told that we would have to stay in Quiberon for our safety but that it would be only for a little while, until we could reunite with the family. Mother arranged to leave us with Simone's parents, who would be paid for our room and board. Our apartment belonged to members of the Le Bourhis family. During this separation we received mail from our mother and were aware of what was happening to our family. We were becoming accustomed to living with the Le Bourhis family, sharing the life they led, and it now seemed normal.

One day in June 1940 we learned that the Germans were only three days from Paris. My parents decided to leave their business and apartment. They knew that, if they wanted to survive, they also had to go in different directions. They realized that the only stable place at this time was Quiberon, so we became the point of contact for our family. My father joined the French army and was assigned to Toulouse. My older sister and brother left Paris one step ahead of the Nazis, in

316

a car packed with Aunt Zina's family, and went to Perpignan. Then, after a little while, they joined Father in Toulouse, where he remained after his discharge from the army. He then started to work and make a home for anyone in our family who could join him. Fira took care of him and Jacques.

The Germans marched down the Champs Elysées, and the whole world was upside down. They confiscated our business in Paris. Everything and everyone was in complete confusion. My mother, who had returned to Quiberon to be with us, was now traveling back and forth to Paris. She was gathering as many of our possessions as she could and always came back to Quiberon with suitcases of materials and notions.

Our mother's absences frightened us since we were becoming aware of the dangers that she faced in traveling with false papers. The whispering among the adults increased. The Germans were nearing Quiberon and soon would take us all over. Finally, my mother realized that she could no longer postpone leaving us completely. Travel had become more and more difficult, and her presence in Quiberon brought more attention to us. So on October 17, 1940, she left us once more. However, by this time we had become so accustomed to our lives with the Le Bourhises that her departure didn't trouble us too much.

Our new "Maman Bourhis" and "Papa Bourhis" were very understanding and tried to make us feel at home from the beginning. They were honest, hardworking people who opened their hearts to us and simply and completely loved us from the very beginning. They were very special human beings. Our new sister, Simone, was gentle and kind, and her attitude toward us was one of acceptance and normality. We were now Bretons and members of this family. Traditionally, all the people in Quiberon were Catholics. Quiberon is made up of many small villages, and the people wore clothing denoting the villages they came from. We had to learn to go to church every Sunday, in our own costumes, wearing wooden shoes, and to sing their songs and to read the Bible. We learned to play this part beautifully.

For Paulette and me, being left behind, even for our own good, left us with a tremendous feeling of insecurity for our whole lives. The fifteen months we spent together bound us closely to one another until her death in 1999. Our relationship was one of the most precious experiences in my life.

When the Le Bourhis family had to leave their home, the family, including Paulette and me, was taken to L'Usine Amieux. This empty sardine cannery had been requisitioned by the government to house older French soldiers called *Territoriaux,* who formed a type of home guard. It was a large two-story building with a courtyard in the middle and very large, long rooms. We lived in a house just inside the entrance of this complex. When the gates were closed, we too were closed in. Not only were these *Territoriaux* living with us, but we seemed to be the stopping place for other French soldiers fleeing from the advancing Germans. While the soldiers were there, they played with us, happy to see children in the courtyard. They used the second story of the factory for sleeping and the bottom part for their horses. The factory had a lookout tower that we would climb, and we could see bombs exploding in neighboring towns. One day, as we were watching with our French soldiers, we saw motorcycles driven by Nazis entering the main road in town. Before we knew it, they had taken over our town without a struggle.

No one can describe the incredible feeling of loss of self that an invasion creates. The invaders came and no one stopped them. They marched in as if everything there belonged to them, and from then on we would be living under new laws—theirs. We were all at their mercy. The villagers were proud people, and it wasn't long before many of them went underground and tried to fight this invasion.

What happened next may be totally unbelievable but is absolutely true. The Germans picked our factory for their headquarters! They rode into our courtyard and took all the French soldiers as their prisoners. Within minutes at least a hundred Germans came in and started to settle into our home. We were all horrified at this unbearable situation, but there was nothing we could do or say about it.

Oddly enough, our lives became almost normal, routine. Though we were—so to speak—in hiding, we did not hide. We lived openly with our new family as their children. We went to school every day, walking through the village. By then we had already adopted their ways and blended in nicely.

Our adopted family was an average one in the village. Papa Bourhis was a very handy man. He knew how to fish for sardines from big fishing boats and how to garden. This was very strange for us city dwellers, who thought that everything one needs can be bought at a store. He knew how to kill chickens, rabbits, and pigs, a totally new experience for us. Maman Bourhis was a typical loving mother and a wonderful homemaker, including watching over the homework and hygiene of her "two little girls."

The house had a second floor and all the bedrooms were there. Our bedroom had two large windows overlooking the ocean. The factory was situated right on the beach, and we came to know the sounds of the ocean very well as time went by. Whenever I have felt anxious or undecided about certain feelings within my soul, I must hear the sound of the ocean. I have retained the love I felt for the sea.

The Germans who took our Quiberon lived within our gates, and we were able to observe them every day. They were harsh with themselves and with others, even within their own group. But whatever they were, living so close to us every day in the courtyard made us see different faces of this terrifying army. The Germans tried to be friends with us, especially with us children. We reminded them of their own children back home. I must say that many were still very young and children themselves.

While we lived with our parents in Paris, we had never had any religious upbringing. Yet here we were, learning not only about a new religion but how to function and understand what this really meant to our new family. We also had to learn how to integrate ourselves into the school system and how to understand what the sea and the land could offer us, not just as things to enjoy but as a source of food. To this day I have always tried to live in rural areas, as I feel more comfortable in that atmosphere.

School was a very important part of our daily activities. Our school was quite different from our old one in Paris. Here in Quiberon, teaching and learning were serious but more casual. We were taught in large sunny rooms, in a one-story building, with well-kept outside play and sanitary facilities. Almost everyone rode bicycles or walked to school. Paulette and I walked back and forth twice a day. In France the midday break is two hours long. We soon grew accustomed to the routine and did fairly well.

For Jews, going to school in Paris had not been easy. Since we were born to Russian Jewish immigrants who did not speak French, we had some difficulty at first in communicating. It wasn't until I started kindergarten that I realized that our family was different; we spoke a combination of Russian and Yiddish. It didn't take me long to learn French, and I was reluctant to speak any other language after that. There was a lot of anti-Semitism in France, and even children felt it very strongly. But going to school in Quiberon, as part of a Catholic family, meant total acceptance. I know that I liked it very much, and at that time I could not understand why one needed to be a Jew rather than a Catholic anyway.

We all went to church every Sunday. The church in Quiberon is very old and very beautiful. Going to church meant a couple of hours of quiet praying, singing lovely songs, waving to friends from other areas, and then, when it was over, standing outside the church, just spending time with one another. My sister and I learned all the prayers, and I still know some of them by heart today.

At home, with our new parents, we learned the ways of self-reliance. With Maman Bourhis I learned to knit, and it served me well for many years into my adult life. With Papa we learned the ways of gardening, to grow vegetables for our table. From time to time Papa took us on one of his fishing trips to catch sardines. We learned to appreciate and eat what we caught. We brought along bread and drinks from home, but the fish we caught were eaten raw on the spot. I enjoyed many a meal taken from the sea, including mussels from the rocks that bordered our seashore and, especially after a rain, snails. We would bring them all to Maman, and she would make marvelous dishes out of them.

This was a strange time for us. Our parents wrote to us and sent money to our new family for our care, and we answered them. But they took on a secondary role in our lives. The only family we had was where we were; our real family had faded in our memories and had become almost unreal to us.

One cold night, January 20, 1941, our mother showed up without warning in the middle of the night and demanded that we prepare immediately to leave with her to rejoin the family in unoccupied France. Our reaction at that moment has haunted me for many years, and, although understood, it still stirs a strong emotional reaction in my soul when I think of it. It was a definite no. Our refusal brought pain to our mother's eyes, and the pain was felt not only by her but by all who would be affected by her demands. We couldn't believe that our new family could give us up, and we were hesitant to go with a woman who was almost a stranger to us. We had found security, of a sort, in our new roles.

My mother, for her courage in dealing with our wartime situation, had always been loved and respected by our adoptive family. They knew, however, that there was no alternative, and so they packed a little suitcase for each of us, hugged us tearfully, and sent us on our way. Our trip, with false papers, was an adventure filled with fear and despair. No longer would we be part of an accepted family, with our religion and security. By the sole act of being retrieved by our mother, we became Jews again.

Our family decided to get us because of the hope of leaving France for a new life, a trip it refused to make without us, at the risk of all the family's lives. After a night train ride Paulette and I, huddled together, quiet and obedient to our mother, arrived in Paris. We waited there for two weeks with an aunt until the word came early in February to prepare for another trip. We were put on another train and traveled south to reach the Loire, which separated occupied from unoccupied France. We arrived in the middle of the night in a wooded area and were met by members of the resistance, who hid us in a cellar, dark and hushed, for what seemed many hours, with many other Jews.

The Germans were patrolling the river. Resistance members had been observing their routine and finally told us to walk down to the river as quietly as we could. We reached the shore and boarded small boats. We were packed in very tightly. On a river full of ice we started our crossing. We were terrified. As we reached the middle of the river, the Germans discovered us and started to shout and shoot. Though none of us was hit, the boats were not as lucky, and leaks developed in their sides. The icy water started to seep in, and soon many of us could no longer feel our frozen legs.

How can I describe what takes over in such desperate situations? Our determination to make it to the other side was so fierce that, even though we knew the Germans were trying to kill us, we were almost oblivious to them. Our thoughts were fixed on the shore that we had to reach. We finally reached it and people were waiting for us. Some money changed hands, and we were taken to a house to rest. In the morning we took a train with our mother and the family of Joseph, Fira's boyfriend.

We were taken to a house that our family was renting in a small town called Salies du Salat. Jews at this time in Vichy France were assigned to towns. The people of these towns only tolerated us. If we wanted to visit another town, we had to request official permission. Salies du Salat had a schoolhouse, a movie house, a grocery store, and so on but nothing really distinctive. Paulette and I tried to adapt ourselves to our new surroundings, but we were full of anger and resentment at this unwanted change. I don't think we made life easy for the rest of the family, but they understood and treated us with love and patience.

After a while my father requested permission to move to a larger neighboring town, Muret. The authority granted his request on the condition that the males would agree to work for local farmers. He accepted, and so my brother and father were assigned to a farm in Muret.

By now I was thirteen and Paulette was ten. It is now, so many years later, that I realize how very important it was to have her with me during this period. We had already gone through so much together, and here we were, once again, finding strength in our mutual trust, learning our real roles once again. This was not the sort of freedom that we had hoped to find. No longer surrounded by Germans, we now lived in restricted areas for Jews, but we did move freely within the town. We lived in Muret for almost a year, in a small apartment on the second floor of an apartment building. I remember our preoccupation with food. We all had ration coupons, but that didn't necessarily mean that the food was available. We focused on how to get it, where to get it, how to ration oneself until we could buy some more.

My father's services as a tailor were in demand. Since he was not permitted to work officially, he had to be very careful. He was very selective in what he chose to do and worked for others only if he could exchange that talent for groceries or whatever the family needed for our survival. My mother was also very talented beyond the making of tasty meals. Her courage and strength always held us together as a loving family. She was also a born diplomat and could charm officials and shop owners into whatever they could offer to make our daily life easier. Grandma Anna also lived with us, and she helped take care of us. And I began to knit, either for money or for goods.

While in Muret our lives took on a normality in the daily struggle of our new situation. We went to school and made friends. The circus came to town and I met boys from school there. I was growing up, and boys were taking an interest in me. I was flattered and showed my interest as well.

Nothing can stop love, and love was flourishing in our household. One day Fira announced that she would marry her boyfriend, Joseph. Joseph's family was assigned to another town, and it was not always easy for them to get together. In addition, we had to get official permission for the marriage. Everything was very complicated. We were all very happy about the marriage, and we started to make arrangements to welcome Joseph's family. Since the ceremony was to take place in our apartment, we wanted everything to be as good as it could be. We started to accumulate food for our guests to eat after the wedding, and my mother and grandmother cooked and baked for days. Joseph's father was a very pious Jew and very knowledgeable about his religion. According to Jewish law, a pious Jew can perform any ceremony if at least ten Jewish men are present. It was decided that he would marry them. Since getting passes to move from one town to the other was so difficult, the whole family crossed the town illegally. The ceremony was very traditional and beautiful.

Finally, in the summer of 1942 the time came for our family to leave Muret. We felt nothing, no regrets. We were leaving nothing behind. We were eager to be on our way, perhaps for the last time. The train ride from Muret to Marseille is short, only a couple of hours. We had mixed feelings during that time: excitement at the prospect of a new life for us in America, and sorrow that our newly married Fira would not be coming with us. Her new husband's passport had not come through, and she decided that she would stay with him. They lived with false papers in a small village in Belgium. After the war they joined us with their small daughter, Corinne, in America.

There was a strange kind of excitement in Marseille. It was very crowded. Jews with and without passports were everywhere. Those without passports were frantically trying to obtain whatever could get them out of France. Also, since our family didn't have any money for the trip, our father was searching for financial aid. The Hebrew Immigrant Aid Society (HIAS) was helping many Jews financially, Jews who would not otherwise have had a chance at life. We were one of those families helped by the HIAS, for which we have always been grateful. For the first few years of our lives in America, this debt was continually on my father's mind. He faithfully repaid every penny that the HIAS had given to us.

We finally were notified that everything was in order. We packed our small suitcases and marched toward a large passenger ship. Fira and Joseph were there, waving good-bye to us, and we were all very upset at leaving them behind. The ship took us to Oran, in Algeria, and there we disembarked and boarded a train that took us to Casablanca. We arrived exhausted a week later and were taken to an enclosed and guarded area. There we stayed, once again, waiting. All the adult passengers were interrogated. This internment camp had minimal facilities. After about a week we left the tents and boarded a truly large Portuguese ship, the *Nyassa*. We had paid the minimum necessary to get us onboard and our facilities showed it. But we were very excited. This was it.

During the first three days it seemed as if the whole boat was suffering from seasickness. In fact, our family was so sick and looked so terrible that the captain of the ship took pity on us and moved us to one of the cabins on an upper deck for the remainder of the trip. We were very grateful. After three days our stomachs seemed to settle down, and after all the months of rationing and eating small portions, we all went a little crazy on the food, which was plentiful. It was wonderful. We traveled on this ship for almost a month, including a weeklong stopover in Bermuda. The fear that had been part of all our lives while we were in France was starting to subside, and we all felt more relaxed and happier.

Baltimore was our first sight of America. The excitement on the boat cannot be described. This was freedom. This was the beginning of a new life. And then an unbelievable thing happened, something that we thought we had left behind forever: we were led into an internment camp. The men were separated from the women and children. You cannot imagine our frantic cries. We were terrified. Since we did not speak English, we couldn't understand what this all meant.

It took days for us to calm down and realize that no harm would come to us. This was another interrogation center. Since we were all arriving from war zones, the Allies were being careful. Spies were infiltrating countries in the guise of refugees escaping persecution, so interrogations were necessary. This time even Paulette and I were called in by the officials. Since we had been in the occupied part of France and had lived among German soldiers, we were questioned for several hours. We told exactly what we did and what we saw, and they seemed to be satisfied. We were allowed to see our father and brother at special times, and that reassured us that they were all right. The separation was painful nevertheless, especially for our mother. One day we were released and finally on our own.

My aunt Zina, my mother's younger sister, and her family had been in America for a couple of years and were living in New York, so this was our destination. We arrived at Grand Central Terminal, into the arms of my aunt. What a joy to see the family again—and to feel the security of being with someone who knew her way around. For the first time in our lives we were taking a subway, to Washington Heights. My aunt took us to their apartment. Uncle Ifsiah Swidler (known as Sam), his wife, Sonia, and two children lived just a few blocks away from my aunt's. My father was very anxious to see his brother, and so, after a brief rest at my aunt's place, we left to walk to my uncle's apartment.

My father had not seen his brother for twenty-five years, so you can imagine the joy they felt at being reunited. For us it was quite a different experience, since we had never met our cousins. Now, of course, our newfound family became very important to us, as they were part of the security that we needed in our new country. Our first meeting was very hard because of the language barrier. However, my father spoke to his brother's family either in Russian or Yiddish. We didn't stay long, as we had made plans with Aunt Zina to leave for the country, to a bungalow colony in Connecticut.

My father and Jacques stayed in town. Uncle Ifsiah's wife had a brother who had a room for rent. Mr. Dinkin was not only willing to rent us the room, but he was also willing to give my father and brother jobs. He was a tailor and had his own shop, and, as he needed help, their coming was very convenient for him and for us. My father was very grateful to find work right away, since that had been his first priority. He was, of course, an experienced tailor and a great asset to Mr. Dinkin. My brother was just starting to learn the trade, and this was a good beginning for him, working with his father.

We were very appreciative of the wonderful help that we received from that family. It certainly made our transition easier. This was the beginning of our establishing ourselves as self-sufficient. Jacques stayed with us only three months since he was then drafted into the U.S. Air Force. For four years he was a mechanic on B-29s out of Guam. After that he tried working as a tailor, but tailoring was truly not his vocation. He married Miriam, had two children, Marc and Claudine, and eventually operated a very successful clothing store in Poughkeepsie, New York. He died in Florida on March 18, 2005.

Every day was a new experience and a new emotionally charged reaction to our new surroundings. Nearby was a Jewish community center. For us it was an entry into some of the possibilities of a new social life. I spent many hours there, trying different clubs, getting known, and making friends. The neighborhood was populated by many Jews. At the start of Hitler's rule, some German Jews had emigrated to the United States with their belongings. Since they had money, they were able to afford better neighborhoods, and Washington Heights had nice apartments. Then, before the United States entered the war, other European Jews arrived. They had already lost most of their possessions, and they wanted to settle in known Jewish areas.

Upon our return from Connecticut we were taken to our neighborhood school. Paulette was eleven and registered at the local grammar school. I registered at George Washington High School, since I was fourteen. My high school education in America was a most unhappy time in my life. The school system was not prepared for the influx of foreigners. We had to learn the language as best we could, and it was very difficult to be in a class all day where you understood absolutely nothing. Every test was a failure and every day was sheer torture. Fortunately, someone eventually thought of having me take first-year French, and in translating the French into English, I started little by little to learn. I received As in French and Fs in most other subjects. The one class where I learned a useful skill was typing. I took to it quite easily, and it helped me tremendously in learning the alphabet and therefore the language. Still, I couldn't speak the language. I was held back in every class except French and typing.

I learned how to play hooky. The friends I made were always after me to go someplace with them, either downtown to Times Square to see a show or just to a park to play. At first I was horrified at the prospect of not telling my parents what I was doing, but I soon got over that. I started to work after school in the garment district of New York. My first job was on an assembly line of a factory that made children's overalls, and I would spend hours bent over the machine. The factories in the garment district were owned mostly by Jews, and there I found that I could communicate with a little Yiddish and Russian, which I spoke very badly.

By 1946 our family had become somewhat Americanized, and our lives were pretty routine. My dad worked for Klein and Klein Sportswear, cutting and making their samples. He was very well paid for his talents. Since he worked from his very first day here in different clothing enterprises where Yiddish was spoken, he never really had a chance to use English and therefore learned it very slowly.

My mother, on the other hand, was very gifted in languages and went to night school to learn. It wasn't long before she was speaking English fairly well, with her beautiful Russian accent. She was also working in the garment district, but she was on piecework. There was a great difference between weekly pay and piecework pay. Not only did she work hard at her sewing machine all day, but when she came home she did all that was necessary to keep her family together. She was not a great housekeeper, and many times when we got home from school we would have to clean up quite a mess. However, she was a great cook—of solid, stick-to-the-ribs types of meals—in the Russian style. After a while she started to teach me how to cook so that she could get some relief, and this started my cooking for the family. Soon I was working as a telephone operator-receptionist-typist for Klein and Klein Sportswear, a job that my dad had helped me to get, right in the middle of the garment district. Paulette was still going to school. Jacques came home from the service and was looking for a job.

My mother's shop had many other workers, and among them was a lady named Gertrude Mershon. She always talked about her son Norman, who was in a naval hospital, recuperating from tuberculosis. During Thanksgiving of 1946 we received a dinner invitation from the Mershons and met Norman there. Soon he was discharged from the navy and began attending New York University. On September 28, 1947, we were married by a justice of the peace in Yonkers. My father understood but was horrified. He, who was not a religious man, felt that we had not been properly married. He talked of my dowry of $1,000, which he had set aside to help us get settled into our own place. We decided to cooperate in the planning of a second wedding ceremony, out of respect for our parents and also out of our need for my dowry. And so plans were made for about three hundred people whom my father wanted to attend this wedding. We were married in a religious ceremony, and everyone had a wonderful time.

Norman continued his schooling at NYU and I kept working. Within three months I became pregnant. It took us almost six months of intensive searching to find an apartment in Inwood, Queens. Our son, Gerard, was born on September 18, 1948. This was a great event in our families. To my family he was the first American-born citizen. It was a happy period in our marriage.

For the next couple of years, however, our lives were a struggle, not only financially but also because I did not understand how to take care of a family. Norman studied day and night, and I was in charge of everything else. He got a monthly GI Bill allowance, and this continued through our time together. At twenty and unsure of myself, I was easily controlled by my husband and mother-in-law. They continually impressed upon me that the most important thing I could do was to free my husband from all responsibilities, since his education would mean a better future for all of us. During the summer of 1949 one of us had to have a job. Norman had no skills and failed in job hunting, so I went back to the garment district and found a job the very first day. But every night after work I still had a meal to prepare, and I had to take care of the baby. Moreover, when school started again in the fall, I had to quit my job.

Norman's graduation in the summer of 1950 brought big changes. Norman had been accepted at the University of California–Los Angeles (UCLA) for graduate work. We sold our furniture, and with what remained we set out for Los Angeles by car. We left everything and everyone we knew in New York and moved into university GI housing.

From the beginning I knew that this new environment would be difficult for me to adjust to because of my own insecurities. I was still learning English and spoke with a strong accent. I had not only missed out on schooling in Europe because of the war, but I had quit high school before graduation with no diploma. Being surrounded by educated people on a university campus was very intimidating. My efforts to educate myself were exhausting. I felt, as always, like an outsider. We also could not manage with the GI Bill allowance, and I went to work for Douglas Aircraft in Santa Monica. In 1952 Norman lost his mother to colon cancer. Also in 1952 I became pregnant with our second child. Douglas Aircraft did not allow any pregnant woman to work past her fifth month, so I lost my job. Gale was born on June 20, 1953.

Typing my husband's dissertation was the culmination of six years of hard work, and he reached his goal of obtaining a PhD in microbiology. It was with mixed feelings that we prepared to leave. The only job offer he received was for a two-year postdoctoral fellowship at NYU. We eagerly accepted it. We went back to New York and were glad to be once more near our families. But our marriage was constantly faltering. Keeping us together became my primary goal. I was terrified to be left alone with my two children, because I was unsure how I could take care of them. Also, no one in my family had ever had a divorce, and the thought proved a terrible weight on me. The tension in our apartment was almost unbearable. My greatest fear was that my family would learn of my situation.

After NYU, Yale appointed Norman assistant professor in the Department of Microbiology. We put our few belongings in the car and drove to New Haven to start anew, only an hour and a half from New York and easily accessible to our families. I found a part-time position and worked for six years in the Department of Pathology at Grace Memorial Hospital, which was associated with Yale Medical School. My ability to handle this job and the respect I received from the other employees gave me new confidence in myself. I had improved my education and speaking skills in several night classes, and they served me well. However, after much turmoil Norman and I decided to separate.

My father, who was the sample maker for Christian Dior in the New York garment district for many years, died of a stroke in 1962, after he had retired. My mother also worked in the garment district for a while after the family arrived in New York.

For the first time since I left Quiberon in 1942, I started to think about religion. I had never been in a synagogue. The only religious upbringing I had ever had had been as a Catholic in France. Now I wanted my children to have a base for their future beliefs. I enrolled in Mishkan Israel, a reform synagogue headed by Rabbi Robert Goldberg. I did not want my children to feel as insecure as I did, though I did not feel the need to go to synagogue. I had always felt Jewish, but that had always been as far as it went. And so, for the first time, my children were exposed to a Jewish environment.

At this time an old interest of mine surfaced. We went to a folksinging concert at Yale. We enjoyed it so much that we all decided to learn to play the guitar and sing. This new way of life seemed to be doing us a lot of good, and we enjoyed it very much. After learning the guitar and many songs, I started to sing in coffee shops, and an audience for my songs began to grow, partly because I was the only one at that time who could sing in different languages. Some of the parents of the children who heard me asked me to teach them. I agreed and became a teacher of folk songs and music. My son, Gerry, who was then twelve, could tune my guitar with no problem, and he helped me with the students. This was supplemental income for us.

After a year, Norman decided to come back to his family. That year on my own had taught me that I was strong and able, and the relationship between us changed. But my European upbringing had made me a very submissive wife, and, though I tried to be more independent, when Norman was with us it was almost impossible. Before long he also picked up the guitar and started to play with the rest of us. However, his contract had been for six years, and Yale did not renew it, so it was time to move on.

The Biology Department at the State University of New York at Buffalo offered Norman an associate professorship. I had never heard of Buffalo, but it was to be our next home. So in 1964 we bought our first house, after sixteen years of moving from one place to another. We were all very excited and looking forward to a settled family life. I applied at the personnel office of the university, and almost immediately I got a job in the Chemistry Department. My training in scientific terms was excellent, since I had typed Norman's doctoral thesis and had spent six years in the Pathology Department at Yale.

My job was easy and I did it well. My reputation as a secretary, administrator, and organizer grew during my year in the Chemistry Department. Then, after two years more, this time in a job at the University Archives, people on campus were aware that I was an efficient and trustworthy person. No one can truly understand what the respect in which I was now held meant to me. In January 1967 I became an assistant to the director of the Concert Office in the Music Department. This was a full-time job, but it was flexible. It allowed me to go home at 3 P.M. to wait for my children. This job carried me into a whole new world that I loved from the very beginning. At the age of thirty-nine I felt that I had found a place where I would want to stay. It took me no time at all to learn the many facets of putting on a concert. The years that I spent in the Music Department were also years of education. I went back to school, passed my high school equivalency exam, and started college. The more confident I felt, the more my marriage deteriorated. There were no jobs that I could not undertake with success at work, yet I could do nothing right at home.

Norman was due for a sabbatical in 1971. He applied for a year in Paris, where he would be able to do research for a French laboratory. Now that the children were grown and partly on their own, I also took a year's leave from the Music Department. I entered the University of Paris–Sorbonne for that year. During our off-hours we explored Paris. We made some friends and on the surface all seemed to go well. However, I became aware of the almost complete deterioration of our marriage.

Back in Buffalo in 1973, I asked my husband to move out. Powerless to get him to leave the house, I packed my things. I was forty-six, and this was the first time in my life that I found myself alone. The divorce was finalized a year later. I felt free to leave. My son was in the air force, and my daughter was working and living with friends. The adjustments to this new life were very difficult, but having my job and the confidence of my colleagues made it more bearable.

The summer of 1974 was very important to me, as I met two people who would eventually change my life. The first was Pauline Oliveros, a professor of music at the University of California–San Diego. She had come to Buffalo to give a workshop and we became friends. In March 1975 I went to San Diego to be a guest in her home. I had a wonderful week there and wanted to return for good. Back in Buffalo, I realized that I no longer wanted to be in the same town as my ex-husband. After eight happy years in my department I resigned my position. The second person I met that summer was the new supervisor in the Typographic Department at Buffalo, Clarence Scott. We had daily contact in our jobs, and a friendship was born out of working together. The friendship grew and a deep caring developed.

On June 1, 1975, I packed my things in my car and started out across the United States, with a friend, to start anew. Somehow, this did not seem overwhelming. Once I left, nothing but the destination seemed to matter. After we arrived in Leucadia, California, where Pauline lived, my friend Bess returned to Buffalo. Now I was truly on my own and all my ties to Buffalo were cut. It was a sad day.

I needed to rest from the trauma of my failed marriage, my years of tension, and the trip to California. Pauline did not pressure me. I took advantage of my newfound freedom and spent a few months on the beach, walking, swimming, and relaxing. At times I explored possibilities of employment.

Encinitas is a small community on the coast, very near Leucadia. I found a position there as a typist at a Western Union office that was owned by Margo Watson. She was a gentle and kind boss, and we hit it off and worked well together. In time she revealed that she belonged to a Spiritualist movement and invited me to visit the "Chapel of Awareness." It had a very pleasant atmosphere and seemed to fulfill my spiritual need. The organization's philosophy of positive thinking and action appealed to me. It did not require one to be anything but a spiritual human being. I attended this chapel for several years and even took classes on psychic development. Meditation brought a certain quiet and peace in my heart.

Meanwhile, Clarence Scott was writing and calling from Buffalo, and in August 1975 he came for a month's visit in Pauline's home. A position in graphic arts became available at Grossmont Community College, and a couple of months later he was offered the job. He resigned from SUNY Buffalo and came back to San Diego. In January 1976 we found an apartment only three miles from each of our jobs. Within the year I was hired as a bilingual secretary in the French and Italian Department at San Diego State. It was wonderful to be able to speak French again full time.

From 1976 to 1989 I was privileged to learn many wonderful new things at San Diego State. Meeting students who would be lifetime friends and some who became extended family was very rewarding. As the administrative assistant, I found much joy in the efficiency and the excitement that our department generated. The department gave me a feeling of belonging, perhaps because it offered me a return to the familiar years and language of my childhood.

When Clarence arrived in San Diego, I took him to the Chapel of Awareness so we could form a strong spiritual bond between us, and we belonged to it from 1975 to 1982. A minister of the Chapel of Awareness married us in 1982 in our home, surrounded by family and friends. It was a wonderful time.

This changed quite suddenly in 1982, when Clarence became a born-again Christian and looked for a more traditional church that was related more to the teachings of the Bible. This was a very hard time for me as I was satisfied with my life, and I became insecure again. I did not want to belong to a synagogue but did not feel particularly comfortable in a church. Because we discussed this problem honestly, Clarence knew how this whole situation was affecting me. His steadfastness and loyalty in our relationship made me understand that nothing could damage it. The security of this marriage was something that I had never experienced before, and I felt blessed by it.

Through the years, we did not live in a vacuum. Clarence brought three daughters into our lives, and I brought a son and a daughter. There were many visits back and forth with family and friends, and the years passed pleasantly and peacefully. In 1989, at sixty-two years of age, I retired. At first I slept and read a lot and just puttered around the house. Then a temporary position opened up at Dor Hadash, a Reconstructionist synagogue, and I took the job. Since I wanted exposure to what it was to be a religious Jew, I thought that this job would be ideal.

Thrice during the next couple of years I was requested to help. Each time I covered the office to the best of my ability. The rabbi, Ron Herstik, a man of unusual warmth and charisma, was also a child of survivors of the Holocaust, and I was able to open my heart to him and tell him of my experiences. After a couple of years I decided to join the synagogue as a regular member. Clarence came with me to Friday night services, and I continued to go with him Sunday morning to his church. This seemed to work, although it was difficult. Much of the service was conducted in Hebrew, and we found ourselves just mouthing what we truly did not understand.

The people at the synagogue were very nice and very accepting, and we soon formed some relationships there, including an interfaith *havurah* (fellowship). I took classes on the Torah and tried very hard to understand what was being taught, but it was not easy and many times even uncomfortable. Little by little Clarence stopped coming, and though I continued on my own, it was not the same and my attendance there dwindled.

In October of 1995, my husband realized that I had to find a way to resolve my unhappiness and need to find myself, so he encouraged me to go to a conference in Los Angeles called Child Survivor/Hidden Child, run by Holocaust survivors. This conference had a very great impact on me. Upon my return to San Diego I contacted several people I had met there, and we formed a support group with

Madeleine Scott, San Diego, Mother's Day 2002.

other child survivors. Since then we have been meeting every other month for discussion and lunch.

Soon after this conference, in February 1996, Steven Spielberg's Survivors of the Shoah Visual History Foundation contacted me. On March 1, 1996, I gave my testimony. The questions of the interviewer, John Kent, and my answers were very revealing, even to me. This was not an easy task. Nevertheless, I was glad that I was able to endure the two-hour taping. A new feeling came over me of openness and sharing. I knew that my family would understand me now, better than ever before.

The rabbi of my synagogue asked me to share my story from the podium. Each time I spoke, it was for the most part a very emotional and draining experience. Some members of the synagogue who had children in grammar school wanted me to talk to their classes. I accepted several invitations and spoke in classes to very responsive and respectful audiences. However, each experience left me so depressed that I had to reduce my talks and eventually end them.

I decided to go to the next conference. This one had workshops for children of child survivors (the second generation), and I invited my daughter, Gale, to come with me. I really never communicated to her what my years in the war zone had been like, and I had always felt a kind of uneasiness with my children that I could not explain. This conference took place in Teaneck, New Jersey, on October 24, 1996. We hoped not only to get to know each other better but also to get a better understanding of how our life together, as a family, had played out. It was indeed very helpful to both of us. A year after this conference, I decided that I had had enough and that I would not attend another one. My San Diego group of survivors still meets, and these relationships are enough for us at this time.

The year 1999 was a terrible one for our family. My dear sister Paulette and her husband, Neil, were killed in a car accident with four of their friends in Boca Raton, Florida, where Neil and Paulette moved after their retirement. No words can describe the terrible pain and loss felt by all the relatives of the three couples.

And then we lost four more members of our immediate family. Our trips back and forth to New York for funerals left us totally exhausted and emotionally drained. That was when I decided that I didn't want to belong to the synagogue any more. I felt that it did not meet any of my needs. To be honest, I really did not know what my needs were, nor do I now.

My French adoptive relatives, who are still living in Quiberon and Paris, are very close to us and in regular contact. My adoptive sister, Simone, her children, grandchildren, and great-grandchildren are a permanent part of our family. They have been to the United States a few times. They visited Paulette and Neil in New York and Florida. My French relatives have come to visit us in San Diego and have been received with open arms and much love. We have returned from time to time for visits in France and have been received equally warmly. Through more than sixty years we have shared much of our lives with each other. The loss of my little sister was very painful to them, and their letters of love and support cannot be measured in the comfort that they have brought us. Till the end of my days I will always think of them as family.

My husband still goes to church every week, but I accompany him as seldom as once a month. My attempts to be Jewish and religious have not been too successful. My children both identify themselves as Jews, but Gerard married a Gentile and his two sons are being raised as Catholics with knowledge of their Jewishness. My whole life has been one of insecurity and turmoil, and I feel that the cause of this was the war years, when my identity was not only questioned but lost, and I have never recovered from that feeling, no matter how hard I try.

In the twilight of my life I am searching for a path to pleasantness and peace. I hope to find it and with it be satisfied about the meaning of my journey.

331

Commentary on Group 3

ROBERT KRELL

The narratives of the "older" survivors reflect the experiences of those who went through the Holocaust as adolescents and youths. Their formative developmental years were behind them. They were stricken by disaster in that period of life where schooling and schoolmates comprise the normal routine, where romance first blossoms, career decisions are made, and traditions and values solidified.

Their memories are vivid, for these child survivors had reached the age when conceptual and abstract thought are fully developed. Whereas in the accounts of the younger children, some experiences may have been obscure, even dreamlike (Did it really happen? to me?), this group of young people had no doubt about what they had witnessed and endured. Their level of maturity during the ordeal later led them to envy younger survivors as "lucky" not to remember, for these older survivors were not fully aware that younger children could suffer as they did, even if the suffering was not similarly perceived or interpreted.

Such conceptual differences are found in stories where an older sibling and a younger one survived together, and each thinks his actions saved the other. For example, a thirteen-year-old boy looking after an eight-year-old brother in the camps refuses to give up in order to remain the responsible "adult." However, because he perceives the desperation of the situation clearly but the eight-year-old does not, the optimism of the younger child boosts the morale of the older, when he might consider surrendering to what appears to be inevitable. No wonder each thinks he is the one responsible for their survival.

In these older adolescents the variety of experiences expands from the younger children's accounts of hiding, resistance, escapes, and concentration camps. This older group of survivors, although mostly adolescents during the Holocaust, emerged as young adults old enough to marry, as so many did in the late 1940s and early 1950s. They often obtained professional degrees or went into business. Most enjoyed successful careers. Of course, there were considerable numbers of survivors who did not do well, and one would not have been surprised if fewer had succeeded, given their life-shattering experiences.

Kuba and Helen Beck's recollections of survival under Schindler's protection are those of a relatively mature young man and woman who confirm Schindler's heroic role in the rescue of Jews. They married in a displaced persons camp in Germany on December 1, 1946. Their common experience may well have provided a foundation for emotional health, given the depth of understanding of each other's losses and suffering. This is not always the case. Some survivors experience relief in being with a nonsurvivor spouse, a person from the "normal world," even though that person may never come to understand the demons that plague the survivor spouse.

As a general observation, the younger child survivors seem to have done better if they married a person not personally touched by the Holocaust, whereas youths and young adults such as Kuba and Helen Beck managed to move forward despite, or perhaps because of, the background they share. In fact, of the nineteen survivors whose stories we are sharing in addition to the Becks', only Sara Munic married another Holocaust survivor. Eva Benda married a man who had spent the war in a Japanese internment camp in the Dutch East Indies. Both Benda and Munic are in this oldest group.

Whereas the younger child survivors may speak of lost childhoods, disrupted education, and fragmented memories, the older adolescent survivors speak of emotional damage and of wounds to the soul. Everything that makes up one's soul—values, traditions, faith—in G-d, in human beings—was turned upside down and inside out. Eva Benda states, for example, "I try to pretend it didn't happen, that it doesn't matter any more. But it is seared into my soul." Madeleine Swidler Scott provides another example. For most of her life she moved back and forth among faiths, exploring a Spiritualist movement and Reconstructionist and Reform synagogues, as well as her husband's church. The years spent comforted by the safety and security of being Catholic and without a strongly established Jewish identity left her uncomfortable with practicing Judaism in later life. This is common to many Jewish children hidden as Christians.

Another coping story is that of Sara Munic. She has remained an observant, if not Orthodox, Jew, as her prewar family was. From the age of fifteen Sara's life was a relentless nightmare, filled with fear, hunger, and the loss of her beloved family, yet by the time she was nineteen, she had somehow rallied. When she was twenty-two, she married and started her own family. One must assume that she did not allow this massive traumatic disruption of her life to deter her from building on the success of her first fourteen years of a relatively secure and comfortable life. It is important to appreciate the sustenance derived from a good beginning and how influential pleasant memories, even those tinged with sadness, have been in the postwar adaptation of this group of adolescents and young adults.

Charles Gelman says in his narrative that "I have never had any psychological problems deriving from my Holocaust experience." That may sound strange in light of the loss of his entire family and his witnessing of the obliteration of thousands of fellow Jews in organized and brutal slaughters. The difference in Gelman's experience, which may account for his comparatively good emotional health, is his life as a partisan. Those who found a way to fight back against the enemy, and exact both revenge and justice for their murdered families, on the whole have experienced less guilt and shame than those who could not and were forced to endure, through no fault of their own, the entire spectrum of degradation and victimization. After the war people like Gelman may have seen themselves less as victims and more as fighters.

Similarly, Kuba Beck says, "We have not suffered any bad psychological effects, nor have any of our survivor friends." But Sara Munic reports: "I'm on Prozac now. It helps a little, but now that I live alone, it's even harder. . . . Sometimes I have to lie down during the day because I can't sleep at night." And Madeleine Swidler Scott: "My whole life has been one of insecurity and turmoil, and I feel that the cause of this was the war years, when my identity was not only questioned but lost." Among the youngest group of child survivors, four of the seven report having experienced trauma serious enough to require medication, psychotherapy, or both. But none in the middle group has reported such serious psychological problems. Clearly, we still have a lot to learn about the long-term effects of psychological trauma on individuals.

Child survivors' conferences and gatherings have become common since 1983–84 at regional levels and, since 1991, internationally. These meetings, held annually throughout North America, as well as in Jerusalem, Prague, and Amsterdam to date, attract several hundred participants and provide a safe venue for the "children" to speak with one another and discover lives lived similarly. They have learned that the problems of identity confusion, the need to keep silent, and the fragmentation of memory are not in themselves unique but reflect themes common to their unique experiences. More than half the contributors to this book have participated in such events, and they all testify to their value, from encountering long-lost friends to learning more about the Holocaust to expressing themselves through writing and art and to educating their offspring, the second and third generations.

What about child survivors as parents? How do people robbed of childhood view the raising of children? Comparatively little is known, but a recent study sheds some light on this matter.* Questionnaires distributed at two child survivor gatherings (Montreal and Los Angeles) elicited fifty-seven responses. The two main questions in the Los Angeles questionnaire were: What were the major principles that you tried to follow in raising your children? How are the relationships between you and your children now?

---

*Robert Krell, Peter Suedfeld, and Erin Soriano, "Child Holocaust Survivors as Parents: A Transgenerational Perspective," *American Journal of Orthopsychiatry* 74, no. 4 (October 2004): 502–8.

We predicted that the probable answer to the first question would center on issues concerning vigilance; being prepared for possible catastrophe; suspicion of others (particularly non-Jews); an emphasis on education, independence, and material security; an appreciation for living life to the fullest; and an enduring commitment to Holocaust remembrance.

The actual responses involve primarily the importance of teaching their children respect for and acceptance of others, being honest and open, providing an education for their children, and demonstrating their love for their children. In response to the second question the child survivors described their relationships with their children as mainly loving, with good communication. In a smaller survey five of twenty-two parents considered their relationship with their children to be strained or poor. A question in the Montreal survey asked respondents what the best thing that ever happened to them was. The overwhelming answer was "my children." We concluded that "the general perception of parent-child relationships as loving and open with some strain" is not dramatically different from such relationships in the general community, especially considering the hardships endured by the child survivor parents in early life.

The children see it differently. The so-called second generation reveals a great sensitivity to the pain of their parents and a desire not to upset them further. Therefore, they became the bearers of good news, high marks, and evidence of popularity and tried to avoid potentially painful questions. They were kept in the dark about the Holocaust. Their fantasies were occasionally more horrifying than the truth.

For the most part the second generation complains that the parental pride was not communicated to them, whereas lavish criticism was. And whereas the survivor parents felt that they were providing nonmaterialistic values, the children felt their parents were preoccupied with work and providing material necessities.

The mystery is why the children of *adult* survivors are disproportionately represented in the helping professions, a phenomenon more readily explained in the children of *child* survivors, who are themselves frequently engaged in professions that involve the care of children or the aged or in researching topics concerning the human condition. Of course, the parents credit themselves with the achievements of their children, who confirm that their parents indeed transmitted certain core values.

We do know that in large-scale studies, Holocaust survivors and their children function within the normal range when compared with Jews born in North America and elsewhere, safely away from Nazi-occupied Europe.

In fact, in the accounts that comprise this book most survivors do reveal an inherent pride in their families, for children represent, either consciously or unconsciously, a victory over the attempt to annihilate the Jews.

Tikkun Olam

HILDE SCHERAGA

The stories in this collection have much in common, including that all the survivors succeeded in coming to a new country and starting a new life. Given the trauma they experienced, it seemed miraculous to them that they were able to reenter a "normal" society, this time one that did not consider being Jewish a crime. Most found ways of creating new families of their own and integrating into the American way of life. Yet we know that on another level, in their inner hearts and souls, the horrors they endured never left them. The victimization, the inhuman murder of millions of innocent people, bestowed an invisible veil of ongoing suffering on all who were caught by the greatest and most infamous of murderers and torturers.

Are human beings destined to continue to impose atrocities on minority populations for believing in different religions or different modes of conducting the business of their nation? Will there ever be an end to man's inhumanity to man?

I see a ray of hope for the future of mankind. It is a very faint ray, but at least it is always present—everywhere. If man's inhumanity to man seems to live and thrive, so does the ability to focus on people's extraordinary creativity, which has manifested itself since the beginning of history. Music, art, poetry, operas, novels, tragedies, comedies—old and new—that nourish the soul and the heart are never absent from our lives. Who can live without being inspired and nurtured by the unbelievable creative endeavors that play a vital part in all societies? This positive vitality is present in all modern societies. Our job is to focus on the enduring values of these treasures, which are seldom given the importance that they deserve. We must search for meaningful endeavors that unite all human beings in every corner of the earth, rather than focusing on what divides us. Perhaps this is naive, but is there a better way of *tikkun olam* (repairing the world)?

SELECTIVE CHRONOLOGY

1933

January 30	President Paul von Hindenberg swears in Adolf Hitler of the National-sozialistische Deutsche Arbeiterpartei (NSDAP, or Nazis) as chancellor (prime minister) of Germany after a Reichstag (Parliament) election in which the Nazis received about 33 percent of the vote.
February 27	The Reichstag building in Berlin is set on fire, giving Hitler an excuse to suspend civil rights and allow a wave of arrests and terror throughout Germany.
March 11	Storm troopers attack Jewish-owned department stores, beginning the massive violence against Jews.
March 20	The Nazis open the first concentration camp, at Dachau, near Munich.
March 24	The new Reichstag passes the Enabling Law, which permits Hitler to rule by decree for four years.
April 1	Nazis proclaim a boycott of all Jewish-owned businesses.
April 7	The Reichstag enacts laws that require the dismissal of all "non-Aryan" civil servants, prohibit the admission of "non-Aryans" to the bar, and apply quotas for Jewish students in higher education.
May 10	Nazis publicly burn thousands of books that oppose Nazism, were written by Jews, or are considered degenerate.
September 22	Jews in Germany are fired from positions in literature, music, art, broadcasting, theater, and the press.

1934

January 26	Germany and Poland sign a ten-year nonaggression pact.
July	Organized by Zionist groups, Jews from central and eastern Europe begin to emigrate illegally, many to Palestine.
August 2	President Hindenberg dies; Hitler becomes head of state and commander in chief of the armed forces.

1935

January 13	Germany regains the Saarland from France.
May 21	Non-Aryans prohibited from enlisting in the German armed forces.
September 15	Hitler announces the Nuremberg Laws at a Nazi Party rally in Nuremberg. The key provisions effectively make German Jews stateless and prohibit marriage and even sexual relations between Jews and people of "German and related blood."

1936

March 7	German troops reoccupy the Rhineland with no significant reaction by the major powers.
April 19	Arabs rebel against the British in Palestine, leading to a substantial reduction of quotas for Jewish immigration into Palestine.
June 30	Polish Jews stage a general strike to protest anti-Semitism.
October 25	Benito Mussolini and Hitler sign pact creating the Rome-Berlin Axis.
November 25	Germany and Japan sign the Anti-Comintern Pact against the Soviet Union.

1937

July 16	Buchenwald concentration camp opens.
August	Jews in Poland suffer some 350 attacks.
December 28	Anti-Semitic government installed in Romania.

1938

March 13	Hitler announces the Anschluss, the annexation of Austria to Germany. Nazis begin applying anti-Semitic laws in Austria.
May 16	The first group of Jews begins forced labor in Mauthausen concentration camp in Austria.
May 29	Hungary enacts its first anti-Semitic law.
June 25	Nazis forbid German Jewish doctors to treat Aryan patients.
July 6–15	Representatives of thirty-two countries meet at the Evian Conference in France to discuss the European refugee problem but do little about it.
September 29	Britain, represented by Neville Chamberlain, and France agree at the Munich Conference to German annexation of the Sudetenland, the strategic mountain area of Czechoslovakia.
October 6	Germany annexes the Sudetenland. Czechoslovak Republic established, with autonomy for Slovakia.
November 9–10	Kristallnacht pogrom in Germany and its territories destroys Jewish personal and business property and 267 synagogues; Germans intern thirty thousand Jews in concentration camps.
November 15	Jewish children expelled from German schools.
December 3	Field Marshall Hermann Goering issues the Decree on Eliminating the Jews from German Economic Life.

1939

January	Illegal emigration from Germany to Palestine begins.
March 2	Eugenio Pacelli becomes Pope Pius XII.
March 4	Decree leads to forced labor of Jews in Germany.
March 14	Slovakia declares its independence—under a pro-Nazi puppet government.
March 15	German forces occupy Prague; Bohemia and Moravia become a German protectorate; many Jews and others arrested.
March 16	Germans apply racial laws in Bohemia and Moravia.
March 28	Germany abrogates nonaggression pact with Poland.
May 15	Nazis establish Ravensbrück concentration camp for women in Germany.
August 23	Nazi-Soviet Nonaggression Pact signed, provides for partition of Poland between them.
September 1	All Jews in Germany subjected to 8 P.M. curfew. Germany invades Poland, igniting World War II.
September 2	Germany annexes the Free State of Danzig (Gdańsk in Polish), establishes Stutthof concentration camp just east of Danzig.
September 6	Germans occupy Kraków. SS Einsatzgruppen, mobile killing units, begin mass murder of Jews.
September 17	Soviet Union invades Poland and soon occupies all the area designated as Russian in the Hitler-Stalin pact.
September 21	Reinhard Heydrich begins concentration of Jews into the cities and creates Jewish councils in German Poland.
September 28	Warsaw surrenders to Germany.
September 29	Germany and Soviet Union formally partition Poland. Intense persecution of Jews by Germans begins.
October 5	Poland surrenders.
October 8	First Jewish ghetto established in Piotrków Trybunalski, Poland.
November 23	Hans Frank, Nazi ruler of the Generalgouvernement (Poland), orders all Jews to wear yellow stars and to mark Jewish businesses with yellow stars.
December 5–6	German authorities seize Jewish property in Poland.

1940

January–February	Jewish youth movements in Poland begin underground activities.
February 8	Nazis decree establishment of Łódź ghetto.
April 9	Germany invades Denmark and Norway.
April 12	Hans Frank, Nazi ruler of Poland, orders that Kraków be made Judenrein (free of Jews) by November.
April 27	Heinrich Himmler, head of SS, orders establishment of Auschwitz concentration camp.
May 10	Germany invades Belgium, Luxembourg, and the Netherlands. Winston Churchill replaces Neville Chamberlain as prime minister of the United Kingdom.
May 12	Germany invades France.

June 10	Italy declares war on Great Britain and France and invades France.
June 15	Soviet Union occupies the Baltic states (Estonia, Latvia, and Lithuania).
June 22	Germany and France sign an armistice.
June 27	Romania cedes Bessarabia and Bukovina to the Soviet Union.
August 30	Hungary annexes northern Transylvania from Romania.
September 27	Germany, Italy, and Japan sign the Tripartite (Axis) Pact.
October 3	Vichy (unoccupied) France enacts the first anti-Jewish laws.
November 15	Nazis seal the Warsaw ghetto.
November 20–25	Hungary, Romania, and Slovakia join the Axis.

1941

March 1	Bulgaria joins the Axis.
March 25	Yugoslavia joins the Axis.
April 6	Germany invades Greece and Yugoslavia.
June 22	Germany invades the Soviet Union.
June 23	Einsatzgruppen begin mass murders of Jews in the Soviet Union.
September 29–30	Germans massacre nearly thirty-four thousand Jews from Kiev at Babi Yar.
October 11	Romanian authorities establish ghetto for fifty thousand Jews in Cernauti.
October 12	German forces reach the outskirts of Moscow.
October 15	Mass deportations of Austrian and German Jews to "the east" begin.
November 24	Heydrich establishes Theresienstadt (Terezin) as a "model camp" near Prague.
December 1	First transports arrive at Majdanek death camp.
December 6	Soviet counteroffensive begins outside Moscow.

1942

January 20	In a Berlin suburb Heydrich presides over the Wannsee Conference attended by top Nazi officials to coordinate the "Final Solution of the Jewish Problem."
February 23	A Soviet submarine sinks the *Struma,* a ship loaded with 768 Romanian Jewish refugees that was refused entry into Palestine and Turkey. One refugee survives.
March 17	Mass murder begins in Belzec, the first of the camps to become operational under Aktion Reinhard, the code name for the plan to kill all the Jews in occupied Poland.
May 4	First "selection" for gassing takes place at Auschwitz/Birkenau.
May 7	Sobibór death camp opens.
May 27	In Prague members of the Czech resistance shoot Reinhard Heydrich, wounding him fatally.
June 10	Germans obliterate the Czech village of Lidice in reprisal for assassination of Heydrich.
July 22	Treblinka death camp completed.
July 28	Zydowska Organizacja Bojowa (ZOB, Jewish Fighting Organization) formed in the Warsaw ghetto.

August 4	Germans deport Janusz Korczak and the children in his orphanage from Warsaw ghetto to Treblinka, where all are gassed.
August 11	Gerhart Riegner of the World Jewish Congress in Geneva manages to contact Rabbi Stephen S. Wise in New York and Sidney Silverman, a member of the British Parliament, about Nazi plans to annihilate the Jews of Europe, but the U.S. State Department holds up delivery of this message to Wise, who finally receives it from Silverman on August 28.
August 12	Battle of Stalingrad begins.
October 28	Deportations of Jews from Theresienstadt to Auschwitz begin.
November 2	British take El Alamein in Egypt from the Germans.
November 8	American and British forces invade North Africa.
November 11	Germans and Italians occupy southern France.
November 24	Rabbi Wise makes public the news contained in the Riegner telegram.
December 17	Allies condemn German "bestial policy of cold-blooded extermination."

1943

January 14	U.S. President Franklin Delano Roosevelt and Churchill meet at Casablanca and declare that a central aim of the war is the unconditional surrender of Germany.
February 2	The German Sixth Army under Friedrich Paulus surrenders to Soviets, ending the Battle of Stalingrad.
February 26	First transport of Roma (Gypsies) reaches Auschwitz.
April 19–May 16	Heeding the call of the ZOB, the Jewish Fighting Organization, to resist the transports, Jewish fighters hold off German troops and police in the three weeks of fighting known as the Warsaw ghetto uprising. Only a few Jews escape and fewer survive. Germans destroy the ghetto.
July 9	Allies invade Sicily.
July 25	King Victor Emmanuel III and high command overthrow Mussolini in Italy. Field Marshal Pietro Badoglio, a Fascist war hero, forms new government.
August 2	Prisoners rise up in Treblinka; only seventy survive.
August 20	Germans crush Jewish rebellion in Białystok.
September 8	New Italian government signs armistice agreement with Allies.
October 1–2	Danes rescue seventy-two hundred Danish Jews from impending deportation.
October 13	Italy declares war on Germany.
October 14	Prisoners at Sobibór death camp rebel; few survive.
November 9	A forty-four nation conference at the White House creates the United Nations Relief and Rehabilitation Administration (UNRRA).

1944

January 26	President Roosevelt establishes the War Refugee Board.
February 27	Soviets end the siege of Leningrad.
April 7	Alfred Wetzler and Rudolph Verba escape from Auschwitz and reach Slovakia, bearing detailed information about the mass murder of Jews in Auschwitz. Their report, known as the Auschwitz Protocols, reaches the West in June.

June 6	Allies land in Normandy.
June 23	Swedish International Red Cross team visits Theresienstadt.
July 9	Swedish diplomat Raoul Wallenberg arrives in Budapest.
July 20	German army officers' attempt to kill Hitler fails.
July 24	Red Army liberates Majdanek.
August 25	Allies liberate Paris.
October 7	The Sonderkommando, Jews forced to incinerate gas chamber victims at Auschwitz, rebel and burn Crematorium IV.
December 16	The Battle of the Bulge begins.

1945

January 16	Red Army enters Budapest.
January 17	Soviets arrest Raoul Wallenberg and he disappears. Red Army liberates Warsaw.
January 27	Red Army liberates Auschwitz.
February 4–12	Churchill, Roosevelt, and Stalin meet at Yalta in the Crimea.
March 7	U.S. forces cross the Rhine into Germany.
April 1	U.S. forces invade Okinawa.
April 11	U.S. troops liberate Buchenwald.
April 12	President Roosevelt dies.
April 13	Soviet troops liberate Vienna.
April 15	British troops liberate Bergen-Belsen.
April 25	The United Nations meets in San Francisco. U.S. and Soviet troops meet on the River Elbe.
April 28	Italian partisans shoot Mussolini while he is trying to escape to Switzerland.
April 29	Red Army liberates Ravensbrück; U.S. forces liberate Dachau.
April 30	Adolf Hitler and Eva Braun commit suicide.
May 2	Soviet forces take Berlin. German forces in Italy surrender to the Allies.
May 3	Germans hand over Theresienstadt to the International Red Cross.
May 5	U.S. troops liberate Mauthausen.
May 7	Germany surrenders to the Allies, ending the war in Europe.

GLOSSARY

Aktion **(German):** Any German military action for political or "racial" purposes. Most commonly used to describe murderous German campaigns against Jews for the purpose of deportation or execution.

American Jewish Joint Distribution Committee (JDC, the Joint): Founded in November 1914 to coordinate relief shipments to the Jews of Europe and Palestine after World War I began. Its Web site (www.jdc.org) describes its efforts during World War II: "As Hitler consolidated power between 1933 and 1939, JDC accelerated its aid to German Jewry. JDC helped 250,000 Jews flee Germany and 125,000 to leave Austria. As German armies approached Paris in 1940, JDC transferred its offices to Lisbon. From there, we helped thousands escape from Europe. JDC maintained thousands more in hiding. . . . JDC aid reached Jewish prisoners in labor battalions in France. Some 250,000 packages . . . sustained Polish and Ukrainian Jews in Asiatic Russia." It continues its work today, promoting emigration from Europe to Israel, reconstructing Jewish life in Europe, caring for needy Jews in Israel and in Muslim countries, and aiding Jews in distress elsewhere.

Anschluss (German): Literally, "connection"; the German annexation of Austria on March 13, 1938, which reduced Austria to the province of Ostmark.

anti-Semitism: A term coined by the German journalist Wilhelm Marr in 1879 to distinguish between traditional anti-Jewish hatred based on religion and a more inclusive definition based on "race" and nationality.

Appell, Zahlappell **(German):** Lineup, counting, or roll call, the most feared part of the day for inmates of concentration and slave labor camps. It frequently continued for hours while the prisoners stood at attention and were inspected for signs of illness.

Armja Krajowa (AK) (Polish): Home Army, Polish underground affiliated with the Polish government in exile in London. Carried out operations against the Germans and, even after the war, the Jews.

Arrow Cross Party: Hungarian National Socialist Party. Founded in 1937 by Ferenc Szalási, it assumed power in October 1944. It was responsible for the deportations and mass murder of eighty thousand Jews until January 1945.

Aryan: The hypothetical parent of the Indo-European language family. Perverted by the Nazis to mean a non-Jewish racial grouping. Has no validity in biology or anthropology, but the Nazis claimed that Aryans constituted a superior non-Jewish "race."

Auschwitz (German): Largest and most notorious annihilation camp in the German camp complex, located near the Polish town of Oswieçim. Established on April 27, 1940, its main components were:

> Auschwitz I—original and main camp, served first as Polish military barracks, then as a concentration camp largely for Gentiles.
> Auschwitz II—also called Birkenau in German, Brzeźinka in Polish. Opened in October 1941, chiefly for the massacre of Jews and Roma (Gypsies), it was the site of four gas chambers.
> Auschwitz III—also known as Buna-Monowitz, refers to both the slave labor camp producing synthetic rubber for the chemical giant I. G. Farben and to thirty-six subcamps.

Altogether, probably 1.1 to 1.3 million people were murdered here, 90 percent of them Jews, and nearly 75,000 Poles, more than 20,000 Roma, 15,000 Soviet prisoners of war, and more than 10,000 others. The Red Army liberated Auschwitz on January 27, 1945.

bar mitzvah, bat mitzvah (Hebrew): Literally, son or daughter of the covenant, a Jewish child who has performed a coming-of-age ceremony, generally at age thirteen for boys and twelve for girls.

BBC: British Broadcasting Corporation. People all over German-occupied Europe depended on its regular news programs for factual information about the course of the war and other important matters. It also broadcast coded messages to resistance groups and helped to sustain the morale of the conquered peoples.

Birkenau (German): See Auschwitz.

Bricha (Hebrew): Literally, "escape." This was a project of the Jewish Agency for Palestine, the Haganah, and the Jewish Brigade of the British army to help displaced Jewish survivors immediately after the war to get out of Europe and—when possible—into Palestine.

displaced person (DP): At the end of World War II in Europe, perhaps eleven million people were living, mostly involuntarily, in places other than the homes they occupied before the war. The Germans had moved them to about one thousand concentration camps and subcamps, factories, and other industrial enterprises. By September 1945 about six million had returned to their homes, but few Jews were able or willing to do so.

ghetto (Italian): First used in Venice in 1516, the word derives from the local dialect for *foundry* and originally referred to a city area occupied only by Jews who had congregated there. The Nazis, however, revived the long-disused term and applied it to sections of most Polish and Lithuanian cities and towns and a few other centers of Jewish population where the Nazis had forced all Jews to live before deporting them to slave labor centers or death camps. The first Nazi ghetto was established in Piotrków Trybunalski, Poland, on October 8, 1939, and by the end of 1943 most ghettos had been liquidated.

Haganah (Hebrew): The clandestine Jewish defense force in Palestine during the British mandate. Though busy combating Arab hostility and attacks at home, and training for future operations, the Haganah, which was founded in 1920, provided personnel for both the Jewish Brigade and secret missions to aid the Jews of Europe during the war. As the war ended, the Haganah also participated in the Bricha and formed the nucleus of the Israeli army after independence in 1948.

Hebrew Immigrant Aid Society (HIAS): Founded in 1927, its principal functions have been to assist Jewish immigrants in the United States, both before and after their arrival. Although it was able to rescue few Jews during World War II because of U.S. immigration quotas, after the war it helped evacuate the DP camps and resettle about 150,000 people in the United States, Canada, Australia, and South America, according to its Web site (www.hias.org). Today it often works closely with other agencies, such as the United Nations High Commissioner for Refugees and the U.S. Departments of State and Justice.

High Holidays: Rosh Hashanah (New Year) and Yom Kippur (Day of Atonement).

Jewish Agency for Palestine: The executive arm of the World Zionist Organization, charged with helping Jews to settle in Palestine, it was the chief institution of the Yishuv, the Jewish community in Palestine, and represented it before the British mandatory authorities. Now called the Jewish Agency for Israel, it continues to assist Jews emigrating to Israel.

Jewish Brigade: An infantry brigade group consisting of about five thousand of the thirty thousand Jewish volunteers from Palestine, it formed as part of the British army in September 1944 in response to the insistent demand of the Jewish Agency. When finally allowed into combat against Germany, the brigade fought in northern Italy in early 1945. While still in British uniform, the men also played an important role in helping Jewish survivors of the Holocaust to escape from Europe after the war through the Bricha, to revive Jewish communities in Europe, and to mete out summary justice to a number of Nazi perpetrators of the Holocaust.

Judenrat (German): Council of Jewish leaders established by the Germans in ghettos to assist them in carrying out their plans for murdering Jews. In the meantime, such councils were to keep order in the ghetto, contain infectious diseases, allocate limited resources, meet German demands for victims for deportation, and so on. Many council members tried to mitigate the horrors of ghetto life and to save as many Jews as possible under extraordinarily difficult conditions.

***Kapo* (German):** From *Kameradschaft Polizei,* "community policeman" or *Kamp Polizei,* "camp police." A concentration camp inmate appointed by the SS to assist in administration and keep order in return for additional rations and better living conditions.

kibbutz (Hebrew): A communal settlement in Israel in which the land, buildings, equipment, and so on are owned collectively. Some Jewish youth groups in the Diaspora in the 1940s and 1950s formed kibbutzim for practice before making aliyah (emigrating) to Palestine/Israel.

Kindertransport (German): A program under which nearly ten thousand Jewish children from Germany, Austria, Poland, and Czechoslovakia were allowed to emigrate without their parents to the United Kingdom, Belgium, and the Netherlands in 1938–39. Most of these children never saw their parents again.

Kristallnacht (German): Literally, "Crystal Night" or "Night of Broken Glass." Government-sponsored pogrom that occurred throughout Germany, Austria, and the Sudetenland on the night of November 9–10, 1938. The Nazis and police destroyed hundreds of synagogues, smashed the windows of and looted merchandise from thousands of Jewish-owned stores, invaded homes, killed many Jews, and incarcerated about thirty thousand Jewish men in prisons and concentration camps. This marked a watershed for many German Jews, a true wake-up call, for henceforth officials would not only tolerate but encourage violence against Jews. Persecution increased dramatically, and tens of thousands tried to emigrate. For many it was too late.

Ladino: A Judeo-Spanish language written in Hebrew characters, widely spoken from Italy to Turkey, Bulgaria, and Egypt.

Nuremberg Laws: Laws announced by Hitler in a speech in Nuremberg and formally adopted by the Reichstag in September 1935 that disenfranchised the Jews of Germany. One effectively reduced the status of Jews to stateless people. Another prohibited, among other things, marriage and even sexual relations between Jews and people of "German and related blood."

Organization for Rehabilitation through Training (ORT): Founded in 1922, ORT is the American branch of the Russian Obshtchestvo Remeslenovo Truda (Society for the Encouragement of Handicraft), begun in 1880. After the war ORT offered vocational training in the DP camps. Today ORT has programs in Europe, Israel, the Americas, Australia, and elsewhere.

partisans: Underground resistance fighters against German occupiers, especially in rural areas of central and eastern Europe. They often organized along formal military lines and sometimes worked closely with the Soviets. Partisans were generally hostile toward Jews, but perhaps twenty thousand Jews served in partisan units, including all-Jewish units, and after liberation many were honored for their service.

pogrom (Russian): Literally, "devastation." An organized massacre, or persecution, especially with government collusion, against any person or class, especially Jews. The word was first used in English in 1905, and since 1881 it has often been applied to early Russian outbreaks of violence.

Purim: Holiday (usually in March) celebrating Jews' escape from massacre in Persia at the hands of Haman, an evil adviser to the king.

Righteous Gentiles, Righteous Among the Nations: Israel officially honors non-Jews who, at the risk of their own lives and without financial remuneration, helped Jews to survive the Holocaust. They are given the title Righteous Gentile and awarded a medal, and a tree is planted in their honor at Yad Vashem in Jerusalem.

seder: Ritual meal that is part of the Passover observance.

Sephardi: From *Sepharad,* the Hebrew word for Spain. A Jew of Spanish origin, often speaking Ladino. The other major group of Jews are the Ashkenazi, who settled in central and eastern Europe and speak Yiddish, an offshoot of German, written in Hebrew characters.

Shabbat (Hebrew), *shabbos* **(Yiddish):** The Sabbath day for Jews (and for some Christians), from sundown Friday to sundown Saturday.

Shoah (Hebrew): The word appears in Isaiah 10:3 and means "destruction, complete ruination." Israelis prefer this term to *Holocaust,* which is derived from the Greek meaning "burnt offering," or sacrifice to God.

SS (Schutzstaffel) (German): Translated literally as "protective detachment," the Schutzstaffel was founded in 1925 as Hitler's bodyguard. It became an independent organization under Heinrich Himmler in 1929. By the end of 1932 he had expanded it from a few hundred members to more than fifty thousand in 1933 and then to 200,000. After the SS participated in the slaughter of the SA (Sturmabteilung, Hilter's paramilitary storm troopers) leadership in 1934, the status of the SS grew, but it was still part of the Nazi Party. In June 1936 Himmler became the head of all German police and, with Heydrich, gradually changed the police into an instrument of Hitler. The SS assumed responsibility for implementing the Final Solution, and both ran the camps and their associated enterprises and provided personnel for Einsatzgruppen. The SS also organized an elite military arm, the Waffen SS, which engaged in heavy combat throughout the war, and trained personnel for leadership in the SS and other police agencies.

tallith: Prayer shawl generally worn by Jewish males aged thirteen and older.

Talmud Torah: A religious school for young boys where the concentration is on study of the Torah, the Five Books of Moses.

Theresienstadt (German), Terezin (Czech): Established on November 24, 1941, in an old garrison town in Bohemia, this was widely touted by the Germans as a "model ghetto" where Jews led idyllic lives. In reality, it was a transit camp, receiving 140,000 Jews, of whom eighty-seven thousand were sent to death camps, principally Auschwitz, where they were murdered. When liberated by Soviet troops on May 9, 1945, Theresienstadt held seventeen thousand survivors, most in terrible physical condition, many of whom died within days of liberation.

United Nations Relief and Rehabilitation Administration (UNRRA): Agency formed by the Allies on November 9, 1943, mainly with American funds, to deal with issues involving displaced persons. It performed very well under extremely difficult conditions, led by former New York mayor Fiorello La Guardia. It was closed on September 30, 1948.

Yad Vashem (Hebrew): The Holocaust Martyrs and Heroes Remembrance Authority in Jerusalem. Established in 1962 by the Israeli government, it houses the center for Holocaust archives, a museum, and a memorial. Among those honored are Righteous Gentiles, who helped Jews survive the German massacres.

***Zahlappell* (German):** See *Appell.*

> *Sources:* I am indebted to the following sources for information used in compiling this glossary: Howard Blum, *The Brigade* (New York: Perennial, 2002); Jack R. Fischel, *The Holocaust* (Westport, CT: Greenwood, 1998); Martin Gilbert, *Atlas of the Holocaust* (New York: William Morrow, 1993); *The Holocaust Chronicle* (Lincolnwood, IL: Publications International, 2000); and Walter Laqueur, ed., *The Holocaust Encyclopedia* (New Haven, CT: Yale University Press, 2001).

APPENDIX:
Holocaust Child Survivors of Connecticut Guidelines for Contributors

July 9, 2000
Suggestions and Questions—for items you might like to include in your story:
Please note that what follows are only suggestions.

Part I

Your Childhood

1. Place of birth and year of birth.
2. Describe your family.
3. What was life like at that time—for your family? For you?
4. Your life prior to the onset of WWII.
5. Was your family religious? Describe.
6. Your school experience: Jewish school?
7. Your friends: Jewish only? Why? Why not?
8. Did you experience anti-Semitism prior to WWII?
9. Include interesting and important facets of your life at that time.

The War Years

1. What were the first signs of organized anti-Semitism that touched your life? (For instance, in Germany and Austria the life of Jews changed as early as 1933.)
2. When did things begin to change for you and your family?
3. Write about the occupation of your country by the Germans or the Russians.
4. If your country was not physically occupied at the onset of the war, because it had a Nazi-friendly government—such as Italy, Vichy France, Slovakia, Hungary, Romania, etc.—how did you experience the first signs of anti-Semitism? What dangers did you and your family experience?
5. If you left on a Kindertransport, who arranged your escape? How did you feel about leaving your family, your home, your friends for a foreign country? Did you understand why you were being sent away?
6. If you were on the SS *St. Louis,* what were your experiences when the ship was sent

back to Europe?

7. If you escaped to Switzerland, describe how that came about.
8. Describe the war years. How did you survive? Which family members survived? If you were sent to a ghetto, labor camp, concentration camp, describe your life there. What happened to your education?
9. If you survived in hiding or passed as a Christian, who helped? How did you feel about your rescuers? What were the conditions (i.e., shelter, food, basic needs, etc.)?

Part II

Your Life after WWII

1. What happened after liberation? Where did you go? What did you do?
2. Write about your feelings, your hopes, and your dreams for your life after the Holocaust. How did you resume (if that is the case) a relationship with relatives—some of whom you may never have met before the war? If you were reunited with close relatives, write about that. If you separated from your rescuers, how did you feel about that?
3. How did you feel vis-à-vis your relatives who did not experience the Holocaust?
4. How did you feel about speaking, thinking, and reflecting on the events of the 1930s and 1940s?
5. Write about your education/career/marriage/children.
6. Write about the impact of the Holocaust on your personal life.
7. Reflect on how the Holocaust affected your thinking and your feelings.
8. Can you reflect on the permanent impact the Holocaust had on your life and that of your family, including your spouse and children?
9. If you were separated from your parents at a young age, what happened to your ability to form trusting and warm relationships?
10. As you continue to reflect on your Holocaust experiences, describe how the overwhelming impact of those experiences affected you.

Note: For our purposes in this particular project (our third), Part II is the more important and should be detailed more than Part I.

CONTRIBUTORS

KUBA AND HELEN BECK divide their time between Poughkeepsie, New York, and Florida. Kuba retired in 1988 from IBM, where he was an advisory engineer. He continues to lecture on their experiences during the war and remains active in Jewish affairs. They have two sons and four grandchildren.

EVA BENDA has an MA in psychology and is a retired psychiatric social worker at a children's home. She lives in North Haven, Connecticut. She does volunteer work at the Greater New Haven Jewish Community Center and is a board member and editor of the newsletter of the Holocaust Child Survivors of Connecticut. She is also writing her autobiography and talking to community groups and schools about her Holocaust experience. She has a son and a daughter in Washington, D.C., and they have three children between them.

EVA METZGER BROWN has a PhD from Columbia University and is a clinical psychologist and divorce mediator, with a home and private practice in Amherst, Massachusetts. She founded Intergenerational Healing in Holocaust Families, a project of the University of Massachusetts, in 1993 and works with survivors and the second and third generations. She is also a professional writer. Her essay "One Step Along the Way" appears in the book *Becoming a Bat Mitzvah: A Treasury of Stories* (2003). She is married to Dr. Norman Brown, a retired gastroenterologist. They have three married children and seven grandchildren, six of whom are named for relatives killed in the Holocaust. All of the grandchildren are being raised Jewish.

NICHOLAS FRIEDMAN is treasurer of the Holocaust Child Survivors of Connecticut and lives in Norwalk with his wife, Judy. He is retired from the presidency of his manufacturing company and is a passionate tennis player. He and Judy have two children and three grandchildren.

IRENE FRISCH (née Bienstock) is a retired medical librarian, living in Fort Lee, New Jersey, with her husband, Eugene. She is a devoted and proud mother of two and grandmother of three. She enjoys traveling, painting, writing, and reading.

RENÉE FRITZ lives with her husband, Jesse, in Naples, Florida. She is a wardrobe consultant in the women's fashion industry and an interior decorator. She gives seminars on the Holocaust for teachers and speaks to school and community groups on the subject. Jesse was a printing broker before he retired and is now a handyman. They both enjoy golf and other physical activities.

CHARLES GELMAN, a retired cantor and insurance salesman, died on May 24, 2004. He lived with his wife, Sydonie, in New Haven, Connecticut, and in Florida, where they took courses at Florida Atlantic University. In both places they volunteered at the local Jewish community center and shared their experiences with survivor friends. Their daughter and son live in New York.

MARTIN IRA GLASSNER is a university professor emeritus of geography at Southern Connecticut State University and is still very active professionally. A native of New Jersey, he holds a BA from Syracuse University, an MA from the California State University at Fullerton, and a PhD from the Claremont Graduate School. As a U.S. Foreign Service officer, he served in Washington, D.C., Jamaica, and Chile. He did graduate work in Mexico and has taught in Israel, Chile, and China. He served as an adviser to the government of Nepal in Kathmandu in 1976 and 1989 and as a consultant to the United Nations Development Programme, including missions to South and Southeast Asia (1979), southern Africa (1984, 1990), and Northeast Asia (1997). Since 1982 he has represented the International Law Association (headquarters in London) at the United Nations. He has lectured around the world and is the author of sixteen books and numerous articles and published papers. He is a member of Temple Beth Sholom in Hamden, Connecticut, and lives in Hamden with his wife, Renée.

RENÉE GLASSNER is a retired high school teacher of Spanish and French. She holds a BA from the State University of New York at Albany and an MA from California State University at Fullerton. A resident of Hamden, Connecticut, since 1968, she has given talks and interviews about her Holocaust experience as far from home as Rarotonga in the Cook Islands. She is married to Martin Glassner; they have three daughters and ten grandchildren, eight of them in Israel.

FELICIA GRABER is a retired public high school teacher and lives in St. Louis, Missouri. She is the founder and director of the Hidden Child/Child Survivor Group of St. Louis and is a docent at the local Holocaust Museum and Learning Center. She speaks about her experience during the war to various groups and is a member of the center's Docent Advisory Committee.

ROBERT KRELL is a professor emeritus of psychiatry at the University of British Columbia (UBC). He was born in The Hague, Holland, on August 4, 1940, and was hidden there from the Germans by the Munnik family from 1942 to 1945. His parents also survived in hiding, but all their relatives were murdered in Auschwitz and Sobibór. In 1951 the Krells moved to Vancouver, where Robert received his medical degree in 1965. After psychiatry training in Philadelphia and California, he returned to UBC, where he was appointed to the faculty in 1971. For ten years he was director of residency training and for twenty-five years was director of child and family psychiatry at UBC. He has written or contributed to twenty-five books and forty journal articles. In his private practice he has treated Holocaust survivors and Dutch survivors of Japanese concentration camps. As an outgrowth of his private practice, he began videotaping the stories of Holocaust survivors in the Vancouver area in 1978, and by 1984 he had recorded 120 eyewitness accounts. He served on the International Advisory Council of the Hidden Child Conference in 1991. In 1985 he founded the Vancouver Holocaust Centre Society for Education and Remembrance and in 1994 established the Holocaust Education Centre. He continues to treat aging survivors of massive trauma and to participate in programs against racism and prejudice. He lives in Vancouver with his wife, Marilyn. They have three children.

DORI LAUB is an associate clinical professor of psychiatry at Yale University, where he has taught since 1969; he lives in Woodbridge, Connecticut. He has published extensively and received many honors for his work on trauma, genocide, and the Holocaust. He cofounded the Holocaust Survivors Film Project in 1979 and the Fortunoff Video Archive for Holocaust Testimonies at Yale University, in which he remains very active. He has served on the staffs of Connecticut Valley Hospital and the Connecticut Mental Health Center and maintains a private practice in psychoanalysis and general psychiatry, working especially with victims of trauma and their children. From his first marriage he has a son and a daughter who have two children between them. He is married to a German Gentile, a journalist who came to Yale to write about the Fortunoff Video Archive and continues to study the Holocaust.

ASHER J. MATATHIAS lives in Woodmere, Long Island, New York, with his wife, Anna. He holds an MA from the New School and has completed coursework there for a PhD in political science. He is a retired New York City public school teacher and is an adjunct professor of political science at St. John's University. He has been president of his B'nai B'rith lodge since 1983 and is active in other Sephardic and community affairs. He and Anna have three daughters.

SARA MUNIC retired in 1988 from an insurance company and began taking college courses. She is still an avid reader. She lives in West Hartford, Connecticut, and is a life member of Hadassah. She has two sons, two daughters, and seven grandchildren.

MARIAN NACHMAN has lived in Greenwich, Connecticut, since 1967. She teaches English as a Second Language at the Stamford branch of the University of Connecticut and in the Adult Education Program of the Town of Greenwich. She is active in the Holocaust Child Survivors of Connecticut. When not working, she enjoys travel, especially to Washington State, where both of her children live.

RUDY ROSENBERG is married to the former Rosette Wauters and has a son and two grandchildren. He now lives in Williston Park, Long Island, New York, and runs a small biotechnology company in Westbury. His narrative in this volume is adapted from his booklet, "And Somehow We Survive," and he continues to work on his memoirs, the working title of which is *An Unorthodox Life.*

CONTRIBUTORS

HILDE SCHERAGA, who died on April 26, 2004, was a retired teacher and active volunteer in Stamford, Connecticut. She was president of the Holocaust Child Survivors of Connecticut (HCSC); served on the executive committee of Jewish Family Service, of which she was a past president; and was a member of the interfaith committee of the Interfaith Council of Southwestern Connecticut. She preferred causes that serve to heal those in need. She was an active speaker for the HCSC and received many awards, including the Hannah G. Solomon Community Service Award of the National Council of Jewish Women. She is survived by her husband, Mort, and three daughters.

MADELEINE SWIDLER SCOTT lives in San Diego with her husband, Clarence. Both are retired and enjoy walking, swimming, traveling, and keeping fit. Madeleine remains busy with her work for the Advocates for Classical Music, Children Survivors of the Holocaust, and many other creative projects. She and Clarence look forward to many more years of a peaceful and healthy life and visits with their children and grandchildren.

ZAHAVA SZÁSZ STESSEL, a librarian, has a PhD from New York University and is retired from the New York Public Library. She and her husband, Meier, live in Brooklyn and have two daughters and several grandchildren. Her book, *Wine and Thorns in Tokay Valley: Jewish Life in Hungary: The History of Abaújszántó,* was published in 1995 by Fairleigh Dickinson University Press.

JUDITH TRAUB lives in Great Neck, Long Island, New York, and the West Side of Manhattan with her dentist husband, Gerald. They have a son, a daughter, and three grandchildren. She retired in 1995 as a teacher-librarian. She is a member of the Great Neck Synagogue, a docent at the Nassau County Museum of Art, a facilitator of a local book review group, and an involved grandmother.

GIORGINA VITALE has a BA degree (magna cum laude) in comparative literature from Southern Connecticut State University and has done graduate work in gerontology. She taught Italian at the Berlitz School of Languages and worked for fifteen years at the Jewish Federation of Greater New Haven. She is active in her synagogue and in several Jewish and community organizations. She is a founder, board member, and coordinator of the support group of the Connecticut chapter of the ALS Association, an organization dedicated to the fight against Lou Gehrig's Disease. She lives in Branford, Connecticut, and has four daughters and seven grandchildren.

JULES WALLERSTEIN, a mechanical engineer, retired in 1989 from Perkin-Elmer and lives in Norwalk, Connecticut, with his wife, Helen. They have two daughters and five grandchildren and celebrated their fiftieth wedding anniversary in 2003. He is a member of the American Legion and the Disabled American Veterans and a past commander of the Jewish War Veterans. He does volunteer work for many organizations and lectures at schools, churches, clubs, and synagogues about his Holocaust experience.